THE
EUCHARIST
MAKES
THE CHURCH

THE EUCHARIST MAKES THE CHURCH

Henri de Lubac and John Zizioulas in dialogue

by
Paul McPartlan

T&T CLARK
EDINBURGH

T&T CLARK
59 GEORGE STREET
EDINBURGH EH2 2LQ
SCOTLAND

First Published 1993

ISBN 0 567 09640 8 HB
ISBN 0 567 29241 X PB

British Library Cataloguing-in-Publication Data
A catalogue record for this book is available
from the British Library

Typeset by Trinity Typesetting, Edinburgh
Printed and bound in Great Britain by Biddles Ltd, Surrey

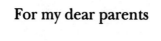

For my dear parents

Contents

Part Two. John Zizioulas

Part Three. Dialogue

Note

Most patristic references are given from J. P. Migne, *Patrologia Latina* (PL; Paris, 1844-1864) and *Patrologia Graeca* (PG; Paris, 1857-1866). The practice of both Henri de Lubac and John Zizioulas in rendering the titles of Greek patristic works in Latin has been followed.

Unless an offical translation is indicated as the source of a quotation, translations are mine throughout.

Foreword

This is a book about two of the most important ideas in modern ecumenism as worked out by two of the most important theologians of recent times.

The ideas both concern the Church. The first is that the Church is most truly itself, not in its organisation or its teaching or its moral guidance or its works of mercy or as the champion of the poor, but in the celebration of the Eucharist. The liturgy, according to the Second Vatican Council, especially the Eucharist, is 'the outstanding means by which the faithful can express in their lives, and manifest to others, the real nature of the Church' (Decree on the Liturgy, n. 2). The second idea is that the nature of the Church is most fully defined as communion, the fellowship of those united by what they share: one body, one Spirit, one Lord, one faith, one baptism, one God and Father (Eph: 4.4-5). This insight lay at the heart of the Anglican – Roman Catholic International Commission's statement *Church as Communion*, and has featured in a number of other agreements which involved a wide range of Christian traditions, including Orthodox, Lutherans, Methodists and Pentecostals, and the World Council of Churches.

The two theologians span the period since the beginnings of the second World War. It was in 1938 that Henri de Lubac wrote his great book *Catholicism*, in which he expounded a theology of the Church based on the Eucharist: 'the Eucharist makes the Church.' Nearly half a century later John Zizioulas's exciting and original work *Being as Communion* developed de Lubac's eucharistic ecclesiology in the light of the understanding of communion as a fundamental ontological category: 'being means life, and life means *communion*'. (A revealing light is cast on the difference between Eastern and Western theology if one compares that saying with the principle that was fundamental to J. H. Newman's thought: 'to live is to change, and to be perfect is to have changed often'.)

Paul McPartlan's profound study of de Lubac and Zizioulas, showing as it does how the thought of these two great theologians, one Roman Catholic, the other Greek Orthodox, is interlocking and complementary, has a special value for the ecumenical movement. It illustrates Pope John Paul's saying that, separated from the Orthodox Church, the Catholic Church is breathing with only one lung. It also shows the tragic futility of the present suspicious rivalry between Catholics and Orthodox in the countries newly liberated from communism.

Edward Yarnold, S.J.
Campion Hall, Oxford

Introduction

On 10 September 1991, a personal message from Pope John Paul II was read at the funeral of Henri de Lubac in Notre Dame Cathedral in Paris. The pope nominated de Lubac as a cardinal in 1983, when the great theologian was approaching his eighty seventh birthday, but still at work and writing. In his message, Pope John Paul said that he had given him this honour in order 'to acknowledge the merits of a tireless scholar, a spiritual master and a jesuit who was faithful during the various difficult moments of his life'.

'With perspicacity he plumbed the teaching of the Fathers and the medieval authors and found support in a penetrating knowledge of great modern writers, to nourish a personal reflection which in a brilliant way became part of living Tradition. All this enabled him to make a valuable and fruitful contribution to the Second Vatican Council.'[1]

De Lubac's influence, however, has certainly not been restricted to the Catholic Church. One young man greatly indebted to him as he began his own theological research in the 1950s was John Zizioulas (born 1931), a member of the Orthodox Church and now himself a leading theologian, memorably described by Yves Congar as 'one of the most original and most profound theologians of our age'.[2] One of the founding members, in 1979, of the international Joint Commission for Theological Dialogue between the Roman Catholic Church and the Orthodox Church, Zizioulas was

[1] *L'Osservatore Romano* (English edition), 16 September 1991, p. 12. De Lubac was created Cardinal Deacon of S. Maria in Domnica on 2 February 1983. We shall refer a number of times to the Second Vatican Council, or Vatican II, and particularly to its Dogmatic Constitution on the Church, *Lumen Gentium.*

[2] Yves Congar, 'Bulletin d'ecclésiologie' (1982), p. 88.

called from the ranks of the laity to be a bishop in 1986 and he continues to be one of the principal figures in the modern ecumenical movement.[3]

The book which Zizioulas particularly remembers from that time,[4] and which he still regularly cites,[5] is de Lubac's tome on the relationship between the Eucharist and the Church, *Corpus Mysticum.*[6] The principal point that Zizioulas draws from de Lubac's monumental historical survey is that this relationship entered a new phase in the West in the thirteenth century. Until that time, the Eucharist constituted 'the sacrament of the Church, that which expresses the Church's unity and which makes the body of Christ and the body of the Church identical'.[7] Thereafter, at the hands of scholastic theologians, 'the treatment of the Church became separated from the treatise on the sacraments and . . . the treatise on the "Mystical Body" was cut off from the treatise on the Eucharist'.[8]

In due course, after the fall of Byzantium in 1453, the East followed the West into a phase of scholasticism, which Zizioulas, like his teacher Georges Florovsky, regards as a period of 'Babylonian captivity'.[9] Orthodoxy's escape has been effected in this century, Zizioulas maintains, through reestablishing a link with its 'roots'. He is clear about who deserves the credit.

'The first important factor responsible for new, positive and creative developments in Orthodox theology in our century is,

---

[3]For a full account of Zizioulas' ecumenical activity up to the time of his ordination as Metropolitan of Pergamon on 22 June 1986, cf. Gaëtan Baillargeon, *Perspectives orthodoxes sur l'Église-Communion, L'oeuvre de Jean Zizioulas,* pp. 34-58.

[4]I draw here, as at many points in my presentation of Zizioulas, on personal discussions with him.

[5]E.g. *EPH,* pp. 336-337; *TLU,* p. 165; *EFEL,* p. 2; cf. *BC,* p. 20. The abbreviations used for the works of de Lubac and Zizioulas are indicated below in their respective bibliographies, pp. 306-309 and 310-314, with a 'Note' about how they may readily be distinguished, p. 306.

[6]First published in 1944; second edition, 1949.

[7]*EPH,* pp. 336-337.

[8]Cf. *TLU,* p. 165.

[9]*ORT,* p. 6; cf. *BC,* p. 20. For Florovsky's considerable influence on Zizioulas, see below, Chapters Six and Ten.

rather curiously, the work of "Western" theologians . . . . [The] return to the ancient patristic sources, which has characterised Western theology in our century, is largely responsible for the Orthodox theological renaissance.'

Henri de Lubac is one of the few Zizioulas chooses to name whose works 'in the field of patristics and ecclesiology . . . have allowed modern Orthodox theologians to return to their own sources'.[10]

De Lubac is unquestionably one of the pioneers of this century's patristic revival in the West and his work on the Church and the Eucharist has been particularly seminal. His conclusions and even his words have become theological currency, often without attribution. B. Sesboüé says that he saw the celebrated double principle coined by de Lubac, that 'the Church makes the Eucharist' and 'the Eucharist makes the Church', quoted here and there as a patristic formula![11] In fact, this double principle appeared for the first time only in de Lubac's *Méditation sur l'Eglise,* in 1953. There, while he says that the Church and the Eucharist stand 'as cause to each other', it is clearly the second half of the principle that he regards as having been more neglected: 'the Church makes the Eucharist, but the Eucharist also makes the Church'.[12] The Church, indeed, gathers to celebrate the Eucharist.

> 'But if the sacrifice is accepted by God and the Church's prayer listened to, this is because the Eucharist, in its turn, *makes the Church,* in the strictest sense.'[13]

De Lubac's *Corpus Mysticum* may be regarded as an extended defence of the principle that 'the Eucharist makes the Church'[14] and a weighty appeal for its restoration to the

---

[10]*Ibid.,* p. 6. The others he names in this field are Emile Mersch, Jean Daniélou, Yves Congar and 'the Benedictines of Chevetogne'.

[11]B. Sesboüé, 'Eucharistie: deux générations de travaux', p. 101.

[12]*Splendour,* p. 92, amended translation (cf. *Méditation sur l'Eglise,* p. 113). Throughout, I shall translate *'fait',* as in *'fait l'Eucharistie'* and *'fait l'Eglise',* by 'makes' in preference to 'produces'.

[13]*Ibid.,* p. 106, amended translation, incorporating de Lubac's original italics (cf. *Méditation sur l'Eglise,* p. 129).

[14]De Lubac states the principle with emphasis in *CMys,* p. 104.

prominence it had before the full rise of scholasticism. In fact, the principle was already implicit in de Lubac's programmatic work, *Catholicisme,* published in 1938, in which he endorsed the medieval teaching that '*sacramenta faciunt ecclesiam*', the '*sacramentum sacramentorum*' being 'the Eucharist'.[15]

It is largely the success of this appeal that Zizioulas acknowledges when, after describing 'the traditional scholastic vision according to which it is the Church which makes the Eucharist and not vice versa',[16] he rejoices that we have now, in 'our contemporary era', entered a third phase in the history of this relationship, a phase in which 'the ancient link between Church and Eucharist' has been 'recovered'.[17] It is striking that, as we have just seen, Zizioulas uses the terminology of de Lubac's double principle in *Méditation sur l'Eglise* to outline the various ecclesiological options and that he echoes de Lubac's title for the eucharistic chapter of this book, 'The Heart of the Church',[18] when he himself describes the Eucharist as 'the heart of all ecclesiology'.[19]

Thus, both de Lubac and Zizioulas would assert that *the Eucharist makes the Church*. The aim of this study is to explore and compare what they, respectively, mean by this assertion and thereby to compare their theologies, in both of which this assertion occupies a central position, as we shall see. However, it is not a static comparison, with the two theologies simply placed side by side. Rather, with an awareness of the early influence of de Lubac upon Zizioulas regarding the role of the Eucharist in the Church, our ultimate purpose is to investigate how Zizioulas can be said to have carried forward de Lubac's own results and intentions, not only on this point, but more generally.

For instance, while bearing the above marks of de Lubac's influence, Zizioulas' summary of his own position moves beyond de Lubac's sequential ordering of the two halves of his double principle, whereby the Church makes the Eucharist

[15] *Catholicism,* pp. 34-35.
[16] *ORT,* p. 8.
[17] *EPH,* p. 339.
[18] *Splendour,* Chapter 4.
[19] *BC,* p. 131, n. 19.

which, *in its turn*, makes the Church, and indicates a significant integration. Rejecting both the unilateralism of scholasticism and what he sees as the opposite unilateralism of Nicolas Afanassieff's 'eucharistic ecclesiology',[20] Zizioulas says emphatically: '*the Church constitutes the Eucharist while being constituted by it*'. Indeed, he presses on to a total integration, whereby Church and Eucharist 'coincide, and are even in some sense identical'.[21]

There is, then, a certain development to be discerned as we move from the stance of de Lubac to that of Zizioulas on this point. As we expand from this vital centre, we shall discover that it is one of a number of interrelated developments, all of which, taken together, show that Zizioulas has taken up the baton from de Lubac, so to speak, and made remarkable progress in the race to achieve some of the primary objectives which he shares with de Lubac, such as the eradication of individualism in Christianity.

In fact, as we shall see, there are several occasions on which de Lubac readily admits that there are gaps in his account and targets he has left unattained. With pioneers, it is always so. The next generation must continue their work. I wish to show that a leading theologian from the East has much to offer to the continuing purpose of this great Western master. I undertake this task with an ecumenical intention, in line with the urging of Pope John Paul II that 'the Church must once again learn to breathe with its two lungs — the Eastern one and the Western one'[22] and the desire of the late Ecumenical Patriarch Dimitrios I that 'our two worlds may meet and find their identity in one Lord, one faith, one baptism, one God and Father of all, in him who is above all and through all and in us all'.[23]

[20]*EPH*, pp. 340-341; *ORT*, p. 8; *ENO*, p. 173. Cf. below, p. 227.

[21]*Ibid.*, p. 341. Cf. *BC*, p. 219: 'the concrete local community . . . is to be understood a something constituted by the very event it constitutes'.

[22]Pope John Paul II, address to the Roman Curia in the presence of a delegation from the Ecumenical Patriarchate, 28 June 1985, published in *L'Osservatore Romano* (English edition), 15 July 1985, p. 5. The image was coined by Yves Congar (cf. *Diversity and Communion*, p. 89).

[23]Ecumenical Patriarch Dimitrios I, address, with reference to Eph 4:5-6, in the presence of a papal delegation, 30 November 1986; quoted by E. Fortino, 'Pan-Orthodox decision on the Catholic-Orthodox dialogue — Towards the next meeting of the joint commission', p. 8.

The theological worlds of de Lubac and Zizioulas have actually met very little hitherto. Apart from the indications already given, and the important reference he also makes to de Lubac's *Catholicism* as a work reinforcing the assertion of his own teacher, Florovsky, that ecclesiology is 'a chapter of Christology',[24] Zizioulas refers to de Lubac very little,[25] and de Lubac refers to Zizioulas hardly at all.[26] The point of this book is to bring them together. Accordingly, the encounter which follows has three parts. Part One presents the theology of de Lubac, not hesitating to highlight the gaps and tensions therein. Appropriate elements from Zizioulas' approach will be introduced at these points, to indicate his possible contribution. Part Two clarifies the position of these elements in Zizioulas' theology, as his overall vision is examined. The momentum from Part One into Part Two then continues into Part Three, where the major lines of our comparison are developed as the two theologians engage with one another most directly and vigorously. Though, given our overall purpose, this study tends to bring strengths of Zizioulas' theology to bear upon weaknesses in de Lubac's, criticism of Zizioulas is not absent; it is expressed particularly as our findings are drawn together in the Conclusion.

Again in line with our approach, attention is restricted, with regard to Zizioulas, to what he has contributed, by means of its

---

[24] *ORT*, p. 8. Cf. below, pp.212-213.

[25] Zizioulas cites de Lubac only twice more, both times referring to *Les églises particulières dans l'Eglise universelle* (to which we refer in translation as *Motherhood*); first, in *BC*, p. 202, n. 113, on whether the bishop belongs first to his particular church or to the episcopal college (cf. *Motherhood*, pp. 250-251, n. 43, and below, p. 110), and secondly, in *PDC*, p. 148, n. 13, on the interchangeable use of *ekklesia* for both the whole Church and the local church (cf. *Motherhood*, pp. 171f.).

[26] De Lubac cites Zizioulas only four times, on three occasions referring to the article by Zizioulas which became chapter 4 of *BC*, regarding the fulness of the Church's presence in each particular church, the difference between episcopal collegiality and collectivity and Cyprian's doctrine that each bishop answers to God for his church (*Motherhood*, pp. 177, n. 23; p. 259, n. 6; p. 269, n. 20, respectively). De Lubac's final reference is in *SComm*, p. 24, n. 45, to Zizioulas noting the liturgical practice of the *fermentum* in the East as well as in the West in the early centuries (cf. *EEE*, p. 40).

appearance in Western languages, to the ecumenical encounter of East and West, in the form either of published writings or of unpublished conferences and lectures in the West, where he lived for a long time and still regularly teaches. This study has benefited greatly from access to a considerable amount of Zizioulas' unpublished material, which he has generously allowed to the present author. Further, we must recognise as beyond our scope here a thorough appraisal of de Lubac's and Zizioulas' respective fidelity to their many patristic sources. This is not primarily a study in patristic theology. Our task is to compare the visions of de Lubac and Zizioulas themselves.

A comparison between de Lubac and Zizioulas would not be worthwhile if their similar statements on the Eucharist in the Church were either unintegrated or peripheral in their respective theologies. However, though Zizioulas has written much less than de Lubac, both men's writings cover a wide range of theological issues, evidencing a truly global vision, and though de Lubac made much less effort to systematise his vision than Zizioulas has, both visions are ecclesiological[27] and therefore, at heart, eucharistic. The Eucharist therefore constitutes a powerful means of comparing these visions and bringing the respective traditions from which they emerge into dialogue.

Parts One and Two, which endeavour to set the Eucharist in its context for each of de Lubac and Zizioulas and to show its centrality in their theologies, have been structured in parallel, so as further to promote, even implicitly, the dialogue between the two theologians. Chapters One and Six examine their programmatic writings and the similar priorities and methodologies apparent in them, particularly their common existential concern to address the predicament of man by a creative return to the doctrine of the Fathers. Chapters Two and Seven treat the fundamental distinction between the uncreated God and His creation which both de Lubac and Zizioulas emphasise

---

[27]Both de Lubac and Zizioulas see the Christian life as essentially ecclesial. With reference to the teaching of Origen, de Lubac says: 'the life of the spirit reproduces in the soul the mystery of the Church herself' (*Splendour*, p. 272). Zizioulas draws on the doctrine of Maximus the Confessor to assert that 'in the same Spirit the very structure of the Church becomes the existential structure of each person' (*PDC*, p. 152).

in order to safeguard God's freedom. Once this distinction is made, then the way in which God in Christ encounters His creation can be progressively unfolded.

The pivotal Chapters Three and Eight propose and examine for each of de Lubac and Zizioulas a unifying motif in their writings, the Augustinian dictum, '*Nec tu me in te mutabis, sicut cibum carnis tuae, sed tu mutaberis in me*',[28] for the former, and the scriptural notion of corporate personality, the one and the many, for the latter. Because de Lubac regards the Augustinian dictum as eucharistic and Zizioulas considers the Eucharist to be the event in which corporate personality is realised, we appreciate the focal role played by the Eucharist in their two visions and we advance into an examination of how the Eucharist makes the Church in Chapters Four and Nine.

Zizioulas' integration of the two parts of de Lubac's double principle means that the structure of the Church which makes the Eucharist necessarily forms part of the considerations involved in Chapter Nine. However, de Lubac's separation of these parts leads us to examine his understanding of the Church's structure in a separate Chapter Five, which culminates in his response to the stance of the Russian Orthodox theologian, Afanassieff. The parallel chapter of Part Two, namely Chapter Ten, therefore examines Zizioulas' critique of Russian theology, and particularly strives to reveal the primary reason for his frequent criticisms of Afanassieff.

Though much research on de Lubac's theology and specifically on his ecclesiology has been done, none has yet taken the recurrent Augustinian dictum as an interpretative key to his vision. I believe that its potential is immediately apparent, given, first, that the dictum is eucharistic for de Lubac[29] who stresses that the Eucharist makes the *Church*, secondly, that he considers the dictum to be accomplished in Heaven, when the natural desire for the vision of God is realised, this desire being his constant theme in his treatment of *Grace*,[30] and, thirdly, his

---

[28]Augustine, *Confessions* 7, 10, 16 (PL 32, 742): 'You will not change me into you, as food for your flesh, but you will be changed into me.'

[29]Cf. below, Chapter Three.

[30]Cf. below, Chapter Two.

lament that 'these two great doctrinal themes' of the Church and Grace were for a long time 'studied in two separate treatises', with the result that 'the ecclesiological synthesis was sought for but not found'.[31]

Only one extended study of Zizioulas' theology has so far appeared, namely that by Gaëtan Baillargeon.[32] Though Baillargeon opens his presentation of Zizioulas' ecclesiology with a section entitled '*L'«Un» et le «multiple»*', which refers to the equivalent exegetical concept of 'corporate personality' and affirms that here is 'the heart, the central core of the ecclesiological perspective of John Zizioulas', this section is very short,[33] and the two interchangeable terms, the one and the many and corporate personality, appear only infrequently thereafter. It is striking that neither term appears in Baillargeon's chapter on 'The Pneumatological Dimension of the Church',[34] even though Zizioulas notably says of the one and the many that it is 'the mystery of Christology and Pneumatology, the mystery of the Church and at the same time of the Eucharist'.[35] Such a statement leads me to give the notion of corporate personality, or of the one and the many, great prominence in my exposition here, as the interpretative key to Zizioulas' vision.[36]

Thus, it is a sustained encounter of de Lubac and Zizioulas that is offered here, based on a new focusing of their respective theologies. Although tensions have arisen again between Catholics and Orthodox in the recent years of sweeping political changes in eastern Europe, new freedoms have brought the exciting possibility of unprecedented personal contact and genuine theological dialogue. It is my hope that this book may contribute to mutual understanding and *rapprochement* as we work and pray for the day when the two Churches will be visibly united at one altar.[37]

---

[31] *Splendour*, p. 65.

[32] Baillargeon, *Perspectives orthodoxes sur l'Église-Communion*.

[33] *Ibid.*, pp. 65-66.

[34] *Ibid.*, pp. 99-122.

[35] *EPH*, p. 346. Cf. below, p. 167.

[36] In Chapter Twelve I make substantial criticisms of Baillargeon's appraisal of Zizioulas, cf. below, pp. 265-270.

[37] For a full documentation of the growing contact between Rome and Constantinople in recent times, cf. E. J. Stormon, *Towards the Healing of Schism.* Also, soon to appear is P. McPartlan (ed.), *One in 2000? Towards Catholic – Orthodox Unity. Agreed Statements and Parish Papers* (St Paul, Slough, 1993).

This study began life as a doctoral thesis at Oxford. Its publication gives me, as a priest of his diocese, the opportunity to renew my thanks to the Archbishop of Westminster, Cardinal Basil Hume, for generously having given me the opportunity to pursue this research. I would like again to thank Fr Edward Yarnold, who was my principal supervisor and who has kindly written a Foreword for this book, and Bishop Kallistos Ware, who also supervised me. Bishop John Crowley has always been most considerate and the interest and advice of Fr Yves Congar have been much appreciated. Particular thanks are due to Stratford Caldecott, whose firm desire to publish this work gave me encouragement and was finally realised. Many friends have helped me along the way; I would specially thank Fr Anthony Meredith and Dr Bernard Attard, for companionship amid the rigours of research and writing, and Fr David Manson, for fraternal support throughout. For their constant love and prayers, I owe a great debt to my family, especially my parents to whom I gratefully dedicate this book.

To both Henri de Lubac and John Zizioulas themselves, I am profoundly thankful for inspiring me and for honouring me with the opportunity for lengthy discussions. With Metropolitan John, happily, the many conversations which have borne fruit in important points of clarification noted in the text can continue, whereas my several meetings with Cardinal de Lubac now become a treasured memory. As a token of my thanks and esteem, I was glad to be able to present a copy of this work to him in September 1990, and I would wish to be counted among the company to which Pope John Paul referred in his funeral message, as he recalled one of de Lubac's favourite scriptural passages.

> 'With all those who remember him in hope and gratitude, I entrust him to the infinite mercy of God. After having been attentive to the "prophetic message" as to "a lamp shining in a dark place", may he be able to see the morning star rising!'[38]

Paul McPartlan
Easter 1992

---

[38] *L'Osservatore Romano* (English edition), 16 September 1991, p. 12, with reference to 2 Pet. 1: 19. Cf. de Lubac, *Mémoire*, pp. 84-85.

Part One

Henri de Lubac

Chapter 1

The Programme: Catholicisme

Considering the extensive *corpus* of Henri de Lubac's writings, Hans Urs von Balthasar says the following.

'At the beginning stands the programmatic *Catholicisme* (1938), a work which was intended to be and actually became a major breakthrough. The major works which followed grew from its individual chapters much like branches from a trunk.'[1]

The Fathers and Ecumenism

In *Catholicism*, de Lubac diagnosed that the real reason why the ecclesial sense of the Eucharist was lost lay in a change 'gradually wrought in men's habits of mind' after the age of the Fathers.

'Just as they would no longer see the spiritual reflected in the sensible or the universal and particular as reciprocally symbolical, so the idea of the relationship between the physical body of Christ and his Mystical Body came to be forgotten.'[2]

The Fathers of the Church who feature most prominently in de Lubac's writings from the beginning are Origen and Augustine, from East and West respectively. He later admitted that, both in Origen and Augustine, 'historical data are frequently

---

[1]Hans Urs von Balthasar, 'The Achievement of Henri de Lubac', p. 12. As a student at Lyons, von Balthasar sought guidance from de Lubac when he began his own study of the Fathers; cf. 'Cento domande a von Balthasar', pp. 14-15.

[2]*Catholicism*, pp. 41-42.

given short shrift, and serve as springboards rather than as terms for thought'. There was, thus, 'a rather dangerous climate of thought' brought about by Origen's 'brand of Alexandrian Platonism', in which the springboard itself could be seen as incidental, lacking 'any real solidity'.[3] De Lubac clearly implies in these comments that the springboard must be strictly associated with what it can launch us into. We already perceive his sacramental understanding of the relationship between springboard and further reality, that is between the sensible and the spiritual. He maintains that both Origen and Augustine escaped the danger and had 'a profoundly historical view of life'.[4]

Elsewhere, with regard to the Augustinian dictum which he frequently recalls, he recognises that 'it would not be difficult to assign a Platonic origin' to elements of Augustine's teaching also. The theme of the eater being eaten bears obvious similarities to the Platonic principle that 'the soul which feeds on the Beautiful is assimilated by the Beautiful', but, says de Lubac, it 'adapted itself so marvellously to the data of revelation'.[5] Here we see the heart of de Lubac's attachment to Origen and Augustine. Their Platonism led them to refer every created thing beyond itself and to see life as but the threshold of the Mystery into which we are to be assumed. In contrast, as de Lubac said in *Catholicism*, the 'Aristotelian logic' which influenced the formulation of theology in the Middle Ages 'showed itself unsuited to those organic, unitary ideas which had formerly, in some respects, found an ally in the Platonic mentality'; 'logical intelligence' is 'impatient of any idea of mystery' and makes *its own* connections 'artificially' between the objects it itself has separated.[6] Thereby, intelligence ceased to be 'a power of penetration into the heart of reality' and became merely 'a tool for constructing architecture of the mind'.[7]

---

[3] *Sources*, p. 3.
[4] *Ibid.*, p. 3.
[5] *CMys*, pp. 200-201 and n. 64. Cf. below, pp. 67-72.
[6] *Catholicism*, pp. 162-163. Cf. below, p. 58, n. 34.
[7] *Paradoxes*, p. 104. Cf. de Lubac's criticism of dialectic, below, pp. 57-58.

De Lubac wishes us to understand Origen and Augustine as having a *sacramental* view of life and its data, which their Platonism supported. This life and its data open up into the Mystery, they are not the end. What the Mystery is and how it impinges sacramentally upon this life will prove to be major questions in our comparison between de Lubac and Zizioulas, but *that* this life is sacramental is a view which they would share.[8]

There was in de Lubac a profoundly ecumenical spirit, even though he was not much involved in explicitly ecumenical activity during his life.[9] 'The splendid name of Catholic', he says, signifies 'the fulness of the Christian spirit' which is quite contrary to the 'distrustful and factious sectarian spirit' which has at times existed in some of those wearing this title as a denominational label.[10] Maurice Villain acclaimed *Catholicism* as '*un grand livre oecuménique*' on two grounds. First, because 'his broad exposition' offered something to 'any religious man drawn by the issues of faith' and, secondly, because it 'renounced oppositions and anathemas' and courageously set out 'to find again the axes and the true proportions of the Gospel message'.[11]

In *Catholicism*, de Lubac quoted an unattributed saying which summarised what we may call his *anti-confessionalist* attitude. 'It is a great misfortune to have learnt the catechism against someone.' He said this in the context of lamenting the damage done by 'controversy' to doctrine on the Church and on the Eucharist. The risk is that what was learned in this way 'was but half learned'.

> 'For if . . . heresy is an occasion of progress for orthodox doctrine, there follows in its train the danger that this progress may be one-sided and the occasion in its turn . . . of further error.'[12]

---

[8]Cf. e.g., our comparisons below, pp.86-89, 262-264.

[9]Von Balthasar notes that, in *The Splendour of the Church* (pp. 112-113), de Lubac expresses his belief that a 'genuine' Eucharist can exist only within the Church and he comments: 'Here as little as elsewhere does de Lubac go more closely into ecumenical problems arising' ('The Achievement of Henri de Lubac', p. 44 and n. 10).

[10]*Catholicism*, p. 169.

[11]Maurice Villain, 'Un grand livre oecuménique: *Catholicisme*', p. 328.

[12]*Catholicism*, pp. 164-165.

Of 'the theologian who makes too many concessions to the demands of controversy' de Lubac pointed to something 'less often noticed' and, he implied, the more damaging in consequence.

> 'In his struggle against heresy he always sees the question, more or less, willingly or unwillingly, from the heretic's point of view. He often accepts questions in the form in which the heretic propounds them, so that without sharing the error he may make implicit concessions to his opponent, which are the more serious the more explicit are his refutations.'[13]

De Lubac made clear that his commitment was to the Catholic Church which, he stipulated, is 'neither Latin nor Greek, but universal'[14] and to her Tradition, the 'constitutive thinking' of Christianity, which is more fundamental than her dogma, the 'constituted thinking' of Christianity.[15] He appended to *Catholicism* nearly fifty texts, mainly patristic and hitherto not easily accessible,[16] in his endeavour to set forth what Villain called 'the great patristic tradition in which he [de Lubac] is so perfectly at home', a tradition 'which embraces East and West together'.[17] Villian said the following about de Lubac's exposition.

> 'It is first of all an encounter with our Orthodox brethren, to whom it gives such a fine place [*une si belle part*], by reinstating in the place of honour the Greek and Syriac Fathers and by penetrating with their breath the great dogmas of faith: Creation, Incarnation, Redemption, Church.'[18]

---

[13]*Ibid.*, pp. 166-167.

[14]*Ibid.*, p. 156.

[15]*Ibid.*, p. xvii.

[16]In an introductory note to the first edition (reproduced in *Catholicism*, p. xiv), de Lubac said it seemed that such a selection could be useful, given that the French public still faced an 'extreme shortage of patristic editions and translations'. Seven more texts had been added by the fourth edition (1947), but no more have been added in subsequent editions, up to the seventh in 1983.

[17]'Un grand livre oecuménique: *Catholicisme*', p. 320.

[18]*Ibid.*, p. 328.

Soon afterwards, de Lubac undertook the direction of a series of patristic texts, which began to appear in 1942 as 'Sources Chrétiennes'. The series began with many works of the Greek Fathers.[19] De Lubac tells how it realised the plan of Victor Fontoynont for such a project as 'a means of *rapprochement* with the Orthodox Churches'. It was one way of showing them 'that the Catholic Church still recognised the ancient Fathers as her own'.[20] However, de Lubac then had to counter suspicions of imbalance in the series by explicitly affirming that 'no patristic author is excluded from it'.[21]

We may note that de Lubac wrote *Catholicism* on the insistence of his friend Yves Congar[22] and that it appeared as the third volume in another greatly influential series, 'Unam Sanctam', which had been inaugurated in 1937 with Congar's own study, *Chrétiens Désunis*, subtitled: *Principes d'un 'oecuménisme' catholique*.[23] Villain commended the fulness and equilibrium which de Lubac derived from the Fathers for his exposition of 'catholic doctrine' in *Catholicism*.

> 'Thereby, without ever directly seeking to be, he was a precursor of catholic ecumenism.'[24]

Neopatristic Synthesis

> '[O]ur Fathers in the Faith . . . received from the Church of their time the means to nourish the Church of our times as well.'[25]

In these introductory words to *Catholicism*, de Lubac emphasised the present relevance of patristic doctrine. He reiterated

[19]The first ten texts were works by Gregory of Nyssa, Clement of Alexandria, Athenagoras, Nicholas Cabasilas, Diadochus of Photike, Gregory of Nyssa (again), Origen (*Homelies on Genesis*, with an Introduction by de Lubac), Nicetas Stethatos, Maximus the Confessor and Ignatius of Antioch, respectively.

[20]De Lubac describes the background in *Souvenirs*, pp. 10-11.

[21]In *Souvenirs*, de Lubac reproduces a 'Note a propos de la collection patristique «Sources»'; the quotation is from §1 of this Note (p. 12).

[22]H. Vorgrimler, 'Henri de Lubac (L)', pp. 422-423.

[23]The second volume in the series 'Unam Sanctam' was J. A. Moehler, *L'Unité dans L'Eglise* (Cerf, Paris, 1938).

[24]'Un grand livre oecuménique: *Catholicisme*', p. 320.

[25]*Catholicism*, p. xix.

them with an admonition in 1942: 'the thought of the first
Christian centuries is ever-living [*toujours vivante*], . . . if we no
longer live from it, the fault is our own'.[26] Again, over thirty
years later, introducing a new study of grace, he said:

> 'nothing solid can be achieved in theology without tested
> materials, with which the long history of Christian reflection
> supplies us. All research must be first of all a revival through
> Tradition. All renewal supposes continuity, even in the face of
> new situations'.[27]

Over the years, new situations drew from de Lubac numerous adapted treatments of the theme which overarches his
whole theological endeavour, namely that of the relationship
between nature and grace. Again in 1980 he warned of the
errors of the theory of 'pure nature',[28] as he had done first, and
so controversially, in *Surnaturel* in 1946. But we must realise
that this book was itself the result of thirty years' reflection,
which began when Auguste Valensin, his friend from when he
entered the Society of Jesus in 1913, introduced him to Maurice
Blondel and, in 1919, to all the papers of Pierre Rousselot (killed
at Verdun in 1915), and which became active investigation,
specifically encouraged by his professor Joseph Huby, when he
began his formal studies of theology in England in 1924.[29]

---

[26] *STPDieu*, p. 715.

[27] *Athéisme*, p. 10.

[28] *BCat*, p. 185; in footnote 16, de Lubac indicates the different contexts of
several of his studies of Grace. In 1984, he said that the only real 'novelty' of
MSup in 1965, over *Surnaturel* in 1946, 'consists in a preface which intends to
show that the traditional doctrine . . . responds to the theological situation of
the 1960s as well as it did to the sometimes opposite situation of the 1930s and
1940s' (*TOcc*, p. 113). We may interpret that the prevalent error of the earlier
period was the view that from the natural orientation of all towards a natural
end, some were called to a supernatural destiny, whereas the error of the later
period was to assume that the one supernatural destiny of all was to be
achieved without conversion and a gratuitous 'second gift' from God, and
that it was therefore no longer *super*-natural. In 1986, de Lubac specified that
the error of the later period, which led to the restatement of his position, was
'secularism' (*Lettres*, pp. 62-63).

[29] H. Vorgrimler, 'Henri de Lubac (L)', pp. 423-424. Cf. de Lubac, *Mémoire*,
p. 16; *EVat*, p. 11.

'De Lubac set himself to study the history of the doctrine of the supernatural. Thus the theory of the relation between nature and grace, with which Blondel had been so preoccupied, without however supplying all the explanations hoped for, and which Rousselot related to the act of faith studied scripturally, came to de Lubac to be supported historically, with the help of a better distinction between sound theological tradition and the extrinsicist deformations of neo-scholasticism.'[30]

In *Catholicism*, de Lubac stated the single theme on which he subsequently wrote many variations: 'the vision of God is a free gift, and yet the desire for it is at the root of every soul'.[31]

Yves Congar does not hesitate to say that the two areas of the supernatural and the Eucharist are those in which the principal influence of de Lubac on modern theology is to be found, but that *Surnaturel* is his key work.[32] Angel Antòn, a *peritus* at Vatican II, considers it unfortunate that *Surnaturel* was actually published *after* de Lubac's great historical study of the relationship between the Eucharist and the Church in *Corpus Mysticum*, since this order suggests the wrong priority between the works and disguises de Lubac's fundamentally *anthropological* concern, *within which* his ecclesiology ought to be situated.[33] De Lubac himself says of the mystery of the supernatural, 'which is the mystery of our divine destiny', that it 'appears rather like the framework in which all the other mysteries of revelation have their place'.[34]

Accordingly, we shall examine de Lubac's ecclesiology[35] after studying his anthropology.[36] In both of these areas he

---

[30]Vorgrimler, 'Henri de Lubac (B)', p. 809. For biographical details of de Lubac, cf. Vorgrimler, 'Henri de Lubac (B)' and 'Henri de Lubac (L)'; G. Chantraine, 'Esquisse biographique', in H. U. von Balthasar and G. Chantraine, *Le cardinal Henri de Lubac: l'homme et son oeuvre*, pp. 9-41; and also now de Lubac's own, long-awaited, *Mémoire sur l'occasion de mes écrits*.

[31]*Catholicism*, p. 178.

[32]I am indebted to Yves Congar for personal discussions, from which this point is taken.

[33]I gratefully draw on personal discussions with Antòn.

[34]*MSup*, p. 217.

[35]See below, Chapters Four and Five.

[36]See below, Chapters Two and Three.

professedly set out to make himself the 'echo' of Tradition,[37] never 'in a frenzy of archaism',[38] but in order to bring its wisdom to bear upon current issues. This wisdom is found in paradox.[39] Regarding ecclesiology and the Eucharist, de Lubac said in *Catholicism* that we must hold together the 'symbolism of unity' and the 'Eucharistic reality'.[40] Regarding anthropology and Grace, he most recently said that we must acknowledge both 'the essential ordination of the created spirit to the "vision of God"' and 'the strictly supernatural and completely gratuitous character of the latter'.[41] Moreover, Tradition then requires that these two areas themselves be 'put together' if 'the ecclesiological synthesis' is to be found.[42] The re-establishment of this grand patristic synthesis for our own times is what de Lubac strove to enable.

Existential Emphasis

'[F]or about three centuries, faced by the naturalist trends of modern thought on the one hand and the confusions of a bastard Augustinianism on the other, many could see salvation only in a complete severance between the natural and the supernatural. . . . Such a dualism, just when it imagined that it was most successfully opposing the negations of naturalism, was most strongly influenced by it, and the transcendence in which it hoped to preserve the supernatural with such jealous care was,

---

[37]Said of his work on nature and the supernatural in *TOcc*, p. 113 and of his contribution to ecclesiology in *Splendour*, p. ix. In the latter, as he had done in *Catholicism*, p. xviii, he offered this as an explanation of the numerous footnotes to be found in the book.

[38]*Catholicism*, pp. xviii-xix.

[39]Cf. *MSup*, pp. 217-219.

[40]Cf. *Catholicism*, p. 171.

[41]*Spirito*, p. 269. This volume, published in 1981, as vol. 13 of the Italian *Opera Omnia* of de Lubac, is one of those which contains specially revised material, which may thus be taken as de Lubac's final word on the matters concerned. Here, in the second part, entitled 'Spirito e libertà nella tradizione teologica', de Lubac augments the second part and the conclusion of *Surnaturel* and then adds a '*Nota finale*', pp. 269-270.

[42]Cf. *Splendour*, pp. 64-65; above, pp. xx-xxi.

in fact, a banishment. The most confirmed secularists found in it, in spite of itself, an ally.'[43]

The urgency with which de Lubac wishes to reject 'separated' theology is well communicated in this passage from *Catholicism*. He is pointing out perhaps the most damaging example (because it has rendered Christianity quite irrelevant for many) of heresy dictating the terms of orthodoxy:

> 'nowadays, seeing the matter in its proper perspective, don't we realise that the "separated" philosophy of recent centuries has found its correlative in a "separated" theology?'

The hallmark of this 'separated' theology was that 'the supernatural, deprived of its organic links with nature, tended to be understood by some as a mere "super-nature", a "double" of nature'.[44] Central to separated theology was the theory of *pure nature*, according to which, as de Lubac more recently said:

> '"nature" and "[the] supernatural" each constituted a complete "order", the second being in fact super-added [*surajouté*] to the first, without any link between them except, in our nature, a vague and general "obediential potency" to be, as it was said, "elevated"'.[45]

Clearly, de Lubac considers that the remedy lies in restoring the 'organic links' between nature and the supernatural; theology must be properly rooted in philosophy and philosophy must open into theology. In stating that 'the end of a reasonable creature is to attain to beatitude, and that can only consist in the kingdom of God',[46] Aquinas was bridging philosophy and theology, and de Lubac thinks that the 'main impulse' for 'Latin theology's return to a more authentic tradition' in this matter within the last century 'came from a

[43] *Catholicism*, pp. 167-168.

[44] *Ibid.*, p. 167.

[45] *Athéisme*, p. 97. Cf. the interpretation of Aquinas by Cajetan (below, p. 32, n. 41), whom de Lubac critically regards, with Suarez, as principally responsible for the theory of pure nature (*AMTh*, pp. 164, 176).

[46] *Catholicism*, p. 59; quotation from Thomas Aquinas, *Contra Gentiles*, 4,50,5. Cf. *ibid.*, p. 167, where de Lubac contrasts Thomism with 'separated' philosophy and theology, and below, pp.33-34.

philosopher, Maurice Blondel'.[47] Elsewhere, de Lubac commended the 'personalist' and 'existential' ('though not existentialist!') character of the authentic tradition, which dealt not with abstract essences but with 'the nature of the humble human being that we are'.[49]

De Lubac believes that only Christ provides the key for the self-understanding of man as he is: 'Christ completes the revelation of man to himself'.[49] Furthermore, 'salvation . . . for humanity consists in its receiving the form of Christ'[50] and this happens in the Church, which is 'Jesus Christ spread abroad and communicated'.[51] Thus, the Church is the existential location of the salvation sought by all.

> 'In her [the Catholic Church], man's desires and God's have their meeting-place. . . . It [Catholicism] is the form that humanity must put on in order finally to be itself.'[52]

Fifteen years later, de Lubac elaborated these foundational statements with his *Méditation sur l'Eglise*, which von Balthasar says provides 'the spirituality for the theology of *Catholicisme*'. 'The mystery of the Church is set in relief against the entire mystery of salvation as its existential centre.' Von Balthasar particularly draws attention to the two 'existential' chapters, seven and eight, in which 'consequences are . . . drawn for Christian life'.[53] De Lubac there describes the characteristics of a '*vir ecclesiasticus*', 'a man in the Church; better, a man of the Church' and he praises Origen. 'He thought — and rightly —

---

[47] *BCat*, p. 37. In the same year as *Catholicism* was published, de Lubac wrote a short but notable article on Blondel, 'Le motif de la création dans «L 'Etre et les êtres»' (= *Motif*). For a full study of Blondel's influence on de Lubac, cf. Antonio Russo, *Henri de Lubac: teologia e dogma nella storia. L'influsso di Blondel.*

[48] *MSup*, pp. 82-83. The latter quotation is from Maximus, *Ambigua* (PG 91, 1361A).

[49] *Catholicism*, p. 187. Cf. *MMys*, p. 68; *Athéisme*, p. 109.

[50] *Ibid.*, p. 111.

[51] *Ibid.*, p. 14; quotation from Bossuet, 'Allocution aux nouvelles catholiques', *Oeuvres oratoires*, vol. 6, p. 508. Cf. below, p. 60.

[52] *Ibid.*, pp. 156-157.

[53] Von Balthasar, 'The Achievement of Henri de Lubac', pp. 43, 44.

that there was no other way of being a Christian in the full sense.'[54]

De Lubac's statements enable us to be still more specific about the existential location of salvation. His stress in *Catholicism* that theology ought to draw primarily upon the Church's *worship* implies that it is *at prayer* that the Church is most herself:

'the necessary defence of threatened truths, with its *operosae disputationes*, may deflect attention, unless we are careful, from the *orationes quotidianae*, what the Church "has never ceased to proclaim in her prayers" can thus disappear for a time from some theological treatises'.[55]

The Church's prayers focus on the Eucharist and the fact that de Lubac is able to say both that 'the New Testament is Christ'[56] and that 'the Eucharist is itself, as in a summary, the New Testament'[57] indicates that, for him, life in Christ translates immediately, *here and now*, i.e. existentially, into a life centred on the Eucharist: 'Christ *in his Eucharist* is truly the heart of the Church'.[58]

We have seen de Lubac acknowledge the debt of Christian philosophy to Blondel. De Lubac's existential focusing of salvation not only on the Church but particularly on the Eucharist follows that of Blondel himself, of whom Peter Henrici says not only that he 'wished to show that man's deepest volition finds its fulfilment only in the practice of the Church', but also that '[t]he Eucharist became the centre of his spiritual life (and of his philosophical thought)'.[59]

---

[54] *Splendour*, pp. 178ff. See below for de Lubac's understanding of the Christian's *participation* in the life of the Church (pp.90-93).

[55] *Catholicism*, p. 165.

[56] *Sources*, p. 105, with reference to Bede, *Quaestiones in libros regum*, 1, 1 (PL 93, 431A): '*Novum Testamentum . . . qui est Christus*'.

[57] *CMys*, p. 76.

[58] *Splendour*, p. 113 (my italics); cf. de Lubac, *ESPaul*, pp. 482-483, n. 12, where he says of the title 'the centre and origin of the Christian world' that it 'is true in general of the real body [of Christ], but, in a more precise way [it is true] of the real body given in mystery, present in the *assemblée cultuelle*'. For further comment on de Lubac's contribution to making the Body of Christ *concrete*, cf. P. McPartlan, 'Eucharistic Ecclesiology', p. 318.

[59] P. Henrici, 'Blondel and Loisy in the Modernist crisis', p. 363.

Catholicity and Personhood

De Lubac's programmatic work, *Catholicism* was a sustained attack upon individualism in Christianity,

'True eucharistic piety . . . is no devout individualism. . . . With one sweeping, all-embracing gesture, in one fervent intention it gathers together the whole world. . . . [I]t cannot conceive of the action of the breaking of bread without fraternal communion.'[60]

Among the factors by which he said believers had contributed to the impression of observers that the Christian is one 'who withdraws from the converse of men, exclusively preoccupied with his own salvation, which is a matter between God and himself'[61] were 'the swamping of the spiritual life by the detestable "I"' and 'the failure to realise that prayer is essentially the prayer of all for all'.[62]

De Lubac referred to 'a general development of individualism' which 'appears to coincide with the gradual dissolution of medieval Christianity'.[63] Among those preparing the way for a revival of traditional doctrine, 'the Catholic school of theology at Tubingen', with Drey, Möhler and their disciples, stands out.[64] He took the words of E. Masure as a summary of what he wished to elaborate. 'Fundamentally the Gospel is obsessed with the idea of the unity of human society.'[65] He subtitled *Catholicisme*, 'Les aspects sociaux du dogme'. De Lubac's reason for reasserting there the teaching of the Greek Fathers is

----

[60] *Catholicism*, p. 48.

[61] *Ibid.*, p. xiv; quotation from Gabriel Seailles, *Les affirmations de la conscience moderne* (1906³), pp. 108-109.

[62] *Ibid.*, pp. xv-xvi.

[63] *Ibid.*, pp. 163-164.

[64] *Ibid.*, pp. 172-173. De Lubac notes the 'definition of the Spirit and Essence of Catholicism' attempted in the 1819 prospectus of the school's official organ, the *Theologische Quartalschrift*: 'The central fact is the revelation of the plan realised by God in humanity: this plan is an organic whole with a progressive development in history.'

[65] *Ibid.*, p. xv; quotation from E. Masure, *Semaine sociale de Nice* (1934), p. 229.

quickly apparent: he finds mainly among them Fathers who 'in dealing with the creation were not content only to mention the formation of individuals, the first man and the first woman, but delighted to contemplate God creating humanity as a whole'.

'For Irenaeus, . . . as indeed for Origen, Gregory Nazianzen, Gregory of Nyssa, for Cyril of Alexandria, Maximus, Hilary and others, the lost sheep of the Gospel that the Good Shepherd brings back to the fold is no other than the whole of human nature. . . .

'They [the Fathers] seemed to witness its birth, to see it live, grow, develop, as a single being. With the first sin it was this being, whole and entire, which fell away, which was driven out of Paradise and sentenced to a bitter exile until the time of its redemption. And when Christ at last appeared, coming as the "one bridegroom", his bride, once again, was the "whole human race".'[66]

Of great importance for our purpose here is how de Lubac envisages the unity of Christ's bride. Here, she is the 'whole human race' and elsewhere de Lubac often refers to the *Church* as the Bride of Christ.[67] Though de Lubac emphasises that these two brides must not be confused,[68] he draws attention at the outset of *Catholicism* to the likeness between what we might call their respective *patterns* of unity.

'[The] unity of the Mystical Body of Christ, a supernatural unity, supposes a previous natural unity, the unity of the human race.'[69]

Let us clarify the pattern of unity which he envisages. With regard to 'this human nature, from its beginning to the end of the world', de Lubac immediately asks: what is 'the principle of its unity'? In reply, he first makes the general remark that Genesis teaches that 'God made man in his own image'.

[66] *Ibid.*, pp. 1-2 (cf. pp. 199-200); including short quotations from 'Pseudo-Chrysostom (Hippolytus?)', *In Pascha*, 1 (PG 59, 725).
[67] Cf. below, pp. 29, 90-93, 258-259.
[68] *Catholicism*, p. 213, n. 27.
[69] *Ibid.*, p. 1.

'[T]he divine image does not differ from one individual to another: it is all the same image. The same mysterious participation in God which causes the soul to exist effects at one and the same time the unity of spirits among themselves. Whence comes the notion, so beloved of Augustinianism, of one spiritual family intended to form the one city of God.'[70]

This remark helps us to appreciate that de Lubac's understanding of Augustinianism is markedly Platonic, in that he suggests it is *one and the same* image stamped from above identically upon each which makes all one; in other words, the principle of unity lies *above*, it is not to be identified with any of the particular images here below. De Lubac reads Gregory of Nyssa likewise.

'[T]he doctrine of Gregory of Nyssa . . . makes a distinction between the first individuals of our kind, coming forth "as by degrees" from their causes, at their time, "by a natural and necessary genesis" in the fashion of all other living creatures, and Man made according to the Image, the object of a direct creation out of time, who is in each of us and who makes us so entirely one that we ought not to speak of man in the plural any more than we speak of three Gods. For "the whole of human nature from the first man to the last is but one image of him who is [*una eademque veri Dei imago*]".'[71]

This pattern of unity is one in which all are united by what they each have identically from above. It is *not* the same as that which underlies the following statement which de Lubac simply juxtaposes, thereby implying that the two patterns of unity are identical. 'By the sacrifice of Christ the first man was saved, that man who is in us all.'[72] From the latter point of view, the principle of the unity of the human race lies not above but here among us; it is the first actual man, Adam. With regard to the analogous unity of the Church, our subsequent chapters will show the importance of distinguishing between a unity

---

[70] *Ibid.*, pp. 2-3.

[71] *Ibid.*, p. 3; quotations from Gregory of Nyssa, *De hominis opificio* 6 (PG 44, 147B-C) and 16 (PG 44, 188). The first two of de Lubac's lengthy appended patristic texts are from Gregory of Nyssa, *De hominis opificio*, 16 (PG 44, 181-5) and 22 (PG 44, 204-5) (cf. *Catholicism*, pp. 229-232).

[72] *Ibid.*, p. 2; quotation from Pseudo-Chrysostom, *In Pascha*, 2 (PG 59, 725), cf. 1 (PG 59, 723).

caused by the same individual Christ[73] being in each from above and the unity of the corporate personality Christ, in which Christ himself stands as one of the many, in their midst.

For the present, let us see how de Lubac presents the unity, communion or *koinonia* of the Church in *Catholicism* and let us continue paying particular attention to the *pattern* of unity. De Lubac's is a *rooted* theology, the very opposite of a 'separate' theology.

> 'The Creator and the Redeemer . . . are one and the same God.
> . . . The Word that became incarnate to renew and complete all things is also he who "enlighteneth every man that cometh into this world".'[74]

Thus, there is a natural attraction to unity in Christ. False religions occur more where this attraction has *strayed*, perhaps disastrously, rather than where utter falsehood reigns.[75] Catholicism is this attraction fulfilled. 'Catholicism is religion itself.'[76] 'On every side . . . in our divided world there are appearing desires for unity' which the Catholic can 'use' in order 'to lead men of good will to the threshold of Catholicism, which alone can effect this unity in its highest sense'.[77] Importantly, de Lubac points out that, as well as the 'metaphysical' obstacle of our individuality, the 'moral' obstacle of our 'egoism' also blocks our passage over the threshold.[78] These obstacles, barring the way into the 'personal life' which is the '*vocation*' of all,[79] are 'naturally impassible'.[80]

---

[73] In referring to Christ as an 'individual', we are following the terminology of Zizioulas and intending Christ who can be considered apart from his relationship with the Church (Zizioulas, *BC*, pp. 108, 182; cf. below, p. 167). See also below, p.23, n. 114.

[74] *Catholicism*, pp. 147-148. Cf. *Splendour*, pp. 174-175: '[God] made us to be brought together into the heart of the life of the Trinity'.

[75] Cf. *ibid.*, p. 147.

[76] *Ibid.*, p. 157. De Lubac interprets the axiom, 'outside the Church, no salvation', to mean that the visible, Catholic Church is 'the "natural place" to which a soul amenable to the suggestions of grace spontaneously tends'. To be so tending, even implicitly, is what imparts salvation (cf. *ibid.*, pp. 119-122).

[77] *Ibid.*, pp. 195, 197. On p. 30, de Lubac says that 'the Catholic spirit' is 'a spirit . . . of the broadest universality coupled with the strictest unity'.

[78] *Ibid.*, p. 189; cf. *DGod*, pp. 25-26.

[79] Cf. *ibid.*, p. 181 (de Lubac's italics).

[80] *Ibid.*, p. 189.

Across that threshold lies a 'new world', and de Lubac
quotes the succinct description of its life by his close friend,
Jules Monchanin: it is a world 'ruled by the mysterious
immanence of one in all, and of all in each one'.[81] Such is the
proper relationship between 'Person and Society';[82] such is
the relationship which exists in Catholicism. De Lubac describes it as the relationship between 'the personal and the
universal' and speaks of the need to grasp the unique relationship involved.

> 'There must be basically a real apperception which seizes at a
> single glance, beyond all spatial intuition, the bond between the
> personal and the universal'.[83]

The mutual 'immanence' we have mentioned takes the person
out to the world, the person is 'a centrifugal centre',[84] and
brings the world into the person, 'a person is a whole world';[85]
exterior and interior realms open up simultaneously and
correlatively.[86] A person is 'fully realised' when 'perfectly
universalised' and only Christ makes this possible.[87] It is effected by 'his Spirit' whom 'Christ promised to send to his own'
and whose work de Lubac summarises as follows.

> 'He creates in man new depths which harmonise him with the
> "depths of God", and he projects man out of himself, right to the
> very end of the earth; he makes universal and spiritualises, he
> personalises and unifies.'[88]

---

[81] *Ibid.*, p. 189; quotation from J. Monchanin, 'De la solitude à Dieu', in
Médecine et Adolescence (1936), p. 293.

[82] This is the title of Chapter Eleven of *Catholicism*, in which de Lubac is as
critical of false collectivism as we have seen him being of individualism.

[83] *Catholicism*, p. 188.

[84] *Ibid.*, p. 182. Cf. Zizioulas' description of the person as both ecstatic and
hypostatic (*BC*, p. 53, n. 47; *HCH*, p. 425, n. 1).

[85] *Ibid.*, p. 182; quotation from J. Maritain, *Humanisme intégral*, p. 17.

[86] Cf. *ibid.*, p. 186. In *Splendour*, de Lubac says: 'Christianity is universal not
only in the sense that all men have their Saviour in Jesus Christ, but also in the
sense that the whole man finds his salvation in Him' (p. 144).

[87] *Ibid.*, p. 189.

[88] *Ibid.*, p. 186.

To grasp the pattern of the unity of the Church, we may look to St Paul, whom de Lubac presents as perfectly expressing the 'new depths' wrought by the Spirit. De Lubac stresses Paul's statement that God revealed His Son '*in me*'.[89] The indwelling Christ is thus the key. De Lubac describes Christ as 'taking possession of man . . . and penetrating to the very depths of his being'. It is Christ whom Paul has 'discovered within himself'.

> 'Henceforth the idea of human unity is born. That image of God, the image of the Word, which the incarnate Word restores and gives back to its glory, is "I myself"; it is also the other, every other. It is that aspect of *me* in which I coincide with every other man. . . . It is our very unity in God.'[90]

We see, therefore, that the Church is supernaturally united, as Christ's Bride, by each of her members having within them the identical indwelling Christ, who restores in each the identical imprinted image which is the basis of humanity's natural unity, since each human being possesses it 'whole and entire and undivided'.[91] Both natural and supernatural unities have the pattern of what we may call a *coincident unity-of-identity*.

De Lubac stresses that such a unity does not merge beings.

> 'True union does not tend to dissolve into one another the beings that it brings together, but to bring them to completion by means of one another. . . . Union differentiates.'[92]

However, we must say that if the union is effected by something they have identically in common (such as the same image in each or the same Christ in each), then the differentiation cannot be complete and the relationship between the beings cannot *define* them. In de Lubac's presentation, it is what human beings have identically in common that makes them unite (indeed, as we have just seen, 'coincide') and so relate; it is not their relationships which make them unite. All of

---

[89] *Ibid.*, pp. 186-187 (de Lubac's italics); cf. Gal. 1: 15-16.

[90] *Ibid.*, pp. 187-188 (de Lubac's italics).

[91] *Ibid.*, p. 3; quotation from Ruysbroeck, *Mirror of Eternal Salvation*, 8.

[92] *Ibid.*, pp. 180-181. In *RTeil* (p. 149), de Lubac quotes J. P. Blanchard, *Méthode et Principes du Père Teilhard de Chardin* (1961), p. 15: 'As the famous "I think therefore I am" *is* Descartes, so "union differentiates" *is* Teilhard.'

their relationships pass through Christ or God, as is clear in the letter from one medieval monk to another from which de Lubac approvingly quotes: 'if you love the image of God, you love me as the image of God; and I, in my turn, loving God, love you'.[93] We may ask whether, given such a middle term, the two monks can really be said to love each other with the specificity which that term would normally imply. Further, if this is how de Lubac understands what he calls the 'circumincession' of persons in the *Civitas Dei*, the question arises of whether he envisages the circumincession of the Persons of the Trinity, to which he also refers, in the same way, especially since he says that the human 'unity of circumincession' is 'in the likeness of the Trinity itself'.[94] It appears that de Lubac considers the circumincession of the divine Persons to be the result of something they have in common, namely the divine nature, rather than as itself what determines their nature.[95]

The insights of mystical solitude pervade *Catholicism*. Clearly, the monks whose correspondence has just been recalled were separated from one another, but de Lubac regards their words as exemplary for *all* Christians.[96] One of the texts appended by de Lubac is Peter Damian's eleventh-century instruction to his eremitical monks that, in their solitude, they could still celebrate the Liturgy, saying both 'The Lord be with you' and the response, 'And with thy spirit'.

> 'In fact, he who prays alone may say "we", and the multitude may say "I". For, by the power of the Holy Spirit who dwells in each

[93] *Ibid.*, p. 31; quotation from (St Bernard ?) *Meditationes piisimae de cognitione humanae conditionis*, 5, 15 (corrected reference) (PL 184, 495B). Cf. below, pp. 276-277.

[94] *Ibid.*, p. 183. Cf. above, p. 17, n. 74, and below, pp. 93-94.

[95] In the French edition of *Catholicisme* (1983[7], p. 7, n. 2), a footnote to the extract quoted at note 70 above (p. 16) cites the explanatory article by R. Arnou, 'Unité numérique et unité de nature chez les Pères après le concile de Nicée'. In this article, Arnou says, with reference to the teaching of Basil, which he likens to that of Gregory of Nyssa, that the unity of the divine nature 'is found in each of the three Persons' (p. 251).

[96] Cf. *Catholicism*, p. 31. We may compare the circumstances in which Afanassieff developed his eucharistic ecclesiology, in which *communities* are linked invisibly (cf. P. McPartlan, 'Eucharistic Ecclesiology', p. 327).

and fills us all, the individual is a multitude and the multitude is an individual.'[97]

De Lubac quotes from this text in *Catholicism* and elsewhere, to express the mutual immanence of Christians:

'just as man is called a microcosm, so each one of the faithful is, so to say, the Church in miniature'.[98]

Accordingly, the '*anima ecclesiastica*' may be more strictly defined as 'that soul which *is* the Church'.[99]

Moreover, de Lubac named as '*inspirateurs immédiats*' of *Catholicism* three remarkable priests: Yves de Montcheuil, Pierre Teilhard de Chardin and Jules Monchanin.[100] Teilhard and Monchanin led lives involving much separation from their Christian brothers, in travels for research and the founding of a Benedictine ashram in India, respectively, and de Lubac regarded both as mystics.[101] De Montcheuil gave the ultimate witness in the isolation of execution.[102] All three certainly qualify as *viri ecclesiastici*, for they were by no means individualists. De Lubac quoted in *Catholicism* the 'magnificent simile' of Teilhard, who spoke of the *activity* of 'pure souls', likening them to 'the snowy summits whose impassive peaks continually breathe *for us* [*aspirent . . . pour nous*] the invigorating currents of the higher atmosphere'.[103] In his tribute to Monchanin, de Lubac said of those who, like Monchanin, chose the contem-

---

[97] *Catholicism*, pp. 289-290: quotation from Peter Damain, *Liber qui dicitur Dominus Vobiscum*, 6 (PL 145, 236B). For the context of this work, see e.g. P. McNulty, *St Peter Damian, Selected Writings on the Spiritual Life*, pp. 17-18.

[98] *Ibid.*, p. 168; quotation from *Liber qui dicitur Dominus Vobiscum*, 10 (PL 145, 239D). Cf. *Splendour*, pp. 105, 272, 274; below, p. 93, n. 96.

[99] *Splendour*, p. 274 (my italics).

[100] In a note for the edition of *Catholicisme* as no. 13 of the 'Foi Vivante' series (Cerf, Paris, 1965), p. 15.

[101] Said of Teilhard in *RTeil*, p. 84, and of Monchanin in *Images*, p. 45.

[102] Having been taken from his cell by the Gestapo at 22.00 on 10 August 1944; cf. de Lubac, *Trois*, p. 71.

[103] *Catholicism*, pp. 191-192 (corrected translation and my italics), cf. *RTeil*, p. 222; quotation from Teilhard, *Le milieu divin*, p. 125. De Lubac was not uncritical of Teilhard; his many misgivings are listed by von Balthasar, 'The Achievement of Henri de Lubac', p. 33, n. 2.

plative life, that 'their desert is the place of communion with their invisible brothers . . . they present to the Father the oblation of the whole world'.[104] He explicitly calls Monchanin 'a man of the Church', whose heart 'beat in unison with the universal Church'.[105] Finally, again in posthumous tribute, de Lubac quoted the words of de Montcheuil. 'Each Christian must carry within him the whole Church.'[106]

However, we must note that mystical solitude has no *fundamental* place for a specific community or local church in its vision of the Christian life. Such a structural unit is superfluous when one man, as priest, can utter the words of Christ and, as Christian, can respond in the name of the whole Church. This scheme relies on the priest retaining a generic identity as a Christian underneath his additional ordination as a priest, rather than his being a Christian precisely as a priest. In the former view, the priest stands out from his fellow Christians to utter his priestly words and then stands among them to respond. In the latter view, he stands among them as a priest.

De Lubac established a theological milestone in *Catholicism* by his description of the Church as 'the sacrament of Christ': 'she really makes him present'.[107] S. Wood concludes that he never 'precisely developed *how*' this is so.[109] We may see two ways. First, the priests of the Church, standing out from the people, make Christ present. But secondly, they join the people in response, forming, together with the people, that

---

[104]*Images*, p. 111.

[105]*Ibid.*, pp. 35, 39.

[106]*Trois*, p. 95 (no reference given).

[107]*Catholicism*, p. 28; de Lubac's footnote reference to Möhler, 'Letter to the Countess Stolberg (1834)' (*Catholicisme* (1983[7]), p. 50, n. 3), does not appear in the English translation. Cf. *Splendour*, p. 147. De Lubac was the first theologian this century to develop the sacramental view of the Church, which, after further elaboration by German and Dutch theologians, found expression at Vatican II in *Lumen Gentium*, nn. 1, 9, 48 (W. Kasper, *Theology and Church*, pp. 113-114; cf. comments by C. Moeller in John H. Miller (ed.), *Vatican II. An Interfaith Appraisal*, p. 177). P. Smulders notes the link between this theme's appearance in *Catholicism* and the commemoration of Möhler's centenary ('L'Eglise sacrement du salut', p. 315).

[108]S. Wood, *The Church as the Social Embodiment of Grace in the Ecclesiology of Henri de Lubac*, p. 299.

sacramental veil, woven by the circumincession of persons indwelt by Christ,[109] as we have already seen, within which alone Christ may be encountered. The second view seems to be that which accords with what de Lubac described in *Catholicism* as 'the first principle of Augustinian mysticism'.

> 'Each individual needs the *mediation* of all, but no-one is kept at a distance by any intermediary.'[110]

This interpretation is confirmed by his later repetition that the Church is 'the sacrament of Christ' and clarification that a sacrament 'is not something intermediate, but something mediatory'.[111]

'God does not love us as so many separate beings',[112] said de Lubac in *Catholicism*. The Church is the circumincessory context of His loving of each. De Lubac's great purpose in *Catholicism* and thereafter, was that of promoting the de-individualisation of Christians, by urging an understanding that 'grace which is produced and maintained by the sacraments does not set up a purely individual relationship between the soul and God or Christ';[113] rather, the soul has this relationship necessarily in the context of the Church, the Bride of Christ.

In contrast, the 'de-individualisation of *Christ*' is the main purpose of Zizioulas.[114] In his vision, Christ no longer stands

---

[109]Cf. below, pp. 80-81.

[110]*Catholicism* (de Lubac's italics), p. 183. De Lubac adds that Augustine 'completely transformed' the neo-Platonist hierarchical vision of a scale of degrees of being, which 'pseudo-Dionysius only partially rectified'. Augustine's own faith taught him that there were no intermediaries between God and us in a hierarchy of being.

[111]*Splendour*, p. 147.

[112]*Catholicism*, p. 183.

[113]*Ibid.*, p. 32.

[114]*MCO*, p. 299 (my italics); cf. *HCH*, p. 441, also BC, p.113, n. 116. Rowan Williams gives a caution about Zizioulas' refusal to apply the term, 'individual', to Christ, but recognises that he has no intention of denying Christ's human particularity ('Review', p. 103). Zizioulas himself stresses this point: '"de-individualisation" does not mean the dissolution of personal particularity but, on the contrary, the condition for the emergence of true personal otherness and identity' (*HCH*, p. 441, n. 2).

out from the Church, engendering in her members a coincident unity-of-identity, instead he stands among them, constituting them and constituted by them, in what we may contrastingly call a *differentiated unity-of-complementarity*. The consequence of this different pattern of unity, communion or *koinonia*, which flows from Zizioulas' different understanding of Christ, is his stipulation of a carefully structured assembly for the proper celebration of the Eucharist. A private Mass is inconceivable for him.[115]

[115]Cf. below, p. 178.

Chapter 2

Nature and the Supernatural

'It would be too paradoxical, and even a little ridiculous, to acclaim the topicality of a subject which was first chosen for the lack of topicality it offered.'[1]

De Lubac wrote these words in 1955, in the middle of 'the long period in which he was proscribed within the Church because of *Surnaturel* (1946)',[2] or, more specifically, because this study was generally thought to have been implicitly criticised in Pope Pius XII's encyclical letter, *Humani Generis*, in 1950.[3] Their ironic tone springs from the fact that, in the appropriately uncontroversial topic of Buddhism which he was researching,[4] he had discerned the 'hidden but active presence' of 'the eternal problems', namely those of the relationship between nature and the supernatural.

---

[1] *Amida*, p. 9.

[2] Hans Urs von Balthasar, 'The Achievement of Henri de Lubac', p. 8. For details of this period and its immediate prelude, cf. de Lubac, *Mémoire*, particularly, pp. 61-115.

[3] De Lubac later maintained that, far from criticising his view, *Humani Generis* actually incorporated a phrase of his, from 1949, into its teaching (cf. *EVat*, p. 13; *Lettres*, p. 79). The phrase is: '*Si Dieu l'avait voulu, il aurait pu ne pas nous donner l'être, et cet etre qu'il nous a donné, il aurait pu ne point l'appeler à Le voir*' (*MSur*, p. 104). *Humani Generis* condemned the following error: '*Alii veram «gratuitatem» ordinis supernaturalis corrumpunt, cum autument Deum entia intellectu praedita condere non posse, quin eadem ad beatificam visionem ordinet et vocet*' (Denzinger-Schönmetzer, *Enchiridion* [hereafter, DS], n. 3891). Cf. *MSup*, p. 169, n. 54.

[4] Cf. H. Vorgrimler, 'Henri de Lubac (B)', pp. 814-816.

'Rarely has man seemed to experience his destitution more keenly [*mieux*] and moreover to approach a religion of grace. Few symbols are so evocative of the supernatural world and of its sovereign invasion than the Amidist pictures of the "Descent", with their colossal Amida, luminous and calm, silently advancing, a Force at once compassionate and implacable. Nevertheless, how far all of this remains from the Christian supernatural! Freed from the puerilities of its fable, Amidism still remains deeply sunk in that twilight thought and spirituality which belong to all "natural" religion, as to all "natural" mysticism.'[5]

De Lubac considers that the nature/supernatural problematic is omnipresent in human experience and that Buddhism expresses, perhaps most honestly,[6] the wisdom of those who face it without Christ. He says that what Buddhists lack, quite simply, is 'the only Revelation, which culminates and finishes with Jesus Christ'. Significantly, he rephrases this as follows: they have not had 'the decisive experience from which arises ... the world of persons'.[7] 'For the Buddhist ... every individual nature is "an embryo of Tathagata", and is therefore destined to become a buddha'.[8] But 'the Buddhas themselves have no real being; they are simply aspects of an impersonal and insubstantial buddhahood which absorbs them all into one single Dharmakaya'.[9] There is thus an 'idealistic monism which lies at the bottom of Buddhism'.[10]

Sharply to be contrasted is Christian belief. As de Lubac stated elsewhere, 'for Christians created nature is no kind of divine seed'.[11] We may approach the vital theme raised here of

---

[5]*Amida*, pp. 9-10. Amidism is the largest Buddhist sect in Japan. The important theme of *descent* will recur, e.g. below, pp. 43-44.

[6]In the untranslated 'Avant-propos' to the original French edition of *Aspects du bouddhisme I*, de Lubac referred to Buddhism as, aside from Christianity, '*sans doute le plus grand fait spirituel de l'histoire*' (p. 8).

[7]*Amida*, p. 10.

[8]*MSup*, p. 108.

[9]*Aspects*, p. 45.

[10]Von Balthasar, 'The Achievement of Henri de Lubac', p. 22 (cf. p. 23), in summary of de Lubac's analysis of Buddhism.

[11]*MSup*, p. 109.

creation as follows. There is, he says, 'a gulf between Buddhist charity and Christian charity'.[12] Buddhist charity, or rather *pity*, is 'all the more perfect, the more abstract and general it becomes', whereas 'Christian charity is directed towards human beings in all their particularity'. The latter is universal precisely in its particularity: 'general and universal are as different as abstract and concrete'.[13] Buddhism lacks 'unitive charity' because, ultimately, 'there are no beings to give themselves to each other'.[14] De Lubac diagnoses the root cause of this fluidity when he says that, in Buddhism, beings lack 'ontological solidity deriving from a Creator'.[15]

We may therefore summarise that the Christian doctrine of creation fundamentally rejects *monism*. The distinguishing of particular beings from one another relies upon them all being primarily distinguished from a Creator. Their mutual love relies upon their all having been created out of love, by a God whose 'very Being' is love. What Buddhism feels 'most painfully' is 'the absence of a real God, a living God, a God of Charity'. The Christian believes that '*Deus est Caritas*' and that it is the imprinted *image* of God which 'forms the fundamental solidity of his [man's] being'.[16] Christianity has, indeed, a place for 'negative theology'.

'In Christianity, nevertheless, affirmation always triumphs in the end. If this is not true of Buddhism, it is because it lacks the only possible Foundation: God, creative Love.'[17]

De Lubac here traces Christianity's contrast with Buddhism's monist oblivion back *via* the doctrine of creation into God's own inner life. Elsewhere, he confirms the concrete and personalist style of his response to Buddhism by stressing that creation should be explicitly related to the divine *Persons* and

[12] *Aspects*, p. 37.
[13] *Ibid.*, pp. 38-39.
[14] *Ibid.*, p. 50.
[15] *Ibid.*, p. 41.
[16] *Ibid.*, p. 41. We shall return to examine the affirmation that 'God is love' in Chapter Eleven.
[17] *Ibid.*, p. 51.

thereby acknowledged as a *free* act. If '*Deus creans est Deus ut natura*' then 'God would create — if the word is still appropriate at all — of necessity'.[18] Moreover, with regard to God's own being, he endorses Blondel's rejection of any notion of 'divine nature' as something given (a '*fatum*'), which would be antecedent to God's 'primordial freedom'. God 'owes nothing to anyone except Himself'.[19] Though de Lubac never explicitly speaks of the *Father's* freedom, he does point out that the 'one and only God', in whom the first article of the Creed professes belief, 'is certainly not, directly and formally, the divine substance common to the three Persons: it is . . . the Father . . . as the principle of the other two Persons'.[20]

Thus, the key which opens up the Christian world of persons is the doctrine of creation by a free God, with its implicit recognition of a fundamental distinction between the created and the uncreated, that is, between nature and the supernatural. Commenting forcefully on the need for a distinction between 'human nature' and the 'supernatural', the latter being not strictly God but 'the divine order considered in its relationship of opposition to, and of union with, the human order', de Lubac says the following.

> 'To deny this fundamental distinction . . . would be to deny as well and in its very principle every notion of revelation, mystery, divine Incarnation, redemption or salvation. That would be to deny the Christian faith itself. . . . [O]ne would no longer believe in the living God who reveals himself to man, who intervenes in man's history, who "became man so that man might become God".'[21]

Once God is distinguished from creation, the two come together in Christ. How de Lubac envisages this occurring will occupy us greatly. We may note immediately, however, as a

---

[18]*MSup*, p. 82, n. 23.
[19]*Spirito*, p. 263, n. 12; quotations from M. Blondel, *L'action* (1936), vol. 1, p. 164. De Lubac adds a further quotation from *L'action* (1936), vol. 1, p. 180: 'Pure Act does not bear [*ne subit pas*] a nature by some sort of fate [*fatalité*]; it is freely necessary and necessarily free.'
[20]*Faith*, p. 35.
[21]*BCat*, pp. 20-22; cf. below, p. 55.

prelude to our discussion in Chapter Three of the topic of mysticism, which focuses and personalises consideration of nature and the supernatural, that de Lubac prizes the nuptial image of the Church as the Bride of Christ because it preserves the vital distinction without which Christianity would collapse into monism. 'Christian mysticism', he says, derives much from the symbolism of 'spiritual marriage'.

> 'Because between the human soul and its God, as in the wedding of the Church and the Lamb, it is always a matter of union, not of absorption (whether this be in one sense or the other); of unification, if you like, but not of identification. It is a case of mutual love — even though the whole initiative is God's.'[22]

As the last sentence of this quotation indicates, de Lubac is concerned to paint a *theocentric* picture, clearly attributing all initiative to God as He creates and calls humanity to Himself. De Lubac sees a breakdown of this traditional picture at the time of Baius, when *both* sides took *man* as the starting point and considered the supernatural in accordance with its etymology:

> 'partisans and adversaries of Baius agreed too often on defining [the] supernatural extrinsically and relatively, by reason of its inaccessibility or gratuity, without getting through to the ultimate reason for this gratuity . . . namely its intrinsically divine character'.[23]

The terms '(human) nature and the supernatural' are even less happy today because of 'their abstraction' and the 'very different usage' which they have in modern life. However, de Lubac says that he retains them 'because they are imposed upon us by history'.[24]

---

[22] *MMys*, p. 65; cf. M. Figura, 'Henri de Lubac: teologia della pienezza della fede', p. 79. De Lubac says that to seek 'the realisation of the Absolute' beyond a mere 'union with God' would be to pursue 'the supreme illusion', which ends in a *nirvana* where all finite reality is lost, rather than in a fulness where it is transfigured (*MMys*, p. 66).

[23] *Surnaturel*, p. 154.

[24] *Athéisme*, pp. 96-97.

It was in the papal condemnation of Baius that the term 'supernatural' first appeared in an ecclesiastical document.[25] De Lubac summarises the case against Baius as follows.

> The supernatural is not owed to nature; it is nature which, if it is to obey God's plan, owes itself to the supernatural if that supernatural is offered to it.'[26]

If we focus on *man*, then we can easily find ourselves, with Baius, regarding grace as necessary simply to *complete* man in himself, in his nature. If we focus on *God*, then we see grace as His gift to *perfect* man, that is to draw him to the end for which he was made by God Himself, namely the beatific vision.

> 'The difference between these two verbs, to complete and to perfect, indicates the whole, radical difference between Baius and St Thomas.'[27]

Before turning to St Thomas Aquinas, we may note de Lubac's repeated qualification of nature as *human* nature.[28] It appears that, in his concern to present the authentic teaching of Aquinas, that God calls all humanity to one supernatural beatitude, no purely natural beatitude being conceivable for some, de Lubac has considered man in isolation from the rest of the created world. He admitted with regret that he had excluded consideration of 'man's solidarity with the universe' in his first book, *Catholicism*.[29] However, it is an omission which he never remedied.[30]

Thomas Aquinas

It is the conviction of de Lubac that Aquinas' doctrine on nature and supernatural was in line with all the great scholastics, who in turn derived their teaching from Augustine. He summarises a survey of this common doctrine in the following

---

[25] *BCat*, p. 20. Cf. Propositions 21, 23 of the Bull, *Ex omnibus afflictionibus*, in 1567 (DS, nn. 1921, 1923).
[26] *MSup*, p. 123; cf. below, p. 45.
[27] *Ibid*., p. 122, n. 92.
[28] Cf. above, pp. 28-29.
[29] *Catholicism*, pp. xvi-xvii.
[30] Cf. below, Conclusion.

fundamental principle. 'The spiritual creature does not find its end in itself, but in God.'[31] He repeatedly recalls the statement by Augustine which manifestly gives rise to this principle and which runs as a motif through de Lubac's treatment of this theme.

> *'Fecisti nos ad te, [Domine] et inquietum est cor nostrum, donec requiescat in te.*[32]

He stresses that neither Augustine nor any of the scholastics who followed him even hint that the spiritual creature thereby constrains God. God's freedom is implicit in the recognition of His absolute priority.

> '[T]he will of God is the first thing here, and therefore God's liberty is total. It is this will which, at every moment of each of our lives, remains first, acts first. His sovereign liberty encloses, surpasses and causes all the bonds of intelligibility that we discover between the creature and its destiny. Nature and the supernatural are thus united, without in any sense being confused.'[33]

De Lubac highlights the 'very Augustinian phraseology' which Aquinas used when he expounded the restless '*desiderium*' in man.[34] The opinion which Aquinas was opposing, which it is important to identify (for it was not that of Baius), was that of the philosophers who could not entertain the possibility of the beatific vision.[35] Contrary to the fundamental principle stated above, it has always been the view of 'common sense' that: '*desiderium autem naturale non potest esse nisi rei quae naturaliter*

---

[31] *MSup*, p. 129.

[32] 'You have made us, (Lord) for yourself and our heart is restless until it rests in you.' Augustine, *Confessions*, 1,1,1 (PL 32,661); quoted in *MSup*, p. 84; also pp. xiv, 49 and on p. 251, n. 20, with an additional allusion on p. 162. Cf. *Faith*, pp. 70, 79, 82, 83, 162.

[33] *MSup*, pp. 128-129. The scheme of unity without confusion evokes the Chalcedonian dogma of Christ. We shall see how de Lubac makes what we shall call the 'Chalcedonian shift' from the original dogma to its existential impact upon Christians in Chapter Three.

[34] *Ibid.*, p. 251; reference to Aquinas, *Summa contra Gentiles*, 3, 50, 4: '*Nihil finitum desiderium intellectus quietare potest*'.

[35] *Ibid.*, pp. 33-35; cf. p. 217.

haberi potest.[36] Aquinas quoted such views in order to reject the common sense application of them to *all* created natures, man included. '[T]here is nature and nature' and 'the nature of spirit created by God's free decision for a supernatural end freely chosen is not comparable in every way . . . to the nature of material beings'.[37]

> 'Man's longing for God is in a category of its own; we cannot apply univocally to it any of the patterns of thought which we generally use to try to define relationships between beings in this world.'[38]

De Lubac stresses that Aquinas refused to apply the common sense view 'automatically to the case of created spirit in relation to its last end'.[39] However, the theory of pure nature arose when those who claimed to be interpreting Aquinas *did* so apply it. De Lubac calls them 'our "common sense" theologians'.[40]

While the common sense view may be derived from Aristotle's *De caelo*,[41] so may 'the universal, fundamental law of high scholasticism',[42] which Aquinas, after formulating it, immediately applies to the situation of man before God. Thereby, ingeniously, 'he manages to use the Philosopher [Aristotle] to refute him, without appearing to attack him'.

> 'St Thomas excelled at this . . . [M]any of those who came after him have been deceived by it.'[43]

---

[36] *Ibid.*, p. 210: 'there can be no natural desire except for something which can naturally be had'; quotation from Aquinas, *In 3 Sent.*, dist. 27, q.2, a.2, ad 4um. Cf. *MSup*, p. 178.

[37] *Ibid.*, pp. 178-179.

[38] *Ibid.*, p. 114.

[39] *Ibid.*, p. 210

[40] *Ibid.*, p. 210. Cf. below, pp. 34-35, 45.

[41] Cf. *Ibid.*, p. 179, n. 90 and *AMTh*, pp. 184-185, where de Lubac refers to Cajetan's use of book 2 of Aristotle's *De caelo* (actually, 2, 8, 290a) to this end in his commentary on Aquinas', *Summa theologiae, In Primam*, q.12, art.1 (cf. Aquinas, *Opera omnia* (Rome, 1882-1971), vol. 4, p. 116). Cajetan continues in the same place (n.9): '*Apud s. Thomae quoque doctrinam . . . homo non naturaliter, sed obedientialiter ordinetur in felicitatem illam.*'

[42] Von Balthasar, 'The Achievement of Henri de Lubac', p. 26.

[43] *MSup*, pp. 198-199; cf. p. 154.

The law is as follows.

> '[A] nature which can attain the perfect good [*perfectum bonum*], although it needs outside help, is of a higher condition than a nature which can attain without such recourse only a lesser good. . . . Likewise it is better to be a rational creature who can reach perfect happiness [*perfectum beautitudinis bonum*], though needing divine help, than a non-rational creature which is not capable of this happiness [*boni*], but arrives at some partial good under its own natural power.'[44]

De Lubac considers that Aquinas' own achievement, not matched by all of his disciples, was to use Aristotle in the service of the Christian Gospel. Aquinas' view was that the philosopher and the theologian deal with 'two series of complementary, but not contradictory, truths'.[45] 'Pure nature', for Aquinas, would be nature 'considered in itself', that is, 'independent of all reference to God'.[46] As such, it would be the legitimate study of the philosopher, who might also consider man, though necessarily 'abstractly and statically'. What Aristotle lacked, de Lubac crucially points out, was a knowledge of the fact of 'creation'. This fact means that knowledge of a thing in itself is not *exhaustive* knowledge of it. The philosopher needs the theologian to contextualise *all* of his findings in terms of how God has *actually* constituted men and things 'in their concrete reality', with a particular end in view. In the *actual* order, God has created man with a 'natural desire' to see Him. With this doctrine, Aquinas built a 'bridge' between Aristotle and Chris-

---

[44]Aquinas, *Summa Theologiae*, I, II, q.5, a.5, ad 2um; quoted partially by de Lubac in *MSup*, p. 179, n. 90 and fully on pp. 197-198 and in *Surnaturel*, p. 119, n.3. In the latter place, de Lubac also recalls Aquinas, *De malo*, q.5, a.1, which he renders as follows: 'it is greater to be able to do more with external help than to be able to do less by oneself'. Aquinas' reference in the *Summa* is to Aristotle, *De caelo*, 2, 12, 292a.

[45]*AMTh*, p. 211.

[46]Cf. *MSup*, p. 16. Since, as we are about to see, de Lubac does acknowledge 'the God of the philosophers', presumably we are to understand him here to mean independent of all reference to the true God as He has actually revealed both Himself and our destiny.

tianity.[47] In it 'is summarised all of the teaching of St Thomas about the relations between nature and the supernatural'.[48]

The place which Aquinas wished carefully to give to Aristotle is precisely shown in his doctrine of a '*duplex hominis bonum ultimum*'.[49] By this expression, Aquinas intended not two alternative possible ends for man, one for some and another for the rest, but one *twofold* end for all. There is not 'a double possible orientation', but 'an actual duality'; *both* ends are to be achieved. The happiness of the philosopher is the end which man 'can attain by himself'.

'In fact, only the second truly merits the name of a last end and only it transcends the earthly horizon.'[50]

The former happiness consists in coming to know '[t]he God of the philosophers', who 'completes the formula of the world' and so satisfies man's reason.[51] However, Aquinas' 'greatness' was to recognise that man as he actually is desires *more*. He cannot escape 'the nostalgia of Being'. His intelligence is 'steeped in' his spirit and reaches further, to the *vision* of God.[52]

However, in that Aristotle analysed the actual state of man and envisaged his actual end totally within this world, we may judge that Aquinas' attempt to make use of him purely abstractly was precarious. It does appear that he was risking the eventual misinterpretation of his own doctrine in terms of a double possible orientation in the actual created order. This is, in fact, the 'error' which de Lubac attributes to his stern critic, R. Garrigou-Lagrange, and which he traces back through many theologians to Suarez.[53]

---

[47] Cf. *Surnaturel*, pp. 130-132.

[48] *Ibid.*, p. 477; cf. *DGod*, p. 146.

[49] Cf. *DHBeat*, for de Lubac's fullest treatment of this doctrine, based on Aquinas, *Summa Theologiae*, I, II, q.62, a.1. In *AMTh*, p. 212, he refers to its occurrence in Aquinas, *De veritate*, q. 14, a.2. Cf. G. Vass *The Mystery of Man and the Foundations of a Theological System* (hereafter, *Mystery*), pp. 60-62, for a brief account of the role of this doctrine in Aquinas.

[50] Cf. *Surnaturel*, p. 110.

[51] *DGod*, p. 144; reference to Aquinas, *Summa theologiae*, I, q. 32, a.1.

[52] Cf. *ibid.*, p. 147.

[53] *DHBeat*, p. 291. Garrigou-Lagrange was one of the strongest opponents of the *nouvelle théologie*, cf. his article, 'La nouvelle théologie où va't'elle?'. We may note that '*nouvelle théologie*' was the term which de Lubac himself had first critically applied to the theory of pure nature, cf. *Surnaturel*, pp. 125, 135, 140.

In contrast with these *common sense* theologians, who include man within their 'absolute principle' which matches natural desires to natural powers in creation,[54] there stands Aquinas, who perceived that man is a 'special case'.[55] Unlike other creatures man has what must be diagnosed as an 'unstable ontological constitution'.

> '[He is] a creature made out of nothing which, astoundingly, touches God. . . . At once, and inextricably, both "nothing" and "image"; fundamentally nothing, yet none the less substantially image.'[56]

We shall see that de Lubac's understanding of the relationship between nature and the supernatural hinges upon a triad of elements. Here he indicates the first two of three things which he would distinguish. The phrase 'substantially image', which indicates the second element, is highly significant. Being the image of God is not *accidental* in man, but *substantial*. We may compare what de Lubac said in *Surnaturel*, namely not that man *has* a desire for God, but rather that, as a created spirit, he '*is* desire for God'.[57] The comparison, which suggests that man's desire for God is the image of God, which is *substantial* in him, is confirmed by de Lubac's statement that the desire to see God 'constitutes us'.[58] 'St Thomas held that finality is something intrinsic, affecting the depths of the being.'[59] Nevertheless, de Lubac still distinguishes this finality as a *second* element, by referring to it as something *imprinted* when man's *nature* (the first element) is actually created.

> 'The Creator's power imprints a movement "deep within his creature, in the heart of the created being, at the moment of its

[54] In *Spirito*, p. 255, n. 1, de Lubac specifically criticises Suarez' '*assioma contestabilissimo*': '*appetitus naturalis non fundatur nisi in naturali potestate*' (*Tractatus de gratia Dei, Prolegom*, 4,1,8, in Suarez, *Opera omnia*, vol. 7, p. 181).

[55] *MSup*, p. 198.

[56] *Ibid.*, pp. 147-148.

[57] *Surnaturel*, p. 483 (my italics).

[58] *MSup*, p. 217.

[59] *Ibid.*, p. 92.

creation" . . . a movement not of this or that individual, but of the nature all have in common.'[60]

By attaching the movement or desire so resolutely to the nature which all men have,[61] de Lubac anchors his conviction that there is one *destiny* for all, though we must also say that the risk which he then runs is of a *confusion* between the first and second elements.

Introducing now a *third* thing to distinguish, de Lubac says that the desire exists so that it may be transformed into *love*.

'Before loving God, and so as to be able to love Him, it [the human spirit] desires. Made for God, the spirit is attracted by Him.'[62]

Does the desire cease if and when it is transformed into love? De Lubac's negative answer shows us not only that the second element permanently retains its distinction from the third, but also that the first permanently retains its distinction from the second. De Lubac delicately presents them as *nested* realities,[63] with the first and second permanently supporting the second and third, respectively. He says that the desire 'is in us the *permanent* action of the God who creates our nature'.[64] The starting point is man's 'uneliminable creaturely condition'.[65] We may then say that man's being always a creature, means that God is *permanently* creating him, in which action God also actually imprints the desire for Him and calls man to the beatific vision.

---

[60]*Ibid.*, pp. 176-177.

[61]De Lubac notes that Aquinas referred not just to man's '*desiderium naturale*', but also to his '*naturae desiderium*'; cf. *MSup*, p. 75 and n. 13; with reference, for example, to Aquinas, *Summa contra Gentiles*, bk. 3, ch. 48, resp. 2. De Lubac repeatedly quotes from bk. 3, ch. 57, n. 3: '*omnis intellectus naturaliter desiderat divinae substantiae visionem*' (*MSup*, pp. 73, 256).

[62]*Surnaturel*, p. 483.

[63]Cf. man's intelligence being 'steeped in' his spirit (above, p. 34).

[64]*Surnaturel*, p. 487 (my italics). Creating our nature and imprinting the desire are *distinguishable* actions. That the desire does not cease when transformed into love is de Lubac's meaning in stating that the *donum perfectum* does not deprive man's spirit of 'its original impulse' (*DGod*, p. 110; cf. below, p. 40, n. 83).

[65]*Spirito*, p. 257, n. 3; cf. the quotation given below, p. 43, n. 102.

'If there is in our nature a desire to see God, this can only be because God wills for us this supernatural end which consists in seeing Him. It is because, so willing and not ceasing so to will, He lodges and does not cease to lodge the desire for it in our nature. Thereby, this desire is nothing other than His call.'[66]

The following statement may serve to indicate the full delicacy of de Lubac's triad.

'God alone is simply love without desire, because God's nature is not imposed upon Him: pure Being, pure Act, He is also pure Love.'[67]

We see that desire pertains to the *creature* and expresses the permanent dependence of the one who only receives his nature. It then follows that, if love is the third element of the triad, the existence of desire as a distinct second element depends crucially upon there being a clearly acknowledged first element, namely created nature itself. Without this first element, a *monist* scheme is unavoidable, in which man and God belong to a closed system where man's desire must be fulfilled by God and the gratuity of its fulfilment cannot be maintained.

Compromising this gratuity was precisely the allegation made in various quarters against de Lubac. Karl Rahner associated de Lubac with the anonymous author, D., whom he took as representative of the *nouvelle theologie* 'circle' or 'school'. Rahner said he could not accept their view that man's '*desiderium*', the '*potentia oboedientialis* of nature', is 'a *constituent* of his "nature" in such a way that the latter cannot be conceived without it, i.e. as pure nature'.[68] In other words, Rahner requires that there be something *left*, which may be termed *natura pura*, after the *desiderium*, to which he refers elsewhere in the same article as the 'vocation to supernatural communion with God',[69] is abstracted from man. He distinguishes

[66]*Surnaturel*, pp. 486-487.

[67]*Ibid.*, p. 483, with reference to Blondel, *L'Action* (1936), t. 1, pp. 163-164. Cf. above, p. 28, n. 19.

[68]Cf. Karl Rahner, 'Concerning the Relationship between Nature and Grace' (hereafter, 'Relationship'), p. 303. Vass understands D. to be D. Delahaye (*Mystery*, p. 171, n. 4).

[69]*Ibid.*, p. 300.

man's 'concrete quiddity' from his 'nature' and admits that the
end which God has actually decreed for man must be '*eo ipso* an
interior ontological constituent of his concrete quiddity "ter-
minative", even if it is not a constituent· of his "nature"'.[70]
However, he asserts that, if such a *natura pura* does not exist, as
a 'remainder'[71] or '*Restbegriff*',[72] then it is impossible to maintain that grace is unowed ('*ungeschuldet*').[73]

Rahner emphasises that grace must be 'an unexpected
miracle of his [God's] love', whereas D. makes it no more of a
miracle than creation itself.[74] Because D. considers the 'disposition' as 'belonging to nature', it follows that, although the
creature man is not owed his existence, once created he *is* owed
grace.[75] In short, unless the disposition/*desiderium*/*potentia
oboedientialis* is a gift beyond that of nature itself, grace cannot
be another, second gift:

> 'the longing for, the ordination to, God's Love, this existential
> for supernatural grace, only allows grace to be unowed when it
> is itself unowed'.[76]

Therefore, *three* things must be distinguished: nature, the
disposition and grace.

However, this is exactly de Lubac's own point in so painstak-
ingly distinguishing his own triad, with particular emphasis on
the distinction between the first and second elements. Already
in 1949 (that is, before *Humani generis* in 1950) he had made
the latter vital distinction by speaking of the '*double* initiative

[70] *Ibid.*, p. 302.

[71] *Ibid.*, p. 302.

[72] *Ibid.*, p. 313.

[73] *Ibid.*, pp. 304-306; cf. pp. 312-315. I restore the correct translation of
ungeschuldet as 'unowed'; cf. *ibid.*, p. 304, n. 2.

[74] *Ibid.*, p. 305. De Lubac's difference from D. is therefore already implicit
in his description of the gift of God as 'the marvel of marvels and the miracle
of miracles' (*Surnaturel*, p. 488).

[75] *Ibid.*, p. 308.

[76] *Ibid.*, p. 313; cf. above, n. 73. This description of the 'existential' as
something *interior* to man, namely his 'longing', serves to refute the criticism
of Rahner by de Lubac in *MSup*, p. 132, n. 2 and by E. Schillebeeckx in
'L'instinct de la foi selon s. Thomas d'Aquin', p. 397.

which brings him [created man] into being and calls him',[77] a statement which he repeated in 1965, with further clarification: 'in effect this brings him into being in order to call him'.[78] Confirmation of the proximity of de Lubac and Rahner in this matter was provided by de Lubac in 1965 when he distanced himself from the article by D. and lengthily quoted Rahner.[79] Further confirmation is provided by the fact that both have to face the same difficulty. With regard to de Lubac's account, we may wonder how, if man is '*substantially* image', this image can be said to be itself imprinted upon something prior, namely man's nature.[80] Likewise, Rahner, who describes this 'potency' in man as 'what is inmost and most authentic in him, the centre and root of what he is absolutely', realises that he must defend himself against von Balthasar's objection that if this is so, 'one can no longer disregard this inmost centre in favour of the possible concept of a pure nature'.[81] However, for Rahner, as for de Lubac, such a disregarding would be a purely theoretical exercise, for no-one actually lives according to such a pure nature; it is posited purely to acknowledge man's 'uneliminable creaturely condition'.[82]

It was in 1965 that de Lubac specified his triad. By what he called 'a legitimate and indeed necessary process of analysis', he distinguished three things:

> 'the fact of the creation of a spiritual being, the supernatural finality imprinted upon that being's nature, and finally the offer presented to his free choice to share in the divine life'.

We must recognise, he said, that in this triad, 'the first thing does not necessarily imply the second, nor the second the third, in any sense that would inhibit God's utter independ-

---

[77]*MSur*, p. 104.
[78]*MSup*, p. 106.
[79]*Ibid.*, pp. 138-139.
[80]Cf. above, p. 35.
[81]'Relationship', p. 311 and n. 1; cf. Vass, *Mystery*, p. 71.
[82]Cf. above, p. 36.

ence'.[83] The gratuitousness of grace is what is asserted in saying
that the second does not necessarily imply the third, but the
theory of pure nature strives to defend it by an argument which
in fact asserts that the first does not necessarily imply the
second. Therefore the theory is 'insufficient' for its professed
purpose.[84]

> 'It remains to be shown that the supernatural is absolutely freely
> given to *me*, in my condition now. Otherwise nothing at all has
> been said.'[85]

De Lubac understands our actual condition now to be one
in which we have an unquenchable desire for God. What is
needed is a viewpoint which will show that, even so, God's gift
of the supernatural is utterly gratuitous. As we shall see below,
what the theory of pure nature does is to minimise man's desire
for God to a mere *velleity*. However, Like Baius himself, against
whom it was used, the theory understands God as *owing* an end
to man in the *natural* order. De Lubac endorses the opinion
that this in itself invalidates the theory,[86] for God cannot owe
anything to anyone.[87] His implication is that, out of respect, the

---

[83] *MSup*, p. 105. The triad offers a way of classifying the *five* terms which de
Lubac actually uses in his complex discussion of this theme in *MSup*, namely
'creation', man's 'desire', God's 'call', the 'offer' of the second gift and the
'gift' itself. The 'offer' is the third element of the triad. Clearly, it cannot be
separated from the second gift itself, which is actualised by acceptance of the
offer. De Lubac identifies man's desire and God's call with the imprinted
image of God which imprints a supernatural finality upon man (cf. above, pp.
36-37), this being the second element of the triad. Creation remains, or rather
createdness, expressing man's fundamental contingency. On occasion, de
Lubac refers to the *call* as if it were the *offer* (e.g. *MSup*, pp. 98-99). The
explanation is that the distinction between the two is only logical and not
temporal; in fact they are given *together*. Elsewhere, he combines the first and
second elements of the triad as the '*datum optimum*', on to which is grafted the
'second gift', namely the '*donum perfectum*', which is the third element of the
triad (cf. *DGod*, pp. 110-111).

[84] *Ibid.*, p. 80; cf. pp. 42, 67, 94-95.

[85] *Ibid.*, p. 71.

[86] Cf. *ibid.*, p. 62, n. 52 and p. 193.

[87] In *Surnaturel*, p. 488, de Lubac states that 'one of the first axioms of the
Christian faith' is '*Deus nulli debitor est quocumque modo*'.

theory only makes the more modest claim upon God, namely that He confer a natural beatitude on man, but that in so doing it concedes the fatal point that man can entertain any claim before God. Renouncing this notion frees us to recognise God's claim upon man in the actual created order, which is one in which He has created man so as to share His life with him.

The possibility that such a sharing can occur outside the visible Church is clear in de Lubac's acknowledgement that 'every man can be saved through a supernatural that he anonymously possesses'.[88] Although grace 'reposes by right' in the visible Church alone, it is 'poured out all around her' and can 'attain in mysterious fashion the souls even of those who know her not'.[89] We must always recall that it is the *theocentric* aspect which de Lubac regards as 'essential'. To anthropocentric terms from the theology of grace such as *possession*, he himself applies the following corrective:

> 'beatitude is service, vision is adoration, freedom is dependence and possession is ecstasy'.[90]

Christianity's unique understanding of God's creative call to all causes it to steer what de Lubac professes to be a paradoxical middle path between the two logical positions 'known to the Gentiles',[91] who consider either that 'to admit creation *ex nihilo* would be to admit by that very fact the final annihilation of every being born, for what has had a beginning must also have an end'[92] or that 'if the intelligent soul is eternal in the future . . . then it is eternal in the past'.[93]

> 'Alone against all these systems, refusing to be talked into either of their two opposing solutions, Christian philosophy opens up for man the prospect of a new kind of life, which has been

---

[88] *Catholicism*, p. 110 (corrected translation; cf. *Catholicisme* (1983[7]), p. 183).
[89] *Ibid.*, p. 109. Cf. above, p. 17, n. 76.
[90] *Surnaturel*, p. 492.
[91] Chapter Six of *MSup* is entitled, 'The Paradox Unknown to the Gentiles'.
[92] *MSup*, p. 160; quotation attributed to R. Guénon.
[93] *Ibid.*, pp. 158-159; quotation from 'the Averroist Siger of Brabant'.

promised to him, and establishes the essential conditions that make it possible.'[94]

Christianity believes in a 'unilateral eternity'.[95] Christian Revelation alone has stood against the common sense view expressed throughout history that 'every nature must find in itself, or in the rest of the cosmos of which it is an integral part, all that it needs for its completion'.[96] In its light, Christian philosophy has developed 'the concept of a human nature which is open to receive a supernatural gift'. De Lubac emphasises the utter newness of this notion, which Aquinas faithfully expounded.[97]

> 'Such a concept was unknown . . . in ancient philosophy. There is nothing Aristotelian about it . . . . [N]or is it Platonic or Plotinian.'[98]

However, again we note de Lubac's qualification of 'nature' by *human*.[99] Eternal life is, for him, something only for man, as a spiritual creature, and not for the material creation. Man's distinctness lies in his being the image of God. But this distinctness is fulfilled not, as for Zizioulas, in man being already the *priest* of creation, exercising a responsibility which is 'crucial for the survival of nature'.[100] Rather, as we shall now see, the image looks towards fulfilment in an escape from the world, particularly in an escape from *time*.

Space and Time

Like de Lubac, Zizioulas pays much attention to a *drive* which he analyses in man. When man asks 'Who am I?' Zizioulas says, he manifests his desire 'to raise the particular to the level of ontological primacy', that is, to recognise the enduring uniqueness and ultimacy of *persons*. It is a 'drive to personhood', but man is powerless to fulfil it; 'only in God' are

[94]*Ibid.*, p. 160.
[95]Cf. *ibid.*, p. 157.
[96]*Ibid.*, p. 155; cf. above, pp. 31-32.
[97]*Ibid.*, p. 154; cf. above, pp. 32-33.
[98]*Ibid.*, p. 154.
[99]Cf. above, p. 30.
[100]Zizioulas, *PGC*1, p. 3; cf. below, Chapter Nine and the Conclusion.

its conditions fulfilled. There are clear echoes of de Lubac when Zizioulas says of this drive:

'Is that the *Imago Dei* in man? I believe it is.'[101]

Like de Lubac, he believes that the image of God in man is man's restless drive to share God's personal life, a drive which can only be fulfilled by a further gift from God. Both believe this further gift to be *Christ*. We shall see that the difference between them lies in their understanding of Christ.

De Lubac comments that the virtue which 'classical antiquity' notably lacked was *humility*. Christianity worked a 'complete moral revolution' in advocating it,[102] not as 'a *passive* virtue' but as an active 'readiness to welcome God "who comes down"', that is, 'to accept what is born "not of blood, nor of the flesh, nor of man's will"', namely *Christ*.[103] Moreover, the Christ conveyed by this graphic description is the individual Christ in himself. We have seen de Lubac's endorsement of Blondel's account of God's 'primordial freedom', which arises from God not being *given* His nature.[104] We may note the remarkable likeness of Zizioulas' statement that, in God, 'nature is not primary [i.e. prior] to the particular being'; 'being is not "given" — this is what "uncreated" means'.[105]

Like Zizioulas, de Lubac is particularly interested in what being God's image means for man's *freedom*. He speaks of freedom as 'that prerogative of man created in God's image',[106] this image, we recall, being what Christ restores.[107] However, unlike Zizioulas, de Lubac is unable to translate this conviction

---

[101]*OBP*, pp. 42-43.

[102]*BCat*, p. 57; cf. *Spirito*, p. 256, n. 3: 'If Christian Revelation, united with the power of the Holy Spirit, has come to change radically the spiritual attitude on which salvation depends, it has nevertheless not changed human nature, nor released it from its ontological laws.' We may compare Zizioulas' similar comments about *theosis* (below, pp. 152-153).

[103]*Ibid.*, p. 56; quotations from Eph. 4:9-10 and Jn. 1:13, respectively; cf. below, p. 57, n. 29. Zizioulas likewise says that Christology is necessarily 'one *from above*' (*OBP*, p. 43).

[104]Cf. above, p. 28.

[105]*OBP*, p. 43.

[106]*BCat*, p. 122. Cf. below, p. 148.

[107]Cf. above, p. 19.

into an account of *how*, through Christ, man attains a freedom which is fully the image of God's freedom. Such an attainment must involve man overcoming the givenness of his own being. Because Christ is intrinsically *corporate* for Zizioulas, man's free affirmation of Christ is at once also his free affirmation of himself in Christ.[108] De Lubac cannot say this because, as we have just seen, in his view it is Christ *as an individual* who comes down to man.[109]

Nevertheless, Zizioulas rejects as firmly as de Lubac any notion that man's createdness is ever surpassed. De Lubac insists that creation relates not just to 'our origin' but rather to 'our essence'.[110] Zizioulas criticises the 'poor quality Aristotelianism' which led 'medieval Western theology' to give the impression that 'the act of creation' is 'in some way surpassed [*depasse*] . . . by a kind of "created grace" imparted to creation such that it has 'the possibility of existing by itself'. He interprets this 'created grace' as 'a drive [*elan*] . . . imprinted by God in the nature of creation so as to assure it eternally of existence'.[111] In that he understands this drive to be an '"innate force" belonging to [*propre à*] the nature of what is created',[112] the view he is criticising aligns with that of D., which de Lubac disowns as we have seen. Moreover, in a memorable image, de Lubac explicitly rejects any view of 'created grace', which he uses as a synonym for 'the supernatural' (that is, the third element of his triad, not the drive or desire, which is the second), as something which can impart an independent survival.

> 'There is no question of conceiving it as a sort of entity separated from its Source, something like cooled lava — which man would appropriate to himself.'[113]

[108]Cf. below, pp. 150, 168, 189, 225, 243.
[109]Cf. also, below, pp. 53-54.
[110]*Surnaturel*, p. 485; cf. *MSup*, pp. 25-26.
[111]*CEE*1, p. 163.
[112]*Ibid.*, p. 163.
[113]*BCat*, p. 41-42 (corrected translation). De Lubac uses a Blondelian term in referring to grace as 'unnaturalisable' (*BCat*, pp. 32, 41 and already in *Surnaturel*, p. 154).

De Lubac considers that neglect of the radical consequences of 'our situation as creatures' leads to an understanding of God and man as 'two things *face to face* with each other, . . . equals in some fashion', both within a single universe of interrelated beings. Then, if there is 'some coherence' in this universe then any *desire* of man must constitute an *obligation* upon God. The violence which such a notion does to 'divine sovereignty' causes us to put 'a brake on man's desire' and reduce it to a mere 'velleity', or non-resistance to the call to the vision of God if it were to come, rather than a dynamic openness to this destiny. Such is the path which led to the theory of *pure nature.*

> 'A more precise attention to the links which the creature maintains [*soutient*] with its Creator would have saved us, it seems, from the path we have just described and the barely satisfactory solution which is its outcome.'[114]

Recognising the difference between Creator and creation requires us to distinguish God from the universe and then to interpret the desire for God which is in man as man's obligation not *on* God but *to* God. It is 'the expression of God's right', that is '*une exigence divine*'.[115]

Though Zizioulas has never read *Surnaturel,* from which these latter statements are taken, nor any of de Lubac's writings on its theme,[116] he echoes de Lubac remarkably when he himself criticises the perception of man as 'a "partner" of God on equal terms'. Such as perception, he says, results from understanding human nature 'in itself', failing to heed that '*creaturely* being' is understood only in relation to God and that it finds its fulfilment only 'in giving itself up to God's love'.[117]

There is clear similarity between de Lubac's and Zizioulas' dynamic understandings of the drive of created man towards personal fulfilment in the uncreated God. However, we have

---

[114]*Surnaturel,* p. 486. In *MSup,* de Lubac notes that 'early Greek tradition contains no such idea' as that of 'pure nature' and hence that it is unknown in Eastern theology (p. 7).

[115]*Ibid.,* p. 489.

[116]I draw here on personal discussions with Zizioulas.

[117]Cf. *BC,* p. 219 and n. 27.

seen one important difference between them, relating to the
Christ who comes down from above.[118] There is another difference, which is linked to the first in that it relates to what we
might call the place from which Christ comes. It is to do with
the manner and location of our fulfilment, which is indicated
by the way in which each of the two theologians describes
man's ontology, that is, his substance or hypostasis. Let us
recall the assertion of de Lubac that man is 'substantially
image'.[119] This is a description of man not in himself, but as the
created object of God's continual call to communion, a call
which generates man's desire.[120]

> 'This desire is in us, yes, but it is not of us, for it does not satisfy
> itself except by mortifying us. Or rather, it is so much in us that
> it is us ourselves, but it is we who do not belong to ourselves: *non
> sumus nostri.*'[121]

We belong to God who is outside time and our fulfilment, for
de Lubac, lies outside time. 'Of necessity we must find a
foothold in time if we are to rise into eternity.' The Word of
God 'came to deliver us from time, but by means of time';[122]
'the Incarnation . . . in time, saves us from time'.[123] He
translates the Apocalypse text to read: 'Then time shall be no
more.'[124] We must accordingly understand man in the Church
to feel particularly keenly the desire to 'go up'[125] to where the
roots of his being lie.

Let us now contrast the statement of Zizioulas that, in the
Church, man has a 'paradoxical hypostasis, which has its roots
in the *future* and its branches in the present'.[126] Like de Lubac,
Zizioulas will not envisage our destiny as the outcome of an

[118]Cf. above, p. 44.
[119]Cf. above, p. 35.
[120]Cf. above, pp. 36-37.
[121]*Surnaturel*, p. 488; cf. *MSup*, pp. 99-101.
[122]*Catholicism*, p. 68; cf. *Athéisme*, p. 143, where de Lubac wonders about the
relationship 'between the (always relative) temporal freedom of man and his
freedom from time'.
[123]*CPég*, p. 99.
[124]*Catholicism*, p. 67; cf. Apoc 10:6.
[125]*MSup*, p. 174.
[126]*BC*, p. 59 (my italics) and n. 58.

historical evolution. Our destiny is transcendent and God-given. It is all the more unusual, then, that he should so single out *futurity* as the prime characteristic of its location. He evidently means much more than simply that our destiny is future in the trivial sense that it has not yet arrived; de Lubac would, of course, agree to *such* futurity. It would seem that he is making our destiny *future* so as to involve the axis of history in it. Here time is not being escaped but *redeemed*[127] and brought, entire, into the Kingdom. It is being given ontological content, so that the future can literally be the ontological ground of the present.

Both de Lubac and Zizioulas say that personhood involves relationships, both with God and with other human beings.[128] But Zizioulas points out the role of *time* in sustaining particular created identities. He approves the analysis of Augustine who, 'for the first time stated clearly that time as a concept is introduced automatically with Creation and cannot be applied outside it'.[129] Time has nothing to do with the uncreated God, nor, on our side, is it the result of the Fall. It pertains to *createdness*, being, with space, what enables creatures to be *distinguished*. Paradoxically, it thus both divides and unites identities.[130]

> 'This means that if you love a human being so much as to want its identity to be eternal, you cannot but wish at the same time that the spatio-temporal context which has formed the identity of this person be saved too.'[131]

These words sharply contrast with those of de Lubac, who says of the gift of eternal life 'poured out by the Holy Spirit into the depths of the human heart' that it 'cannot flower fully save in circumstances wholly other than those of space and time;.[132]

---

[127]Cf. *ESLT*, particularly pp. 18-22.

[128]For de Lubac, cf. *Catholicism*, pp. 181-182, but see below, p. 48, n. 136. For Zizioulas, cf. below, p. 48, n. 137.

[129]*ESLT*, p. 4. 'Such a view seems to lie behind the mainstream of the Greek Fathers too.'

[130]*Ibid.*, pp. 5, 6; cf. *CEE*1, pp. 164, 166.

[131]*Ibid.*, p. 9.

[132]*BCat*, p. 100.

Zizioulas, nevertheless, is adamant. 'Eternity cannot be an alternative to time, time is its condition.'[133]

We have seen de Lubac's conviction both that our created-ness is never surpassed and that our destiny lies outside time. Zizioulas would find a contradiction in this pairing, since time is part of the matrix of createdness. Time, for Zizioulas, is *constitutive* of created being,[134] essential for the distinction of created beings. It serves the necessary function, so to speak, of holding beings apart, such that they can be themselves. To dispense with it would result in beings *collapsing upon each other* as coincident atoms, rather than complementing each other in what we might appropriately describe as a *molecular* unity. We have indeed noted, in de Lubac's description of unity, an atomistic coincidence,[135] which effectively means that personhood is imparted solely by the vertical relationship with God,[136] rather than by the combination of this with a horizontal component of relationships with other persons. Whereas time would enter into this horizontal component, de Lubac tell-ingly locates salvation in a vertical escape from time. Zizioulas holds firmly to the *combination* of vertical and horizontal components as the source of personhood[137] and therefore, in order to stress the neglected horizontal axis, he refers to our destiny as *future*. Our transcendent destiny is *ahead* rather than just *above*; it draws us *through* time rather than *out* of it.

Like Zizioulas, de Lubac speaks of this transcendent destiny in terms of the '*caelum novum, nova terra*'.[138] However, his

[133]*ESLT*, p. 9.

[134]Cf. *ibid.*, p. 5.

[135]Cf. above, p. 19.

[136]De Lubac makes strong statements about coming to personhood which indicate the role only of the vertical dimension; e.g. God is the 'personalising Personality' (*Motherhood*, p. 154, quoting an expression of Teilhard), Christi-anity offers 'a personalising union with God in Christ' (*BCat*, p. 163).

[137]E.g. *BC*, p. 230, where Zizioulas speaks of the ordained person essentially related simultaneously both to God and to man in the definitive context of the celebrating community. He is the 'mediator', not by 'presupposing or establishing a distance between these two but by *relating* himself to both'.

[138]*Catholicism*, p. 67. For Zizioulas, cf. *CMBC*, p. 13: in the Eucharist 'the new heaven and the new earth of the Kingdom are anticipated'.

admitted neglect of the relationships between man and the universe[139] and his readiness, unlike Zizioulas, to speak of our destiny as that of *souls*[140] indicate that he has not adequately taken into account either our space/time solidarity with the rest of nature, which, as Zizioulas says quoting St Paul, '"groans and is in travail"... awaiting the salvation of man',[141] or indeed the space/time matrix of our communion with each other. De Lubac himself admitted the unanswered questions that he found in these two areas, such as how to conceive 'the final integration of this terrestrial world into the eternal Kingdom', how to elaborate 'the transfiguration from which must emerge "the new heavens and the new earth"'[142] and how to understand 'the bond which must exist between collective eschatology and the personal destiny of each one'.[143] All in all, following Vatican II's Pastoral Constitution on the Church in the Modern World, *Gaudium et Spes*, promulgated in 1965, de Lubac stated that one of the questions which presented itself 'to the theology of tomorrow' was the development of 'a more explicit, more comprehensive and more rigorous eschatology'.[144] Such is precisely the contribution that Zizioulas has sought to make.

---

[139]Cf. above, p. 30.

[140]E.g. *TMAp*, p. 99, with reference to Augustine, Aquinas and Teilhard. Zizioulas is emphatic: 'God does not want only souls to be saved ... but he wants also the salvation of bodies and of the whole world' (*CEE2*, p. 67); cf. Christ 'saves man *and the world*' (*VEM*, p. 85, my italics).

[141]*BC*, p. 119, with allusion to Rom. 8:19-23.

[142]*Athéisme*, p. 149.

[143]*Ibid.*, p. 144.

[144]*Ibid.*, pp. 149-150. cf. P. McPartlan, 'In my end is my beginning'.

Chapter 3

Mysticism and the Eucharistic Motif

'But I shall not write this book. It is beyond me in every way, physically, intellectually and spiritually. I have a clear vision of its structure; I distinguish and virtually situate the problems which ought to be treated in it, according to their nature and their order; I see the precise direction in which the solution of each of them ought to be sought — but I am incapable of formulating that solution.'[1]

Henri de Lubac made this frank admission in a memo of 1956 and reiterated it twenty years later, adding that he was still no further forward with regard to this project. The statement is all the more remarkable in that he was referring not to a marginal work which he would have liked to complete, but rather to the book which, as he said in the same memo, 'for a long time now . . . has inspired me in everything'.

'It is from here that I draw my judgements; it is this that gives me the means to arrange my ideas in order.'

---

[1] *Mémoire*, p. 113. The quotations in the following paragraph are from the same page. The manuscript of these recently published memoirs was actually circulated by de Lubac to Hans Urs von Balthasar and a number of other friends around the time of his eightieth birthday, in 1976. Von Balthasar had written an article, 'The Achievement of Henry de Lubac', to mark this occasion. To this article, he added a Foreword (hereafter 'Foreword'), quoting and commenting upon extracts from the manuscript, for his contribution, 'Une oeuvre organique', in H. U. von Balthasar and G. Chantraine, *Le cardinal Henri de Lubac: l'homme et son oeuvre*, published in 1983; cf. particularly, pp. 45-48.

He was referring to 'my book on mysticism'.[2]

In fact, although his intense interest in mysticism dates from the 1950s, de Lubac's first published item, in 1925, was a review about mysticism.[3] This subject, like that of nature and the supernatural, was a lifelong preoccupation. De Lubac's only synthetic treatment of the subject appeared in 1965, appropriately in the same year as his definitive, two-volume expansion of *Surnaturel*.[4] To a collective work edited by André Ravier, *La Mystique et les mystiques*, de Lubac contributed an Introduction, in which, as he commented in retrospect: 'I summarised some of the ideas which, according to my original plan, would have been developed in several volumes'.[5] Though it is short, this introductory study is clearly of the utmost importance for understanding the framework of de Lubac's theology.

If the theme of nature and the supernatural is personalised by that of mysticism, we shall see that this study gives a strong indication that, in turn, the latter is concretised in the Eucharist. Yet, as von Balthasar said, in comment on our opening quotation, de Lubac viewed his writings as 'approximations to a centre never attained'.[6] We shall end this chapter by asking whether a narrow understanding of the Eucharist prevented de Lubac from finding in it the mystical synthesis he sought.

The Chalcedonian Shift

In his 1965 text, de Lubac said that there is 'an essential passivity in true mysticism' and that the Catholic position hinges upon the distinction and relation of the two terms in his

---

[2] *Ibid.*, p. 113.

[3] Namely, *QMys.*

[4] Namely, *AMTh* and *MSup.*

[5] *Mémoire*, p. 113; cf. von Balthasar, 'Foreword', p. 47, footnote. We shall refer to *MMys*, which is an expanded version of this Introduction (cf. *TOcc*, p. 37, n. 1).

[6] 'Foreword', p. 48; he added that this gives to the reader the possibility of understanding 'apparently disparate' elements of de Lubac's work 'in their secret intention' and making them 'converge to an Archimedean point'. (With reference to the principle of the lever, Archimedes is said to have announced: 'Give me a place to stand and I will move the Earth.')

title, 'Mysticism and Mystery'. His account bears the marks of his study of grace in the same year, with its painstaking precisions. In the actual order of things, human nature is everywhere the same, created in the image of God. This image is a gift received with man's being itself. God gives it with a view to leading man to His likeness, which is consummated in the 'beatific vision'. The likeness is realised 'under the action of the Holy Spirit, . . . by union with Christ'. Man is 'made for this union' and therefore his nature must have both an 'ontological' desire for it and 'a certain capacity for the intussusception of the mystery which is both given and revealed to us in Christ'. The capacity itself is 'empty and powerless to provide itself with its object'; it is 'a faculty of welcome [*acceuil*]' which can be properly understood only 'in its correlation with the mystery'.[7]

'Intussusception' is a term that de Lubac takes from Blondel, who refers to the 'intussusception of supernatural life' in the context of the third phase of the 'three-fold birth of Christ' which the Liturgy celebrates, namely: '[his] birth in souls by a mysterious but certainly [*bien*] real extension of Emmanuel into the depths of faithful hearts'.[8] De Lubac refers to this three-fold birth and says of the 'spiritual Christian' reflecting upon 'the mystery of Christmas':

> 'he understands that this historical coming of the Word of God among men was yet only a beginning: the Word of God must now be born in him, so that the purpose for which he came to our earth might be realised'.

With particular mention of Origen, Augustine and others, de Lubac adds that this theme is widespread in Christian tradition 'from the first centuries to our days'.[9]

Christ is born again in each of his faithful. Raising an important theme for de Lubac, we may say that it is the

[7] *MMys*, pp. 56-57.

[8] Blondel, *Exigences philosophiques du christianisme* (hereafter, *Exigences*), p. 54, a page to which de Lubac refers in *MMys*, p. 72.

[9] *MMys*, p. 71; cf. *ExMéd* II/2, pp. 513-516; *Motherhood*, pp. 79-82. De Lubac regards the doctrine of the birth of Christ in souls as 'the common possession of both Eastern and Western spirituality' (*Motherhood*, p. 82).

Church's *maternal* task to bring about this birth. Immediately after Vatican II, de Lubac stressed that this was the function not just of the hierarchy.

'The *Ecclesia Mater* is not only the hierarchical Church: every holy man engenders the Logos and contributes to its diffusion around him.'[10]

In his 1965 text, de Lubac quotes Blondel drawing attention to the fact that Jesus considered not only as his brothers, but indeed as his *mother*, 'whoever welcomes [*accueille*] his word and puts it into practice'. The remarkable quotation actually combines a *paternal* element with the maternal theme. Blondel describes how we become '*divinae consortes naturae*':

'only by reproducing in ourselves that which is the divine mystery *par excellence*, that is by engendering the Son and breathing the Spirit; . . . thus, the Christian is essentially θεότοκος [*sic*]'.[11]

Blondel here aligns the Father and Mary, the Trinity and the Incarnation, with the implication that, since we are creatures, the way in which we engender the Son and breathe the Spirit, in imitation of the Father, is Marian and incarnational. The assumption is that the desire of man is nothing less than to imitate the Father engendering the Son and that the way in which it is fulfilled is by imitating Mary and engendering the Son enfleshed.

'Christ is the mystery', quotes de Lubac, and 'mysticism wholly consists in living Christ'.[12] His evocation of the Bethlehem scene clearly implies that it is the individual Christ himself whom he is envisaging, indwelling the Christian. We may note the directness of his criticism of Karl Barth's remark that 'the bible says nothing about the birth of the Saviour in our soul'.

[10] *ChPM*, p. 46; with reference to the final pages of *ExMéd* II/2. See next note.

[11] *MMys*, p. 72; quotation from *BWCorr*, vol. 2, p. 400. We see that de Lubac uses 'Logos' and 'Word of God' interchangeably with 'Christ'; cf. below, p. 59, n. 41.

[12] *Ibid.*, pp. 57-58; quotations from D. Barsotti, *Vie mystique et mystère liturgique* (1954), p. 17.

He comments: 'if Barth is right with regard to the words, he is greatly mistaken with regard to the fact'.[13] The specificity of the Mystery, as the incarnate Christ himself, is again evident when de Lubac recognises that it is Protestant theologians' suspicion of immanentism that leads them to 'a radical opposition between all mysticism and Christian faith'.[14] He stresses the *otherness* of the Mystery; it is 'the singular reality to which he [the Christian mystic] adheres by faith' and which thereby is 'infinitely fruitful' in him and others. This Mystery is 'the fleshly birth at Bethlehem in Juda' and the historical Redemption won in Christ.[15] Its otherness is *permanent*: 'here the mystery is first and last'. De Lubac alludes to one of his favourite quotations in order to summarise his understanding of the Christian mystic's distinction from, yet interaction with, the Mystery.

> 'Eternal life itself will make him penetrate more deeply into the interior of this Mystery; thus will the saying of St Augustine be realised most fully [*le mieux*]: assimilating the mystery, he will instead be assimilated by it'.[16]

De Lubac's exposition makes it impossible to maintain any mystic élitism, as if mysticism were the privileged path of only a few Christians. Mysticism is for all: 'mystical experience . . . is Christianity itself' and St Paul is its 'master' not because he was once lifted to the third Heaven but because, on the road to Damascus, he received the Mystery of Christ who comes down.[17]

---

[13] *Ibid.*, p. 55; quotation from Barth, '*Avent*, p. 43'. In comparison with de Lubac's view (cf. the references above, p. 52, n. 9), the absence of any reference to Christ's birth in Christians in Barth's meditations on the meaning of Christmas (cf. *Christmas*) is striking.

[14] *Ibid.*, p. 51, with reference to Barth's rejection of mysticism in *Church Dogmatics*, I/2, p. 751.

[15] Cf. *ibid.*, pp. 72-73. See below (p. 64) for the interiority of the Redemption to the incarnate Christ in the thought of Bérulle, to whom de Lubac refers here.

[16] *Ibid.*, p. 73: cf. '*Nec tu me in te mutabis, sicut cibum carnis tuae, sed tu mutaberis in me*' (*Confessions*, 7, 10, 16; PL 32, 742). See below, pp. 67-72; also P. McPartlan, 'Tu seras transformé en moi'.

[17] Cf. *ibid.*, pp. 60, 64-65. Zizioulas says that 'the Eucharist is the mystical experience of the Church par excellence' (*CMBC*, p. 13), understanding it as the regular mystical experience of all Christians.

Moreover, the distinction-but-interaction which characterises Christian mysticism bears a *Chalcedonian* imprint. Mysticism shows the relevance of Chalcedon for everyday Christian life, that is, its *existential* bearing. De Lubac says elsewhere that the definition of Christ at Chalcedon is 'the nexus of all [definitions]'.[18] Having carefully described the supernatural as 'the divine order considered in its relation of opposition to, and of union with, the human order',[19] he turns to consider, in personal terms, 'the union of these two incommensurables: God and man'.[20]

> '[T]he two elements which we deal with here, nature and the supernatural, have not become an intermixture or confusion but have been joined in intimate union in dependence on and in the image of the two natures in Christ.'[21]

Since the supernatural is God as He unites with the human order, or, in a word, is *Christ*, who is God's '*Geste d'Amour*' towards humanity,[22] we may interpret de Lubac as saying that the Chalcedonian union of divine and human natures in Christ, without division or confusion, is now the pattern for the union between the incarnate Christ (the Mystery) and each Christian. Moreover, we may add that the decisive weighting of the Chalcedonian formula, such that in the union of natures the *I* of Christ is divine, is mirrored in the '*sed tu mutaberis in me*' of the Augustinian formula for the union of Christ and the Christian.[23] Thus, *mutatis mutandis*, the pattern of the Chalcedonian formula may be used to describe the being of the Christian, as it is to describe the being of Christ. We shall

[18] Cf. *AMys*, p. 204, '*elle est au noeud de toutes*'. In this passage, de Lubac expresses 'humble astonishment before the mystery'. Again, the Mystery is clearly that of the Incarnation itself, the Mystery of the Chalcedonian Christ; cf. below, n. 22. For Zizioulas, the Chalcedonian definition is also central; cf. below, pp.150-153, 212. The definition may be found in DS, nn. 301-302.

[19] *BCat*, p. 20. Cf. above, p. 28.

[20] *Ibid.*, p. 83.

[21] *Ibid.*, p. 85.

[22] *AMys*, p. 201: '*Ce grand Geste d'Amour, Jesus, c'est Vous-même.*' Cf. *ibid.*, p. 211: '*[C]e Geste de l'Amour. . . . C'est Dieu fait homme, c'est l'incarnation de Dieu.*'

[23] Cf. above, p. 54, n. 16.

refer to the *Chalcedonian shift* from the original application of this definition to Christ himself to its existential application to the Christian animated by the Mystery of Christ.

Universal Concrete and Corporate Personality

De Lubac frequently refers to the Christian *newness*, recalling the words of Irenaeus, to which 'we must always return'.[24]

> '*Quid igitur novi veniens in terram Dominus attulit?* — *Omnem novitatem attulit, semetipsum afferens.*'[25]

In these words, de Lubac sees not just the newness of Christ with regard to what went before, but his final newness with regard to the future, that is, Christ is not just totally new, but the whole newness.

> 'Christianity's transcendence is not only relative to this or that prior reality. It is not just a provisional originality, superiority [or] newness, opening the way for some further invention destined to surpass it. It is an absolute transcendence. *Omnem novitatem attulit.*'[26]

The obverse of the frequency with which de Lubac recalls this saying of Irenaeus is the firmness with which he rejects the doctrine of Joachim of Fiore, for whom Christ was just the 'second-last word of God's love for men', the last word being the gift of the Spirit.

> 'If the Incarnation is something real, it can only be the last word, which, under the action of the Spirit, must never cease to spread out [*se déployer*], to manifest, as St Paul says, "its unsearchable riches".'[27]

---

[24]*AMys*, p. 210; cf. Yves de Montcheuil, *Leçons sur le Christ*, pp. 14, 185.

[25]E.g. *MMys*, p. 69; quotation from Irenaeus, *Adv. haer.*, 4, 34, 1 (PG 7, 1083).

[26]*AMys*, p. 196.

[27]*PSpir*2, p. 474; cf. *Splendour*, pp. 149-151. De Lubac thinks that the start of joyful hope for 'a new age on this earth' marks the transition from the Middle Ages (with their 'often anxious' wait for the 'final catastrophe') to the Renaissance and beyond and characterises the spiritual 'posterity' of Joachim, which he traces at length in *PSpir*1 & 2 (cf. *PSpir*1, pp. 16, 32).

Christianity is new and final because Christ is new and final. In this sense, Christ is *eschatological*, since the ultimate enduring Mystery will still be nothing but the incarnate Christ; this Mystery, we recall, is first *and last*.

The Mystery *overarches* time. De Lubac criticises Cullmann's interpretation of the once-for-all (*ephapax*) aspect of the Christ-event. He sees it, says de Lubac, situated in the ongoing succession of events in human history, having a uniqueness which is simply that of every event, in that it happens only once. De Lubac wishes to single out the Christ-event:

> 'this unique Event, inscribed in time once-for-all, dominates [*domine*] the whole of time; in this sense that it possesses a specific and transcendent uniqueness, which makes it a mystery, or rather the Mystery'.[28]

Thus, more precisely, we may say that the Mystery of the incarnate Christ *rises* to overarch time, for it originates in a specific historical location. Christ ascended from there, *ut impleret omnia.*[29]

Before examining how Christ, the Mystery, comes down to fill all things, let us note the way in which de Lubac indicates the *otherness* of Christ, as he stands over the world. He does so by means of his highly characteristic theme of *paradox*. We may start with the otherness of God.

> 'Once the idea of the living God has fallen like a seed into consciousness . . . it certainly is subjected, like all other ideas, to dialectic.'[30]

De Lubac implies that dialectic moves horizontally outwards, like ripples from where the seed has fallen. Dialectic, he says, is 'the alternation of "for" and "against"'. It involves 'contrari-

---

[28] *MMys*, p. 73, n. 115; reference to O. Cullmann, *Christ and Time*, p. 121. Cf. *Sources*, p. 217.

[29] We have seen de Lubac apply Eph 4:9-10 to the necessary humility of the Christian in accepting Christ who comes down to indwell him (above, p. 43). De Lubac refers to the text as 'the one which Fr Teilhard loved most' (*BCat*, p. 56, n. 3; cf. *EFem*, p. 235, n. 76): '*Descendit, ascendit, ut impleret omnia.*' (*BTCorr*, p. 162, n. 8, cf. p. 146 and *EFem*, p. 175). Cf. below, p. 64, n. 75.

[30] *DGod*, p. 37.

ety and negation', 'one term is always called forth by another'.[31] De Lubac's preference is for *paradox*, which, he says,
'has more charm than dialectics':

> 'its function is to remind the dialectician when each new stage
> is reached in the argument, that however necessary this forward
> movement is no real progress has been made'.[32]

Real progress is to be found only *upwards*, not *forwards*. Whereas
dialectic moves from a '*for*' to an '*against*', as it seeks in its own
plane, paradox recognises 'the *simultaneity* of the one and the
other', such that they give each other 'vigour'.[33] The paradoxical *pair* may then act as a 'springboard'.

> 'We have to promote, not a horizontal progression, but a
> vertical movement, that very movement which of old was called
> "anagogy". . . .'[34]

De Lubac does not explicitly link the fragmentation of
reality into all these different items or terms with sin. It seems
to be simply a feature of the created order. 'The universe itself',
he says, 'is paradoxical'.[35] However, as we have seen, God does
not stand among these items, rather the idea of God falls into
this dialectical world. Reversing this movement, God is found
not by following a dialectical chain of affirmation and negation
but by paradoxically pairing them as springboards of what we
might call pure affirmation. This seems to be de Lubac's first
meaning in recalling Paul's words about Jesus: 'There is only
Yes in him.'[36]

However, he implies that there is also a second meaning,
namely that Jesus 'reveals the Heavenly Father's love in and

---

[31] *Ibid.*, p. 36.

[32] *Paradoxes*, pp. 9-10.

[33] *Ibid.*, pp. 11-12 (my italics).

[34] Cf. *ibid.*, pp. 196-197. The title which de Lubac gave to Chapter Ten of
CMys, 'Du symbole a la dialectique' indicates how drastic a decline in
eucharistic doctrine he attributes to the scholastic period. M. J. Nicolas, O.P.,
sought to defend the theological method of this period against de Lubac's
charges ('Théologie de l'Eglise, Etude critique', pp. 385, 388-389).

[35] *Ibid.*, p. 10.

[36] *DGod*, p. 38, with reference to 2 Cor. 1: 19.

through his own person'.[37] In other words, Jesus is the Father's Yes to creation. As there are no gods which can stand alongside the true God,[38] so Jesus does not stand amongst fragmentary items. Rather, he stands *over* them, offering the '*Life* . . . in which all life is eminently contained'.[39] If '[p]aradox is the search or wait for synthesis',[40] he himself is the synthesis. De Lubac says to Jesus: 'You yourself are the Kingdom.'[41]

In principle, de Lubac joins with Teilhard and Monchanin[42] in specifying the Eucharist as the means by which Jesus gathers the whole creation into himself. He sees the influence of Teilhard on Monchanin's view that the Eucharist 'will transubstantiate the universe'.[43] For both of them, he says, the Eucharist is 'the efficacious sign, the pledge and seed of the hoped for transfiguration of the universe' and he comments: 'nothing is more strictly in line with Catholic faith'.[44] However, perhaps again manifesting his admitted lack of integration of human beings with the rest of creation and of creation in general with the Kingdom,[45] in practice, de Lubac ventures to explain only Jesus' gathering of *humanity* into himself. The gathering pri-

[37] *Ibid.*, pp. 37-38. De Lubac says: 'In that sense, too, the Apostle's words are verified. . . .'

[38] *Ibid.*, p. 38, n. 31; reference to Barth, *Dogmatics in Outline*, p. 40.

[39] Cf. *Paradoxes*, p. 197.

[40] *Ibid.*, p. 9.

[41] *AMys*, p. 206. In n. 1, de Lubac quotes Origen's term, '$α\dot{v}τοβασιλεία$'; *In Matthaeum*, 14, 7 (PG 13, 1197B). However, de Lubac's readiness to refer, interchangeably, to Christ or the Logos or the Word of God (cf. the quotations above on pp. 52-53) causes doubt about whether the Incarnation is intrinsic to this title or not, particularly since, in the same place, de Lubac refers to Jesus as 'the Truth and the Life' (*AMys*, p. 206), names which Augustine applies to the pre-incarnate *Word*, who additionally became the Way when he took flesh (Augustine, *In Joann.* 34, 9; PL 35, 1656); cf. below, p. 292. Similar doubts about '$α\dot{v}τοαλήθεια$' (Origen, *In Joann.* 6, 6; i.e. 6, 3 in PG 14, 209D) prompt strong criticism of Origen by Zizioulas (*BC*, p. 76). Cf. below, pp. 156-157.

[42] Cf. above, pp. 21-22.

[43] *Images*, pp. 141-143; quotation from 'a Note on *Eucharistie-Parousie-Corps glorieux*'. Cf *FTeil*, pp. 56-61, for Teilhard.

[44] *Ibid.*, p. 144.

[45] Cf. above, pp. 30, 48-49.

marily occurs through the Eucharist, as de Lubac shows in the following statement about Teilhard, in which the narrowing of perspective from the cosmos to humanity is implicit.

> 'He [Teilhard] believed, as St Augustine believed, whose formulas he revives, in the "devouring power of the Eucharist" — "the little host as devouring as a glowing crucible" — which, far from being assimilated by him who receives it, assimilates him itself.'[46]

We shall return to this narrowing in the next section when we consider the Augustinian dictum to which de Lubac again alludes in this quotation.

The key to de Lubac's explanation of the gathering of humanity is the indwelling Christ. He says of Christian mysticism that 'it develops under the action of the mystery received in faith, [the] mystery which is that of the Incarnation of the Word of God'.[47] As we saw above, Christ was born of Mary so as to be born in us.[48] It is significant that de Lubac quotes the statement of Bérulle, 'the mystery of the Incarnation . . . is a permanent mystery and not a temporary action [*une action passagere*]', in the context of this birth of Christ in Christians,[49] for he would seem thereby to indicate his understanding of two descriptions which he favours for the Church: first, 'the permanent incarnation' of the Son of God[50] and second, 'Jesus Christ diffused and communicated'.[51] In this context, these descrip-

---

[46]*FTeil,* p. 58 (no specific source for the quotations is given).

[47]*MMys,* p. 63.

[48]Cf. above, p. 52.

[49]*MMys,* p. 72, cf. *Motherhood,* p. 82. The quotation, from Bérulle, seems to be a conflation by de Lubac of part of the introduction to *Oeuvres de piété,* n. 79, with part of the text of this *oeuvre* (79, 7), using the Eucharist as a bridging term. Bérulle says, first, ' *Le Mystère de l'Eucharistie est comme une restauration du Mystère de l'Incarnation',* then later, ' *ce Mystère [de l'Eucharistie] ne consiste pas en une action passagère, mais en un état permanent'.*

[50]J. A. Möhler, *Symbolism,* p. 259; quoted by de Lubac in *Splendour,* p. 27, n. 6. Cf. 'the Incarnation continued', in *ChPM,* p. 24 and *Moehler,* p. 374. In *CMys,* he says that the Church is 'Christ continued', but that this continuity is not always 'distinctly analysed' (p. 34).

[51]Bossuet, 'Allocution aux Nouvelles Catholiques', *Oeuvres Oratoires,* vol. 6, p. 508; quoted by de Lubac in *Catholicism,* p. 14, *Splendour,* p. 27, *ChPM,* p. 24.

tions respect the uniqueness of Christ's historical ministry and do not seek to prolong it romantically (e.g. in an equally sinless Church), as has sometimes been alleged.[52] They recognise that there is a *shift* between Christ and the Christian. But they express that this shift is *Chalcedonian*, that is, that Christ ascended *so as to fill all* and that in this new phase of history the principle of life in his followers is nothing less than the incarnate Christ himself, the Mystery received.

The Church is then, as it were, the *wider* Mystery.

> 'By an "extension of the sense", imposed somehow by virtue of an inner logic, St Paul applies to her [the Church] this same word "mystery" which he had first used of Christ.'[53]

In his 1965 text, de Lubac twice quotes a passage from Louis Bouyer which expresses this extension.

> 'The centre around which St Paul's whole spirituality is ordered is what he calls "the mystery". He defines it in the Epistle to the Colossians as: "Christ in you, [the] hope of glory".'[54]

For de Lubac, the extension marks a *second phase* of the plan of salvation, when Christ *becomes* corporate; the first phase considers Christ apart from the Church, that is, as an individual. That there is a genuine *deepening* of the Mystery as it enters a second phase may be seen from the following statements by de Lubac. The Incarnation is a paradox,[55] but the Church is *more* paradoxical than Christ[56] and, in the 'mystical life', de Lubac hails the 'triumph' of paradox.[57] It would seem that he is emphasising the *structure* of the paradox which develops from that of the unity of divine and human in Christ to that of the unity of the

[52]Cf. Congar's criticism of both descriptions in 'The Church: The People of God', p. 13.

[53]*ChPM*, p. 24.

[54]*MMys*, p. 55, n. 52, also p. 59, n. 64; quotation from L. Bouyer, *The Spirituality of the New Testament and of the Fathers*, p. 88, incorporating Col. 1: 27.

[55]*Splendour*, pp. 26-27.

[56]*Ibid.*, p. 28: 'the Church is even more compact of contrast and paradox than Christ'. Cf. *Catholicism*, p. 27: 'the mystery of the Church is deeper still, if that were possible, than the mystery of Christ'.

[57]*Paradoxes*, p. 10.

divine/human Christ and the human being in the Christian. As the structure changes (in what we have called the Chalcedonian shift), so the Mystery extends and deepens, from that of the incarnate Christ himself into that of the Church.

De Lubac stresses that, since man is not just a creature but also *sinful*, God's *Geste d'Amour*[58] towards him must be one not just of Incarnation but also of Redemption.[59] He bids us focus upon the Cross.

> 'If it is true that all of Christ's activity reveals him, can we not however think that only by the Cross does incarnate Charity reveal itself entirely?'[60]

The Cross is thus the climax of the Mystery of the Incarnation which is both new and final.

> 'The coming of Christ marked the plenitude of the ages. No fulness or depth will ever exhaust the *Geste* of Calvary.'[61]

It is the *Geste* of Calvary which, in effect, having been inscribed in history, now 'embraces all worlds, as it shines above all times' with a glow which is that 'of eternal Life'.[62] This *Geste* is the Mystery actually to be received, as de Lubac makes clear in a more specific comment than the one we noted earlier about what is 'first and last':

> 'what is first and last is the redemptive Act, the gift which God makes to us of Himself in His Son'.[63]

De Lubac is correspondingly more specific that it is this Act of Christ which dominates time and which 'towers over [*domine*] the constitution of his mystical body'.[64]

Thus, when the Mystery is present, it is the incarnate Christ of *Calvary*. There were echoes of the work of Yves de Montcheuil when,

---

[58] Cf. above, p. 55.
[59] Cf. *BCat*, pp. 117-122.
[60] *AMys*, p. 202, n. 1.
[61] *Ibid.*, p. 212.
[62] *Ibid.*, p. 213.
[63] *PDDog*, p. 156. Cf. above, p. 54.
[64] *Sources*, pp. 205-206. Cf. above, p. 57.

in *Catholicism*, de Lubac lamented an excessive stress in the eucharistic doctrine of recent centuries upon the Real Presence itself.

'The very connection between this Presence and the reality of the sacrifice was too little regarded for all its lessons to be drawn from it.'[65]

Prompting unwarranted criticism that he was questioning the Real Presence and neglecting Transsubstantiation,[66] de Lubac added, in *Corpus Mysticum*, that the ingrained separation between the sacramental and sacrificial aspects of the Eucharist should now be forgotten. The Mass is 'the daily sacrament of which the "*res*" is the one Sacrifice accomplished by Christ in the days of his flesh'.[67] Christ is sacramentally present in the fruitful reality of his one sacrifice. The single, historical *Geste* of Calvary has been lifted up (therefore the Resurrection and Ascension are implicit in de Lubac's account), so as to overarch history and condition it by coming down into it again. In his 1965 text, de Lubac specifically applied this path, which 'mystical realism' recognises, to 'Catholic doctrine of the Mass and the sacraments'.[68]

De Lubac's incorporation of a passage from Olier's explanation of the Mass in his account combines with his quotations from Bérulle to indicate his attachment to what John Saward calls 'the French School of post-Reformation Catholic spirituality'.[69] The passage speaks of our Lord entering into the bosom of the Father[70] and thus highlights, again, the fact that

[65] *Catholicism*, p. 171. De Montcheuil stressed the link between the sacrificial and sacramental aspects of the Eucharist, which the Council of Trent treated separately; *Mélanges théologiques*, pp. 49-70. Cf. B. Sesboüé, 'Eucharistie: deux générations de travaux', p. 101.

[66] Vorgrimler, 'Henri de Lubac (B)', p. 813. Cf. below, Chapter Four.

[67] *CMys*, pp. 70-71; cf. p. 80.

[68] *MMys*, p. 72, n. 109.

[69] J. Saward, 'Bérulle and the "French School"' (hereafter, 'Bérulle'). Saward describes Bérulle, Olier and Condren as the 'masters' of this school. Bérulle's highest esteem was for Augustine (pp. 386-388). De Lubac favourably refers to the seventeenth century 'French School' in *Splendour*, pp. 108, 251.

[70] *MMys*, p. 60; quotation from Olier, *Explication des cérémonies de la grand'messe de paroisse* (1687), pp. 250-251.

considerable emphasis upon Calvary does not mean that the Resurrection and Ascension are being neglected. Indeed, de Lubac says: 'the sacrifice of Jesus is fulfilled in the Resurrection, from which his death is inseparable'.[71] The Resurrection has, as it were, lifted Christ's sacrifice to a point from which it can have universal efficacy.

> '[The] external aspect of the Mystery is past, as is true of everything which pertains to time — Christ, having now entered into his glory, suffers and dies no more — but its internal aspect remains'.[72]

The almost identical way in which Saward describes the stance of the French School manifests de Lubac's rapport with it. Saward says that the wounds of Calvary are 'the primordial example' of the following doctrine.

> 'Bérulle's great insight is that, while the exterior circumstances of [the] various states and mysteries of Christ's life are past, the interior state or living disposition within Christ's human soul remains, and it is this disposition which can have an effect, as *vertu* or *mérite*, on us.'[73]

De Lubac quotes Bérulle's comment that these mysteries are not 'things past and extinguished, but things living and present',[74] and he stresses that they have a universal presence and efficacy because a *concrete* achievement has been *universalised*. He aligns with Blondel, von Balthasar and Teilhard in their application to Christ (and even, by Teilhard, to Mary) of the notion of a 'universal concrete'.[75]

---

[71] *Sources*, p. 111.

[72] *Ibid.*, p. 215. De Lubac refers not only to numerous patristic sources for this doctrine, but also to the modern liturgical theology of Odo Casel.

[73] 'Bérulle', pp. 390-391.

[74] *MMys*, p. 73; quotation from Bérulle, *Oeuvres de piété*, 76, 1.

[75] *Ibid.*, p. 73, n. 113; with particular reference to *EFem*, de Lubac's study of Teilhard's poem, 'The Eternal Feminine'. Given the clear sense of the term, 'universal concrete' seems a better rendering of '*universel concret*' than 'concrete universal'. I shall alter the translation accordingly. De Lubac notes Teilhard's application of the Ephesians passage (cf. above, p. 57, n. 29) to Mary (*EFem*, p. 125) and remarks on 'the boldness of Teilhard's Mariology' (*EFem*, p. 122). Cf. below, p. 67, n. 90; also P. McPartlan, 'Mary for de Lubac and Teilhard'.

We have seen that de Lubac envisages the unity imparted by the universal concrete as belonging to a second phase. Christ can, at least in principle, be considered in himself, apart from the Church. He becomes corporate when, having descended and ascended as an individual, he then fills all. '*Translatus est Christus ad Ecclesiam.*'[76] For Zizioulas, in contrast, Christ is immediately and by definition corporate. He points to Johannine evidence that the one who *first* descended was the Son of Man, that is, a *corporate personality*.[77]

> 'Christ's "I" is of course the eternal "I" that stems from his eternal filial relationship with the Father. But as the incarnate Christ he has introduced into this eternal relationship another element: us, the many, the Church. If the Church disappears from his identity he is no longer Christ, although he will still be the incarnate Son.'[78]

Whereas the one constitutes the many in Christ as a universal concrete, in Christ as a corporate personality it is also true that the many reciprocally constitute the one. The one and the many are mutually constitutive.[79]

De Lubac says that Teilhard and Blondel give 'the same fundamental meaning' to the notion of the universal concrete, and he quotes Blondel.

> 'True unity consists in the presence in us and in all things of one and the same real mediation, of a universal concrete which, without being involved in the imperfections of creatures and their finite mode of being, is nevertheless, itself and complete, in all things.'[80]

For Christians, added de Lubac, this universal concrete is 'Christ, man and God'.[81] There could hardly be a clearer

---

[76] *Sources*, p. 220 ['Christ has passed over (in) to the Church']; quotation from Paschasius Radbertus, *In Iam. Jer.*, 2 (PL 120, 1119A; corrected reference). Cf. *CMys*, p. 34.

[77] Cf. below, p. 181.

[78] *MCO*, pp. 299-300.

[79] Cf. below, Chapter Eight.

[80] *EFem*, p. 120; quotation from Blondel, *Exigences*, p. 185.

[81] *Ibid.*, p. 120.

statement of the unity which we have termed 'atomistic';[82] it is the same (incarnate) Christ (the Mystery) in each that makes all unite. Christ, the one, certainly here constitutes the many, but Zizioulas considers that this must also be true reciprocally for there to be a corporate personality: the many must also constitute the one.[83] In the passage above, Blondel is in the course of distinguishing 'two sorts of unity', that of Christianity and that of *monism*.[84] Zizioulas would suggest that Christianity offers *another* vision of unity, which is not only non-monistic but non-atomistic, too. It is a vision of Christ as one of the Church, holding the many apart in a differentiated unity-of-complementarity.[85]

Having so firmly rejected 'the swamping of the spiritual life by the detestable "I"',[86] de Lubac is clearly aware that his own exposition can seem to move straight from Christ to the individual, for, after presenting the indwelling of Christ in souls as 'the very essence of Christian mysticism', he immediately adds: 'this doctrine, while interiorising the mystery, does not itself lead to any individualistic distortion'. It is 'more important and . . . more immediately consistent with patristic thought' to consider, rather than this maternity of each Christian soul, the maternity of the Church.[87] 'Christian mysticism . . . is necessarily an ecclesial mysticism.'

> 'All that will be said of the Christian soul concerns first of all the Church as a whole . . . and that is why the Christian soul must be called *"anima ecclesiastica"*.'[88]

[82]Cf. above, p. 48.

[83]Thus when, for instance, Joseph Ratzinger apparently identifies the concepts of universal concrete and corporate personality, while describing the latter only in terms of the identity which the one gives to the many, he is *not* using the notion of corporate personality as Zizioulas understands it (*Das neue Volk Gottes*, p. 81). Ratzinger is actually referring not to Christ but to Adam. The Old Testament, he says, considered Adam as a '*konkret Universale*' and, correspondingly, the people as a '*GroBpersönlichkeit*'.

[84]Cf. Blondel, *Exigences*, p. 185: their respective understandings of unity are '*tout à fait différentes et même opposées*'. Cf. Chapters Two and Seven for the firm rejections of monism by de Lubac and Zizioulas, respectively.

[85]Cf. above, p.24.

[86]*Catholicism*, pp. xv-xvi. Cf. above, p. 14.

[87]*Motherhood*, p. 83.

[88]*MMys*, p. 67.

However, Christ here stands outside the Church (as the one brought to birth by the Church). The Church is then united by the coincidence of her members because of the same Christ indwelling each. But the rendering identical of all her members is a return to *individualism*.[89] It would appear that the victory over individualism is not won until Christ stands in the midst of the Church, not only constituting the many but also constituted by the many.[90]

'Nec tu me in te mutabis, sicut cibum carnis tuae,
sed tu mutaberis in me.'

Already in *Catholicism*, de Lubac quoted the text of Augustine which recurs throughout his writings, either directly or, as we have seen twice already,[91] in echoes, and he immediately gave it a *eucharistic* interpretation.

'When, with St Augustine, they [our forebears] heard Christ say to them: "I am your food, but instead of my being changed into you, it is you who shall be transformed into me", they unhesitatingly understood that by their reception of the Eucharist they would be incorporated the more in the Church.'[92]

Again in *Corpus Mysticum*, calling it 'the famous formula', de Lubac saw this text expressing 'the genius of Augustine' in synthesising the Pauline and Johannine interpretations of the

[89]Cf. A. Louth's comment, with regard to liturgical participation, that when everyone does the same the result is *individualistic* (*Denys the Areopagite*, p. 132).

[90]If Christ stands outside of the Church, then there will be a tendency to find a focus in the Church herself. De Lubac describes the Church as 'the great body from which Christ took his body' (*CMys*, p. 34), implicitly directing attention to Mary, with regard to whom he elsewhere quotes Isaac of Stella's summary that what is said *universaliter* of the Church, is said *specialiter* of Mary and *singulariter* of each faithful soul (*Sermo* 51, *In Assumptione beatae Mariae*, PL 194, 1865C). De Lubac comments that the roots of these modulations lie deep in Christian mysticism (*Splendour*, pp. 277-286, particularly p. 285, n. 6). Teilhard's account of *Mary* as a *universal concrete* (cf. above, p.64) accords with this approach.

[91]Cf. above, pp. 54, 60

[92]*Catholicism*, p. 42.

Eucharist.[93] Finally, in *Christian Faith*, he referred to it as 'the famous declaration *about the Eucharist* which St Augustine puts into the mouth of Christ'.[94]

The original context of the Augustinian text is *not* eucharistic; Augustine is recalling his encounter in individual contemplation with the Word of God.[95] It would seem, then, that it is de Lubac's deliberate intention to make it refer to the *concrete* encounter with the *incarnate* Word which takes place in the Eucharist. All of the locations in which de Lubac quotes or echoes this text accordingly acquire *eucharistic* overtones. In particular, his use of the text to express the climax of the mystical life of the Christian in eternity[96] implies that reception of the Eucharist is the Christian's prime anticipation of his end and the practical point of his entry into and progress along the way to it. Though de Lubac's writings are unsystematic, the number and variety of such locations act as confirmation that, as de Lubac indicates in the opening comments of this chapter, he has been attempting to expound a single, coherent vision. Moreover, they suggest that the Eucharist is its practical key.

Let us see how the text occurs in de Lubac's writings on exegesis and grace and verify both the internal links of his theology and also the latter's eucharistic key. M. Figura summarises as follows the view which de Lubac derives from the Fathers. 'Christianity is a unity of exegesis and mysticism.'[97] De Lubac himself clarifies:

> 'the mystical or spiritual understanding of Scripture and the spiritual or mystical life are, at root, the same thing. Christian mysticism is this understanding pressed to its end, following the four traditional dimensions, each of which governs the next: history, "allegory" or doctrine, morality or "tropology" and anagogy.'[98]

[93] *CMys*, p. 200; cf. pp. 191-192.
[94] *Faith*, p. 134 (my italics).
[95] Its context precedes Augustine's Baptism in the *Confessions*. Cf. below, p. 293. A. Sage does not even mention the text in his study of 'L'Eucharistie dans la pensée de saint Augustin'.
[96] Cf. above, p. 54.
[97] M. Figura, *Der Anruf der Gnade*, p. 88.
[98] *MMys*, p. 63.

Allegory properly refers to the passage from the Old Testament to the New.[99] It is 'a passage to Christ' who both separates and unites the two Testaments 'in himself'.[100] In particular, Christ separates and unites on the Cross.[101] 'Jesus is Exegete of Scripture pre-eminently in the act by which he fulfils his mission.'[102]

The relationship of Israel to Christ, that is, of the Old to the New, expresses the relationship between 'nature as it exists', that is, human nature with the imprinted image of God, and 'the supernatural for which God destines it'.[103] Since the New Testament is not just *novum* but *novissimum*, it cannot itself be allegorised.[104] The two further senses of Scripture beyond allegory remain dependent upon the Mystery of Christ's Incarnation, and especially of his Cross, 'and cause us to explore it in depth'.[105] The Mystery is indeed *figurative* of further realities, but in a way utterly different from Old Testament figures.

> 'Here it is figure which is the *dominant* reality, a reality not only active and efficacious, but also *assimilating*. The life of the Church, the life of the Christian soul, the life of the eschatological kingdom are . . . wholly constituted by man's assumption into the heart of the mystery of Christ. . . . [This] figure says to each of those which it signifies: "You shall not change me into yourself, but you shall be changed into me."'[106]

[99] Cf. *Sources*, pp. 11-12, 100-101.

[100] *Ibid.* p. 103.

[101] *Ibid.*, p. 180.

[102] *Ibid.*, p. 109.

[103] Cf. *MSup*, p. 107. Moreover, just as the second gift does not quench the created nature and imprinted image which comprise the first gift (cf. above, p. 36 and p. 40, n. 83), so the New Testament does not dispense with the Old. The Old Testament is cherished by the Church as the essential *ground* of the Gospel (cf. *Sources*, pp. 8, 120): 'as the seed gives way to the fruit in which the seed again appears . . . the Old Testament lives on, transfigured, in the New' (*ibid.*, p. 175). For the practical implications of this conviction, in a resolute stand against anti-semitism, cf. *NFRel*, p. 11 and p. 155, n. 3; also, more recently, *RCAnt*.

[104] Cf. *Sources*, pp. 89, 198-199; *Catholicism*, p. 85.

[105] *Sources*, p. 201.

[106] *Ibid.*, pp. 203-204 (my italics).

We have suggested that whenever de Lubac incorporates this Augustinian text into his account, he does so with eucharistic overtones. In this case, the implication would be that it is by the Eucharist that we encounter the New Testament mystery and, by receiving, are assumed into its heart. Such, indeed, is exactly de Lubac's view. He says that '[t]he new Covenant was established at the Last Supper'[107] and that 'the Eucharist is itself, as in a summary, the New Testament'.[108] If the modulated path of Christian mysticism is mapped by the three-fold spiritual exegesis into which the letter of Scripture opens up, then the Eucharist is its gateway. In the Eucharist we have 'the whole of the Bible in substance . . . in a single mouthful'.[109]

'Christ *in his Eucharist* is truly the heart of the Church',[110] said de Lubac, taking the important step of making *concrete* and *public* the principle of the Church's life and hence the Church herself.[111] The Church is the public presence of Christ himself, 'the sacrament of Christ'.[112] She is 'the *great* Sacrament which contains and vitalises all the others',[113] the home, as it were, of all that sacramentally gives access to the Mystery of Christ and the context necessary for such access. She is the great epiphany of the Mystery in the world and the great springboard into the Mystery for us. Thus, for instance, the Scriptures come to life in the Church.[114]

De Lubac seems to give the suffix '-ism' to views which in some way deny what he has spent his life expounding, namely that there is only one end, which is supernatural, and that nothing natural has purpose in itself; it must be assimilated to

---

[107] *Ibid.*, p. 211.

[108] *CMys*, p. 76. Significantly, it is to *CMys* (p. 200) that de Lubac refers after his quotation of the Augustinian text in *Sources*, pp. 203-204 (cf. above, n. 106).

[109] *Sources*, p. 188.

[110] *Splendour*, p. 113 (my italics).

[111] Cf. McPartlan, 'Eucharistic Ecclesiology', p. 318, in which I refer to an article by Ratzinger republished as Chapter One of *Church, Ecumenism and Politics*, particularly pp. 7, 14.

[112] *Catholicism*, p. 28. Cf. above, p. 22.

[113] *Splendour*, p. 147 (my italics).

[114] Cf. *ibid.*, p. 204.

the Mystery of Christ. He says that the Church's ministry which comes from Jesus is fully historical, but instituted to realise 'a communion victorious over all historicity'.[115] We may deduce that *historicism* looks towards an end *in* the course of history rather than an end above, of which history is but the threshold. Also, de Lubac laments those 'who have constructed for themselves not a too literal, but a purely literalist, idea of dogma'.[116] We are to understand *literalism*, therefore, as the view which fails to appreciate Dogma as 'sign of the Mystery'[117] and which considers instead that Dogma contains truth in itself. 'Revealed truth' is 'intrinsically supernatural and mysterious'. 'Properly speaking we do not possess it: it possesses us.'[118]

Moreover, the revelation of the Mystery of God's whole purpose ought not to be separated from the Mystery itself, which is '*le Tout du Dogme*'.[119] Dogmatic definitions are, 'in a sense, totally constructed from human materials', but they express divine truth 'on condition that they are always related back to . . . the living Centre, to the divine Centre from which everything radiates and to which everything must lead us: to Jesus Christ'.[120] This Centre is not consumed but consuming. The eucharistic motif strikingly reappears in the following statement by de Lubac precisely about key dogmatic definitions.

> 'The word "consubstantial" at Nicaea, the union of the two natures at Chalcedon, marked the triumph of the primitive faith against the attacks of a hellenism that sought to engulf it. *Non me in te mutabis, sed tu mutaberis in me.*'[121]

Once again, we may verify that de Lubac does indeed intend, by quoting the Augustinian dictum, to convey a *eucharistic* association, in this case with the definition of Dogma, for he

---

[115]*Motherhood*, p. 35 (corrected translation).

[116]*Images*, p. 145.

[117]*Ibid.*, pp. 144-145; quotation from Monchanin, 'Théologie et mystique du Saint-Esprit', p. 74.

[118]*PDDog*, p. 147.

[119]*Ibid.*, p. 156.

[120]*AMys*, p. 210.

[121]*BCat*, p. 69. Cf. *Faith*, p. 134; *SPChr*, p. 135.

says elsewhere that those who have a literalist idea of Dogma poorly understand explanations of the 'extensions of the Eucharist'.[122]

However, this very point may serve to disclose a weakness in de Lubac's position, for, in short, *how* does the bond between the Eucharist and the definition of Dogma function in practice? De Lubac gives no answer. How can the glowing presence of Christ in the eucharistic elements, the consecrated bread and wine, *actually* extend so as to be a glowing presence in Dogma except through the mediation of human beings, whose own conversion 'can never be said to have been fully achieved' in this life,[123] and who therefore are not adequate vehicles for this extension? The extension *would* work if, for instance, Dogma received its ratification by human beings in a privileged context in which the presence of Christ in them was on a par with his presence in the elements, as if the gathered community was itself the eucharistic presence of Christ. Zizioulas believes that such a privileged context does actually exist, it is the eucharistic celebration, in which the people present are mystically identified with the corporate Christ of the Parousia.[124]

Also, we have seen de Lubac present the four-fold exegesis of Scripture as the pattern for the modulated advance of the mystical life of the Christian, whose practical starting point is the Eucharist.[125] However, he also presents the Scriptures *themselves* as a practical starting point for the Christian's mystical life. He says, of the Scriptures and the Eucharist, that 'in one as in the other it is the same Logos of God who comes [down] to us and raises us up to himself'.[126] This biblical view of the Christian life compromises de Lubac's constant stress, reflected in his repeated reference to the Augustinian dictum, on the Eucharist as the *single* focus of the Church. A solution would be to understand the Eucharist itself more broadly as the assembled *community* and to specify more precisely the Church

[122]*Images*, p. 145.
[123]*Sources*, p. 21, cf. p. 17.
[124]Cf. below, e.g., pp. 135-136, 169, 193-194; also p. 197.
[125]Cf. above, p. 68.
[126]*HEsp*, p. 356.

within which the Scriptures come to life as the Church in this assembly. Then, both the eucharistic elements and the Scriptures would be at home within this single focus. Zizioulas does consider the Eucharist 'as a community',[127] but de Lubac strongly rejected such a view.[128]

Perhaps de Lubac was unable to forge the mystical synthesis because, while emphasising the practical centrality of the Eucharist in the Church's life, he had to acknowledge other practical *springboards* into the Mystery, such as Dogma and the Scriptures, which, since he saw the Eucharist primarily as the transformed elements,[129] had to stand *alongside* the latter without a satisfactory integration. All of them are at home simply in the *Church* as the great Sacrament. However, integration is possible if the great Sacrament is the Eucharist as the assembled *community*, which professedly has a privileged identity in this celebration that it does not bear at other times. Then, indeed, *within* the Eucharist, not only the other sacraments, but also Dogma and the Scriptures, give access to the Mystery. Moreover, it becomes possible then to see how, by the members of the community bringing creation into their celebration, the Eucharist, which they there *are*, may extend to embrace all that God has made.[130]

If de Lubac's achievement was to redirect attention from the external *works* and *actions* of Christ to the total saving Mystery of his *Person*,[131] Zizioulas takes the further step of unfolding the

---

[127] *BC*, p. 213; *CECB*, p. 1. For Zizioulas' understanding of Scripture within the Eucharist, cf. below, pp. 133-134. 'If the Word of God comes from the future and not from the past, its proper place is the eucharistic context' (*CMBC*, pp. 16-17).

[128] In personal discussions, de Lubac emphatically said 'No, that is not true' to the suggestion that the Eucharist is the assembled community!

[129] De Lubac's emphasis on linking the Real Presence with Christ's sacrifice (cf. above, pp. 62-63) does not prevent a retained focus upon the eucharistic elements, now understood as the primary access to his sacrifice (cf., e.g., below, pp. 78-81).

[130] Cf. above, p.59.

[131] E.g. *AMys*, p. 201 (cf. above, p.55, n. 22); *Sources*, p. 190; *RDiv*, p. 177; also the comments of de Lubac and his colleagues in M. Labourdette, *et al*, *Dialogue théologique*, p. 90. Cf Zizioulas, likewise, in *BC*, p. 212, n. 9; *EQA*, p. 55.

Mystery of this Person as an essentially *corporate* personality, indeed as *the* corporate personality. That this further step was not unthinkable for de Lubac is implicit in his recognition that Pneumatology, which Zizioulas would see as the key to a corporate understanding of Christ,[132] is underdeveloped in the West. After the Second Vatican Council, de Lubac quoted without protest the following comment.

> 'The Latin Church's Christology is very advanced, but its theology of the Holy Spirit is still at the stage of adolescence.'[133]

---

[132]Cf. below, p. 167

[133]*ChPM*, p. 35, n. 22; quotation from Mgr Ignace Ziadé, Maronite Archbishop of Beirut, on 16 September 1964.

Chapter 4

_____

The Eucharist makes the Church

'Memorial, anticipation, presence: the Eucharist is . . . indeed a "mystery" in each of its three essential aspects which it has had from the beginning, each of which may in turn be cast into greater relief, but which always remain inseparable [*indissociables*].'[1]

This summary of eucharistic doctrine by de Lubac justifies us in taking as a measure of the satisfactoriness of his own exposition the extent to which he secures the inseparability of these three aspects.

We have seen his complaint, in *Catholicism* and *Corpus Mysticum*, at neglect of the link between Christ's sacramental Presence and his Calvary sacrifice.[2] His even greater complaint in *Catholicism* was against such a stress 'on the proof of the Real Presence' that the 'symbolism of unity' in the Eucharist was treated secondarily, as a mere 'edifying consideration', often relegated to an appendix.[3] He gave his overall view in *Corpus Mysticum*: the Church's offering of the Body of Christ, present '*in mysterio panis*', is inseparably both a memorial, '*in mysterio passionis*', and an anticipation, '*in mysterio nostro*'.[4] We both look back to Christ's Passion and look forward to our unity as we offer Christ's *Mystical Body*, that is, when we gather liturgically for 'the celebration of the holy Mysteries'[5] around the altar and

[1] *CMys*, p. 83.
[2] Cf. above, pp. 62-63.
[3] *Catholicism*, p. 171.
[4] *CMys*, pp. 83-84.
[5] *Ibid.*, p. 60.

specifically around the eucharistic elements, for de Lubac describes Christ's Mystical Body as follows.

> '[The] Body to which the symbol of the bread mystically refers and which it mystically envelops.'[6]

In fact, the latter quotation is more than a description of the *corpus mysticum*, it is a *definition*. De Lubac draws attention to the linguistic 'menu' according to which '*corpus mysticum*' was broadly equivalent to '*sacramentum (mysterium) corporis*',[7] that is, to 'the Body present and received "*in mysterio*",'[8] in other words, liturgically, 'under . . . material or ritual appearances'.[9] To summarise, the *corpus mysticum* is the Body of Christ *in the Eucharist*. De Lubac's exhaustive study entitled *Corpus Mysticum* is an historical investigation[10] of a phenomenon which he had noted in *Catholicism*,[11] namely the transfer of this term during the eleventh and twelfth centuries from its original application to the Eucharist in order to apply it to the *Church*.[12] The original term for the Church, namely the *corpus verum* of Christ, was correspondingly transferred back to the Eucharist.

There is a twofold dynamism implicit in celebrating the holy Mysteries: first, the dynamism of Christ's own sacrifice and secondly the dynamism of our communicating in it. With reference to the patristic period, de Lubac says that 'many texts concerning the Eucharist would be more deeply understood' and that 'certain of them would offer fewer exegetical difficulties to defenders of the "Real Presence"' if it were remembered that 'the essential perspective of these texts is not that of a presence or of an object, but that of an action and of a sacrifice'.

---

[6] *Ibid.*, p. 69.

[7] *Ibid.*, p. 95.

[8] *Ibid.*, p. 84, cf. pp. 63-64, 68, 74, 281.

[9] *Ibid.*, p. 68.

[10] A. J. Lindsay notes de Lubac's 'deliberate' indication, 'Etude historique', on the title page of *Corpus Mysticum*, as also 'Etudes historiques' on that of *Surnaturel; De Lubac's Images of the Church*, pp. 81-88.

[11] Cf. *Catholicism*, p. 42.

[12] De Lubac says that the adjective 'mystical' was dropped in reference to the Eucharist in the mid-eleventh century, in reaction to Berengarius (cf. below, p. 84). Then followed a period in which both the Eucharist and the

'Their aim is not at all, directly, the link between the body of Christ considered "in itself" and the "sacramental species".'

The whole 'eucharistic complex' is linked to Calvary: '*sacramentum corporis quod pependit in ligno*'.[13] In what is again effectively a *definition*, de Lubac says that the *corpus mysticum* is 'the Body engaged in a mystical action, [the] ritual echo indefinitely multiplied in space and time of the single Action from which it takes its meaning'. As de Lubac continues his description of the *corpus mysticum*, we see that communicating is taking that action as food.

'It is the Body by which one communicates [*communie*] in the Passion of the Lord. "*Hoc accipite in pane, quod pependit in ligno; hoc accipite in calice, quod manavit de latere*". This Augustinian formula, quoted by Paschasius Radbertus, is something quite different from a certification of identity; it makes us penetrate the intimate meaning of the mystery.'[14]

We have seen de Lubac's assertion that the *res* of the sacrament of the Eucharist is Christ in his Calvary sacrifice.[15] However, this *res* is, in turn, the *sacramentum* of something further, on which de Lubac directly focuses when he acknowledges Augustine's teaching that our eucharistic food and drink is the '*societas ipsa sanctorum*'.[16] In a study to which de Lubac refers, P.Th. Camelot describes Augustine's tendencies to move straight from what later theology would call the *sacramentum tantum* to the *res tantum*, without an intermediate step (the *res et sacramentum*), and to refer to the sacrament of something as the thing itself.[17] De Lubac states

---

Church were simply called the *corpus Christi*, with the adjective *mysticum* unattached. It was during the second half of the twelfth century that, in order to distinguish the *ecclesial* Body of Christ, *it* came to be qualified as the *corpus mysticum* (*CMys*, pp. 95-96; 116-121).

[13] *CMys*, pp. 78-79 (unattributed quotation, but see next note). Cf. above, p. 73, n. 129.

[14] *Ibid.*, pp. 74-75. In footnote, de Lubac clarifies that 'the good Paschasius' quoted this saying 'as from St Augustine' (PL 120, 1354A).

[15] Cf. above, p. 63.

[16] *CMys*, p. 198.

[17] Cf. P.Th. Camelot, 'Réalisme et symbolisme dans la doctrine eucharistique de s.Augustin', pp. 402-403, 408-409. De Lubac's reference to this article occurs in *CMys*, p. 200, n. 58.

that there is 'a fulness of thought' in Augustine. Its sense can be conveyed 'only by an elliptical and paradoxical circuit'.[19] After recalling the Augustinian (eucharistic) motif which we examined in the previous chapter, de Lubac offers the following summary of Augustine's view.

> 'He [Christ] himself is the Body whose food those who eat it become.'[19]

De Lubac specifies analytically elsewhere that Christians are *not* the 'eucharistic' Body of Christ; the eucharistic Body is Christ's 'real, personal Body which lived, died [and] is glorified'.[20] Incorporating the changed terminology, he summarises the eucharistic teaching of the great scholastics as follows: the species of bread and wine are the *sacramentum tantum*, the *corpus Christi mysticum* (i.e. the Church) is the *res tantum* and the *corpus Christi verum* (i.e. born of Mary) is the *res et sacramentum*, that is, the *res* of the first and the *sacramentum* of the second.[21] While this scholastic formulation does preserve what de Lubac would see as the correct causal progression, this presumably being the reason why he pays it the compliment of being 'structurally Augustinian',[22] his objection is that the terminological change has altered the doctrine's 'centre of gravity',[23] which, we may interpret, naturally falls on the *corpus* which is understood as *verum*. If this is, as at first, the *Church* then the Eucharist is unfailingly seen as that which exists to edify the Church. However, if it is the Eucharist, then the progression

---

[18] *CMys*, p. 199.

[19] *Ibid.*, p. 201, '*Il est lui-même le corps dont ceux qui le mangent deviennent l'aliment.*' The eucharistic motif appears on the previous page.

[20] *Splendour*, p. 112.

[21] *CMys*, pp. 125-126 (cf. *Splendour*, p. 92); the group summarised includes Albert the Great, Bonaventure and Aquinas. Edward Yarnold surveys the different views of Catholic theologians on the *res et sacramentum* of the Eucharist, showing that Rahner and Schillebeeckx consider it to be the sacrament's social effect in the (visible) Church (*The Second Gift*, p. 171, n. 31). We see that de Lubac differs from these other proponents of the sacramentality of the Church on this point.

[22] *Catholicism*, p. 40.

[23] Cf. *CMys*, p. 275.

tends to stop there. Historically, from being the defining source of the Church, the Eucharist became an end in itself; 'the mystery to understand' became 'the miracle to believe'.[24] Alternative definitions of the Church were then necessary. Accordingly, the opening of the fourteenth century saw, in the first treatise on the Church, the metaphor of the Kingdom preferred to that of the Body of Christ, and increasingly sociological definitions followed.[25]

De Lubac's aim was to reinstate *the Church* as the 'marvel' and to understand the Eucharist as 'the mystical principle, permanently active' to realise it.[26] The Church makes the Eucharist, but she does so because 'in the strict sense . . . the Eucharist makes the Church'.[27] In *Corpus Mysticum*, de Lubac identified as a pressing need of our time a return, 'so as to steep ourselves in it again, to the sacramental origins of the "Mystical Body"'.

'The Church and the Eucharist make each other, every day, each by the other: the idea of the Church and the idea of the Eucharist must likewise be promoted and deepened each by the other.'[28]

There is, then, a definite causal sequence in de Lubac's view of the Eucharist. 'The mystery of communication is rounded out in a mystery of communion.'[29] What is communicated is Christ.

'Fed by the Body and Blood of the Saviour, his faithful thereby all "drink of the same Spirit" who truly makes of them one Body.'[30]

[24] Cf. *ibid.*, p. 269.

[25] *Ibid.*, pp. 129-135. James of Viterbo's *De regimine christiano* (written, 1301-1302) heralded a sudden spate of (mainly juridical) treatises on the Church. Cf. Yves Congar, *L'Eglise de saint Augustin à l'époque moderne*, pp. 270-271, and 'Ecclesia ab Abel', pp. 92-93.

[26] *Ibid.*, p. 103.

[27] *Ibid.*, p. 104; cf. *Splendour*, p. 106.

[28] *Ibid.*, pp. 292-293; cf. *Splendour*, p. 92.

[29] *Splendour*, p. 108.

[30] *CMys*, pp. 103-104; with reference to Chrysostom, *In 1 Cor.*, hom. 30, n. 2 (PG 61, 251).

Thus it is that the *corpus mysticum*, which strictly is Christ's own glorified Body *in mysterio*, can by extension be the *ecclesial* Body of Christ, but only if this latter is being considered *precisely in her edification by the Eucharist*.[31] Christ and the Spirit are at work in the Eucharist, forming the ecclesial Body, gathering the Church. De Lubac states that 'eucharistic realism' and 'ecclesial realism' are interdependent, and, perhaps particularly in response to those who would query Augustine's eucharistic realism, he asserts that 'ecclesial realism ensures eucharistic realism'.[32] He summarises the case for Augustine's eucharistic realism as follows: the Presence is assuredly 'real', because it is 'realising'.[33]

What Christ would realise in the Eucharist was perceived and strikingly expressed by Augustine in a text which de Lubac quoted in *Catholicism*. The very host which offers Christ's sacrificial action to the communicant for the latter's active consumption itself conveys, by its own composition, the fact that there is no merely individual edification taking place.

> '"The Body of Christ", you are told, and you answer "Amen". Be members then of the Body of Christ that your Amen may be true. Why is this mystery accomplished with bread? We shall say nothing of our own about it, rather let us hear the Apostle, who speaking of this sacrament says: "We being many are one body, one bread." Understand and rejoice. Unity, devotion, charity! One bread: and what is this one bread? One body made up of many. Consider that the bread is not made of one grain alone, but of many. During the time of exorcism, you were, so to say, in the mill. At baptism you were wetted with water. Then the Holy Spirit came into you like the fire which bakes the dough. Be then what you see and receive what you are.'[34]

We may readily link these words with the description of the Church which we derived from de Lubac's account in *Catholicism* of her unity, namely as the 'sacramental veil, woven by the

---

[31] *Ibid.*, p. 281.

[32] *Ibid.*, p. 283.

[33] *Ibid.*, p. 284: *'Présence réelle, parce que réalisante.'*

[34] *Catholicism*, pp. 37-38; quotation from Augustine, *Sermo* 272 (PL 38, 1247-1248).

circumincession of persons indwelt by Christ'.[35] The host then appears as the veil or interface between Christ and the individual recipient, which speaks to the latter of the ecclesial unity only within which he may commune with Christ. If he hears, and engages with the sacrament accordingly, then and only then does it happen that he receives Christ and is received by Christ into the Church.

Christ is not to be located in the veil itself, he is not *caught* in the veil, but the veil is the only access to him. We recall that the circumincession of persons is caused by each having the same Christ indwelling.[36] In *Catholicism*, de Lubac showed how the Eucharist serves this pattern of unity with a quotation from Cyril of Alexandria, which implicitly attributes the same pattern of unity to God by concluding as shown.

> 'Within Christ no division can arise. All united to the single Christ through his own body, all receiving him, the one and indivisible, into our own bodies, we are the members of this one body and he is thus, for us, the bond of unity. . . . [A]s Christ is one and indivisible we are all no more but one in him. So did he say to his heavenly Father, "That they may be one, as we are one".'[37]

We might say that receiving the host, which by its constitution itself speaks of the ecclesial dimension of reception, while rejecting this dimension, is simultaneously to reject the host. Eucharistic theology has to have an understanding of Christ's Presence sophisticated enough to cope with such instances of uncharitable reception, without Christ seeming trapped or compromised. De Lubac finds in Augustine precisely such a theology, as we may see from the following brief indication of de Lubac's analysis in *Corpus Mysticum*.

Augustine said: '*secundum quemdam modum sacramentum corporis Christi corpus Christi est*'.[38] There are (at least) two ways of understanding these words; first, that Christ's body exists as

---

[35]Cf. above, pp. 22-23.

[36]Cf. above, p. 19.

[37]*Catholicism*, p. 37; quotations from Cyril of Alexandria, *In Joannem*, 11, 11 (PG 74, 560B) and *De SS. Trinitate Dialogus*, 1 (PG 75, 697B; corrected reference).

[38]*CMys*, p. 105; quotation from Augustine, *Ep.* 98, 9 (PL 33, 364).

a simple entity which the sacrament contains or relates one to *secundum quemdam modum*, or, secondly, that Christ's body exists as a complex entity, whose complexity is paralleled in the sacrament and is itself what is intended by the expression '*secundum quemdam modum*'. Augustine intended the latter. Just as it was possible to look at Christ and understand him only as flesh, so it is possible to look at the Eucharist and understand it only as bread. Just as Christ's visible humanity was filled with his invisible divinity, such that he was only properly understood spiritually, in a faith which penetrated from the visible to the invisible, so the same is true, in parallel fashion, for the Eucharist.

Jerome made a similar distinction with reference to Christ's one flesh.

> '*Dupliciter vero sanguis Christi et caro intelligitur: vel spiritualis illa atque divina, de qua dixit: "caro mea vere est cibus" et "nisi manducaveritis . . .", vel caro et sanguis quae crucifixa est et qui militis effusus est lancea.*'[39]

Jerome intended not two fleshes but 'two different ways of envisaging the same flesh' and also of receiving it. The latter way is 'in its sensible aspect, in its pure "fleshly" reality', in accordance with the sense in which Jesus said to Peter 'flesh and blood have not revealed this to you' and in which Paul teaches that flesh and blood cannot possess the Kingdom of God. The former way is in its vivifying aspect, in accordance with the sense in which he said 'my flesh is real food', requiring both the faith and the correct dispositions of the communicant in order to be discerned and received properly.[40]

We might say that Christ is *really present* as flesh, as bread and, further, as the Church, each of which must be received spiritually; they have an identical *dynamic*. De Lubac gives the following account of the eucharistic doctrine of Alger of Liége, who exemplifies the failure of medieval theologians correctly to understand Jerome's distinction and, likewise, Augustine's *secundum quemdam modum*.

---

[39] *Ibid.*, pp. 140-141; quotation from Jerome, *In Eph.*, 1, 1 (PL 26, 451).
[40] Cf. *ibid.*, pp. 141-142.

'The material flesh, about which he [Jerome] spoke with a pejorative nuance, becomes the historical body of Christ considered in all its states, that is the glorious body, sitting on the right of the Father, as well as the body born of the Virgin, suffering and dying: nothing here recalls any more that flesh and blood "which cannot possess the Kingdom of God". With regard to the "spiritual flesh", it is henceforth spoken of to define the "*corpus in sacramento*", that is to designate the Eucharist in a totally objective sense which is not at all that of Jerome and which is almost the opposite of the thought of the real Augustine.'[41]

De Lubac considers that such a change in understanding the meaning of *spiritual*, from being, as it were, the true quality or context of Christ's visibility, whether as flesh or as bread or as the Church, and hence as the only proper way of receiving and responding to this visibility, to designating a particular objective presence of Christ in the Eucharist, owes something to the influence of Ambrose. Ambrose understood *spiritual* primarily to mean that characteristic of human existence in itself in a particular phase of its history, namely after the resurrection: '*seminatur corpus animale, surget corpus spirituale*'.[42] Christ now has a spiritual flesh and whereas for Augustine this meant still a *localised* flesh or body but 'a flesh submitted to the spirit, in a spirit submitted to God',[43] that is, a flesh which no longer fought with or distracted the spirit, for Ambrose this meant a flesh which enjoyed the freedom of the spirit and was, therefore, by no means localised. With an Ambrosian view, it is perfectly possible for Christ to be objectively present on many altars. The eucharistic body is *spiritual* above all because it is 'the body of Him who rose *totus Spiritus*'.[44] Thus *spiritual* designates a particular objective presence of Christ's body and prescinds from any question about, for instance, the *manner* of discernment or reception.

[41] *Ibid.*, pp. 144-145, with particular reference to Alger of Liége, *De sacramentis*, 1, 17 (PL 180, 790-791).

[42] *Ibid.*, p. 145; quotation from 1 Cor. 15: 44. Cf. p. 150 where de Lubac quotes from Ambrose, *De mysteriis*, 58 (PL 16, 408-409).

[43] *Ibid.*, p. 147.

[44] *Ibid.*, p. 151; reference to Ambrose, *De fide resurrectionis*, 91 (PL 16, 1341).

Ambrose combined 'the most marked realism' with 'the boldest spiritualism' in an equilibrium of which Augustinian doctrine was 'less capable'. Nonetheless, de Lubac regards the latter as 'otherwise more profound'.[45] We may interpret him to mean that the Augustinian notion of Christ fundamentally being now localised in heaven, that is in *one* place, serves to unite in the most rigorous way the three bodies of Christ which, as we saw earlier, have in truth the same *dynamic*. The Eucharist is the mystical veil through which the glorified Christ himself reaches to the Church of this world in order to draw her to himself and embody her in the Church of heaven.[46]

The history of Eucharistic doctrine has two great phases: first, when the main division ('*césure*') was between the first and second bodies and then, secondly, when it moved to stand between the second and third.[47]

> 'The reaction against Berengarius only reinforced a movement which, having begun at the time of Paschasius Radbertus, was identifying more and more the first two of the three "bodies" and, on the other hand, detaching from them the third.'[48]

Berengarius' heretical doctrine of Christ's eucharistic presence '*mystice, non vere*' (mystically, not truly) provoked a response of '*vere, non mystice*' (truly, not mystically), which de Lubac strongly criticises as 'no less exclusive'.

> 'Orthodoxy was perhaps saved, but in return doctrine was surely impoverished.'[49]

The period thus furnishes a prime instance of heresy dictating the terms of orthodoxy:[50] 'it could be said that [the] ultra-

---

[45] *Ibid.*, p. 151.

[46] Cf. *Splendour*, p. 108.

[47] *CMys*, p. 288, the first, second and third being Christ himself, the Eucharist and the Church, respectively.

[48] *Ibid.*, p. 184. We see that M. Cristiani is mistaken in stating that de Lubac locates the crisis in eucharistic doctrine in the eleventh century Berengarian controversy and does not heed the start of the 'new orientation' in the work of Paschasius in the ninth century ('La controversia eucaristica nella cultura del secolo IX', pp. 179-180).

[49] *Ibid.*, p. 251.

[50] Cf. above, pp. 5-6.

orthodox fell into the trap which the heretic had set up for them'. In effect, 'they agreed with him in mutilating the traditional teaching'.[51]

What characterised the second phase was the separation of terms which Augustine distinguished only subtly, namely '*sumere Christum*' and '*sumi a Christo*' and the substitution of a static view of the Eucharist, focused upon the reality of consecration, for Augustine's dynamic view centred upon the fruitfulness of communion. In this changed context, the problem of interpreting Augustine's texts became 'insoluble', because they were asked questions which they could not answer. With regard to the communion of the unworthy (e.g. 'schismatics, heretics [and] the excommunicated'), the question asked was whether they truly *consecrated* the elements. 'Do they have the Body of the Lord upon their altars?' If so then their reception of him automatically followed. Augustine looked rather to *Christ's* action in communion. 'They approach the holy table, they receive the sacrament. What, however, does the Lord do?' His answer was simple; Christ does not receive them. '*Non admittit ad corpus suum.*'[52]

Anticipation

Through the veil of the eucharistic elements, Christ in glory reaches to the Church on earth in order to draw her back through the veil and embody her in the Church of heaven. Thus, when de Lubac says that the Eucharist makes the Church, it is the heavenly Church within the eucharistic veil that he intends. The veil envelops *both* the *res et sacramentum* (Christ) and the *res tantum* (the heavenly Church). De Lubac says that it was only after the mid-twelfth century that the 'ecclesial Body' came to be differentiated as the '*res significata et non contenta*', thereby being 'expelled from the sacrament itself'.[53] Since Christ himself cannot be expelled from the sacrament, this formulation shows de Lubac's understanding of the *res*

[51] *CMys*, p. 251.
[52] *Ibid.*, pp. 289-290; cf. Augustine, *In ps.* 68, 2, 6 (PL 36, 859).
[53] *Ibid.*, p. 276 (my added emphasis).

tantum as an entity which is distinguishable from Christ. It is the circumincession of persons which Christ brings about in the Church but which does not itself contain Christ. Of course, it cannot be considered apart from him, he constitutes it as Head;[54] but de Lubac nowhere indicates that Christ himself is as radically unthinkable without the Church.

We shall now see that de Lubac regards the heavenly Church as a future reality in which we already participate in anticipation. His account of participation further emphasises that it is in the Church as an entity, and indeed as a *person, distinct* from Christ that we participate. This distinction will be seen to endanger the inseparability of aspects of the Eucharist which de Lubac asserted in the opening quotation of this chapter.

He emphasises that 'the Church herself' in her 'mysterious reality' which 'always transcends all those who belong to her and gather to her from all over the earth' does not subsist 'in the manner of a Platonic "idea"'.[55] The heavenly Church, then, is not *already* in perfect existence elsewhere; rather, the earthly Church is her *seed*, she is the latter brought to *future* perfection. While she is truly our Mother, such that it can be said of the Apostles, for instance, that 'they themselves were first conceived by her', it must also be said, since they nurtured her seed, that 'she was born of the Apostles'.[56] In short, assertions about the maternity and present activity of the heavenly Church, are made *retrospectively*, as from the time of the future consummation.

De Lubac maintains that both Origen and Augustine made *retrospective* statements which must clearly be recognised as such. For Origen, 'the hierarchic Church [i.e. the earthly Church] and the heavenly Church are one and the same reality, from different angles'.[57] De Lubac regards this as a 'very important' point of Origen's ecclesiology.[58] He quotes Olivier Rousseau, as follows.

---

[54] Cf. *ibid.*, p. 104.
[55] *Splendour*, p. 76.
[56] Cf. *ibid.* p. 76.
[57] *HEsp*, p. 166, n. 145; quotation from L. Cerfaux, 'Review', p. 148.
[58] *Ibid.*, p. 165, n. 145.

'It is a mistake, I think, to criticise Origen for having applied the idea of motherhood sometimes to the heavenly Jerusalem and sometimes to the Church on earth, as if this were an inconsistency due to an imperfect ecclesiology.'[59]

Rousseau continues in explanation:

'though it is the Church on earth which gives birth, she does so in a heavenly manner, hence the use of the two expressions'.[60]

Ultimately the Church will contain only the 'saints', the 'pure'. To refer to her already in this way is to speak retrospectively, as from the vantage point of the future. De Lubac says that misinterpretation of Origen in this matter 'has marred the interpretation of the whole of his ecclesiology'.[61]

Lest we suspect that predestination is implicit in statements about the present effectiveness of the future heavenly Church, we may note de Lubac's reply to those who charge Augustine with 'determinism'.

'It would be just as fair to regard the apostle John likewise, whose teaching on the opposition of light and darkness, on the man who, born of God, sins no more, on the judgement already pronounced, on those who depart "because they were not of us" . . . is familiar. As much as the evangelist, whose eagle-look lives on in him, Saint Augustine sees in the present moment more than its momentary reality; he refuses to consider a transient reality otherwise than in its relation to the definitive state.'[62]

Already in *Catholicism*, de Lubac made it clear that the Church's definitive state lies in the future[63] and, in *Histoire et Esprit*, he dissociated himself firmly from Origen's notion that the end will, in fact, be 'like the beginning'.[64] The Church in time is the seed of the Church of eternity in genuine historical development. She is the Church of eternity '"*nondum re, tamen*

[59] *Splendour*, p. 79, n. 10 (cf. *Sources*, p. 221, n. 21); quotation from O. Rousseau, 'La Jérusalem céleste', p. 380.
[60] 'La Jérusalem céleste', p. 381.
[61] *Splendour*, p. 79, n. 9; cf. p. 92, n. 3.
[62] *Surnaturel*, pp. 61-62.
[63] *Catholicism*, pp. 26-27.
[64] *HEsp*, p. 44.

spe..." (not yet in reality, yet already in expectancy)'.[65] Already, in anticipation, we participate in the heavenly Church, which will be the eternal context of our relationship with Christ.

Zizioulas also describes a participation which is an anticipation. He says that it is 'the eternal design of the holy Trinity to draw man and creation to participation in God's very life'.[66] The concrete, existential form of this participation is participation in the *Eucharist*, 'understood properly as a community and not as a "thing"'.[67] This community 'portrays the very Kingdom of God here and now',[68] indeed it 'has no meaning in itself apart from its being a reflection — not in a Platonic but a *real* sense — of the community of the Kingdom of God'.[69] As for de Lubac, so for Zizioulas, the reflection is not empty but full of the reality of the heavenly community and that reality lies in the future. In the meantime, Zizioulas says, 'the Church realises its ecclesial identity only sacramentally, i.e. in the form of anticipation'.[70]

However, there is a crucial difference between the understandings which de Lubac and Zizioulas have of that heavenly community. For de Lubac, the heavenly community is *other* than Christ; it is the context of access to him and thereby to the Father.[71] For Zizioulas, the heavenly community *is Christ*, that is, the *corporate* Christ, *simultaneously* one and many, in a *mutually* constitutive way. This corporate Christ is the context of our access to the Father. The eucharistic community, which Zizioulas identifies with 'the worshipping community before the throne of God',[72] is the local church gathered around the bishop, which he says is '*exactly the same as*' the whole Church gathered around Christ.[73] In other words, Christ is not, as for de Lubac, one who stands out from the community, as the

---

[65] *Sources*, p. 221; quotation from Rupert, *In Zach.* (PL 168, 791D).
[66] *BC*, p. 211; such participation being '*theosis*'. Cf. *ibid.*, pp. 94, 228-229.
[67] *Ibid.*, pp. 213-214.
[68] *Ibid.*, p. 229.
[69] *Ibid.*, pp. 232-233.
[70] *CIEI*, p. 12.
[71] Cf. *Splendour*, pp. 147-148.
[72] *BC*, p. 234. Cf. below, p. 170.
[73] Cf. *ibid.*, p. 149 (Zizioulas' italics). Cf. below, p. 169.

medium of its worship before the Father's throne; rather, he stands among the community, as the *centre* of its worship before God.[74] Whereas the many similar grains of the consecrated host can serve as an image of the Kingdom for de Lubac, evoking as they do the unity of the heavenly Church in and through which each will encounter Christ,[75] for Zizioulas the *eikon* of the Kingdom must be intrinsically differentiated into the one and the many; it is painted more broadly by the bishop and the people, together, as the eucharistic community.[76]

Given de Lubac's distinction of the Church from Christ, further evidence of which we shall soon see, he cannot secure, but only urge, as in the opening quotation of this chapter, the inseparability of the anticipatory and the memorial aspects of the Eucharist, because these aspects pertain, respectively, to the two entities distinguished. Christ is present from the past, in the ever-presence of his Calvary sacrifice.[77] The heavenly Church is present from the future, as that into which Christ receives those who respond to him.[78] In de Lubac's theology, the past and the future can be *juxtaposed,* but not *integrated.*[79] Zizioulas' *corporate* understanding of Christ secures absolutely the inseparability of the anticipatory and memorial aspects; their full integration follows from his view of Christ and the Church as only *one* entity. As the heavenly Church is present from the future, so also is Christ; in the Eucharist, he is 'present precisely as the expected one'.[80] The reality which rises to overarch time from a specific source in history, so as to come down and mould history, is not Christ's individual Calvary sacrifice from the past, but the corporate Christ from the Parousia.

[74]Cf. above, p. 22, and, on the ecclesiological dialectic, below, Chapter Twelve.

[75]Cf. above, p. 80.

[76]Cf. above, pp. 72-73, for Zizioulas' broadening of the Eucharist from the elements to the community.

[77] Cf. above, pp. 62-64.

[78]Cf. above, pp. 85-88.

[79]Cf. J. Daniélou's view: '*Juxtaposition d'un passé et d'un futur, tel est le présent chrétien*' ('Christianisme et histoire', p. 183).

[80]*BC,* p. 62, n. 64; cf. Rev. 22: 8-17 and *Didache* 9, 10 (Bihlmeyer, p. 6).

Participation

It is not our purpose here to compare Clement of Alexandria with Maximus the Confessor, nor to evaluate their respective interpretations by de Lubac and Zizioulas, but rather to compare de Lubac and Zizioulas themselves. Accordingly, we may note that the contrast we have indicated here between de Lubac and Zizioulas is well illustrated by statements which they derive from these two Fathers. Describing the Church as the Bride of Christ, and therefore considering her in distinction from him, de Lubac quotes Clement as follows.

> 'In the same way that the will of God is an act and it is called the world, so His intention is the salvation of men and it is called the Church.'[81]

This focus upon the *Church* as God's historical purpose, to which we are to understand the glorified Christ ministering, contrasts sharply with the following perspective, which Zizioulas draws from Maximus and states with his own emphasis.

> ' *The incarnate Christ is so identical to the ultimate will of God's love, that the meaning of created being and the purpose of history are simply the incarnate Christ.*'[82]

Here God's purpose can be stated simply as *Christ,* clearly understood as the corporate Christ, that is Christ surrounded by his own, Christ inseparable from all things in Christ. This eschatological reality is what ministers to history.

It might then appear that, if de Lubac envisages the Christian participating in the Bride of Christ, we could summarise Zizioulas' view by saying that, for him, the Christian participates in Christ-and-his-Bride, as a single, simultaneous reality. However, the fact is that Zizioulas does not adopt bridal terminology for the Church at all, preferring to speak in terms such as those above. Just as the bridal image is prominent in de Lubac's ecclesiology, so its absence is a prime characteristic of

---

[81] *Catholicism,* p. 25; quotation from Clement of Alexandria, *Paedagogus,* 1, 6 (PG 8, 281B).

[82] *BC,* p. 97. Cf. below, p. 149.

Zizioulas'. We must strive to understand this important divergence between the two theologians.[83]

De Lubac's view finds many expressions. Let us note in the
passages which follow that it is the Spouse of Christ, responding to him, which is understood as that which is being formed
and as that in which the Christian participates. De Lubac's
quotation from Clement in *Catholicism* occurs in the context of
elaborating a set of ecclesiological distinctions, most of which,
he says, Augustine has taught us to make, between the earthly
and the heavenly Church. He summarises:

> 'she [the Church] is at the same time both the way and the goal;
> at the same time visible and invisible; in time and in eternity, she
> is at once the bride and the widow, the sinner and the saint'.[84]

De Lubac's fullest account of the Christian's participation in
that which is other than Christ and responds to him occurs in
The Splendour of the Church, where he says that the Word of God
is 'addressed to the Church' and that his 'kiss' is for the Church
and for each of the faithful 'inasmuch as a member of the
Church'.[85] 'Christ loved his Church and delivered himself up
for her'.[86]

> 'It is she who was compassionately sought for by him . . .; she who
> is now reconciled in him to God and whom he feeds daily with
> his sacraments, and who is faithfully united to him as wife to
> husband; she who bears witness to him, prays to him, longs for
> sight of him and waits for his second coming; she, finally, who
> fights in this world and is to triumph in the next.'[87]

De Lubac then adds that individual professions of faith are
only participations, 'to a degree which always leaves something
to be desired', in the faith of the Church, which she receives as
'Christ's gift to her' and from which 'the faith of the individual
is lit'.[88]

---

[83]Cf. below, pp. 258-259.
[84]*Catholicism*, p. 27. Cf. below, p. 282.
[85]*Splendour*, pp. 204, 273.
[86]*Ibid.*, p. 40; reference to Eph. 5: 25.
[87]*Ibid.*, p. 22; cf. *Sources*, p. 22; *Faith*, p. 97.
[88]*Ibid.*, pp. 22-23; cf. *Sources*, p. 120.

What is the relationship between the individual Christian and this Church, the Spouse of Christ, in whose life and faith he participates? We have seen de Lubac invoking Peter Damain's extension of the concept of man as a 'microcosm' to each of the faithful as the 'Church in miniature'[89] and describing the 'unity of circumincession' between Christian persons, after the pattern of the Trinity itself.[90] The way in which, 'while each soul is loved individually, none is loved separately',[91] is by the mysterious immanence of one in all and of all in each one'.[92] De Lubac heightened the comparison with the unity of the Trinity when he, like Congar previously, used the words of Cyprian which Vatican II was subsequently to use early in its account of the Church: she is 'the people united by the unity of the Father and the Son and the Holy Spirit'.[93] Already in *Catholicism*, he said that the unity of the Church is 'both the image and the result of the unity of the Divine Persons among themselves'.[94]

Thus, each Christian is a microcosm of the Church, the Spouse in miniature. The Church's unity is a coincident unity-of-identity, which results from Christ restoring in each Christian the image of God, 'that aspect of *me* in which I coincide with every other man'.[95] All Christians coincide in their identity as the Spouse in miniature. De Lubac explicitly *personifies* this coincident identity of Christians in the Church. Indeed he substitutes *person* for *body* when he renders Peter Damain's teaching on the Church as Christ's Spouse as follows.

[89]*Catholicism*, p. 168. Cf. above, p. 21.

[90]*Ibid.*, p. 183. Cf. above, p. 20.

[91]*Splendour*, p. 273; cf. *Catholicism*, p. 183.

[92]*Catholicism*, p. 189. Cf. above, p. 18.

[93]*Splendour*, p. 175 (substituting 'Spirit' for 'Ghost'); quotation from Cyprian, *De orat. dom.*, 23 (PL 4, 553). Cf. *Lumen Gentium*, n. 4. De Lubac more recently opened a chapter on the *Ecclesia de Trinitate* with this quotation (*Motherhood*, p. 113-114); cf. *Faith*, pp. 30-31. The quotation occurred in Congar's pioneering study, *Chrétiens Désunis* (p. 59, n. 1), in 1937.

[94]*Catholicism*, p. 51.

[95]*Ibid.*, pp. 187-188. Cf. above, p. 19.

'The whole Church forms, in some sort, but one single person. As she is the same in all, so in each one she is whole and entire.'[96]

Elsewhere, he says that when each Christian says the Creed, he speaks '*in persona Ecclesiae*'. Therefore he says 'I believe in God', not referring directly to himself but rather speaking 'as in the name of the whole Church'.[97]

However, this stance which we have elaborated directly from de Lubac's own statements, is *triply* unsatisfactory on his own terms. First, referring to what can truly unite the multitude of beings, he makes the following stipulation.

'Coincidence is no more union than proximity is presence. there is no real unity without persisting difference.'[98]

Yet it is a union based on the coincidence of something common within each, rather than on the complementarity of persisting difference that he has just described for Christians. De Lubac is protesting at the very collapse of Christians into one coincident identity which threatens in his account of the Church's unity. He is seeking a unity between Christians which will distinguish them in unity and, as it were, hold them apart in unity, but he seems unable to formulate it.

The problem becomes even more evident when we consider, secondly, the unity of the Trinitarian Persons, which has

[96]*Ibid.*, p. 168. the quotation appears to be a conflation of the following parts of Peter Damian's, *Liber qui appellatur Dominus vobiscum*, chaps. 5 and 10. '*Tota namque Ecclesia . . . unum procul dubio corpus est.* (PL 145, 239A) [*U*]*t et in pluribus una, et in singulis sit per mysterium tota.* (235A) *Sicut autem homo, Graeco eloquio dicitur Microcosmus, . . . ita etiam unusquisque fidelium quasi quaedam minor videtur esse Ecclesia. . . .* (239D)' The substitution fully accords with Peter Damian's own view of the Church. He himself applies the term '*persona*' to the Church several times (e.g. PL 145, 235B).

[97]*Splendour*, pp. 23-24; cf. *Faith*, pp. 96, 98, 100. There is no contradiction when de Lubac elsewhere says that the community proclaims its faith in the form 'I believe' rather than 'we believe' in order to remind each of his baptismal commitment (*Faith*, p. 30), for he always maintains that what happens in the Church happens dependently in each Christian. What de Lubac is rejecting here is that there is a faith professed by an aggregate 'we'. Faith is professed by the Spouse ('I') and thence by each spouse ('I'). The fifth chapter of *Faith* is entitled, 'The believing Church'.

[98]*Catholicism*, p. 188.

been underpinning de Lubac's account of the unity between Christians, for this unity, 'the highest unity', is emphatically not a unity based upon *coincidence* of Persons. It is quite the opposite: a unity of utter complementarity; coincidence, so to speak, turned completely inside out.

> 'It is impossible to imagine greater distinctions than those of this pure threefold relationship, since it is these very distinctions that constitute them in their entirety.'[99]

Thirdly, the personification of the Church as Spouse uttering her 'I' of response to Christ conflicts with de Lubac's conviction that the 'I' of the Church is *Christ*.[100] Though de Lubac does not quote this conviction from its celebrated formulation in *Das Wesen des Katholizismus* by Karl Adam,[101] it is apparent in his presentation of the teaching of Augustine, whose doctrine of the *totus Christus* was what lay behind Adam's own statement.[102] Regarding the 'I' of the Psalms, particularly voiced by Jesus himself in his question, 'why have you forsaken me?', de Lubac refers to Augustine as follows.

> 'At Gethsemane, on Calvary, Jesus spoke in his own name; yet none the less he spoke at the same time on behalf of humanity. *Sive caput loquatur, sive membra, unus Christus loquitur. Et capitis proprium est loqui* etiam *in persona membrorum.*'[103]

---

[99]*Ibid.*, p. 180.

[100]Congar notes that 'the title of Spouse traditionally given to the Church . . . supposes in her a certain quality of personhood [*personnalité*], *altera persona*'. However, he adds an indication of the attendant difficulties: 'the Fathers and theologians . . . hardly explained themselves regarding the exact content of the term!' ('La personne «Eglise»', p. 625)

[101]K. Adam, *Das Wesen des Katholizismus*, p. 24: '*Christus, der Herr, ist das eigentliche Ich der Kirche.*' In *Catholicism*, p. xvii, de Lubac refers to this study as one of the 'excellent works' which excuse certain gaps in his own presentation.

[102]Cf. *ibid.*, p. 25.

[103]*Catholicism*, pp. 95-96; quotation (with emphasis by de Lubac) from Augustine, *In ps.* 140, 3 (PL 37, 1817). Cf. *ibid.*, p. 189, where de Lubac likens Augustine's *una persona* to St Paul's εἷς, both of which, he says, we must take up again. The Pauline reference is presumably to Gal. 3: 28 in which Paul uses a freestanding 'one' which, notably, is *masculine*: 'you are all one [εἷς] in Christ Jesus'. This text is important also to Zizioulas (*BC*, p. 145).

When de Lubac considers the Church uttering her 'I' to Christ, it is clearly not an utterance that is constitutive of Christ himself. Rather, it is a *response* to his accomplished work. It is significant that when, on the other hand, de Lubac considers the Church's 'I' as that of Christ himself, he still does not consider the Church as constitutive of Christ. He says that it comes about by 'communication of idioms' between 'the Head and the members of the one Body of Christ'.[104] Communication of idioms refers to a situation in which two united realities are nevertheless firmly distinguished, with at least one of them capable of an independent existence, having the characteristics which the union communicates to the other. The union, in other words, is not itself constitutive of the two realities; in the deepest sense, they are *not* ontologically a unity. In this case, the communication from Head to members is what is conveyed by the expression, '*translatus est Christus ad Ecclesiam*', which we have seen de Lubac quote from Paschasius.[105] De Lubac maintains that it is communication of idioms which explains the words which Paul heard: 'I am Jesus whom thou persecutest'.[106]

Thus, the third tension in de Lubac's account, between the two positions which we have just seen, is one in which the two alternatives share an important presupposition, namely that the Church is not constitutive of Christ but is she to whom, in a second phase, Christ communicates himself. It is logical, then, to ask whether the shared presupposition is itself what generates the tension and to seek a possible alternative.

An alternative to this presupposition would be to consider Christ, not above the Church, only constituting her, but in the midst of the Church, as himself one of the many, constituting her and being constituted by her. Each of her members would then be a microcosm of the corporate personality Christ and not a microcosm of the Church as an entity distinct from him. The configuration of Christ in the midst of the Church also dispels the possibility of the collapse of the many Christians into one coincident identity which we saw fuelling the first

---

[104]*Ibid.*, p. 96.
[105]*Sources*, p. 220. Cf. above, p. 65.
[106]*Catholicism*, p. 26.

tension in de Lubac's position, for, while he does not want such a collapse, that is what threatens in his account.[107] If Christ is other than the Church, outside or above the many of whom she consists, and communicating himself to each, then there is a danger that the many will collapse to the one which effectively relates to Christ, this one being Christ's Spouse, the corporate personality *Church*. However, if Christ himself is in the midst of the Church, as *himself* the *one* of her corporate personality, then this collapse simply cannot occur. Christ then does precisely what was seen above to be necessary, namely *he holds the many apart in unity*; personal identities are intact and Christian persons in the Church are in a unity no longer of coincidence but of complementarity.

The focus within the Church, once Christ is distinguished from the Church, tends to become Mary.[108] De Lubac utters a caution against Mariological excesses, but himself accepts what these excesses merely 'over-particularise',[109] namely 'a certain "communication of idioms"' between Mary and the Church.[110] We may say that the excesses are avoided, together with the ambiguity regarding the corporate personality in which Christians participate, which results from referring to a communication of idioms both between Christ and the Church and between Mary and the Church, by locating Christ *within* the Church, as the one at her heart.[111]

Zizioulas would endorse Adam's statement that the 'I' of the Church is Christ,[112] but reject an explanation of their union in terms of communication of idioms.[113] He considers Christ and the Church to be simultaneous and mutually constitutive, a view which we have here seen can resolve tensions in de Lubac's exposition. An indication of the implications of this

---

[107]Cf. above, pp.48, 93.

[108]Cf. above, p. 67, n. 90.

[109]Cf. *Splendour*, p. 251.

[110]*Ibid.*, p. 249 (corrected translation; cf. *Méditation sur l'Eglise* (1953²), p. 285).

[111]Cf. above, p. 66.

[112]Cf. *UC*, p. 14, n. 37; *IED*, p. 144, nn. 12, 13; *CECB*, p. 4.

[113]Cf. below, pp. 250-251.

view for the practical structure of the Church and her celebrations, which we must now consider, may be given as follows. For de Lubac, the visible Church is translucent or transparent to Christ himself.[114] Zizioulas also regards the structures and ministries or orders of the Church as 'transparent',[115] but to 'the very Kingdom of God', that is to Christ *as a corporate personality*, to 'the whole . . . Church united in Christ'.[116] Correspondingly, whereas Zizioulas stresses the need for the presence of *all* of the orders (bishop, presbyters, deacons *and people*) to be present for a faithful portrayal of the Kingdom in its eucharistic encounter with history,[117] de Lubac's emphasis falls on the constitutive role of 'the minister', that is the bishop or priest, whose task is to gather the people and *transmit* life to them.[118]

---

[114]*Splendour*, pp. 147-148, 164.
[115]*CECB*, p. 6.
[116]*BC*, p. 229 and n. 60; cf. p. 206. Cf. above, pp.88-89.
[117]E.g. *EQA*, p. 43. Cf. below, p. 195.
[118]*Motherhood*, pp. 354-356; the community is not 'constituted' without him (corrected translation; cf. *Les églises particulières dans l'Eglise universelle*, p. 244). Cf. *Splendour*, p. 104, n. 5.

Chapter 5

The Church makes the Eucharist

'[*La*] *question du rapport entre l'Eucharistie et l'Eglise ne préjuge en rien l'idée que l'on peut se faire de la structure visible de l'Eglise.*'[1]

De Lubac made this comment in reaction to the likening of his advocacy of the principle that the Eucharist makes the Church to its advocacy by the Orthodox, Afanassieff and Zizioulas.[2] He later reiterated the comment, adding that, although it must be said that 'without the Eucharist there is no Church', the term 'eucharistic ecclesiology' is 'too short'. The Eucharist cannot explain *everything* in the Church; in particular, it cannot explain the Church's *structure*, which exists to meet the need of the Church in history to *spread*.[3] We may deduce that the Church is structured according to pragmatic and specifically *missionary*[4] considerations in order to facilitate

---

[1]Statement of de Lubac in a letter to the present author, dated 4 July 1986: 'the question of the relationship between the Eucharist and the Church in no way prejudges the idea one can form about the visible structure of the Church'.

[2]The following statement prompted de Lubac's response: 'I wish to demonstrate the deep rapport between your work to show that the Eucharist makes the Church and the work of modern Orthodox ecclesiologists, particularly Nicolas Afanassieff and John Zizioulas, to promote the same principle' (Letter to de Lubac, dated 14 June 1986). De Lubac prefaced the quoted assertion as follows. *J'estime grandement, quoique, bien entendu, je ne puisse pas être de tout point en accord avec eux, les travaux des deux ecclésiologues orthodoxes que vous me citez, Mais, je me permets de vous préciser que la question. . . .*'

[3]I draw gratefully on personal discussions with de Lubac.

[4]"The Church is essentially missionary' (*FTMiss*, p. 17). Cf. below, p. 289.

the administration of the sacraments and especially the celebration of the Eucharist so that, 'in turn',[5] the true (i.e.
heavenly) ecclesial life of the participants may be strength-
ened, but that this ecclesial life is not itself directly visible.

Thus, the principle that the Church makes the Eucharist can
be treated, as we are treating it here, distinctly from the
complementary principle, though of course it applies precisely
because of the complementary principle.[6] Having reasserted
the latter principle, that the Eucharist makes the Church,
primarily in *Corpus Mysticum*, de Lubac turned to the former
principle, and to considerations of the practical structure of
the Church, in his subsequent ecclesiological works.[7] This
distinction of material indicates a further influence of Augustine on de Lubac. In 1953 he said that 'in a whole section of the
works of St Augustine' the *Corpus Christi* is treated 'with no
explicit reference to the visible structure of the Church'.[8]

The Bishop as High Priest

De Lubac's numerous quotations from Adrien Gréa's
ecclesiological tome of 1884 in his own ecclesiological studies
of both 1953 and 1971[9] provide one gauge of the remarkable
consistency of his views during this period of great ecclesiological
moment in the Roman Catholic Church, centred upon the
Second Vatican Council (1962-1965). Indeed, his desire to

[5]Cf. *Splendour*, p. 106; above, pp. xv, xvi-xvii.

[6]*Ibid.*, p. 106; above, p. xv.

[7]Namely, *Splendour*, *ChPM* and *Motherhood*, originally published in 1953,
1965 and 1971, respectively. In the following account of the structure of the
Church, as throughout this book, I render 'church' with a small 'c' when it
refers to a particular church, i.e. a diocese, and with a capital 'C' in all other
instances. Although de Lubac advocates reserving the term 'local church' for
groups of dioceses (cf. *Motherhood*, pp. 184-186), I follow the general usage in
which 'local church' and 'particular church' are interchangeable, both
indicating a single diocese.

[8]*Splendour*, p. 65, n. 1.

[9]In *Splendour*, pp. 10, 61, 68, 102 (twice), 104, 107, de Lubac refers to the
1907 reedition of Gréa, *L'Eglise et sa divine constitution*. In *Motherhood*, pp. 190,
206, 250, 278, 314, 317, he refers to the new edition (520pp.) of 1965 (to which
we shall hereafter refer as *L'Eglise*).

amend his 1953 text only by adding 'here and there, some brief, last minute reflections' for its 1985 republication,[10] testifies that there are no substantial changes to be sought in his views over this latter, even longer period.

For instance, regarding his understanding of the principle to which we are now turning, he said the following in 1953.

'The Church makes the Eucharist. It was principally to that end that her priesthood was instituted. "Do this in memory of me."'[11]

In 1971, he reiterated that 'the ministry of the Twelve' was 'instituted in order to "make" the Eucharist' and therefore that it was and is transmissible since the latter 'was instituted by Jesus for the life of the Church up until the parousia'.[12] That this later statement does not indicate a change in his view of the Eucharist from being primarily a *priestly* celebration to having an *episcopal* president, the bishops being the successors of the Apostles, may be seen from the fact that, already in 1953 de Lubac clearly envisaged the bishop as the *High Priest* and, correspondingly, as the primary celebrant of the Eucharist. He associated himself with the intense research of the early 1950s into the sacrament of Orders, which was preparing the way for the teaching of Vatican II that one enters *sacramentally* into the episcopate, which is indeed 'the fulness of the sacrament of Orders'.[13] His 1953 study had a second edition in the same year in order to incorporate new developments.[14] In the second edition, he lifted into the text, from a footnote in the first, Ignatius' description of the presbyters (whom de Lubac calls the *priests*) as the 'precious spiritual crown' of the bishop, and annotated it with references to recent studies.[15]

---

[10]'Preface to the 1985 edition', *Méditation sur l'Eglise* (Théologie 27; Desclée de Brouwer, Paris, 1985), p. 3. The additions are minimal, e.g. a reference in n. 129 on p. 68 and a sentence on p. 203.

[11]*Splendour*, p. 93.

[12]*Motherhood*, p. 341.

[13]*Lumen Gentium*, n. 21.

[14]Cf. *Splendour*, p. xi.

[15]The description, from *Magn.* 13, in P.Th. Camelot's edition of *Ignace d'Antioche, Lettres*, appeared in n. 96 on p. 115 of the first edition of *Méditation sur l'Eglise* and then in the text of p. 128 in the second edition (cf. *Splendour*,

Even earlier, in a wartime lecture, de Lubac anticipated Vatican II's teaching on episcopal collegiality with his assertion that 'the whole episcopal body' is the 'successor of the apostolic college' and 'jointly [*solidairement*] responsible' today for the continuation of the Saviour's mission.[16] He specified in 1953 that the *Eucharist* is the reason for episcopal collegiality when he quoted Cyprian's teaching that '*episcopatus unus est*' immediately after, and in direct correlation with, his assertion that all the bishops offer 'the same and unique sacrifice', albeit in different places.[17]

We may immediately note, therefore, that de Lubac does not exemplify the 'universal ecclesiology' which Nicolas Afanassieff critically attributes to both the Roman Catholic and Orthodox Churches and traces back to Cyprian, contrasting it with the 'eucharistic ecclesiology' which he advocates.[18] Afanassieff considers that Cyprian took the juridical structure of the Roman Empire as his model for the Church's unity and stressed the unity of the bishops. '*episcopatus unus est*', as a universal, juridical unity, standing *above* the merely local unity which the Eucharist manifests.[19]

Moreover, in a general way de Lubac anticipates the criticism which Zizioulas specifically directs towards Afanassieff,[20] when he complains of those who would so exalt the local church that its integration in the universal Church is forgotten. Their ecclesiology, de Lubac maintains, is 'incompletely "eucharistic" and needs '[f]uller attention to the nature of the episcopacy and to the mystery of the Eucharist'.[21] The pairing

---

p. 106), with footnote reference (n. 4), regarding 'the relation of the episcopate to the presbyterate within the unity of the priesthood', to two new articles: E. Boularand, 'La consécration épiscopale est-elle sacramentelle?' and J. Lecuyer, 'Episcopat et presbytérat dans les écrits d'Hippolyte de Rome'.

[16]*FTMiss*, p. 17. Cf. *Lumen Gentium*, n. 22.

[17]*Splendour*, p. 105 and n. 6; quotation from Cyprian, *De unit.*, 5 (PL 4, 501).

[18]Cf. Afanassieff, 'Una Sancta' and 'The Church which presides in love'.

[19]Cf. Afanassieff, 'Una Sancta', pp. 449-454; the Cyprianic quotation occurs on p. 449.

[20]Cf. below, p. 227.

[21]*Motherhood*, p. 204.

of these two remedies makes it plain that de Lubac's statements about bishops are rooted in, and strictly correspond to, beliefs about the Eucharist, of which bishops are the prime celebrants.

Joseph Ratzinger describes the view that High Scholasticism bequeathed to Roman Catholic ecclesiology up to the modern patristic renewal. It understood the sacrament of Ordination as wholly directed towards the *corpus verum* of the Lord, that is, towards conferring the power for transsubstantiation. Every priest had this power; episcopal consecration could not add to it and was therefore not a sacrament. What it conferred was not power of Orders but power of jurisdiction, in other words, not power to make the Eucharist, the *corpus verum* of the Lord, but power to govern the Church, his *corpus mysticum*.[22]

De Lubac's efforts in the 1940s to repair this inversion of the traditional terminology, with the exclusion of the Church from the eucharistic mystery which follows from it,[23] may be seen as preparing the ground theologically for the more specifically *liturgical* research of others in the 1950s. To locate the Church once more *within* the Eucharist is implicitly to recognise the bishop's care of the former as something primarily exercised by celebration of the latter. Summarising the background to *Lumen Gentium*, Ratzinger says that '[f]or modern theology it is again clear that the *corpus verum* and the *corpus mysticum* are ordained one to another' and that service of one cannot be separated from service of the other: 'they constitute a unity of service to the one body of the Lord'.[24] Giving credit to de Lubac, Ratzinger recalls not only *Corpus Mysticum*,[25] but also the programmatic *Catholicism*: 'in everything that it [Vatican II] said on the Church it follows exactly the line of de Lubac's thought'.[26]

---

[22]Ratzinger, 'La collégialité épiscopale: développement théologique', p. 769, cf. p. 767.

[23]Cf. above, Chapter Four, particularly p. 85.

[24]Ratzinger, 'La collégialité épiscopale: développement théologique', pp. 769-770.

[25]Cf. Ratzinger, 'The Pastoral Implications of Episcopal Collegiality', p. 22.

[26]Ratzinger, *Les principes de la théologie catholique*, p. 52.

In 1953, adopting a threefold division of ministry, rather than the admittedly 'more synthetic... and older' division into two powers, of Order and jurisdiction,[27] de Lubac located the hierarchy's powers of jurisdiction and teaching *within* its priestly power of sanctifying. The latter is 'both the origin and final flowering of the other two', in the 'one single mission' which the Church has from Christ and he from the Father.[28] Its 'supreme exercise' occurs in the hierarchy's celebration of the Eucharist, that is, de Lubac says characteristically, when the hierarchy is 'consecrating Christ's body and thus perpetuating the work of the Redemption'.[29] Likewise, in 1971, de Lubac gathered the powers of teaching and jurisdiction into the Eucharist by affirming, first, that the bishop teaches '[i]n order to be able to bring together a Christian people around the Eucharist'[30] and, secondly, that the bishop 'through all his activity, seeks to insure that the unifying reality of the eucharistic mystery over which he presides produces its effect everywhere'.[31]

However, although de Lubac again anticipated Vatican II by his account in 1953 of the priesthood of *every* Christian,[32] he firmly distinguished this priesthood from the ordained or hierarchical priesthood on the grounds that only the latter makes the Eucharist.

'[T]he priesthood of the Christian people is not concerned with the liturgical life of the Church, and it has no direct connection with the confection of the Eucharist. . . . It is the "hierarchic" Church which makes the Eucharist.'[33]

---

[27] *Splendour*, p. 101. Cf. J. Fuchs, 'Origines d'une trilogie ecclésiologique à l'époque rationaliste de la théologie'.

[28] *Ibid.*, p. 102.

[29] *Ibid.*, p. 104.

[30] *Motherhood*, p. 347.

[31] *Ibid.*, p. 208.

[32] *Splendour*, p. 93; cf. *Lumen Gentium*, n. 10 and *Motherhood*, p. 355, Hans Küng refers to *Splendour* regarding the priesthood of all believers (*The Church*, p. 373).

[33] *Ibid.*, p. 96 (amended translation). Likewise in 1971: 'it is precisely so that there can be a Christian people, a priestly people, that it is necessary to have ministers charged with transmitting . . . life' (*Motherhood*, p. 356).

By this action of the hierarchy, 'Christ comes among his own' and 'makes himself their food'.[34] We see that, for de Lubac, the transition between the principles that the Church makes the Eucharist and the Eucharist makes the Church takes place via the presence of Christ in the eucharistic elements. Only the members of the hierarchy bring about this presence, but *then* they themselves receive along with the others the Christ who is present.[35] It is presumably because of the likeness which de Lubac sees between the same Christ in all Christians making all Christians one and the same Christ in all eucharistic gatherings making all the gatherings one, that he applies to these gatherings, without indicating that it is out of its proper context, the saying of Peter Damian about Christians, namely that the Church is 'one in many, mysteriously total in each'.[36]

Thus, we may say that, in de Lubac's view, the presence of the people is not essential for the celebration of the Eucharist, in the strict sense of the very making of the Eucharist. Indeed, all that matters for *fulness* in the Eucharist is the presence of the bishop or priest who makes the Eucharist, as de Lubac conveys in the following words.

> 'What happens in that solemn gathering at the heart of each diocese happens also, with the same fulness and the same effects, in the humblest village Mass or the quiet Mass of the monk in his "desert"; the scale and the setting are of little importance.'[37]

This quotation also reveals that de Lubac does not consider that the presence of the presbyters adds anything to the Eucharist at which the bishop presides. He does not specify them as members of an *ordo* distinct from that of the bishop, but rather refers to them as constituting with the bishop only

---

[34]*Ibid.*, p. 107.

[35]Cf. *ibid.*, p. 97.

[36]*Ibid.*, p. 105; quotation from Peter Damian, *Liber qui appellatur Dominus vobiscum*, 5 (PL 145, 235A). Cf. above,pp. 20-21, 92-93; and below, p. 142. Notably, Gréa applied Peter Damian likewise (cf. *L'Eglise*, pp. 70, 79-82).

[37]*Ibid.*, p. 106.

one *ordo*, namely the '*ordo sacerdotalis* or *ordo ecclesiasticus*'.[38]
One of Zizioulas' criticisms of Afanassieff could, therefore, be
applied to de Lubac, namely that he sees the same fulness in a
presbyteral or parish Eucharist as in an episcopal Eucharist.[39]

We shall see that this view accompanies in Afanassieff, as we
have seen it does in de Lubac, the sequential understanding of
the Eucharist as a presence of Christ first in the elements and
then in the communicants.[40] Afanassieff's basic principle[41] may
have influenced the wording of a passage in *Lumen Gentium*
where it is said that, even in small and isolated altar communities, 'Christ is present through whose power and influence the
One, Holy, Catholic and Apostolic Church is constituted
[*consociatur*]'.[42] However, the Council's appending of a reference to Augustine with which de Lubac himself follows a
similar passage in his own text of 1953,[43] appears to indicate
that the latter's influence was more decisive, especially since
the Council wished, like de Lubac, to emphasise the need for
local communities to be fully integrated into the universal
Church.[44]

The Universal Church and the Particular Church

'In each place the whole Church is present for the offering of
the sacrifice.'[45]

De Lubac says this after describing not only how priests celebrate as extensions of their bishops, but, more importantly,
how the bishops themselves are manifestly united, by being 'at

[38] *Ibid.*, p. 96.
[39] Cf. below, pp. 227-228.
[40] Cf. above, pp. 75-80, 103-104 (for de Lubac); below, p. 228 (for Afanassieff).
[41] Cf. below, p. 226.
[42] *Lumen Gentium*, n. 26 (trans. Flannery). Cf. the comments of O. R. (Oliver
Rousseau), 'In Memoriam: le R. P. Nicolas Afanassieff', p. 295.
[43] Cf. *Splendour*, p. 106. The reference which follows this passage, and which
also occurs in *Lumen Gentium*, n. 26, is to Augustine, *Contra Faustum* 12, 20 (PL
42, 265).
[44] Cf. above, pp. 101-102. For Afanassieff's documented influence on
Lumen Gentium, n. 26, and the stance which the drafters of the text wished to
adopt towards him, cf. P. McPartlan, 'Eucharistic Ecclesiology, pp. 325-327.
[45] *Splendour*, p. 106; cf. p. 100.

peace and in communion' with 'the Bishop of Rome' and by actually mentioning in their eucharistic prayers all their brother bishops 'in other places'.[46]

This reference only to unity with those in other *places*, with no mention of other *times*, strongly implies that de Lubac understands the 'whole Church' which is offering as the current worldwide Church, an interpretation which we shall confirm later in this section, rather than as the whole Church of all times, that is, the eschatological Spouse of Christ. We may note that those who hold the latter view ought to desire the visible unity of local eucharistic communities no less than de Lubac does, though for quite different reasons. For de Lubac, this visible unity of the worldwide Church is necessary because, by the logic of sacramentality, all of those who are offering must be *manifestly* offering and this totality is the worldwide Church. For those of the other opinion, again by the logic of sacramentality, the invisible presence and unity of the Christians of all time in the Christ who is eucharistically present must tally with the visible bonds uniting manifestations of that great final community in the world of today.

The existence of these two positions would seem to account for the fact that de Lubac and John Meyendorff, a disciple of Afanassieff, both criticise Afanassieff's neglect of the need for visible unity between eucharistic communities and yet disagree between themselves. Let us see these points in turn. In 1967, de Lubac noted that the Orthodox belief that the Church is a 'eucharistic communion' indicated 'solid ground for rapprochement between East and West'. But he criticised those who would deduce 'a real priority of the local church over the universal'. The Fathers, he said, would not support such a deduction.[47] Since he refers on the next page to 'the eucharistic and *local* ecclesiology of Fr. Afanassieff',[48] it would seem that the following comment about Cyprian, from whom, as we have seen, Afanassieff maintains that non-eucharistic, *universal* ecclesiology derives, is directed against Afanassieff.

[46] *Ibid.*, p. 105; cf. *Motherhood*, p. 206.
[47] *ChPM*, p. 36.
[48] *Ibid.*, p. 37, n. 33 (my italics).

'"As Christ instituted it," says St Cyprian, "there is only one Church spread in several members through the entire world," and in so saying he did not found a new ecclesiology.'[49]

We have seen that, whereas Afanassieff alleges that Cyprian's stress on the unity of the worldwide episcopacy asserts a unity *above* that of the Eucharist, de Lubac thinks that it is the direct counterpart of eucharistic unity. However, de Lubac's criticism is based on his belief that it is the current worldwide Church which *makes* the Eucharist. Each local community, he says, is 'open on all sides through the bonds of communion' with other members of the worldwide celebrating community 'and preserves her existence as Church only through this openness'.[50] These grounds are unacceptable to Meyendorff, whose following criticism of Vatican II makes plain his understanding of the identification of the local church with all of God's own, in the Church of all ages.

> 'Each bishop, according to the Council, is in fact the pastor of a "part" of the Church, while the bishop of Rome is the head of the "whole" ([*Lumen Gentium*] III, 18). . . . The ancient Church saw in each bishop the head of the "whole" manifested locally, and this "whole" was not a geographical concept — the universal Church of 150 or 1966 — but the Body of Christ which includes infinitely more members than the empirical and visible Church can count today, since it includes the Mother of God, the angels and the whole communion of saints.'[51]

In short, Meyendorff's criticism is that Vatican II understands the universal Church of which the local is a manifestation as the current worldwide Church, led by the bishop of Rome, rather than as the Church of all ages. However, episcopal collegiality follows from Meyendorff's stance no less than from that of Vatican II. Accordingly, he esteems Cyprian as 'the

---

[49] *Ibid.*, p. 37; quotation from Cyprian, *Epist.* 52 (55), 24 (PL 3, 790B).

[50] *Motherhood* p. 202; quotation from Ratzinger, 'The Pastoral Implications of Episcopal Collegiality', p. 22.

[51] J. Meyendorff, *Orthodoxy and Catholicity*, pp. 163-164. The two quoted terms do not actually appear in *Lumen Gentium*, n. 18. '*Tota*' and *portio*' may be found in nn. 22 and 23, respectively.

great doctor of episcopal collegiality'[52] and criticises Afanassieff's 'eucharistic "extremism"',[53] which neglects the 'crucial' correlation of the 'sacramental' with the 'universal' in ecclesiology. It is 'overly schematised and simplified', he says, and 'tends to forget the "universal" dimension of the Church along with all that this implies'.[54]

Thus it is unfair of de Lubac to criticise the 'one-sidedness' of Meyendorff when the latter distinguishes an ecclesiology founded on the local church from 'Roman universalism',[55] as if Meyendorff was content with local churches just in themselves and saw no need for visible unity. Meyendorff's criticisms of Vatican II and Afanassieff make it clear that he strongly requires the unity of local churches, but on the grounds that each manifests the Church of all ages and not just the present worldwide Church under the headship of the Bishop of Rome.

As we have seen, for Meyendorff, the difference between understanding the universal Church of which the particular is a microcosm as the Church of all ages and understanding it as the current worldwide Church is of great importance and consequence. We must now note the highly significant point that de Lubac is also aware of this difference, but that for him it is *not* important. He readily admits that *Lumen Gentium* gives 'less emphasis' to, and makes only one explicit use of, the term 'universal Church' in the sense of the Church of all the ages. Speaking of the glorious completion of the Church at the end of time, it says that all of the just 'from Abel . . . to the last of the elect' will then be 'gathered together with the Father in the universal Church'.[56] Apart from this one text, we may deduce, the universality to which the term 'universal Church' refers is that of worldwide scope. In the conciliar texts, de Lubac

---

[52] *Ibid.*, p. 158.

[53] *Ibid.*, p. 157. Cf Meyendorff's endorsement of Zizioulas' criticism of Afanassieff, in his 'Foreword' to Zizioulas, *BC*, p. 12.

[54] *Ibid.*, p. 160. Cf. Afanassieff's rejection of episcopal collegiality: 'Réflexions d'un orthodoxe sur la collégialité des évêques'.

[55] *ChPM*, p. 37, with reference to Meyendorff, *Orthodoxy and Catholicity*, pp. 104-105.

[56] *Ibid.*, p. 38; with reference to *Lumen Gentium*, n. 2. Cf. Congar, 'Ecclesia ab Abel'.

continues, there is an 'almost total abandoning of the old idea of "the Church of the saints"'.[57] However, remarkably, in his judgement this is 'far from constituting a real infidelity'.[58] Rather, 'it results from a concern for the precision and unification of the concept'.[59]

De Lubac, therefore, regards the two important conciliar texts to which he refers on the page before these comments as referring to the current *worldwide* Church when they speak of the 'universal Church', the 'catholic Church', or simply of the 'Church of Christ', respectively. The first of these texts, from *Lumen Gentium* n. 23, says that the particular churches 'are formed in the image of the universal Church' and that 'it is in and by these that the one and unique Catholic Church exists'. The second text, from *Lumen Gentium* n. 26, states the following:

> 'the Church of Christ is truly present in all legitimate local groups of the faithful who, united with their pastors, also receive, in the New Testament, the name of churches'.[60]

The interpretation which de Lubac here indicates of this latter text confirms our earlier interpretation of his account of the gathering of the whole Church in each place for the Eucharist — it is the whole *worldwide* Church of the *present* time.[61]

It would seem, then, to be *a precision of the concept* which de Lubac is applying when he endorses the Orthodox statement that for the Fathers 'the local Christian community is a manifestation of the whole Church'[62] and then immediately refers to this totality as made up of 'the churches scattered throughout the world'.[63] Meyendorff has made plain the Orthodox understanding that the whole Church manifested in the local church is the Church *of all ages,* the eschatological *ecclesia*

[57] *Ibid.,* p. 38.

[58] *Ibid.,* p. 38 (corrected translation).

[59] *Ibid.,* p. 38.

[60] *Ibid.,* p. 37, with *Lumen Gentium,* nn. 23 and 26 quoted as they are given there.

[61] Cf. above, p. 106.

[62] *ChPM,* p. 36; quotation from O. Clément, *L'Eglise orthodoxe* (1965), p. 7.

[63] *Ibid.,* p. 36.

sanctorum, and de Lubac has made plain his own awareness of this sense of universality. Our conclusion must be that de Lubac is asserting that the eschatological *ecclesia sanctorum* effectively reduces to the current worldwide Church as that which is present and edified in the Eucharist.

In 1971, de Lubac quoted from Congar that there is a 'mutual interiority' between the local church and the universal Church.[64] That Congar meant *worldwide* by 'universal' here is clear from the fact that he is in the process of presenting the Cyprianic evidence for the (worldwide) unity of the bishops in what Congar calls 'the universal college'. Congar says that this mutual interiority means that a bishop becomes such by two inseparable acts: 'consecration for the service of a local church' and 'entry into the universal college'.[65] De Lubac acknowledged Congar's *attempt* to synthesise these two aspects of becoming a bishop[66] and indicated his own desire 'to affirm the connection between the two elements' of becoming a bishop. However, he had to admit that the much debated question of whether either element precedes and causes the other 're-mains open'. Vatican II seemed to favour insertion into the college prior to receiving a particular charge, he said, but he indicated his own reserve by saying that the Council gave this priority in order to highlight its doctrine of collegiality and did not actually 'enjoin it'. The alternative priority, taught by 'those from the East', seemed to be attracting him. He conveyed his perplexity by his admission that the debate involves 'not merely a subtle distinction'.[67]

De Lubac here acknowledges a matter of importance which he cannot resolve. Our suggestion is that de Lubac's appreciation of the Eastern position by which he is drawn but not finally convinced is marred by his *effective reduction* of the universal Church which is present in the particular church to the current

[64]*Motherhood,* p. 201; quotation from Congar, *Ministères et communion ecclésiale* (hereafter, *Ministères*), p. 96.

[65]Congar, *Ministères,* pp. 96-97, cf. pp. 123-140.

[66]*Motherhood,* p. 251, n. 43, with reference to Congar, *Ministères,* pp. 123-140.

[67]*Ibid.,* pp. 250-251, n. 43.

worldwide Church. Zizioulas' detailed elaboration of the Eastern position enables a coherent synthesis of the two aspects of
becoming a bishop, such as de Lubac seeks. Zizioulas describes
this question, on which he notes de Lubac's openness, as 'of
great importance to the Orthodox', and he distinguishes de
Lubac's position from the standard Roman Catholic tendency
'to give priority to the bishop's attachment to the universal
college over his attachment to a particular church'.[68]

Let us continue now our cataloguing of the effective reduction and then ask what underlies it. De Lubac quotes Gréa, as
follows:

> 'the particular church is in substance all that the universal
> Church is'.[69]

To understand Gréa's meaning, we must note that he envisages three descending 'hierarchies':[70] 'God is the Head of
Christ, Christ is the head of the Church or of the episcopate,
. . . the bishop is the head of the particular church'.

> 'But let us declare at the outset that in this particular church we
> revere the whole mystery and the whole dignity of the Church,
> the Spouse of Jesus Christ. The mystery does not diminish [*ne
> se degrade point*] in being communicated. . . . Also the name of
> church belongs to it in full truth. It possesses, without diminu-
> tion or degradation, all the goods and the whole mystery of the
> universal Church.'[71]

Thus, we see that the universal Church is the Spouse of
Christ, a title which evokes the eschatological fulness of Christ's
Bride. However, almost immediately, Gréa refers to 'immuta-
ble integrity' which the particular church of Rome has as a
'special privilege' given with a view to 'the state of the universal
Church',[72] causing us to suspect the effective reduction of the
universal Church, the Spouse of Christ, from the eschatological
Church of all ages to the worldwide communion of particular

---

[68] *BC*, pp. 202-203, n. 113.
[69] *Motherhood*, p. 190; quotation from Gréa, *L'Eglise*, p. 79.
[70] Gréa, *L'Eglise*, p. 69; cf. Congar, *Ministères*, p. 125, n. 4.
[71] *Ibid.*, p. 69.
[72] *Ibid.*, p. 70.

churches at the present time. This suspicion is confirmed by the following statement in which Gréa, who envisages the church of Rome among the other particular churches and therefore her bishop among the other bishops, nevertheless also sets the pope *over* the episcopate in his capacity as *Vicar of Christ*. We recall that Christ is the head of the universal Church. As a striking interchangeability readily substitutes Christ with his vicar in this passage, so the universal Church is effectively reduced to the current worldwide Church, since no pope has authority over the Church of ages other than his own.

> 'Our hierarchies are formed after the type of that society of the Father and the Son; they are its image and reproduce it by a living and faithful likeness. There is in them a head who is the principle: Jesus Christ or his vicar in the universal Church, the bishop in the particular church.'[73]

Gréa's use of 'universal Church' therefore accords with what de Lubac indicated as this term's main usage at Vatican II and as his own usage in his 1971 book. We are, then, doubly sure that it is the *worldwide* Church that de Lubac intends by the 'universal Church' when he twice more quotes Gréa: 'the universal Church is complete in each of the churches'[74] and 'the unity of the hierarchy makes the particular church one and the same thing as the universal Church'.[75]

Lastly, we may note that de Lubac must be understanding *universal* to mean *worldwide* rather than *of all times* when he refers to the pope as 'universal pastor',[76] for, as we noted above, the pope can be pastor only of the Church of his own time. Indeed it is precisely within the Church of his own time that de Lubac firmly situates the pope when he describes him as the 'living bond' existing 'between the Church of today and the Church of the Apostles'.[77] Since de Lubac gives no indication

---

[73] *Ibid.*, p. 130; cf. p. 132. On p. 133, Gréa makes the remarkable statement that 'the Vicar of Christ, head of the Church and of the episcopate, gives [it] to the episcopate to act with him and by him, even though the action . . . is always his own action by its principal title'.

[74] *Motherhood*, p. 205; quotation from Gréa, *L'Eglise*, p. 70.

[75] *Ibid.*, p. 206; quotation from Gréa, *L'Eglise*, p. 289.

[76] *Ibid.*, pp. 276, 312.

that this is an exceptional use of 'universal', we may conclude that the meaning of 'universal Church' throughout his 1971 book, and in its title, is the worldwide Church of today.

Jean Jacques von Allmen and Nicholas Afanassieff

What underpins the notion that the eschatological universal Church effectively reduces to the worldwide Church of today as the community which offers the Eucharist? What is the perspective within which this transition is as automatic as it obviously is for de Lubac? The transition is possible only if Christ is not regarded as inseparable from his Body, the Church. If Christ is inseparable from his Body, then wherever Christ is present so necessarily is his Body, *really* and in its final fulness. As we have seen, this is not de Lubac's view; for him, by sacramental signs and the bonds of communion, it is only the worldwide Church which is really present around Christ. Thus, we may confirm that de Lubac regards Christ as an *individual,* really present from the past, to gather the worldwide Church into the final Church of all the ages, which is still a *projection* for the future.

De Lubac makes the separability of Christ from the Church abundantly clear when he uses 'the compact formulas of St Thomas' to express the activity of the priest at Mass: 'he prays and offers *"in persona omnium"* but consecrates *"in persona Christi"*'.[78] The strong sense of a primary action of Christ himself into which others are subsequently drawn may be confirmed by comparing de Lubac's and Zizioulas' explanations of the eucharistic 'Amen'. De Lubac says that the people 'offer together with the priest', manifesting by their 'Amen' that they 'agree with all that he does and all that he says'.[79] However, this 'Amen' is but a response, by which the people associate themselves with the priest's action which has a certain

---

[77] *Ibid.*, p. 276.

[78] *Splendour*, p. 100; quotations from Aquinas, *Summa Theologiae* III, q. 80, a. 12, ad 3 and q. 82, a. 2, ad 2, respectively.

[79] *Ibid.*, p. 100 and n. 2, with reference to Bossuet, *Méditations sur l'Evangile,* 63rd day.

self-sufficiency.[80] It is not their own specific and *necessary* contribution to the eucharistic action itself, as it is for Zizioulas,[81] whose conviction that when Christ is present so necessarily are his people in a corporate manifestation of the future Kingdom follows from his Pneumatological appreciation of Christ as a *corporate personality*.[82] In the Eucharist, priest (or, rather, *bishop*) and people complementarily act, as we might say, *in persona Christi ecclesialis.*

For Zizioulas, the eschatological reality present in the Eucharist is the corporate Christ, the final *totus Christus*, whereas for de Lubac it is the individual, risen Christ still gathering his people. Accordingly, Zizioulas' view of the Eucharist makes more structural stipulations for this celebration, and hence for the Church herself which is constituted by this celebration,[83] than does that of de Lubac. Indeed, de Lubac's view of the Eucharist makes the minimal structural stipulation, that of a celebrant (primarily the bishop) in apostolic succession to act *in persona Christi.*

Recalling the quotation from de Lubac with which we started this chapter, we may surmise, especially since it was prompted by reflection upon Orthodox eucharistic ecclesiology, that the element of the visible structure of the Church which de Lubac requires but does not find there is the *papal* ministry and that this absence is what leads him to assert that the visible structure of the Church is not 'prejudged' by the relation between the Eucharist and the Church. However, this is an awkward statement for him to make, for his own ecclesiology gives a powerful *eucharistic* justification for the basic structural doctrine of episcopal collegiality[84] and he seems to be striving further, to find a *eucharistic* justification for the *papal* ministry, when he recalls Cullmann's view that there is no Petrine succession[85] and counters it with the words of Jean Jacques von Allmen.

[80]*Ibid.*, p. 104 and n. 5.
[81]Cf. *BC*, p. 218, n. 25.
[82]Cf. below, pp. 166-168.
[83]Cf. below, Chapter Nine.
[84]Cf. above, p. 101.
[85]*Motherhood*, p. 286, with reference to Cullmann, *Saint Pierre disciple, apôtre, martyr;* cf. *Splendour*, p. 200, n. 4.

'Luke situates Jesus' words to Peter about the particular work which will be his *within the framework of the institution of the Eucharist*, that is within the framework of what Jesus wants to see *endure until his return* (Lk. 22: 31ff.).'[86]

The importance of such an observation for de Lubac can be gauged by the fact that, as we have seen, he himself uses the same form of argument for the transmissibility of the ministry of the Twelve.[87]

What, then, prevents de Lubac from embracing fully this point from von Allmen and asserting that eucharistic ecclesiology can ground also the *papal* ministry as part of the Church's structure? An answer lies in von Allmen's premise that '*each* local church is directly [the] sacrament of the heavenly Jerusalem'.[88] While this view corresponds with that of Zizioulas, who does take up von Allmen's insight regarding a eucharistic approach to the Petrine ministry,[89] it is *not* de Lubac's view. For de Lubac, the Church is the sacrament of Christ himself[90] and, as we have seen in this chapter, each local church manifests or *realises*[91] the current worldwide Church whom Christ is present to gather.

Von Allmen stresses that the local churches are all equal, as sacraments of the heavenly Jerusalem.

'There is ... no canonised church [*Eglise-canon*] charged with distributing to the other local churches certificates of ecclesiality. ... No church is [a] *sedes apostolica* more than the others.'[92]

---

[86]Von Allmen, 'L' Eglise locale parmi les autres églises locales' (hereafter, 'L'Eglise locale'), p. 529; quoted in parts by de Lubac, *Motherhood*, p. 287.

[87]Cf. above, p. 100.

[88]Von Allmen, 'L'Eglise locale', p. 518.

[89]Cf. below, p. 210.

[90]Cf. above, p. 97, on 'transparency'; below, pp. 263-264.

[91]Cf. *Motherhood*, p. 251, where de Lubac sets the comment that the universal Church is realised in the particular church in the context of *Lumen Gentium*, n. 23. We have seen (above, pp. 108-109, 112-113) that 'universal Church' almost always in *Lumen Gentium* and always in *Motherhood* refers to the worldwide Church. This is again manifestly its sense in the passage quoted in *Motherhood*, pp. 265-266.

[92]Von Allmen, 'L'Eglise locale', p. 518.

What he says of local churches, that none is 'privileged', applies also to bishops because of 'the parallel, so profoundly biblical [,] between personal apostolate and local church' which he establishes.[93] The most which might be acknowledged in a particular bishop *among* his brothers is the role of being the means whereby the 'mutual recognition of ecclesiality' is made possible and regulated between the local churches.[94]

The situation is different when viewed from de Lubac's point of view, because that which each local church realises, namely the current worldwide Church, is actually committed to the pastoral charge of one of the bishops, namely the bishop of Rome. This does not, however, make of him 'a kind of super-bishop with neither local nor temporal roots' for his ministry.[95] De Lubac firmly rejected the post-conciliar proposal in some quarters that the pope be elected for his worldwide role by a 'representation of the *universal* Church',[96] rather than being elected as bishop of the local church of Rome by, at least in principle, the neighbouring bishops.

> 'Does it not go contrary to one of the most important elements renewed by Vatican II, the value of the particular church based on the bond of the Church and of the Eucharist?'[97]

If the worldwide Church is realised in the local Eucharist, there can be no ministry of wider scope than that of local eucharistic president, so the papal ministry necessarily arises out of the episcopal ministry of a certain local bishop. The pope has pastoral care for the worldwide Church because he has episcopal care for that portion of the worldwide Church which belongs to the local church of Rome.

There are, then, two levels in de Lubac's view of the papal ministry, the worldwide and the local, and the former is rooted in the latter. The pope is not just *over* the other bishops, he is necessarily *among* them also, as Bouyer asserts in a careful

---

[93] *Ibid.*, pp. 518-519.
[94] Cf. *ibid.*, p. 512.
[95] Cf. *Motherhood*, p. 316.
[96] *Ibid.*, p. 319 (my italics). Again, 'universal' clearly means *worldwide*.
[97] *Ibid.*, p. 321.

passage which de Lubac quotes. Peter was not *over* the remaining eleven; he was, as it were, over the *Twelve* of which *he himself was one.*

> 'According to Saint Matthew, it is not so much that Peter is raised by some distinctive power above the rest of the Twelve, but rather that he personally received the same power that will be given jointly to the Twelve (*himself included, therefore*). . . . Peter, in this regard, does not appear as a super-apostle but as the apostle in whom, personally, all that is shared or possessed in common by the entire apostolic college is brought together.'[98]

Both the similarity and the dissimilarity between the pope and the bishops were apparent in the following statement about them by de Lubac in 1953.

> 'As to priesthood and episcopate, he is on the same level as they (he himself addresses them as his "brothers"), though all of them receive their jurisdiction from him.'[99]

However, there is an implicit tension in this view, for how can the pope, from a higher level, give jurisdiction to the bishops if their jurisdiction, like their teaching, is a function of their sanctifying ministry in the Eucharist, which is 'both the origin and the final flowering of the other two [ministries]'[100] and if, regarding this episcopal priestly ministry, as we have just seen, the pope is 'on the same level' as the bishops? This tension can be resolved only if a way can be found whereby the pope gives jurisdiction to the other bishops *precisely by being on the same level with them*, thereby dispensing with the need to assign his worldwide ministry to what we have called a second level. It would then be the case that the pope has a worldwide ministry not growing out of or attached to his local ministry, but precisely *in* his local ministry; his decisive difference from the other bishops would lie not in his being *over* them, but precisely in the uniqueness of his position *among* them, in the worldwide configuration of local churches.

---

[98] *Ibid.*, p. 320 (my italics); quotation from Bouyer, *The Church of God*, p. 379.
[99] *Splendour*, p. 102, n. 3.
[100] *Ibid.*, p. 102; cf. above, p. 103.

The second level constitutes the barrier between de Lubac and von Allmen for whom, as we have seen, the ministry of any bishop, however unique, must nevertheless be exercised *among* his brother bishops and not *over* them. But our opening quotation again reminds us that de Lubac is not convinced that the full uniqueness of the pope can be found if he is placed purely *among* his brother bishops, as a purely *eucharistic* approach to ecclesiology demands (for he and they are equals in eucharistic priesthood). De Lubac's protest against the post-conciliar campaign we have mentioned was that the pope is not simply above the other bishops, he is above because *among* them. Von Allmen would invite him further, to locate the pope *completely* among his brother bishops, but no more than de Lubac can he envisage a real *primacy* in such a location.

The tension in de Lubac's 1953 position reappears in his cautious reaction in 1971 to Afanassieff, but in a manner which indicates de Lubac's readiness to have it overcome. Like von Allmen, Afanassieff would situate the pope completely *among* his brother bishops. He looks to the earliest centuries, and particularly to Clement of Rome, for the definitive exercise of the Petrine ministry. De Lubac himself regards the Letter of Clement to the Corinthians as 'the "eminent prototype" of all Roman interventions',[101] perfectly exemplifying that 'a specifically Petrine succession', which von Allmen himself concedes has to be accepted within the apostolic succession,[102] 'was at first affirmed peacefully by simple practice'.[103] In support of the historical argument for Roman *primacy* which de Lubac sketches, he quotes Afanassieff's account of Clement's action. Afanassieff readily admits that the Roman church 'had no doubt that her priority would be accepted without discussion'.[104] However, Afanassieff refers to this intervention in

---

[101]Cf. *Motherhood*, p. 289; quotation from H. Holstein, *Hiérarchie et peuple de Dieu*, p. 22.

[102]Cf. *ibid.*, pp. 287-288, where de Lubac quotes from von Allmen, 'L'Eglise locale', p. 529.

[103]*Ibid.*, p. 288.

[104]*Ibid.*, p. 283; quotation from Afanassieff, 'The Church which Presides in Love', p. 92.

order to lament that such an effective *priority* of witness, grounded in the need to live out the one Eucharist which each local church celebrates, should have developed into a juridical *primacy,* acting as a unifying power in itself, without immediate reference to the Eucharist and, correspondingly, more patterned after purely human institutions. He says:

> 'the concept of primacy is so enormously different from the concept of priority; indeed either concept almost excludes the other'.[105]

Aware of Afanassieff's distinction between priority and primacy, de Lubac cautiously admits: 'we have not considered here at all the meaning of this dichotomy'.[106]

That de Lubac and Afanassieff regard the same historical manifestation of the Petrine ministry as exemplary indicates their proximity. However, it is clear that they view the same action differently. In his two-level scheme, de Lubac considers that Clement's position as bishop of Rome among his brother bishops is the ground for his authority over them. His cautious comment reveals a certain perplexity in the face of Afanassieff's distinction, but we may say in partial explanation that Afanassieff himself has consolidated de Lubac's two-level scheme, where primacy occupies the upper level, by attributing only a relatively weak *priority* to Clement on the lower level of his relations as a bishop among his brother eucharistic presidents. De Lubac considers that there is more in Clement's action than Afanassieff admits, and if the rigorously eucharistic Afanassieff can find only a priority for the pope then the primacy by which the pope stands out uniquely must be added non-eucharistically. We see again the reason for de Lubac's comment at the start of this chapter.

Zizioulas exposes the weakness of Afanassieff's ecclesiology in not drawing more *structural* implications for the Church out of the Eucharist.[107] We shall see that he opens the way to find

---

[105]Afanassieff, 'The Church which Presides in Love', p. 81.
[106]*Motherhood*, p. 323, n. 28.
[107]Cf. below, pp. 227-228.

a truly unique primacy *among* the bishops on *eucharistic* grounds, thereby rendering de Lubac's second level unnecessary. The eucharistic basis for the papal ministry, which von Allmen's exegetical point indicates, can then be embraced. However, we have already suggested that de Lubac's difficulty with von Allmen's perspective springs from the *effective reduction* which we have investigated and which itself follows from an understanding of Christ as an *individual*.[108] Zizioulas' ecclesiological conclusions derive from his different view on this foundational issue in particular, as we shall now see. By developing Zizioulas' conclusions, we shall offer a resolution of the tension we have here highlighted in de Lubac's exposition.[109]

[108]Cf. above, p. 113.
[109]Cf. below, pp. 208-209.

Part Two

John Zizioulas

Chapter 6

The Programme: 'La vision eucharistique du monde et l'homme contemporain'

In 1966, John Zizioulas gave an address with the above title to a congress in Thessalonika on 'The Orthodox Church and the World'. It was the longest of six contributions, which were hailed when published as signalling 'an authentic theological renewal'.[1] For Zizioulas, this was his first post-doctoral publication.[2] Oliver Clément saw in the collected papers, 'the most striking evidence of young Greek theology', foreshadowing 'the truly Orthodox elaboration of an ecclesial anthropology and cosmology'.[3] As we introduce Zizioulas' synthesis in this chapter, we shall several times recall the programmatic pointers which he gave in this early address.

---

[1]Note on p. 1 of *Contacts* 19 (1967), where the papers were published.

[2]Zizioulas' doctoral thesis for the University of Athens, largely researched in the United States, was published in 1965: Ἡ Ἑνότης τῆς Ἐκκλησίας ἐν τῇ Θείᾳ Εὐχαριστίᾳ καὶ τῷ Ἐπισκόπῳ κατὰ τοὺς τρεῖς πρώτους αἰῶνας (The Unity of the Church in the Holy Eucharist and in the Bishop in the First Three Centuries). There is a substantial review of it by Pier Cesare Bori, 'L'unité de l'Eglise durant les trois premiers siècles'.

[3]O. C. (Olivier Clement), 'Liminaire', *Contacts* 19 (1967), p. 1. For biographical details of Zizioulas' formative theological years, cf. Gaëtan Baillargeon, *Perspectives orthodoxes sur l'Eglise-Communion, L'oeuvre de Jean Zizioulas* (hereafter, *Perspectives orthodoxes*), pp. 27-33.

The Fathers and Ecumenism

Ignatius of Antioch, the Cappadocians and Maximus the Confessor are the Fathers of the Church who feature most prominently in the neopatristic synthesis which, like Georges Florovsky, one of his research supervisors, Zizioulas has undertaken. He is generally critical of Augustine, whose influence he clearly recognises.

> 'An Orthodox with some knowledge of history can identify a Western Christian immediately with Tertullian and Augustine — as soon as he or she begins to take part in ecumenical discussions.'[4]

This comment indicates Zizioulas' own familiarity with ecumenical dialogue.[5] Indeed, much of his bibliography consists of fundamental papers contributed to such dialogue. We may also detect in the quoted comment Zizioulas' impatience with the theological separation of Christian East and West and with the limitations this imposes. Zizioulas attributes an excessive stress on history to the West and on eschatology to the East, and says that these must both be overcome:

> 'the two theologies, Eastern and Western, need to meet in depth, to recover the authentic patristic synthesis which will protect them from the above dangers'.[6]

Significantly, Zizioulas sees strong *ecumenical* characteristics in the Fathers first mentioned above. Ignatius of Antioch, whose writings are often considered to be innovative and different from contemporary texts such as the *Didache* and *1 Clement*, especially because of his understanding of the episcopate, can, Zizioulas maintains, be seen as best translating into practice principles which they all actually shared.[7] Furthermore, this era in general and Ignatius in particular are of particular relevance for us.

---

[4]*EAH2*, p. 65.
[5]Cf. above, pp. xiii-xiv.
[6]*BC*, pp. 20-21; cf. *TSE*, p. 48.
[7]*EEE*, particularly pp. 31-33. Cf. below, pp. 200-202.

'What is common between us and the first three centuries is that we both live in a post-apostolic age. Personally I find the return-to-the-New Testament call in this case as the most deadly method to be adopted by a church which wishes to be alive. The New Testament, or rather the apostolic age, is irrevocably gone and cannot be copied simply because the apostles are gone and cannot be reproduced. We cannot reproduce Paul or Peter who saw the Lord and drew authority from this privilege. If history is of any help to us, it is the post-apostolic rather than the apostolic age that can offer it. Ignatius *can* be reproduced in that he could claim no access to the Lord more than a modern bishop can.'[8]

Commending the Cappadocians, Zizioulas points out that 'Cappadocia, of course, is a "third world" between Alexandria and Antioch'.

'Perhaps a deeper investigation of the history of Patristic thought would show the great merit of the Cappadocians to have been their success in bringing forth a transcendence of the Alexandria-Antioch dilemma that threatened the Church so seriously with division. This would prove these Fathers to be truly "catholic" and "ecumenical" teachers, a title accorded to them by tradition.'[9]

Of Maximus it has been said that he was 'a man who lived between Christian East and West, as familiar with Rome as he was with Constantinople'.[10] Zizioulas particularly notes his role in 'dispelling all suspicions of heresy that the Byzantines had against the Romans concerning the *Filioque*'.[11] With a view to promoting in our own day 'better understanding and, ultimately, an agreement between East and West with regard to Pneumatology', Zizioulas approves as a 'golden rule' Maximus' twofold explanation of the West's position: 'by professing the *Filioque* our Western brethren do not wish to introduce another *aition* [cause] in God's being except the Father', however also, 'a mediating role of the Son in the origination of the Spirit

---

[8] *Ibid.*, p. 41 (Zizioulas' italics, as generally hereafter in quotations, unless otherwise indicated).
[9] *TSE*, p. 39, n. 29.
[10] A. M. Allchin, Foreword to L. Thunberg, *Man and the Cosmos*, p. 9.
[11] *TSE*, p. 49.

is not to be limited to the divine Economy, but relates also to the divine *ousia* [essence]'.[12] He says that these two points 'do not necessarily imply speculations about the *how* or the content of the intra-Trinitarian relations', which in any case 'could be very dangerous'. But 'they imply a great deal concerning the *existential* significance of Pneumatology' and Zizioulas indicates the thrust of his own theology when he concludes: 'this is what, in the final analysis, matters'.

We shall return to examine this recurrent existential emphasis more closely. For the present, we may note that in combining a concern for ecumenism with a return to the Fathers, Zizioulas is following the path of his teacher, Georges Florovsky, one of the leading Russian Orthodox theologians of the diaspora. Florovsky stated at the Evanston Conference of the World Council of Churches in 1954 that 'ecumenism in space' must be complemented by 'ecumenism in time', by which contact is re-established with Tradition.[13]

Like Florovsky, Zizioulas believes that Orthodox theology parted from the authentic Tradition during the 'Scholastic Captivity' of recent centuries. In both Greece and Russia, theological faculties were established after the pattern of Western institutions, both Roman Catholic and Protestant and Orthodox theology became 'basically a variation of Western scholasticism'.[14] Western Europe thereby exported to the East, as it has to the rest of the world, 'an almost catastrophic confusion between the idea of the Church as a local community, which was the only one known to the Early Church, and that of a "Confessional Body"'.[15]

Confessionalism is a malaise that Zizioulas associates with scholasticism. Confessionalism considers that 'Truth is essentially a matter of propositions', that theology both draws on and formulates these propositions, and that 'the Church acquires her identity on the basis of these propositions',

---

[12]*Ibid.*, p. 54, from which also come the remaining quotations in this paragraph. Cf. below, pp. 164-165, 224-225.

[13]Cf. B. Mondin, *I grandi teologi del secolo ventesimo*, vol. 2, p. 295.

[14]*EDO*, p. 33; cf. Florovsky, 'Western Influences in Russian Theology', and above, p.xiv.

[15]*CWU*, p. 29.

tradition being her 'handing down from generation to generation the original faith of the Apostles mainly in the form of creeds and theological statements'.[16]

Zizioulas seeks deeper roots for his theology, as is apparent in the following statement of his approach to ecumenism.

'I personally believe that the greatest contribution the Orthodox can make to the Ecumenical Movement consists of insisting on the point that we are not saved by belonging to a confessional body but to a concrete ecclesial community, to the Church. And theology exists only as a pointer to this mystery of salvation which is the Church.'[17]

Because the Church exists as local churches, Zizioulas clarifies his vision as follows.

'We cannot have a communion of confessional bodies; we can only have a communion of *local churches*.'[18]

More precisely still, each local church is the Church when it celebrates the Eucharist.[19] Therefore, the real roots of theology lie in this celebration, as Zizioulas emphasised in his programmatic address.

'Orthodox theology . . . is fundamentally a doxology, a liturgy . . . it is a eucharistic theology.'[20]

Zizioulas agrees with Florovsky in saying that the basic flaw in Orthodox scholasticism was the severance of theology from these roots: 'the *lex orandi* and the *lex credendi* no longer coincided'.[21] Their return to the Fathers is a return to a theology rooted in the Church's worship.

Neopatristic Synthesis

Why is it that the Fathers are still able to 'speak to all'?

[16]*EDO*, p. 35.
[17]*Ibid.*, p. 39.
[18]*CWU*, p. 28. Cf. *NUS*, pp. 345-346; *CIEI*, p. 18.
[19]Cf. below, p. 133.
[20]*VEM*, p. 83.
[21]*ORT*, p. 6. Cf. Florovsky, 'Western Influences in Russian Theology', pp. 167-168.

Zizioulas answers that the Fathers posed and resolved 'the fundamental problems' in a way which gave theology 'meaning and relevance' for the world of their time, a world 'shaped by Greek thought'. They are important to *us* because, he adds simply, 'such remains our world still today'.[22]

He states elsewhere that what characterises Greek thought is a concern with *ontology*.[23] For Zizioulas, 'ontological' and 'existential' are synonyms.[24] Ontology has to do with 'questions of life and death',[25] in the strongest sense, of being and non-being. As we shall see in the next chapter, he thinks that the achievement of the Greek Fathers lies in that, with them, 'being is traced back not to substance but to person'.[26] They therefore are in a position to respond directly to existentialist philosophers, whose preoccupations are with the person and freedom and who 'have shown in our day . . . that, humanly speaking, the person as an absolute ontological freedom remains a quest without fulfilment'. Zizioulas praises the existentialists for having carried out this analysis of the human predicament 'with an intellectual honesty that makes them worthy of the name of philosopher'.[27] Clearly he regards them as prime spokesmen for what he called above 'our world still today', a world 'shaped by Greek thought'. His comment, then, in his programmatic address, that modern man 'has ceased — and who can blame him? — to think in the anthropological categories of Aristotle and Plato'[28] means not that man today has cast off Greek thought in general, but rather than he is impatient for the product of its *double leavening* by 'biblical faith', namely 'the concept of the person', which Zizioulas calls humanity's 'most dear and precious good'.[29]

---

[22] *ORT*, p. 7.

[23] *BC*, pp. 35, 65; cf. *OBP*, p. 35.

[24] Cf. *ESLT*, p. 3.

[25] These questions are 'totally existential' (*CEE*1, p. 154).

[26] *BC*, p. 42, n. 37.

[27] *Ibid.*, p. 18; cf. *HCH*, p. 424, n. 1.

[28] *VEM*, p. 88.

[29] *BC*, p. 65. Zizioulas adds: 'This and nothing less than this is what the world owes to Greek patristic theology.' Cf. below, Chapter Seven.

Zizioulas looks to Maximus as the inheritor and great exponent of Greek theology in its doubly leavened philosophy, which gave personhood pride of place. He draws attention to the remarkable fact that, while the writings of Maximus and the ascetic Fathers 'were hardly ever quoted in the Orthodox dogmatic manuals of the "academic" type', 'today, on the other hand, the greater part of Orthodox theology is based on such sources'.[30] These Fathers can speak strongly to the present age, for they lived 'intensely and absolutely' the 'tragic aspect' of our fallen existence, which 'contemporary existentialism' has explored. However, they recognised the 'eschatological transcendence' of personhood and so were not overcome by the tragic absence of it in this world. It belongs to the *future* as our *destiny*. Here it can only be *tasted* and such tasting occurs in the Eucharist,[31] upon which Maximus in particular focused monasticism and Christian spirituality in general.[32] The Eucharist 'places creation in the movement — in space and time — towards its proper eschatological end'.[33]

Zizioulas' existential reading of the Fathers is another pointer to the influence of Florovsky, who stated that '[t]he main distinctive mark of Patristic theology was its "existential" character'.[34] This judgement indicates Florovsky's intention when, in 1936, he issued his historic call for a creative return to the patristic synthesis at the First Congress of Orthodox Theology

---

[30]*ORT*, p. 7. Zizioulas cites the 'classical work' of Lossky, *The Mystical Theology of the Eastern Church.*

[31]Cf. *BC*, p. 64 and n. 69. In *CMBC*, p. 21, Zizioulas states: 'The mysticism of the ascetic is . . . in the first instance a participation in the anxiety, the fears, the deaths of all men.' Cf. *HCH*, p. 420: personhood is '*in* this world . . . but not *of* this world'.

[32]*ECC*, p. 43. P. Sherwood comments: 'the Eucharist is at the heart of the Christian life. Maximus supposes it to be so.' (Introduction to St Maximus the Confessor, *The Ascetic Centuries — The Four Centuries on Charity*, hereafter 'Introduction', p. 81).

[33]*Ibid.*, p. 43.

[34]Florovsky, 'Patristic Theology and the Ethos of the Orthodox Church', p. 17.

in Athens, where he was 'the great voice'.[35] He urged his colleagues 'to kindle again the creative fire of the Fathers, to restore in ourselves *the patristic spirit*'.[36] In 1959, he spoke of 'a *neopatristic synthesis*' as 'the task and the aim of Orthodox theology today'.[37] In his Introduction to *Being as Communion*, Zizioulas recalls Florovsky's vision embracing East and West and says: 'these studies are intended to offer their contribution to a "neopatristic synthesis" capable of leading the West and the East nearer to their common roots'.[38]

Florovsky was chosen in 1937 as one of the Committee of Fourteen who had the task of preparing for the World Council of Churches and, in 1950, his influence was decisive in securing Orthodox participation in the Council.[39] Zizioulas himself has been actively involved in the work of the Faith and Order Commission of the WCC,[40] but we may sense the true spirit of the neopatristic synthesis in his assertion that the Orthodox must not be restricted to the 'ghetto' of Faith and Order. He says that they must become involved in the 'social and political concerns' of the Council. It behoves the Orthodox members really to commit themselves to 'bringing to light the existential implications of their faith and traditional structure'.[41]

Existential Emphasis

'The crisis in the relation of modern man with Christ and the incapacity of Christianity to encounter modern man largely derive, without doubt, from the bastard theological tradition

[35]Y. N. Lelouvier, *Perspectives russes sur l'Eglise. Un théologien contemporain: Georges Florovsky*, p. 34.

[36]Florovsky, 'Patristics and Modern Theology', p. 240.

[37]Florovsky, 'Patristic Theology and the Ethos of the Orthodox Church', p. 22.

[38]*BC*, p. 26.

[39]Cf. B. Mondin, *I grandi teologi del secolo ventesimo*, vol. 2, p. 295, with reference to the WCC document, 'The Church, The Churches and the World Council of Churches'. In *ORT*, p. 11, Zizioulas notes the importance of this text for subsequent Orthodox participation in the WCC; cf. D.T.S., 'Chronique religieuse', pp. 442-444.

[40]Cf. Baillargeon, *Perspectives orthodoxes*, pp. 34-43.

[41]*ORT*, p. 13.

that we teach. This tradition has split [*dissocié*] man, made him schizophrenic, suffocated him by dualist concepts and moralising constructs and destroyed his integrity.'

'A vision of the world derived from experience of the Eucharist leaves no possibilities for dissociating the natural from the supernatural, a dissociation in which Western theology has imprisoned [*enfermé*] man by setting him in front of the dilemma of choosing between the two. . . .[T]he Eucharist can save man from the dissociation which drives modern man to reject God, that God whom theology has placed in a sphere which man can no longer understand.'[42]

These spirited words if Zizioulas in his programmatic address speak of his determination to overthrow what we may call *separated* theology. To understand the meaning which this term would have for him, we may note that the choice which he criticises here, between the natural and the supernatural, is also described as one between 'body and soul', between 'spirit and matter'.[43] What he is rejecting is the notion that man acts simultaneously on two stages, as it were, or in two spheres: the sphere of his earthly (natural) needs, important but passing, concerning his body and matter, and the sphere of his heavenly (supernatural) needs, of eternal consequence, concerning the relation of his soul and spirit to God. Elsewhere, it is clear that Zizioulas interprets Augustine's 'two cities' in this way,[44] as a division of the world into 'the secular and the sacred' which, he says, 'does not seem to me to stem from a eucharistic approach to the Church'.[45]

'On the contrary, Orthodox liturgical life pays extreme attention to the body and its needs and matter is present to the point of the bread and the wine being identified with the Lord himself.'[46]

---

[42] *VEM*, pp. 91-92, 86-87, respectively.
[43] *Ibid.*, p. 87.
[44] Cf. *DMJ*, p. 200. Contrary to this view that Augustine is referring to two kinds of activity which each person performs, de Lubac directs us to understand 'two loves' between which each must choose as the guiding principle for the *whole* of their activity (cf. *PSpir*1, p. 62).
[45] *CECB*, p. 5.
[46] *VEM*, pp. 87-88.

Zizioulas later elaborated this firm statement from his pro-grammatic address with an account of how the liturgy in fact 'affirms and clarifies his [man's] *natural life*'.

> 'It [the Eucharist] underlines the fact that nature and creation viewed as a whole must not be rejected on the pretext of some kind of "super-natural". The Eucharist accepts and sanctifies *all* of creation "recapitulated" in the one body of the "first-born of creation".... [I]n the Eucharist, man acts as priest of creation, in the name of and because of the priesthood of Christ, [the] High Priest *par excellence*.'[47]

We may say that the *separated* theology which Zizioulas rejects is that which separates man's body from his soul and, in consequence, separates the material creation from God's eternal Kingdom. Recently, Zizioulas has blamed it for the loss of man's proper identity as priest of creation and hence for the threatened state of the earth.

> 'Man has to become a liturgical being before he can hope to overcome his ecological crisis.'[48]

Thus, unlike de Lubac who counters separated theology by rooting the vision of God in the natural desire of man himself,[49] Zizioulas counters it by rooting man in the material creation, as its priest.[50]

Man exercises this priesthood primarily in the Eucharist. There he assumes his proper identity, his eternal identity. There, in the full sense, he *exists*, he *lives*.[51] For Zizioulas, the Eucharist is the existential location of salvation. It, primarily, is what Christianity offers to the world: 'only the Eucharist in its correct sense is the specific differentiating factor of Christianity'.[52] Only the Eucharist can change the world, as Zizioulas

---

[47]*EQA*, pp. 70-71.

[48]*PGC*1, p. 2. The theme of man as 'priest of creation' is found as early as 1970 in Zizioulas, *OAC*, pp. 188, 192. Also, *HCH*, p. 435; *EPL*, pp. 194-195.

[49]Cf. above, pp. 10-12, 30-42.

[50]Cf. below, pp. 289-295.

[51]Zizioulas considers that 'the entire existential significance of the Pneumatology of the Council [1 Constantinople]' flows from its description of the Holy Spirit as 'life-giver' (*TSE*, p. 53).

[52]*BC*, p. 63, n. 66.

vigorously emphasised in his programmatic address. He attacked what he ironically termed 'our instructive logocracy' which thinks 'that it is sufficient to *speak* to the world in order to change it'.

> 'We offer the *Logos* and the world does not accept it. We forget that the *Logos* is not words but a Person; not a voice but a living Presence, a Presence which is incarnate in the Eucharist, a Eucharist which is above all *gathering* [*rassemblement*] and *communion*.'[53]

Thus, what is primary in Christianity is not a message but a Person. What defines Christianity is a living Presence, to be found in the Eucharist; verbal formulations and propositions are *derivative*, from this source.

Analysis of this quotation from Zizioulas reveals that the Eucharist for him is not something which takes place within a certain gathering or in the context of communion; rather it *is* this gathering and communion themselves. Further, the eucharistic gathering is not just something which the Church, having her definition elsewhere, does; it itself is what defines the Church and is where the Church *is* the Church. 'Already at the time of St Paul, the term Church and those which designate the Eucharist signify the same reality.'[54] In short, the Eucharist is:

> 'that *community* which by coming together . . . to offer and to communicate in the body of Christ most perfectly represents the Church in the world'.[55]

Zizioulas bids us recognise the eucharistic context of the original composition and proclamation of the New Testament. 'Without the Church's liturgical experience we would not have

---

[53] *VEM*, p. 90.

[54] *EFEL*, p. 1. Here as elsewhere, Zizioulas urges 'careful study' of Paul's vocabulary in 1 Cor. 11: 'the eucharistic terms "coming together", "coming together ἐπὶ τὸ αὐτό", "Lord's Supper", etc. are identifed with the ecclesiological terms "ἐκκλησία" or "ἐκκλησία of God"' (*BC*, p. 148). Zizioulas deduces: 'from a structural point of view, the ecclesiality of whatever individual or group in the Church depends on their participation in the holy Eucharist' (*GIE*, p. 271).

[55] *GIE*, p. 271 (my italics).

the New Testament, certainly not in its actual content and form.'[56] Accordingly, we should restore to their *eucharistic* context such pronounced New Testament themes as judgment and reconciliation.[57] He even sees the possibility of progress by setting 'the Petrine task' back into 'the context of the Last Supper' where it is situated in Luke's Gospel.[58]

He also attributes the insights of the early Fathers into the very being of God to their experience as eucharistic presidents of their churches.

'[T]he bishops of this period, pastoral theologians such as St Ignatius of Antioch and above all St Irenaeus and later St Athanasius, approached the being of God through the experience of the ecclesial community, of *ecclesial being*. This experience revealed something very important: the being of God could be known only through personal relationships and personal love. Being means life, and life means *communion*.

'This ontology, which came out of the eucharistic experience of the Church, guided the Fathers in working out their doctrine of the being of God, a doctrine formulated above all by Athanasius of Alexandria and the Cappadocian Fathers, Basil the Great, Gregory of Nazianzus and Gregory of Nyssa.'[59]

The reappropriation of this pre-eminent source of *theo*-logy is a central aspect of the Patristic renewal within which Zizioulas stands.

'[W]hereas in the past no Orthodox theologian would have thought to refer to "sources" such as the Eucharist for doctrinal purposes, a whole branch of modern Orthodox theology has been established with the title of "eucharistic theology". Thus liturgical experience is ceasing to be the speciality of "practical theology" and assuming importance also with regard to speculative or theoretical subjects, such as Trinitarian doctrine, Christology, ecclesiology, etc.'[60]

---

[56] *ESLT*, p. 1.

[57] *EQA*, pp. 58-62; e.g. binding and loosing is a prerogative 'which the Church exercised in eucharistic assemblies' (p. 60). Cf. below, pp. 199-200, 266-268.

[58] *BC*, p. 203, n. 115, with reference to J. J. von Allmen, 'L'Eglise locale parmi les autres Eglises locales'. Cf. above, pp. 114-115; below, p. 210.

[59] *BC*, pp. 16-17. Cf. below, Chapter Seven.

[60] *ORT*, p. 7.

The rigour of Zizioulas' eucharistic synthesis lies in his strict correlation of these apparently different areas of theology, such that one and the same experience is the existential source of knowledge in all three subjects. The implicit principle is that ecclesial life in the Eucharist around the bishop is the life of Christ, in whom we live the life of the Trinity.[61]

Let us focus on the first step of this progression. With reference to Johannine theology, Zizioulas says the following.

'[B]y gathering the community together around the table of the lamb . . . you paint the icon of the kingdom which for John amounts to painting the image of Christ himself. The kingdom in its glory is visible.'[62]

Zizioulas' description of the properly constituted local eucharistic assembly[63] is easily charged with being idealistic. What is the status of a Eucharist celebrated in less than perfect conditions? Is it still a Eucharist? He replies, simply, that it is a less than perfect 'icon of the Kingdom'.[64]

In his programmatic address, Zizioulas said that what exists in the Eucharist is 'the single reality of nature and creation complete *to the point of identification* between heavenly reality and earthly reality'.[65] Zizioulas' later description, above, of painting the icon of the Kingdom shows that we are to understand the 'heavenly reality' in this statement as the Kingdom, and the 'earthly reality' as the icon itself, the local eucharistic gathering. In other words, the Eucharist opens up the earthly gathering not into Heaven as it might be understood *now*, with the saints already there, but into Heaven in its *future* completion, that is, into the Kingdom in its fulness. That Zizioulas can refer to the icon of this future reality simply as 'the image of Christ himself', indicates that, for him, Christ cannot be

[61]We shall frequently refer to this principle, most fully in Chapter Eleven.
[62]*EAH*1, p. 34. As an indication of the second step of the progression, we may note Zizioulas assertion that 'God is not learnt [*appreso*] via the mind, rather He is "seen"' (*ORT*, p. 9). Cf. below, pp. 193-194.
[63]Cf. e.g., below, p. 195.
[64]I draw here on personal conversations with Zizioulas. However, his criticism of *deliberate* imperfection is severe; cf. below, p. 199, n. 75.
[65]*VEM*, p. 87. Cf. below, p. 151.

conceived apart from the whole of creation of which he is the 'first-born'.[66] Christ is always present in the form in which he will come again, namely as a *corporate personality*.[67]

Zizioulas considers this anticipatory aspect of the Eucharist to be of the utmost importance if history is to be fully respected. The Eucharist draws us not out of time, but through time to its consummation. As he said in his programmatic address, in the Eucharist 'we become contemporary with the total history of the pre-eternal plan of God for our salvation in a unity of past, present and future'. The whole of God's historical purpose is set before us, inviting us to a correspondingly 'complete acceptance' of it,[68] in a genuine 'foretaste of Paradise'.[69] Zizioulas is critical of Origen because he interprets him as emphasising 'the eschatological meaning of the Gospel at the expense of the historical'.[70] In what Zizioulas calls a *Neoplatonic* fashion, Origen distinguished, he says, 'between the actual fact and its meaning'[71] and located the latter in an 'extra-temporal' domain, such that what takes place in 'history as a whole' is 'an image and a reflection of something higher which takes place outside time'.[72]

Zizioulas' concern to see the Eucharist not as a distraction from history but rather as that which brings about 'the sanctification of time and history',[73] perhaps manifests a further acknowledgement of existentialism, this time in its critique of Christianity. The existentialist justifiably wishes to find Christianity's 'relevance for his existence',[74] and that means *here and*

---

[66]Cf. above, p. 132.

[67]Cf. above, p. 89, and below, pp. 166-167, 262.

[68]*VEM*, p. 87.

[69]*Ibid.*, p. 86.

[70]*BC*, p. 181 and n. 35.

[71]*Ibid.*, p. 192 and n. 75.

[72]*ESLT*, p. 10. In *HEsp*, p. 292, de Lubac rejects the similar allegation that Origen regarded Christ's earthly sacrifice as 'the shadow' of 'a heavenly sacrifice'.

[73]*VEM*, p. 87.

[74]Cf. *CMOR*, p. 4: Sartre's 'existentialist atheism' has rejected God because the 'impersonalist God' presented to it 'does not have any relevance for his existence'.

now.[75] If the *futurity* of Heaven is emphasised, then it ceases to be a present alternative to this world and becomes the end of which the present liturgy is truly the bearer until it is established permanently.[76] This historical fact *bears* its meaning. In an unpublished paper, Zizioulas summarised his understanding as follows.

> 'In the liturgy matter is not a window to higher things. It is the very substance of a transformed cosmos; it is an end in itself.'[77]

Zizioulas' endorsement of the existentialist conclusion that humanity itself is powerless to realise its quest for free personhood[78] certainly lies behind his radical emphasis that Christianity offers not an *improved* life or a *better* life or a *higher* life, but *life* itself. Christianity's thrust is not *moral* or *ethical* (i.e. for mere improvement of our condition) but *ontological* (i.e. for our very existence itself).[79] We may note a series of synonyms in Zizioulas' exposition. We have seen the equivalence of 'ontological' and 'existential'.[80] He further equates the latter with 'soteriological'[81] and then defines 'soteriology' as 'a realisation of *theosis*'.[82] In short, only God can give what man seeks, because life for creation can only be a participation in His life. Zizioulas says that the state of freedom which man seeks 'obviously can only be realised from outside human existence' and then forcefully adds: '[t]he whole of Christian doctrine ought to be precisely about this'.[83]

Also characteristic of Zizioulas is the use of 'psychological' as a synonym for 'moral' or 'ethical',[84] in contrast with 'onto-

---

[75]'Here and now' is Zizioulas' frequent focus, e.g. *BC*, p. 109, n. 109; also, pp. 175, 179, 188.

[76]The liturgy is *full* of Heaven, that is, 'a reflection — not in a Platonic but a *real* sense — of the community of the Kingdom of God' (*BC*, pp. 232-233).

[77]*CMBC*, p. 15.

[78]Cf. above, p. 128.

[79]E.g. *BC*, pp. 121-122, n. 126. Cf. Sherwood, 'Introduction', pp. 39-40.

[80]Cf. above, p. 128.

[81]Cf. *CWU*, p. 25.

[82]*BC*, p. 211.

[83]*HCH*, p. 433.

[84]E.g. *BC*, p. 109.

logical'.[85] Christianity seeks to work not just a psychological change, a change in the reasoning part of our being, but an ontological change, a change in our very being itself. Given that words relate primarily to our reasoning faculty, we may detect here an echo of Zizioulas' early criticism of Christianity offering the world simply Christ's voice and not his personal presence.[86] We may also discern an attack upon individualism, because whereas a verbal message may be delivered to an atomistic audience of individuals and give to each internally a certain intellectual satisfaction, a personal presence summons to action and interaction, to relationship.

Catholicity and Personhood

In his programmatic address, Zizioulas did indeed complain of the 'pious individualism' which wants to preach to the world instead of celebrating the Eucharist. In reducing the Church's presence to 'an ambo without a sanctuary', it reduces the Church herself to a mere collectivity, 'a sum [*somme*] of Christians without unity or community'.[87] The Eucharist, in contrast, is 'the most anti-individualist act of the Church'. There 'man ceases to be an individual and becomes a person'. Equivalently, he becomes 'Church'.[88]

> 'In the Eucharist, prayer, faith, love, charity (that is to say everything that the faithful practise individually) cease to be "mine" and become "ours" and the whole relation of man with God becomes the relation of God with His people, with His Church. The Eucharist is not just the communion of each one with Christ; it is also the communion of the faithful amongst themselves and unity in the body of Christ.'[89]

[85]E.g. *ESLT*, pp. 20, 22, where Zizioulas stresses that *forgiveness* is ontological, not psychological.

[86]Cf. above, p. 133.

[87]*VEM*, p. 90.

[88]*Ibid.*, p. 88. In Zizioulas' later terminology, to become *Church* is to receive the *ecclesial hypostasis*. This hypostasis 'corresponds historically and experientially *only* to the holy Eucharist' (*BC*, pp. 59-60, my italics). Cf. below, p. 272.

[89]*Ibid.*, p. 88.

It is the Eucharist which the Church must offer to modern man who 'lives every day under the weight of the opposition between the individual and the collectivity' and whose 'social life is not *communio* but *societas.*' Too often, the Church herself has manifested this opposition and failed to give him 'the anthropology which could justify him as a person'. The person 'is not a means to an end; he is an end in himself',[90] as the liturgy is an end in itself,[91] and we are persons in the liturgy. A renewed appreciation of the liturgy must find there true personhood, the key to *communio* or *koinonia.* In the terminology which Zizioulas was soon to adopt, the liturgy subordinates neither the one to the many nor the many to the one; the one and the many are simultaneous.[92] We must clarify the pattern of this unity.

Zizioulas says: 'if one sees a being as a person, one sees in him the whole of human nature.[93] This could be taken to mean that a person has some form of universal human nature, rather than embodying the totality of other persons, but Zizioulas' use of the biblical concept of 'corporate personality' makes it clear that we ought not to interpret him so. He speaks of Adam and of Christ as persons, bearing the totality of their nature, but says of them not that in them *human nature* has died and will live respectively, but, faithfully to biblical teaching, that in them '*the many*' have died and will live respectively.[94] As such, Christ is a 'catholic' man[95] and the desire of each human being to be a person is the desire to be 'a bearer of the totality of its nature', to be, as Zizioulas clarifies, a 'catholic' man.[96] In short,

---

[90] *Ibid.*, pp. 88-89.

[91] Cf. above, p. 137.

[92] The terminology of the one and the many is prominent in Chapter Four of *BC*, which first appeared as an article in 1969, three years after Zizioulas' programmatic address.

[93] *BC*, p. 106; cf. p. 60 where Zizioulas enunciates 'the philosophical principle which governs the concept of the person, the principle that the hypostasis expresses the whole of its nature and not just a part'.

[94] *HCH*, p. 435, n. 1 (my italics); cf. p. 408, n. 3.

[95] *Ibid.*, p. 408, n. 3.

[96] *Ibid.*, p. 441, n. 3.

therefore, the desire to be a person is the desire to be *Christ.* It is Christ who 'realises in history *the very reality of the person*'[97] and, as Zizioulas indicated in his programmatic address, by eucharistic communion, man becomes in Christ what Christ is: 'the total man'.[98]

There is a strong resemblance between Zizioulas' statement that 'the mystery of man reveals itself fully only in the light of Christ'[99] and de Lubac's assertion that 'Christ completes the revelation of man to himself'.[100] However, whereas for de Lubac the Christian is indwelt by Christ and so made one in the Church with all those similarly indwelt,[101] for Zizioulas the Christian *is* Christ and, as we saw earlier,[102] *is* the Church. For de Lubac, Christ unites the Church by being other than the Church and coming identically into each of the Church's members; for Zizioulas, he does so by being *one of the Church*.[103] When Zizioulas says that every Church member 'becomes Christ and Church',[104] he is referring not to two realities, but to one.[105] Likewise, by saying that 'every communicant is the whole Christ and the whole Church',[106] he intends to convey that the whole Christ *is* the whole Church, a differentiated reality, 'parted but not divided',[107] held apart in unity, we might say, by Christ *in its midst.*

A 'catholic' man, then, is a specific person in whom all other specific persons are seen. We may now see this notion in all three of the Fathers, or groups of Fathers, mentioned at the beginning of this chapter as those most frequently encountered in Zizioulas' writings. Ignatius taught that the multitude

---

[97] *BC,* p. 54.
[98] *VEM,* p. 89.
[99] *HCH,* p. 433.
[100] *Cath,* p. 187; cf. above, p.12.
[101] Cf. above, p. 19.
[102] Cf. above, p. 138.
[103] Cf. above, pp. 24, 66, 96; below, pp. 180, 284.
[104] *BC,* p. 58.
[105] Cf. *ibid.,* p. 111: 'All separation between Christology and ecclesiology *vanishes* in the Spirit' (my italics). Cf. below, pp. 166-167.
[106] *Ibid.,* pp. 60-61.
[107] *Ibid.,* p. 60. Cf. below, p. 223.

of the faithful of a place could be seen 'in the person of their bishop'.[108] In so doing, he was working with personal categories, but it was the Cappadocian Fathers who elaborated the necessary ontology; theirs is a 'new philosophical position'. The key thesis is that 'the substance never exists in a "naked" state, that is, without hypostasis, without "a mode of existence"',[109] that is, without *a particular existential state of being*.[110]

Natures are not primary. Human nature exists only because there are particular human beings and exists only *as* these particular beings. Likewise, or rather archetypally, 'it is the Father and the Son and the Spirit that make it possible for "divine nature" to be at all'.[111] Particular beings are primary. But, of course, not all particular beings are *persons*, that is, bearers of the totality of their nature. The Father, the Son and the Spirit are, and Christ is, having been constituted by the Holy Spirit, according to the all-important doctrine of the virgin birth, and thereby made to exist as God exists, preserved from the 'individualisation' which ordinary procreation entails.[112] Other human beings are born as *individuals*, bearing only *part* of their nature[113] and aspiring after personhood. In God, 'nature and person coincide', as Basil saw,[114] but they do not in fallen man; human nature cannot be sought within each. Plato sought above and Aristotle sought below, but both perceived the same point.[115] However, this is not how *person* and nature relate; the true person does not refer elsewhere for his nature, his meaning.

[108]*Ibid.*, p. 153, n. 53; reference to Ignatius, *Eph.* 1, 3 and *Tral.* 1, 1 (Bihlmeyer, pp. 83, 93).

[109]*Ibid.*, p. 41, cf. p. 88, n. 65; reference to Basil, *Ep.* 38, 2 (PG 32, 325f.).

[110]*Ibid.*, p. 236.

[111]*HCH*, p. 435. Cf. *BC*, p. 41: 'Outside the Trinity there is no God, that is, no divine substance.'

[112]Cf. *ibid.*, p. 441, n. 3.

[113]Cf. above, p. 139, n. 93.

[114]*BC*, p. 88, n. 65; cf. *PDC*, p. 147.

[115]I owe this succinct comparison of Plato, Aristotle and the Cappadocians to personal discussions with Zizioulas. Cf. below, p. 176-177.

Zizioulas points out that Maximus the Confessor later used the 'important thesis' of the Cappadocians.[116] He several times refers to Maximus' teaching that 'the catholicity of the Church is to be found in each member personally',[117] a principle which is strongly reminiscent of that of Peter Damian which de Lubac uses, according to which 'each one of the faithful is . . . the Church in miniature'.[118] The 'profound thought' which underlay this teaching of Maximus was that 'in the . . . Spirit the very structure of the Church becomes the existential structure of each person'.[119]

However, the respective uses of these principles by Zizioulas and de Lubac could hardly be more different. De Lubac uses Peter Damian's principle to assert the fundamental *equality* of all Christians, as microcosms of the Church,[120] whereas Zizioulas uses the principle of Maximus to assert the fundamental *complementarity* of the members of each local church, in their corporate manifestation of Christ. De Lubac would say that the same Christ lives in each Christian, However, Zizioulas thinks that each is Christ *in a different way* and thus that to say that each is Christ is *not* to say that each is the *same*, as we may see from the fact that the scriptures show the application to Christ of all the *different* ministries exercised in the early Church. 'He was the apostle, the prophet, the priest, the bishop, the deacon, etc.'[121] Zizioulas' implication is that, for instance, the bishop and deacon are Christ-the-bishop and Christ-the-deacon respectively, distinct and complementary manifestations of Christ, for Christ is himself not an individual who can live in an undifferentiated way in all, but a person, a corporate personality, who is intrinsically differentiated. We may recall that the

[116]*BC*, p. 41, n. 36.

[117]*PDC*, p. 153, n. 26; cf. *ECC*, p. 43: Maximus 'sees the human being as the image of the whole Church'. Also *BC*, p. 58, n. 55: 'St Maximus the Confessor in his *Mystagogy* (4; PG 91, 672B-C) applies the catholicity of the Church to the existential make-up of each believer.'

[118]Cf. above, pp. 20-21.

[119]*PDC*, p. 152; cf. above, p. xix, n. 27.

[120]Cf. above, pp. 92-93.

[121]*BC*, p. 163, with scriptural references.

strictest definition of the *anima ecclesiastica* which de Lubac gave was not, in fact, that such a soul was *Christ,* but that it was *the Church.*[122] There remains ever a distinction between Christ and his members. The same Christ in each brings about a circumcession of the members, but this makes the members the *Church* and not, strictly speaking, *Christ.*

We may indicate this difference between de Lubac and Zizioulas as follows. De Lubac cites the Pauline text that the Mystery is 'Christ in you' in support of his contention that there is a real birth of the Saviour in each Christian soul.[123] Zizioulas interprets the 'you' in this and similar passages not as 'each of you individually', but as 'you corporately', that is the *community* as a unit, *differentiatedly* embodying Christ.[124]

Zizioulas' writings certainly display the 'fresh and somewhat "adventurous" theological thinking' which he considers is needed from the Orthodox involved in ecumenical dialogue.[125] We shall see in the following chapters that he often expresses himself with provocative concision. He is a systematic theologian, primarily concerned with 'the *issues* lying behind the historical developments'.[126] His endeavours to bridge the data and clarify the issues are certainly 'at times over-bold and schematic',[127] but Zizioulas is anchored in a concern for fidelity to the Scriptures and in a conviction that the Greek mediation of the scriptural mind[128] is of enduring existential relevance for our day.

[122]Cf. above, p. 21.

[123]Cf. above, p. 61, with reference to Col. 1: 27.

[124]I draw for this important distinction on personal discussions with Zizioulas. The difference of interpretation cannot be resolved textually, for 'you' would be plural in both cases. Reference must be made to other passages; cf. Zizioulas' view of the use of 'temple' (below, pp. 276-277). Cf. also the difference between de Lubac and Zizioulas regarding de-individualisation; above, pp. 23-24.

[125]*OPB,* p. 56.

[126]*TSE,* p. 29.

[127]R. Williams, review of *BC,* in *Scottish Journal of Theology* 42 (1989) [hereafter referred to as 'Review'], p. 105.

[128]Cf. *BC,* p. 88, where Zizioulas says that the Cappadocians set the being of God 'on a new and more biblical foundation'.

Chapter 7

Greek Philosophy

'The message of apophatic theology was precisely that the closed Greek ontology had to be broken and transcended.'[1]

Zizioulas persistently criticises Greek philosophy's closed ontology. The ancient Greeks subscribed to what he calls 'ontological monism', by which he means that for them 'the being of the world and the being of God formed . . . an unbreakable unity'.[2] This belief 'constitutes . . . the crucial point of conflict between Greek thought and biblical thought in the period of the Greek Fathers,[3] for 'biblical faith proclaimed God to be absolutely *free* with regard to the world'.[4]

Monistic Greek thought, he says, tied God to the world as a single unit, called 'being' and 'posited as an axiomatic or self-explicable principle'.[5] It attributed ultimacy to 'being qua being'.[6]

'Ancient Greek philosophy knew of causation, but it always posited it *within* the framework of being. Everything is caused by something else but the world as a whole is not caused *radically*, i.e. in the absolute ontological sense, by anything else. Plato's creator is an artist and an organiser of pre-existing being, and Aristotle's *nous* is the First Mover causing the world to move

---

[1]*BC*, p. 90.
[2]*Ibid.*, p. 16.
[3]*Ibid.*, p. 70.
[4]*Ibid.*, p. 16 (my italics).
[5]Cf. *OBP*, pp. 37-38.
[6]*HCH*, p. 416.

always *from within* and on the basis of an eternal ὕλη [matter]. The world is eternal; it is not ontologically caused. And so the particular is never the ontologically primary cause of being. This leads to necessity in ontology. Being is not a gift but a datum to be reckoned with by the particular beings.'[7]

Zizioulas considers that Greek thought required and underwent 'two basic "leavenings"'[8] in order for it to be a vehicle for Christianity. We shall consider the two leavenings in detail later in this chapter and find that he associates them, respectively, with the 'two generations' of theological endeavour, those of Athanasius and the Cappadocians, respectively, which were required so as to 'clarify the issues' in the battle with Arianism.[9] The first leavening radically distinguished God from the world:

'with the doctrine of creation *ex nihilo* the "principle" of Greek ontology, the "ἀρχή" of the world, was transposed to the sphere of freedom'.

The result was that 'the being of the world became free from necessity'.[10] The second leavening freed the being of God Himself from necessity, by identifying the 'ontological "principle" or "cause" of the being and life of God' with '*the person of the Father*'.

'God, as Father and not as substance, perpetually confirms through "being" His *free* will to exist. And it is precisely His Trinitarian existence that constitutes this confirmation.'[11]

It is, then, the Father who is 'the "ground" of God's being' and 'the ultimate reason for existence'.[12] Particularity is ultimate, in the person of the Father.

---

[7] *OBP*, p. 38. Zizioulas responds to a complaint that his criticism of Greek philosophy ignores, for example, Plato's notion that the Good 'transcends essence' and is beyond being (ἐπέκεινα τῆς οὐσίας: *Republic*, 509B). This notion he says 'has nothing in common with the idea of a personal God who creates, above all who creates out of nothing' (*CEE2*, p. 63).

[8] *BC*, p. 39.

[9] *NUS*, p. 346.

[10] *BC*, pp. 39-40.

[11] *Ibid.*, pp. 40-41; cf. pp. 121-122, n. 126.

[12] *Ibid.*, p. 89. Cf. above, p. 28.

Freedom is Zizioulas' recurrent existential theme. Indeed, he acknowledges it as his deepest theological preoccupation.[13] The *person* is free from constraint by *givens*, given natures or given beings. Zizioulas particularly highlights *Maximus*' contribution to our understanding of how human beings may, by God's gift of Christ, overcome givenness and enjoy true personhood.

The explanation is in two parts. First, God Himself must be recognised as transcending this fallen world in which freedom is just that of *choice* between givens.[14] Exemplifying apophatic theology, Maximus said that God has 'a simple, unknowable existence, inaccessible to all things and completely unexplainable, *for He is beyond affirmation and negation*'.[15]

> 'In placing God's being . . . above affirmation and negation (Maximus) . . . the Greek Fathers were wishing to situate freedom itself above the limitations inherent in choice and in the "given".'[16]

'Greek monism . . . endangered the absolute ontological freedom of God, i.e. His transcendence.'[17] However, *nothing*

---

[13]I draw here on personal discussions with Zizioulas. Cf. his comment above, p. 137, at n. 83.

[14]God's transcendence of creation in general is implicit in Zizioulas' discussion of His transcendence of *fallen* creation, because he regards the Fall as simply *'revealing and actualising the limitations and potential dangers inherent in creaturehood, if creation is left to itself'* (*BC*, pp. 101-102; Zizioulas' italics). Hence, the 'surprising elision between creation and fall', which Williams notes ('Review', p. 103).

[15]Maximus, *Myst. Praef.* (PG 91, 664C), quoted by Zizioulas in *BC*, p. 90. See next note.

[16]*BC*, p. 121, n. 126. For Zizioulas, affirmation and negation are two sides of the same coin. In a fallen world of *objects* (cf. *BC*, p. 102), the choice of one is at once also the rejection of others. He wishes to point out that God rises above this currency of the fallen world. G. C. Berthold gives a different explanation of the passage in the Preface to the *Mystagogy* to which Zizioulas refers (see previous note). Berthold treats affirmation and negation separately, with God transcending *each*. His footnote to the passage says: 'Dionysius had explained that the universal Cause "transcends all affirmation by being the perfect and single cause of all beings, and transcends all negation by the preeminence of its simple and absolute nature which is free of every limitation and beyond all of them" (*Myst. Theol.*, 5 [PG 3, 1048A]; also 3 [PG 3, 1033C])'; see Maximus Confessor, *Selected Writings*, p. 216, n. 20.

[17]*DGT*, p. 23.

inhibits or compels the transcendent God by being a *given* for Him. He is the source of all. Everything, in its particularity, exists strictly as the object of His will; He knows nothing only in general terms or as examples of a nature pre-set in some blueprint or catalogue of natures. This is Zizioulas' point in laying such stress upon Maximus' teaching that God does not know (or recognise) beings in accordance with their nature but 'as the concrete results of His will' ('*idia thelemata*'). True personhood, 'which is God's way of being', involves not being dictated to in this way: 'to recognise beings in accordance with their nature would amount to a compulsory recognition'.[18]

Such compulsion, in Zizioulas' analysis, is the great suffering of man who wills personhood for himself in his 'quite legitimate desire . . . to be God'.[19]

> 'Man as a person is not content with the presence of beings as they are given to him in the world. In a God-like fashion he wants to recognise beings not "according to their own nature", i.e. according to their compelling givenness, but as "results of his own free will" — as *idia thelemata*, to recall Maximus the Confessor.'[20]

In this predicament, two options seem open to man: 'either to annihilate the "given" or to accept it as *idion thelema*'. Though it presents grave difficulties, 'because *in fact* the world is not man's *thelema*',[21] the solution lies by way of the second option. Experience shows that the first option, namely that of destroying oneself or the world of others, is an illusion. Dostoevsky's Kirilov suggests that killing oneself is the way to complete freedom.

> 'Who dares to kill himself becomes God. Everyone can do this and thus cause God to cease to exist, and then nothing will exist at all.'[22]

---

[18] *HCH*, p. 414, n. 1, with reference to Maximus, *Amb.* (PG 91, 1085A-B); cf. *BC*, p. 97.

[19] *Ibid.*, p. 430, n. 1.

[20] *Ibid.*, p. 420. Zizioulas adds that this lack of contentment is the motivation of Art. Cf. *BC*, p. 42, n. 38: 'Genuine art is not simply creation on the basis of something which already exists, but a tendency towards creation *ex nihilo*.'

[21] *Ibid.*, p. 433.

[22] *Ibid.*, p. 432; quotation from Dostoevsky, *The Possessed.* Cf. *BC*, p. 42 and p. 108, n. 105.

Zizioulas responds:

> 'But the world continues to exist in spite of man's ability to opt
> for non-existence. Freedom thus is shown to be ultimately not
> a matter of decision: its ontological content lies beyond the
> concept of choice, it is indeed incompatible with it.'[23]

There is, as it were, an underlying resistance of the world to
extinction, an irrepressible affirmation of its existence. Zizioulas
points out that there is no more striking proclamation of this
irrepressible affirmation than the Resurrection of Christ. 'The
fact that the Lord is risen has shown that freedom cannot
destroy the world.'[24] The crucial point, we may say, is whether
God Himself is the free source of the affirmation or, with the
world, is part of what is being affirmed. If God Himself is in an
'unbreakable unity' with the world, then He 'offers no real
hope for man',[25] for He is then necessarily affirmed with the
world. As man is the image of God, so man's freedom is the
image of God's freedom. Only if God is transcendent and the
world is His creation *ex nihilo,* 'in an absolute sense', does God's
freedom begin to offer hope to man that his own aspirations
are not vain.[26]

The second part of Zizioulas' explanation of our coming to
free personhood presents Christ as the very summation of all
that God affirms, such that by giving us Christ God is seen to be
giving us the means of *entering into* His free affirmation of
creation, and thereby definitively overcoming the givenness of
all that we encounter. Zizioulas recalls the Pauline doctrine
that all things were created through Christ and for him, and
considers the 'great existential significance of patristic
Christology' to have been the Fathers' translation of this

---

[23] *Ibid.,* p. 432. In spite of all its insights and honesty, Zizioulas points out
here the final absurdity of atheist existentialism. If freedom was ultimately a
matter of decision, then non-existence would be 'ultimately a possibility for
being'. 'By negating God as the affirmation of existence in spite of the
possibility of the choice of nothingness which exists for man, atheistic
existentialism is in fact denying existence altogether.' (*HCH,* p. 432, n. 1)

[24] *CEE2,* p. 70; cf. *BC,* p. 108.

[25] *DGT,* p. 24.

[26] Cf. *CEE2,* p. 65.

doctrine in terms of *personhood*: in the one (Christ) the many are hypostasised and loved.[27] Christ is *himself* God's affirmation of the world's existence and this all-embracing affirmation is precisely what 'God offers in Christ' for us to make our own, by our 'Amen', whenever the Eucharist is celebrated.[28]

As he used Maximus' presentation of God's transcendence in the first part of his explanation, so Zizioulas invokes the 'Christological synthesis' of Maximus for this second part: 'Christ is the *logos* of creation and one must find in him all the *logoi* of created beings'.[29] He particularly highlights the *historical* thrust of this synthesis 'within which history and creation become organically interrelated'.

> '*The incarnate Christ is so identical to the ultimate will of God's love, that the meaning of created being and the purpose of history are simply the incarnate Christ.*'[30]

With this thrust, Christ's presence in the Eucharist, for our *Amen*, is seen to be a presence from the future consummation of history. Zizioulas indicates the fidelity of this view to the perspective of the New Testament.

> 'The breakthrough of the full eschatological reality into historical existence is precisely the characteristic of the Holy Spirit (Acts 2). . . . [T]he Spirit reveals the *whole* truth (John 16: 13) and makes existentially relevant this truth *here and now* in a community of reconciled men.'[31]

The 'full eschatological reality' and 'the *whole* truth' are Christ and all things in Christ, a reality which is so inseparable that Zizioulas can refer to it, in his summary of Maximus above, simply as 'the incarnate Christ'.

As personhood is not of this world,[32] so 'the Eucharist

---

[27] *BC,* pp. 63-64, n. 68, with reference to Col. 1: 16; cf. *ibid.,* p. 54f.

[28] *Ibid.,* p. 121, with reference to 2 Cor 1:19, 20. We have noted the importance of this Pauline passage for de Lubac; cf. above, pp. 58-59.

[29] *Ibid.,* p. 96, with reference to I. H. Dalmais, 'La théorie des «logoi» des créatures chez s.Maxime le confesseur'.

[30] *Ibid.,* p. 97; cf. above, p. 90.

[31] *GRM,* p. 8. Cf. above, p. 136, and below, pp. 189-190.

[32] Cf. above, p. 129, n. 31.

contains an idea of truth which is not of this world'.[33] What we experience ordinarily is a '"truth" . . . opposed to "falsehood"', says Zizioulas, whereas regarding the Logos who is Christ and who contains the *logoi* of creatures we must recognise, with Maximus, that 'there exists nothing which may be examined beside Him and compared with Him'.[34] Nothing can stand alongside the totality of God's historical purpose, since it is a totality. Strictly speaking, Christians themselves are embraced by this totality. They do not stand outside it, which is presumably why Zizioulas says that the Eucharist 'reveals a state of existence free from the possibility of denial'. In this unique state of true freedom, Christ is affirmed from within the communion-event which he is. In the Eucharist, the Spirit gives to 'the community of the Church in history' a 'foretaste' of the freedom which 'is offered to man in Christ as the eschatological "glory" of the "children of God"'.[35]

Now, before moving on to examine Zizioulas' presentation of how the Fathers gave a 'first leavening' to Greek philosophy by distinguishing God from the world and then secured this distinction with a 'second leavening', relating to God's internal being, let us pursue his understanding of how, on the basis of this distinction, God freely encounters the world in Christ.

Christ is the focus in the communication of true freedom from God to man. The Church's most precise formulation of the ontology of Christ is the definition of Chalcedon. This definition may be seen as the kernel of Zizioulas' theological system, as we can now indicate. Echoing the quotations with which we started this chapter, Zizioulas states:

> 'I maintain that . . . monism was always present in classical Greek thought from the pre-Socratics to the Neoplatonists, and that Patristic theology had to wrestle with this issue as the most crucial — perhaps the only one — in its relation with pagan Greek philosophy'.

---

[33] *BC*, p. 121.
[34] *Ibid.*, pp. 90-91, n. 71: accordingly, in a 'profound passage', Maximus referred to the Logos as *above truth*, 'ὑπὲρ ἀλήθειαν' (*Amb.*, 37: PG 91, 1296C).
[35] *Ibid.*, p. 121, n. 126.

To this key issue, *Chalcedon* gave the decisive answer.

'A careful study of the Christology of the Council of Chalcedon would reveal to us that the deeper concern of the Fathers was how to arrive at the unity between divine and human in Christ without falling into mystical monism.'

Chalcedon achieved its goal by saying that in Christ the divine and human natures are united ἀδιαιρέτως (indivisibly) and yet ἀσυγχύτως (without confusion).

'Thus Christology bridges the gap between created and uncreated in a way that avoids monism and maintains the created-uncreated dialectic.'[36]

Most significantly, Zizioulas aligns with this dialectic the other dialectic which strongly marks his theology, namely that between 'the *eschata* and history', that is, between 'this age and the age to come'. The Eucharist, he adds, preserves this latter dialectic.[37] He thereby indicates his understanding that, in each eucharistic event, the age to come decisively *touches* and *lifts* the present age as Christ's human nature was touched by his divine nature and decisively lifted by his 'I' being divine. It is, then, to the Eucharist that we must look in order to find what the *Chalcedonian shift* is for Zizioulas, that is, to understand how, in his view, the dogma of Chalcedon existentially impinges upon Christians today. Whereas the Chalcedonian shift brings the individual Christ to bear upon individual Christians in de Lubac's view,[38] for Zizioulas it brings *corporate* realities into contact, namely the eschatological fulness of Christ and the local eucharistic community, as we may deduce from his following statement about the Eucharist:

'there is no room for the slightest distinction between the worshipping eucharistic community on earth and the actual worship in front of God's throne'.[39]

---

[36] *CMBC,* pp. 8-9.
[37] *BC,* pp. 20, 21.
[38] Cf. above, pp. 51-56.
[39] *BC,* p. 233. Cf. below, pp. 169-170.

Christ is not only the focus, but truly the *locus* of the relationship between God and the world, for all that God affirms, He affirms in the 'communion-event'[40] of Christ. The deepest knowledge we can have of things is to know them as God knows them, not, as we have seen, as natures, but 'as the concrete results of his will'; to know them in the unity with God which makes them most themselves; to know their *logoi*, or life-principles. As we have seen, this deepest knowledge passes through Christ, in whom 'all the *logoi* of created beings' are to be found.[41]

Just as 'true knowledge is not a knowledge of the essence or the nature of things, but of how they are connected within the communion event',[42] so the deepest transformation of a thing is effected by altering this communion. The Fall did not damage the *natures* of things, but broke their *communion* with God; it made difference into division and persons into individuals.[43] Conversely, *theosis* is not about divinising the *natures* of things, but about changing the *way* they exist, by imparting to them divine *communion*. Dalmais summarises Maximus' teaching about 'the "divinisation" which begins for the Christian in baptismal birth' as follows:

> '[it] renews the "mode of existence" (*tropos*) without changing the "essential principle" (*logos*) in accordance with which he was created'.[44]

Zizioulas fully embraces this view. He notes that Maximus distinguished between λόγος φύσεως and τρόπος ὑπάρξεως[45] and states:

> '[the] λόγος φύσεως has no need of transformation; the τρόπος φύσεως demands it'[46]

[40]Cf. *BC*, p. 98.
[41]*BC*, p. 96. Cf. above, p. 149.
[42]*Ibid.*, p. 106.
[43]Cf. *HCH*, p. 425.
[44]I. H. Dalmais, Preface to Maximus Confessor, *Selected Writings*, p. xiii.
[45]*BC*, p. 41, n. 36, with reference to Maximus' teaching that 'the various "logoi" never exist in a "naked" state but as "modes of existence"' (cf. above, p. 141), e.g. *Amb.*, 42 (PG 91, 1341D f.).
[46]*Ibid.*, p. 63, n. 67, with reference to Maximus, *Amb.*, 42 (PG 91, 1340BC and 1341C).

This Maximian doctrine of deifying transformation not of natures but by communion clearly underlay several important comments by Zizioulas in his programmatic address, where he already opened out, as it were, the doctrine of Chalcedon and indicated what we are calling the *Chalcedonian shift*. First, expressing the doctrine itself, Zizioulas said that, in Christ:

'the old Adam is renewed without being destroyed, human nature is assumed without changing and man is deified [*se déifie*] without ceasing to be man'.

Then he said that the Eucharist is the place where, 'in space and time, the very manifestation of the mystery of Christ' occurs now. There the celebrant's offering restores the lost communion and the relational transformation takes place.

'[A]ll that we are, all that we do and all that concerns us in the world can and must pass through the hands of the celebrant as [an] offering to God. Not so that it will remain as it is. Still less so that it ceases to be what it is deep down. But so that *it may become* what it *truly* is and what sin deforms.'[47]

Accompanied indeed by all of creation, we taste our deified state of communion in the Eucharist. At that moment, the world is transfigured without being destroyed and renewed without being recreated, by an encounter with eternity, that is with the future accomplishment of God's plan in Christ. This encounter gives the decisive (Chalcedonian) *lift* to the fallen world.

'In the Eucharist, history and time . . . meet [*se croisent*] with eternity, which . . . becomes precisely the dimension into which time can open.'[48]

The First Leavening

It is to Athanasius that Zizioulas largely attributes the first leavening of Greek ontology.

---

[47] *VEM*, p. 86.
[48] *Ibid.*, p. 87.

'[T]he Son is the εἰκών [image] of the Father precisely because it is in Him that the Father sees Himself as "truth".'[49]

Zizioulas' reference to this as a 'remarkable explanation',[50] and to the following as an 'extraordinary statement', urges us to recognise in Athanasius a radical departure from the philosophy which he himself referred to as that 'of the Greeks'.

'If the Son was not there before He was born, there would be no truth in God.'[51]

Zizioulas says, with emphasis, that this implies that '*it is the Father-Son relationship that makes God to be the truth eternally in Himself*'. Athanasius states that without the relationship between the Father and the Son 'the perfectness and fulness of the Father's substance is depleted (or eliminated — ἀφαιρεῖται)'. 'Has God ever existed without His own (Son)?', he asks. Zizioulas comments as follows.

'To say that the Son belongs to God's substance implies that substance *possesses almost by definition a relational character*. . . . If God's being is by nature relational, and if it can be signified by the word "substance", can we not then conclude almost inevitably that, given the ultimate character of God's being for all ontology, substance, inasmuch as it signifies the ultimate character of being, can be conceived only as communion?'[52]

Athanasius departed from Greek philosophy by rejecting 'any notion of divine substance *per se*', that is, without its relational qualification as 'Father' (which automatically implies also a son). Zizioulas comments: 'it is precisely this that makes the use of "substance" by Athanasius un-Greek'.[53]

---

[49] *BC*, pp. 100-101; reference to Athanasius, *Orat. contra Arianos* 1, 20-21 (PG 26, 53f.).

[50] *Ibid.*, p. 100.

[51] *Ibid.*, pp. 84-85, n. 60; quotation from Athanasius, *Orat. contra Arianos* 1, 20 (PG 26, 53B). Athanasius' reference to Greek philosophy occurs in his *De Synodis*, 51 (PG 26, 784C).

[52] *Ibid.*, pp. 84-85 and nn. 59, 60. The quotations from Athanasius are all from *Orat. contra Arianos* 1, 20 (PG 26, 53).

[53] *Ibid.*, p. 85, n. 60.

Athanasius' inclusion of the Son in the substance of God was part of his anti-Arian strategy of distinguishing substance from will,[54] in order to distinguish between the Son and the created world: the Son's being belongs to the substance of God while the world has its being because of the will of God.[55] Zizioulas notes that Athanasius still regarded substance as ultimate, in the standard line of Greek thought.[56] 'The introduction of the notion of *aitia* (cause) into the doctrine of the Trinity was a necessity which Athanasius had not foreseen.'[57] But his inclusion of the Son in the substance of God introduces the recognition of otherness within one substance which the Cappadocians would pursue to arrive at the ultimacy of the *person*.[58] He decisively broke the 'ontological *syggeneia* [affinity]' of God and the world in 'the closed ontology of the Greeks'[59] and made it possible to recognise the world as God's free creation without implying the createdness of the Son. Moreover, he drew what we might call the existential consequences of createdness: to be created means to be intrinsically threatened by death, by non-being.[60]

Zizioulas quotes Athanasius' direct criticism of Plato for attributing a feebleness to God, by imagining that He had to rely on pre-existing matter for His creative work, such that without it He could have done nothing. Such a God, Athanasius said, is 'simply a craftsman and not the creator', because He is not the *cause* of matter itself.[61] We may see a parallel between Athanasius' contrast of craftsman and creator and Zizioulas'

[54] *Ibid.*, p. 83, with reference to Athanasius, *Orat. contra Arianos*, 1, 33 (PG 26, 80f.) and 2, 2 (PG 26, 149f.) etc.

[55] *Ibid.*, pp. 83-84.

[56] *Ibid.*, p. 83.

[57] *DGT*, p. 25.

[58] Cf. *BC*, pp. 86-87.

[59] *Ibid.*, p. 84.

[60] Zizioulas mentions Athanasius on this point briefly in *CEE*1, p. 163, and at some length in *CEE*2, pp. 66-67, with reference to his *Orat. de Inc. Verbi*, 4, 5 (PG 25, 104-105). He says that Athanasius' position is surely founded on the witness of Scripture, e.g. 2 Thess. 1: 9; 1 Thess 5: 3; Rom. 9: 22; Phil. 3: 10; Heb. 10: 39; Mt. 7: 13.

[61] *CEE*2, p. 61; quotation from Athanasius, *Orat. de Inc. Verbi*, 2 (PG 25, 100A-B).

own contrast between morality and ontology as the thrust of the Christian Gospel.[62] Christianity is not just about morally improving the state of existence with which we are confronted, namely the fallen world of *objects*. It is about rebirth into a new life, which is tasted in the Eucharist when it encounters history in a Chalcedonian fashion. Similarly, God does not just work with material with which He is confronted; He freely creates and gives life, and it is indeed the God whose utter freedom was shown in creation who now freely intervenes in the Eucharist to mould His world for eternal life, which is a life of communion, not of objects.

It appears to Zizioulas that Origen ultimately compromised the freedom of God by conceding some *need* of God for the created world.

> 'Despite his doctrine of creation *ex nihilo*, Origen connected the idea of God so closely with that of creation that he came to speak of eternal creation, arguing that God would not be eternally omnipotent with no object on which to exercise His power.'[63]

Zizioulas associates Origen with Justin as one who risked falling into monism through his belief in a *syggeneia* between God and the soul or *nous* (mind), by his use of the notion of *logos*. Justin was effectively committed to 'the ontologically necessary link between God and the world' and, for Origen, 'the link between the *logos* of God and the *logoi* of creation . . . comes to be organic and unbreakable'.

> 'The application of the *logos* concept in this context led to the crisis of Arianism, which compelled the Church to revise the concept radically.'[64]

We may wonder how, after such a critique, Zizioulas can so applaud Maximus' use of the *logos* concept? The difference which is implicit in Zizioulas' presentation is that whereas the early *logos* theologians link the *logoi* of creatures to the *logos* of

[62]Cf. above, p. 137.
[63]*BC*, p. 75; reference to Origen, *De Princ.* 1, 4, 3. We may note, however, that God's need for the world in Origen is primarily *logical*, lest His unchangeableness be compromised.
[64]*Ibid.*, pp. 73-75.

God, i.e. to the eternal Son, Maximus linked the *logoi* of creatures to *Christ,* i.e. to the Son *incarnate. Christ* is the *logos* of creation.[65] Zizioulas remarks that Maximus parted from Origen and the apologists 'by making the *logos* concept pass from cosmology into the incarnation'.[66]

Zizioulas' vigorous criticism of the theological principle that the immanent Trinity is the economic Trinity is motivated similarly to his criticism of Origen. He considers that this principle concedes some *need* of God for the created world and thus runs the renewed risk of *monism.* He considers that a post-Enlightenment desire to dispense with transcendence lies behind the view that God's revelation 'in Christ and the Spirit as they are involved in history and experience' is *exhaustive.* He thinks that Karl Rahner's *Grundaxiom,* that 'the economic Trinity is the immanent Trinity and vice-versa, the immanent Trinity is the economic Trinity', is 'essentially nothing but a return to the classical monistic view of existence' which endangers 'the absolute ontological freedom of God, i.e. His transcendence'.[67]

Zizioulas objects that, if the principle is applied, then 'the Incarnation is projected into God's eternal being' and, as with 'the Moltmannian "crucified God"', God 'becomes suffering by nature, . . . in constant need of historical reality (involving suffering) in order to be what He *will* be, true God'.[68] He quotes a further consequence, from Congar's 'brilliant' discussion of the issues surrounding Rahner's thesis.

'If all the data of the Incarnation were transposed into the eternity of the Logos, it would be necessary to say that the Son

---

[65]Cf. above, p. 149.

[66]*BC,* pp. 96-97. Zizioulas gives a reference to Maximus, *Amb.* 23. However, there is no mention of the Incarnation in this passage (PG 91, 1257C-1261A). P. Sherwood interprets its meaning as intra-Trinitarian (*The Earlier Ambigua of St Maximus the Confessor,* p. 47).

[67]Cf. *DGT,* p. 23. Zizioulas combines the two formulations Rahner gave of his *Grundaxiom* or 'basic thesis', in *The Trinity,* pp. 21-22, and, earlier, in 'Remarks on the Dogmatic Treatise "De Trinitate"', p. 87.

[68]*Ibid.,* pp. 23-24.

proceeds from the Father and the Holy Spirit — *a Patre Spirituque.*'[69]

We may note that Zizioulas considers the Western *Filioque* to rest upon another 'projection of history into God'. The historical *mission* of the Spirit becomes the basis for Pneumatology: 'the fact that Christ sends the Spirit grounds ontological language about God'.[70] Apophatic theology takes the place of such projections and transpositions, recognising that 'the immanent Trinity is not exhausted in the economic Trinity'.[71] As Congar urges, 'the free mystery of the economy and the necessary mystery of the Tri-unity of God' must be distinguished.[72] Recognition of this *free* initiative of God lies at the centre of the following summary by Zizioulas of his objection.

'The Son *became* man; the second person of the Trinity is not Christ but the Son.'[73]

The following statement by Zizioulas is of great importance for our purpose here.

'[The] economy is the *basis* of ecclesiology, without being the *goal* of it. The Church is built by the historical work of the divine economy but leads finally to the vision of God "as He is", to the vision of the Triune God in His eternal existence.'[74]

The historical work of the Trinity in the economy has been to establish (essentially eucharistic) moments when our final state is opened up to us, when we shall see God as He is. Thus it is diametrically mistaken to think that God must be sought *backwards*, down the line of the historical process.[75] There are *two* ways of praising God, which correspond to *two* kinds of

---

[69] *TSE*, pp. 50-51; quotation from Congar, *I Believe in the Holy Spirit*, vol. 3, p. 16.

[70] *IED*, p. 149.

[71] *DGT*, p. 24.

[72] Congar, *I Believe in the Holy Spirit*, vol. 3, p. 13.

[73] A contribution by Zizioulas, recorded in the official minutes of the BCC/DEA Study Commission on Trinitarian Doctrine Today meeting, 8/9 June 1984, p. 9.

[74] *BC*, p. 19.

[75] Cf. below, Chapter Eleven.

statement about God, in terms of His historical work as we have seen it in the economy and in terms of His future glory when we shall see Him as He is, respectively.

> 'St Basil's two doxologies must be studied in depth because they point to the necessity of two ways of speaking of the Trinity which must remain quite *distinct* from each other. Doxological statements and kerygmatic statements (to remember Schlink's distinction) are of a different nature in theology, and what we can say from God's acts in history is different from what we can say looking at God as He is eternally.'[76]

Zizioulas believes that, in the Eucharist, we stand firmly in history, but not primarily so as to look *backwards* in praise of God's past deeds, rather to praise God Himself for those past deeds brought to their future completion in the eschatological Kingdom which is opened up to us there.

The Second Leavening

Zizioulas' maintains that the first leavening must be followed by a second.

> 'He [God] is the cause not only of beings, but also of being — and even of His own being.'[77]

Indeed, the first leavening *requires* the second, which asserts the ultimacy of the person.

> 'I venture to suggest that unless we admit *on a philosophical level* that personhood is not secondary to being, that the mode of existence of being is not secondary to its "substance" but *itself primary* and constitutive of it, it is impossible to make sense of the doctrine of creation *ex nihilo.*'[78]

Zizioulas' implication is that if God is not free with regard to His own being then His freedom with regard to the world is

---

[76]*DGT*, p. 24; cf. *BC*, p. 191, n. 71. We shall consider Basil's two doxologies further; cf. below, pp. 177-178, 248.
[77]*CEE*1, p. 161.
[78]*HCH*, p. 416.

hollow, for why secure God's freedom with regard to the world only to deny it with regard to Himself?[79]

However, he thinks that Christian theologians have not normally taken this further step:

> 'even the doctrine of God is based normally on the assumption that God is personal because He *first* "is" and *then* "relates" — hence the classical treatment of the doctrine of the Trinity [i.e. *De Deo Uno* first and then *De Deo Trino*] and the problems of intelligibility it has never ceased to present'.[80]

Particularly in Western theology, he says, 'the shift of hypostasis from *ousia* to personhood during the Trinitarian discussion of the fourth century has not yet been fully understood and applied'.[81] Accordingly, Western theology has never unreservedly accepted the notion of *theosis* (deification), because, given the ultimacy of nature, *theosis* seems to involve a loss of humanity, whereas, if the ultimacy of the person is recognised, *theosis* is seen not to impair human nature at all, but rather to cause human beings to exist as God Himself exists, that is, as free persons.[82]

The Cappadocian Fathers were responsible for this shift, which resulted in the conviction that 'the ontological identity of God and the unity of His being were not to be found in divine "substance" but in the *hypostasis of the Father*'.[83] Then the following can be said of God:

> '*He, as a particular being* (the Father) brings about His own being (the Trinity)'.[84]

---

[79]Zizioulas notably develops his reference to the first leavening in the statement quoted above (p. 146, at n. 16) immediately into a statement of the second leavening: 'God is truly free in a positive sense, because "eternally" ... He affirms His existence by a communion-event. He is the Father because He eternally has a Son through whom He affirms Himself as Father, and so on.' (*BC*, p. 121, n. 126). We may note that Zizioulas refers both to the Trinity (here and below, pp. 161, 177) and to Christ (above, p. 152) as *communion-events*.

[80]*HCH*, p. 416.

[81]*Ibid.*, p. 410, n. 2.

[82]Cf. *Ibid.*, p. 440 and n. 1. Cf. above, pp.137, 152, and below, p. 165.

[83]*Ibid.*, p. 410, n. 2.

[84]*OBP*, p. 42.

Zizioulas' dissatisfaction with the equation 'man = man'[85] is but an echo of his rejection of the logical affirmation 'A = A' as 'a dead logic'.[86] 'God = God' is the most resounding example of 'the dead ousianic tautology of something existing because it exists, the logic of the "self-existent"'.[87]

The Cappadocians furthered Athanasius' work to overthrow this dead logic. It seems to be what we have just seen as Athanasius' doctrine of the relationships between the Father and the Son and between God and the world that Zizioulas has in mind in the following statement.

> 'Nothing in existence is conceivable in itself, as an individual, such as the τόδε τί [this particular thing] of Aristotle, since even God exists thanks to an event of communion. In this manner the ancient world heard for the first time that it is communion which makes things "be"; nothing exists without it, not even God.'[88]

Athanasius firmly located the being of the Son in the *substance* of God, but Zizioulas warns against what he would see as a mistaken interpretation of the *homousios* (of one substance) terminology of Athanasius and Nicaea.

> The *homousios* is not to be understood so much as a positive statement, telling us something about God's being, but rather as a negative one, indicating what the Logos is *not*, namely a creature.'[89]

In the next generation, Basil sought to secure the uncreatedness of the Holy Spirit, but, fearing the Sabellian possibilities which *homousios* terminology afforded,[90] he devel-

---

[85]Cf. *HCH*, pp. 447, 445-446: 'Chalcedonian Christology is not to be understood as implying that human nature *per se* is an indication of humanity. ... For Chalcedon the equation "man = man" is unacceptable; it is that of "man = man-in-communion-with-God" that emerges from its Christology.'

[86]*BC*, p. 17.

[87]*DGT*, p. 25; cf. *BC*, p. 17.

[88]*BC*, p. 17; cf. *OBP*, p. 41. This statement indicates how Zizioulas would define an 'individual'.

[89]*TSE*, p. 32; reference to Athanasius, *Orat. contra Arianos* 2,2 (PG 26, 149f.) and 2,20 (PG 26, 188f.), though neither passage actually uses the term '*homoousios*'.

[90]*Ibid.*, p. 35 and n. 14.

oped what we might see as Athanasius' conclusion of the fellowship of the Father and the Son in the divine substance[91] by including the Holy Spirit in this fellowship, that is in the 'κοινωία τῆς Θεότητός' (communion of the Deity) in which the unity of God consists.[92] Zizioulas daringly summarises the preference of Basil for the terminology of *koinonia* rather than *homousios,* [93] by saying that, for Basil, 'the *nature* of God is communion'.[94]

Zizioulas here goes beyond what Basil actually says, which is a putting in parallel rather than an identification of κοινωνία τῆς Θεότητός and θεῖα φύσις (divine nature),[95] and seems to exemplify perfectly the interpretation of Basil for which, on the basis of other articles, A. de Halleux severely criticises him.[96] De Halleux considers that Zizioulas wrongly regards the Cappadocians as having been 'allergic to the language of essence' and that he interprets the 'intra-divine *koinonia*' of which they speak as 'dialogic interpersonal relations', when in fact it simply refers to 'the common nature'.[97] However, imme-

---

[91]Cf. *BC,* p. 89, n. 67: 'Athanasius' relational notion of substance becomes through the creative work of the Cappadocians an ontology of personhood.'

[92]*TSE,* p. 34, n. 13; cf. Basil, *De Spiritu sancto,* 18 (PG 32, 149C; corrected reference). Thereby, though he did not use *homoousios* for the Spirit, as it *had* been used for the Son, Basil nevertheless upheld what Zizioulas calls 'the dogmatic *raison-d'être* of the *homoousios*', namely, 'the faith that the created and uncreated cannot be mixed up and that the Spirit belongs to the realm of the uncreated' (*ibid.,* p. 34).

[93]*Ibid.,* p. 34, n. 13, where Zizioulas cites *De Spiritu sancto,* 63 (PG 32, 184B) (cf. citation of n. 68 (PG 32, 193B) in *BC,* p. 134, n. 23) and *Contra Eunom.* 2, 12 (PG 29, 593C). His reference to *Ep.* 52, 3 (PG 32, 417B) seems inappropriate.

[94]*BC,* p. 134.

[95]Basil, *De Spiritu sancto,* 18 (PG 32, 149C): 'οὕτως ἐπί τῆς θείας και ἀσυνθέτου φύσεως ἐν τῇ κοινωνία τῆς Θεότητός ἐστιν ἡ ἔνωσις' ('thus, in the divine and incomposite nature, in the communion of the Deity, is the union').

[96]De Halleux's criticism is most direct in 'Personnalisme ou essentialisme trinitaire chez les Pères cappadociens?' (hereafter, 'Personnalisme'), pp. 132-155. However, it is based on Zizioulas' book, *EE* (particularly Chapter One), and on his article, *TSE.* The summary of Basil by Zizioulas which we have quoted comes from a chapter which was added to *EE* for the English collection, *BC* (pp. 123-142).

[97]'Personnalisme', p. 289, where de Halleux summarises pp. 142-148 of his analysis.

diately after his summary of Basil, Zizioulas makes an important clarification.

> 'This does not mean that the persons have an ontological priority over the one substance of God, but that the one substance of God coincides with the communion of the three persons.'[98]

In other words, Zizioulas attributes to the Cappadocians not a dispensing with the notion that Father, Son and Spirit are of one substance, but a penetration of it towards understanding the *pattern* of this unity.[99]

Zizioulas considers that, in order to guard against Sabellianism, Basil gave to the term *prosopon* (for each of the persons in the divine communion) real ontological weight. This he did by transferring the decisive ontological notion of *hypostasis* from its Athanasian identification with *ousia* (substance),[100] to the *person*. Zizioulas hails the following statement by Basil as 'strikingly clear and revealing'.

> 'Those who say that οὐσία and ὑπόστασις are the same, are compelled to confess only different πρόσωπα and by avoiding the use of the words τρεῖς ὑποστάσεις [three hypostases] they do not succeed in escaping the Sabellian evil.'[101]

Thus, following Athanasius, again with Basil we are faced with '*something radically new*'; in this case it is '*the introduction of ontological content into the notion of Person*'. This is the development which Zizioulas considers goes unnoticed and tragically so, because it has 'profound philosophical and existential implications',[102] by which we are to understand its relevance for *freedom*.

This development constituted the breakthrough towards the Cappadocian expression of the divine *modes of being*. The

---

[98] *BC*, p. 134.

[99] Cf. above, pp. 139-143; below, pp. 274-276.

[100] *TSE*, p. 36, n. 16, with reference to Athanasius, *Ep. ad afros episc.* (PG 26, 1036B).

[101] *Ibid.*, p. 36, n. 18; quotation from Basil, *Ep.* 236, 6 (PG 32, 884C). Zizioulas comments that this text shows that '*ὑπόστασις was needed precisely in order to add to the relational character of πρόσωπον an ontological content*'.

[102] *Ibid.*, p. 36, n. 18.

ontological ultimacy accorded to *person,* by identifying *it* and not *substance* with *hypostasis,* meant that 'it must be a *Person* — and not a substance — that is the source of the divine existence'.

> 'Thus the notion of "source" is complemented by the Cappadocians with the notion of "cause" (*aitia*), and the idea emerges that the cause of God's being is the Father.'

'Cause' goes beyond 'source', in that it asserts that the divine existence does not just 'spring' from 'an impersonal substance', but rather is actually caused 'by *someone*'. 'Divine being owes its being to a *free person,* not to impersonal substance.'[103] Zizioulas regards the following comment by Gregory of Nyssa as perfectly exemplifying the Cappadocian understanding of *aition* and personal differentiation in the Trinity.

> '[W]hile we confess the invariable character of the divine substance, *we do not deny the difference with regard to the cause and that which is caused, by which we only mean that each person is distinguished from the other* . . . [I]n speaking of the cause and that which is from the cause we do not indicate by these words the nature but the difference in the *mode of being*'.[104]

We may note Zizioulas' ecumenical stance with regard to the *Filioque* controversy. He says that, if Constantinopolitan teaching is interpreted 'in the light of Cappadocian Theology', then *ek tou Patros* must not be taken to exclude 'a mediating role of

---

[103]*Ibid.,* p. 37. In their reviews of *BC,* Saward (p. 46) and Williams (p. 104) both strongly protest at Zizioulas' statement that Western Trinitarian theology, following Augustine and the scholastics, has come to see the divine *ousia* as 'the causal principle (ἀρχή) in God's being' (*BC,* p. 88). Saward perceives this as an allegation of Western 'quaternity', in which the *ousia* would be the cause of the *Father,* as well as of the Son and the Spirit. A footnote to the present passage perhaps indicates that, in spite of appearances, this is not Zizioulas' meaning. He sees Eunomianism manifesting the danger of making 'the Father alone . . . the οὐσία of God', if *ousia* is assumed to be 'ontologically ultimate' (*TSE,* p. 37, n. 21). Eunomianism then made of the *homoousios* 'a Platonic overflowing of God's love' (*DGT,* p. 25).

[104]*Ibid.,* p. 37 and n. 22 (cf. *BC,* pp. 17-18); quotation from Gregory of Nyssa, *Quod non sint tres Dii* (PG 45, 133B, D).

the Son in the procession of the Spirit', providing that the Son does not 'acquire the role of *aition* by being a mediator'.[105]

Let us return to the existential implications of the second leavening. 'Does God exist because He *has to* exist? Does God exist simply because He exists?'[106] Zizioulas notes with concern that Etienne Gilson suggests that medieval scholastic thought linked Being with necessity as the basis of Christian philosophy. If that is so, he comments bluntly, 'it can hardly be called "Christian"'.[107]

> 'If God's existence is determined by the necessity of His *ousia*, if He is, in Gilson's terms, a necessary being, . . . then all existence is bound by necessity. On the other hand, if God's existence is . . . caused by a free person, then there is hope also for the creature which by definition *is* faced by the priority of substance, of "given realities", to be free from these "givens", to acquire God's way of being in what the Greek Fathers called *theosis*. "Theosis" is meaningless apart from the liberation of man from the priority of substance over against the person.'[108]

We have seen that de Lubac would not say that God is a necessary being. He endorses Blondel's importantly different assertion that God is '*freely* necessary' and, moreover, 'necessarily free'. Like Blondel, de Lubac is concerned to protect God's 'primordial freedom' from any notion of an antecedent 'divine nature'.[109] However, in Chapter Eleven, we shall see that de Lubac and Zizioulas do not envisage the *pattern* of God's free Trinitarian life in the same way. In further preparation, let us now consider Zizioulas' view of the participation which humanity has in that pattern of being, in Christ.

---

[105] *Ibid.*, p. 44. Cf. above, pp. 125-126.
[106] *DGT*, p. 25.
[107] *TSE*, p. 45, n. 45, with reference to E. Gilson, *L'Esprit de la philosophie médiévale*, esp. pp.45-66, a chapter entitled, 'L'Etre et sa nécessité'.
[108] *DGT*, p. 25.
[109] Cf. above, p. 28 (my italics).

Chapter 8

The One and the Many

'In order to speak of the identity of Christ, one has to make use of the idea of "corporate personality". This idea, discovered and proposed by modern biblical scholars such as Wheeler Robinson, Pedersen, de Fraine etc., constitutes a scandal to our Western minds, but seems to be the key to an understanding of the Bible.'[1]

Here immediately we note several of the characteristics of Zizioulas' theology which were mentioned at the end of Chapter Six; his boldness of statement, his conceptual bridging of much data and his concern for scriptural fidelity. We see also what Zizioulas means by the need to 'de-individualise' Christ.[2] In the Scriptures, he contends, Christ is not presented as one pursuing a self-contained, individual achievement, even with a view to its subsequent application to all. Rather, from the very beginning, he is corporate; others are part of the definition of his identity. Equivalently, we may say that, from the very beginning, Christ is a *person*, defined by communion with others; he is *one* who is defined by *many*.

---

[1]*MCO*, p. 299. In *BC* (p. 146, n.7; p. 182, n. 38; p. 230, n. 63), Zizioulas specifies the relevant writings of the respective authors; H. Wheeler Robinson, 'The Hebrew Conception of Corporate Personality' (1936, hereafter referred to as 'Hebrew Conception'); S. Pedersen, *Israel: Its Life and Culture* (1926) and J. de Fraine, *Adam et son lignage: Etudes sur la "personnalite corporative" dans la Bible* (1959). He also adds A. R. Johnson, *The One and the Many in the Israelite Conception of God* (1942). Cf. *OBP*, p. 39.

[2]Cf. above, p. 23.

We have seen that Zizioulas refers to the one and the many as 'the mystery of Christology and Pneumatology, the mystery of the Church and at the same time of the Eucharist'.[3] We may now indicate his meaning. He says that there is 'nothing more unbiblical' than starting to consider the Holy Spirit only '*after* the figure of Christ has been completed'.[4] Rather, the Holy Spirit is 'above all the one who makes Christ *be*what he is, i.e. *Christos* — Christ'.[5] The biblical accounts show Christ being 'constituted by the Holy Spirit'.[6] Zizioulas points to two particular characteristics of the Holy Spirit in the Scriptures. First, the Holy Spirit is the gift of the last days, as Acts 2: 17 follows Joel in teaching. Zizioulas interprets this doctrine strictly, to mean not just that when the Holy Spirit is given we are in the final phase of history, but that the Holy Spirit confronts history with its very end. He acts 'to bring into history the last days, the *eschaton*'.[7] How then does history not come to a halt? Because the confrontation occurs *dialectically*; the eschaton is *different* from history and cannot *abide* in history, it *visits* again and again. Secondly, 'the Spirit has always, since the time of Paul, been associated with the notion of *communion* ($\kappa o\iota\nu\omega\nu\iota a$)'.[8] The Spirit's work is 'to open up reality so that it may become *relational*'.[9]

These characteristics have a twofold ontological implication for Christ. 'Christ is inconceivable as an individual: he becomes automatically a relational being',[10] and his relational milieu is eschatological.

> 'The Person of Christ is automatically linked . . . with a *community*. This community is the eschatological company of the "Saints" which surround Christ in [the] kingdom. The Church is part of the definition of Christ.'[11]

[3] *EPH*, p. 346. Cf. above, p. xxi.
[4] *HCH*, p. 441; cf. *BC*, p. 111.
[5] *MCO*, p. 296; cf. *BC*, p. 111; *EAQ*, pp. 22-23.
[6] *EPH*, p. 342.
[7] *BC*, p. 130.
[8] *Ibid.*, pp. 130-131, with reference to 2 Cor. 13: 13.
[9] *MCO*, p. 299; cf. *BC*, p. 112.
[10] *Ibid.*, p. 299; cf. *PDC*, p. 146.
[11] *EPH*, p. 342.

Thus, it is as part of this eschatological milieu that Christ has his personhood, existing as God exists, thanks to his constitution by the Holy Spirit.[12] Moreover, being constituted by the Spirit is what preserves Christ from having (an ultimately tragic) human personhood. Zizioulas considers that the doctrine of the virgin birth expresses negatively what is positively expressed 'in the Chalcedonian doctrine that the person of Christ is *one* and is identified with the *hypostasis of the Son of* [i.e. in] *the Trinity*'.[13] Hence, we may note the important point that, although Christ is fully anchored in the human company of the saints, all danger of Adoptionism is ruled out because, paradoxically, what enables this is precisely the fact that his personhood is divine, being that of the eternal Son.

Zizioulas highlights T. W. Manson's exegesis of the judgement scene in the twenty fifth chapter of Matthew's Gospel. Manson observes that the King (Christ) does not appear as an individual to condemn the wicked for their lack of care for him in the righteous whom he takes to himself. Instead, his brethren appear as a group 'distinct from both parties'. 'The only possible conclusion would seem to be that they are included [with the King] in the concept "Son of Man".' In other words, both the righteous and the wicked are confronted with the 'corporate body' of the Son of Man, 'and judged by their treatment of that body in the days of their power and its weakness'.[14] It follows that, for the righteous, judgement is a dialectical encounter with *themselves* in Christ. Zizioulas says that Christ, 'by his very constitution . . . in the Spirit', 'contains by definition the eschata, our final destiny, ourselves as we shall be; he is the eschatological Man'.[15]

As we shall see, Zizioulas notes the *eucharistic* context of scriptural teaching on the Son of Man. He concludes that we

[12] Cf. above, p. 141.

[13] *BC*, p. 55.

[14] T. W. Manson, *The Teaching of Jesus*, pp. 265, 270. Zizioulas refers to Manson in *EPH*, p. 342, n. 26; cf. *EQA*, pp. 58-59. Robinson notes Manson's corporate interpretation of "Son of Man" in the synoptic Gospels ('Hebrew Conception', p. 57, n. 1).

[15] *BC*, p. 183.

encounter this eschatologial Man, the Christ in whom we are persons, in each eucharistic event. These encounters are regular but transient, hence the 'new hypostasis' of personhood is 'a historical *experience*, even though it is not permanent'.[16] Nevertheless, in their transience they are decisive. The Christian has 'a relationship with God giving eternal life' only by 'constant participation in [the] eucharistic community',[17] that is by living constantly from one Eucharist to the next in an existential rhythm which marks him with the eternal identity he experiences in each celebration.[18]

Zizioulas interprets Ignatius' words to the Smyrnaeans as teaching that, in each eucharistic event, the historical, earthly gathering around the bishop is '"*exactly the same as*" . . . the whole Church united in Christ',[19] that is, the future, eschatological assembly. De Halleux considers that Zizioulas makes here a 'pure and simple identification of the two levels' which reduces Ignatius' comparison to 'a vulgar pleonasm'. The relationship between the levels is, de Halleux insists, 'a complex of identity and difference'.[20] We have already seen that the identification which Zizioulas makes is, in fact, one patterned after the complexity of the Chalcedonian definition of Christ.[21] Accordingly, although the historical (local) church's

---

[16]*Ibid.*, p. 58, n. 53. Cf. below, p. 272.

[17]*ECC*, p. 31, where Zizioulas is setting forth the teaching of Ignatius of Antioch.

[18]Cf. below, Chapter Twelve.

[19]*BC*, p. 149. Zizioulas himself italicises the words shown as his translation of the 'ὥσπερ' in *Smyrn*, 8, 2 (Bihlmeyer, p. 108): 'Wherever the bishop appears, let there the multitude of the people be, just as ['ὥσπερ'] wherever Jesus Christ is, there (is) the catholic Church.'

[20]A. de Halleux, '«L'Eglise catholique» dans la lettre ignatienne aux Smyrniotes', p. 18. De Halleux likens Zizioulas' stance to that of Afanassieff. We shall see in Chapter Ten that Zizioulas criticises Afanassieff for making the local church self-sufficient. His own interpretation does not all *invert the meaning* of Ignatius in this way, as de Halleux implies (*ibid.*, p. 18, n. 76).

[21]Cf. above, pp. 150-153. What Zizioulas rejects is not a *difference*, but a *division* or *distance* (cf. *HCH*, pp. 425-426, 447 for terminology) between the local church around the bishop and the eschatological Church around Christ, such that a *contrast* might be drawn between the two, as, he believes, many have done (cf. *BC*, p. 144, n. 3; p. 149, n. 24; pp. 229-230, n. 60).

identity is truly that of the eschatological Church (as the 'I' of Christ is divine), a firm difference between these two realities (as between Christ's human and divine natures) is nevertheless implicit in his account.

By this strict identification, Zizioulas wants to see each eucharistic assembly as the *bearer*, or *eikon*,[22] of the eschatological assembly until the last day.[23] Until then, the *one* eschatological assembly has its existence only in and as these *many* eucharistic assemblies, each of which is not a part of the eschatological gathering, but that gathering in its fulness. The one is many and the many are one. The one and the many are *mutually constitutive.* '[T]he local churches are *full circles* which cannot be added to one another but *coincide* with one another and finally with the Body of Christ and the original apostolic Church' in 'a *unity in identity*',[24] where all are identified with 'the worshipping community before the throne of God' in the eternal life to come.[25] The inbreaking from the future of this one eschatological reality as many historical events is the work of the Holy Spirit, an activity memorably summarised by Zizioulas as follows.

> 'The Holy Spirit is the one who makes the Church churches and the churches Church, the Eucharist Eucharists and the Eucharists Eucharist.'[26]

Corporate Personality in the Old Testament

So far we have referred only to *Christ* as a corporate personality. However, in the opening quotation of this chapter, we saw

---

[22] *MCO*, p. 300.

[23] '[F]or the Fathers (e.g. Ignatius of Antioch) the local church is in itself a reality in which the "catholic" Church is fully present and real.' (*BC*, p. 233, n. 71) Cf. above, p. 137.

[24] *BC*, p. 158, n. 66. This is the same kind of unity, though here applied to Christian *local churches*, as that which we have been expressing in a slightly different way, as a coincident unity-of-identity, in describing de Lubac's view of the unity of Christian *people* (cf. above, p. 19).

[25] *Ibid.*, p. 234; cf. p. 233, where, with reference to the teaching of John Chrysostom and Maximus, Zizioulas says: 'there is no room for the slightest distinction between the worshipping eucharist community on earth and the actual worship in front of God's throne'.

[26] *PRCE*, p. 50.

Zizioulas refer to this concept as the key to understanding the *whole* Bible. Indeed, he says of the strictly equivalent, and '*paradoxical*', notion of the one and the many that it is 'omnipresent' in the Bible.[27] The Old Testament has many corporate personalities; however, as we shall see, they are all unfulfilled, as the fact that they are *dead* shows. Christ simultaneously fulfils and supersedes them.[28] He is 'the corporate being *par excellence*'.[29]

Of the four studies to which Zizioulas refers[30] when he describes the concept, those of Robinson and de Fraine are his particular sources.[31] However, he makes significant alterations to their presentations. We may suspect his dissatisfaction with de Fraine's account of the meaning of 'corporate personality' when we realise that in Zizioulas' almost verbatim quotation of the fellowship passage, he omits the words in italics.

> 'The term "corporate personality" . . . expresses two things: first of all, that a single individual is truly corporate, *that is to say, functionally identified with a community*; secondly, that despite this "corporate" characteristic he remains an individual person.'[32]

---

[27] *Ibid.*, p. 35.

[28] I owe this important point (and that in n. 41, below, q.v.) to personal discussions with Zizioulas. He regards it as the precise meaning of Irenaeus' doctrine of Recapitulation.

[29] *MCO*, p. 299.

[30] Cf. above, p. 166, n. 1.

[31] Scripture scholars do not fully agree about the concept of corporate personality. Even when de Fraine took up Robinson's early study and wrote at considerably greater length on the theme, in review J. Coppens said that 'a critical study' was still needed ('Review', p. 490) and J. P. Audet referred with understanding to the reader 'who refuses to see an "open Sesame" in the notion of "corporate personality"' ('Review', p. 298). J. W. Rogerson endeavours to show that 'there was from the outset an ambiguity in Robinson's use of the phrase ["corporate personality"]' and that 'this ambiguity has enabled other scholars to make use of the theory in a way for which it was never really suited' ('The Hebrew Conception of Corporate Personality: A Re-examination', p. 2). The ambiguity is between corporate personality as corporate *responsibility* and corporate *representation* (pp. 6-7; cf. also, Rogerson, *Anthropology and the Old Testament*, p. 55).

[32] *PRCE*, p. 35; quotation from de Fraine, *Adam and the Family of Man* (translation of the work given above in n. 1), p. 21 (my italics).

Suspicion that a merely *functional* identification between the one and the many dissatisfies Zizioulas is confirmed when he goes on to stress that the biblical concept is not adequately translated as a *juridical* delegation or authorisation of one to act for many or many to act for one. The latter, he says, rests on the distinction (which was 'the great achievement of the Roman mind') between 'myself as an *ontological* reality and myself *functioning* on behalf of you'. This distinction between 'function and being' is also to be seen in the probable deriva- tion of the word 'person' from the mask worn in a drama: 'the mask is not what one is'.[33] More specifically, we may say that the mask is *added* to what one is, as a role to be played:

> '*persona* is the role which one plays in one's social or legal relationships, the moral or "legal" person which either collec- tively or individually has nothing to do with the *ontology* of the person'.[34]

Clearly, 'functional' is a term to which Zizioulas wants to give 'ontological' weight and status. For him, corporate personality is a matter not simply of *functional* identification but of *ontologi- cal* identification between the one and the many. The same correction may be perceived when he presents the aspects of corporate personality as described by Robinson. He quotes the first aspect which Robinson states: 'the unity of its extension both into the past and into the future'.[35] But Zizioulas does not quote Robinson's clarification of this aspect.

> 'The whole group, including its past, present and future mem- bers might *function* as a single individual through any one of those members conceived as representative of it.'[36]

Instead, Zizioulas gives his own clarification of the aspect as follows, implicitly amending Robinson's account.

> 'It makes the past present and the future present in the past. It makes a unity of men truly, *ontologically* present in one person.'[37]

[33]*Ibid.* pp. 35-36.
[34]*BC,* pp. 34.
[35]*PRCE,* p. 36; quotation from Robinson, 'Hebrew Conception', p. 50.
[36]Robinson, 'Hebrew Conception', p. 49 (my italics).
[37]*PRCE,* p. 36 (my italics).

Zizioulas is not, of course, presuming to correct exegetes in their reading of the Old Testament. Their discovery of functional corporate personality in the Old Testament must be accepted. What Zizioulas' corrections show is not a rejection of this discovery, but a refusal to *define* corporate personality on the basis of it, that is, a refusal to accept that the Old Testament shows corporate personality in its full rigour.

With the exception of Adam, all Old Testament persons exist, by definition, in the state of humanity after the Fall. Zizioulas characterises this state as follows: 'communion is no longer constitutive of being in a fallen state of existence'. It is a fragmented state in which 'beings are particular *before* they can relate to each other: you first *are* and then relate'.[38] In other words, it is precisely a state in which function is added to being. Thus, in fact, the exegetical findings of Robinson and de Fraine, that the Old Testament shows *functional* corporate personality, fully accord with Zizioulas' understanding of humanity's state there from a systematic theologian's point of view. However, Zizioulas is concerned to emphasise that (with the exception of Adam) humanity is there seen in its fallen, rather than its definitive, state and that such a form of corporate personality, merely functional, is a symptom of its malaise.

Robinson does not seem to see corporate personality in the Old Testament as manifesting humanity's malaise. If anything, he sees it as a means of overcoming the death to which we are subject after the Fall, as may be inferred from the optimistic tone of the following remark.

> 'Because it was not confined to the living, but included the dead and the unborn, the group could be conceived as living for ever.'[39]

Zizioulas agrees with de Lubac in thinking that, for humanity faced with death, there is no consolation in the notion of *group* survival.

> 'The fact that beings come and go, live and die, . . . seems to present no existential problem as long as through their death

[38] *BC*, pp. 102-103.

[39] Robinson, 'Hebrew Conception', p. 49; cf. his book, *Redemption and Revelation*, pp. 258-259.

and disappearance other identities arise in a cosmic or biological cycle of being. Thus beings die but being goes on. . . . Such
a thought is often used as a consolation for death. And yet this
sort of escape from the problem leaves unsatisfied everyone
who would find a particular identity, a certain being so dear and
so dearly loved as to be indispensable and irreplaceable. This is
what the Greek Fathers meant by Person: a being so deeply
loved as to be unique and irreplaceable.'[40]

The corollary of any consolation from my survival in the birth
of each new generation must be grief at my demise in the death
of the previous generation. The optimism of Robinson's earlier statement must be tempered by his later recognition that
'Rachel weeps because she dies in her children'.[41]

Though Robinson and de Fraine do not raise the following
point, Zizioulas dwells on *death* as the *downfall* of corporate
personality. He says that corporate personality requires 'a
constant relationship'[42] between the one and the many in their
personal existence. He considers that the Pauline teaching on
the universal effect of the Original Sin of Adam is readily
understood in the category of corporate personality.[43] Death is

---

[40]*ESLT*, pp. 7-8. Cf. *Catholicism*, pp. 197-198, where de Lubac examines the
'humanitarian optimism' that finds consolation in the notion of self-sacrifice
for the furthering of humanity's destiny on this earth. No such immanent
destiny will satisfy, because 'it is not really for humanity that the sacrifice is
made: it is still, despite assertion to the contrary, for other individuals'.

[41]Robinson, 'Hebrew Conception', p. 52, with reference to Jer. 31: 15.
Zizioulas considers that the genealogy of Christ roots him in Adam (cf. Lk. 3:
23-38) in order to show that Adam dies no more, for one of his descendants
has *risen* so as to return life to him. In this way, not only has the 'one', Adam,
given life to the 'many', but, in Christ, they have given life back to him. The
'one' and the 'many' are then mutually constitutive and Adam is fulfilled as
a corporate personality by the Resurrection of Christ, which is the very action
that establishes Christ as *the* corporate personality (cf. *BC*, pp. 113-114, n.
116). The same applies for Abraham (cf. Mt. 1: 1-17). Cf. above, p. 171, n. 28.

[42] Cf. *OBP*, p. 40: said of Adam in relation to 'all the rest of human beings'.

[43]Apart from the other references given, I draw this paragraph from *PRCE*,
p. 39. With reference to 1 Cor. 15: 22 ('as in Adam all die, so also in Christ shall
all be made alive'), Robinson says that Paul's contrast between Adam and
Christ 'draws all its cogency from the conception of corporate personality'
('Hebrew Conception', p. 57). However, P. Lengsfeld says that this concept
is of no great help in the dogmatic explanation of Original Sin, because of its
'fluid contours' (*Adam et le Christ*, pp. 43-44).

not a juridical or ethical *punishment* either for Adam or for us. All *ontologically* shared Adam's fall into subjection to the death which intrinsically threatens created existence,[44] when he opted for 'idolatrous introversion to created being alone'.[45] As a result of the Fall, 'the world consists of *objects*'.[46] Though it seems paradoxical to do so, we may seek in Zizioulas' complaint about Augustine theologising on the basis of 'our fallen condition'[47] the reason for his judgment that with Augustine arose the problem of the transmission of Original Sin.[48] *Transmission* refers to communication between objects; since Original Sin is not something that an object receives but rather is what has made it an object in the first place, the question of transmission does not arise.

In his original communion with the uncreated God, Adam was a corporate personality. His rupture of this communion (through 'idolatrous introversion') necessarily broke also the communion between human beings and caused the corporate personality to fragment into objects. His fall caused the fall of all because his being caused the being of all. Zizioulas summarises the biblical answer to the question of why human beings *are*, as follows. 'What causes the particular human beings to *be* is *Adam*, i.e. *a particular being*.'[49] The one constituted the many, which is one half of the relationship which defines a corporate personality, and since Adam is a corporate personality only in communion with God the Creator, what is said here about Adam implicitly recognises the primary causality of God. God, as it were, causes humanity to exist in this configuration, that is, with Adam as the cause of the many,[50] the particular who

[44]*BC*, pp. 101-102. Also *CEE*1, pp. 163-165; e.g.: 'Death is natural to creation.' Cf. above, p. 155; also p. 146, n. 14.

[45]*HCH*, p. 434, cf. pp. 428-429.

[46]*BC*, p. 102.

[47]Cf. *ibid.*, p. 104.

[48]*PRCE*, p. 39: Zizioulas complains that Augustine inaugurated the interpretation of Original Sin which regards us as being *punished* for Adam's fall, rather than as having fallen with him.

[49]*OBP*, p. 38.

[50]The minutes of the meeting of the BCC/DEA Study Commission at which Zizioulas read the paper, *OBP*, show that Zizioulas' statement about

causes other particulars. Complementarily, the many constituted the one: Adam carried in himself not just his own person,
but all other human persons also, that is, the whole of human
nature in a living, personal unity.

If Adam is dead, this living, personal unity exists no more
and all I have in common with Adam is humanness (i.e. *human
nature* in the sense in which we used it in the previous sentence,
meaning the totality of human existences or persons[51]). Humanness is not located in either of us exhaustively, but is rather
the general which causes the particulars.

> 'What is it that causes particular human beings to *be*? Greek
> philosophy at the time of the Fathers was offering the choice
> between a Platonic οὐσία ὑπερκειμένη [substance existing
> above] and an Aristotelian οὐσία ὑποκειμένη [substance exist-
> ing below]. In other words, the particular human beings *are* in
> so far as they participate either in the ideal "Man" or in the
> "nature" of humanity, its species.'[52]

The bracketed insertions in the following condensed statement by Zizioulas indicate how we have interpreted above his
meaning.

> 'If Adam as a particular human being and not as human nature
> [humanness] is the primary cause of human being, he must be
> in a *constant relationship* with all the rest of human beings, not via
> human nature [humanness] — for this would make nature
> acquire ... the decisive priority — but *directly*, i.e. as a particular
> being carrying in himself the *totality* of human nature [human
> existences], and not part of it [just his own existence]. The
> Fathers noted that this cannot be the case with Adam, since
> death, owing to creaturehood, shows that the particular beings
> carry only part of human nature.'[53]

Adam as the cause of the many seemed to some to displace God. Zizioulas
clarified as follows. '[T]he Biblical doctrine of creation assumes a causation
of the being of the world outside itself. It is then possible to speak of the
causation of man in an analogous way, pointing to Adam not nature.'
(Minutes for 8/9 March 1985, p. 5)

[51]Cf. above, p. 139, n. 93, for Zizioulas' statement of the philosophical
principle governing personhood.

[52]*OBP*, p. 38. Cf. above, p. 141.

[53]*Ibid.*, pp. 40-41.

Death frustrates corporate personality; someone who is dead cannot *personally* constitute me. Death began to take effect through Adam, and thenceforth corporate personality was just an unfulfilled goal for humanity. However, since death intrinsically threatens creation, corporate personality is intrinsically precarious in created existence, as is the desired personhood which it conveys. *Secure* corporate personality was thus not to be found even in our original state. It is what Christ alone brings:

'Jesus Christ . . . realises in history *the very reality of the person* and makes it the basis and "hypostasis" of the person for every man'.[54]

Relationship is the basis of personhood. Temporary or breakable relationship cannot securely ground personhood. I cannot be a person in relation to Adam because he is dead; his 'I' has expired. But I can be a person in relation to Christ for he is risen and lives; his 'I' is the undying because uncreated 'I' of the Son. We appreciate the *existential* significance of this Chalcedonian dogma.[55] The Trinity is the true location of the relationships necessary for corporate personality, as Zizioulas explains in the following, important paragraph.

'In God it is possible for the particular to be ontologically ultimate because *relationship is permanent and unbreakable.* Because the Father, the Son and the Spirit are always together, the particular beings are bearers of the totality of nature and thus no contradiction between the "one" and the "many" can arise. What Adam *should* represent, God *does* represent.'[56]

The *constant relationship* required for corporate personality entails the persons concerned being *always together.* Corporate personality requires *actual personal presence*, in an 'event of communion', which is how Zizioulas often describes the life of the Trinity.[57] It was in order to praise 'God *as He is in Himself* ' that Basil defended the doxology 'Glory be to the Father with

[54] *BC*, p. 54; cf. *HCH*, p. 436.
[55] *Ibid.*, pp. 54-55. Cf. above, p. 174, n. 41.
[56] *OBP*, p. 41.
[57] E.g. *HCH*, p. 446; *TSE*, p. 39. Cf. above, p. 160, n. 79.

(*syn*) the Son, with (*syn*) the Holy Spirit'.[58] This is the doxology, expressing the 'co-presence and co-existence of all three Persons at once', which speaks of God 'in terms of liturgical and especially eucharistic experience'.[59]

In the Eucharist a taste is given of corporate personality. Thus, for Zizioulas, this celebration itself requires the *actual personal presence* of the members of the local church.[60] The private Mass is mistaken[61] because it relies on a ministerial identity outside the *actual personal presence* of the community, one explained in terms of 'representativeness'.[62] Significantly, Zizioulas regards such an understanding of ministry as 'juridical',[63] the term we saw him contrast with a proper notion of corporate personality.[64] He thinks that ultimately it leads to 'a separation of the ordained person from the community':

> 'to act *on behalf* of the community means to stand *outside* it because it means to act *in its place*'.[65]

The Church exists definitively in the eucharistic event.[66] To have an (ontological) ecclesial identity is to have a (functional) relationship and role, *here and now*, in this concrete event, in

---

[58] *TSE*, p. 38; reference to Basil, *De Spiritu sancto*, 1, 3f.; 7, 16 etc.: Basil actually uses *meta* rather than *syn* as the preposition when he says 'with the Son' in these passages (PG, 32, 72C and 93B). Cf. above, pp. 158-159; below, p. 248.

[59] *Ibid.*, pp. 40, 39.

[60] E.g. *EPH*, pp. 347-348. Cf. below, n. 66.

[61] The frequency with which Zizioulas returns to this point is striking; e.g. *EPH*, p. 344; *BC*, p. 152, n. 40 and pp. 216, 250; *EII*, p. 150; *EEE*, p. 39; *EOT*, p. 47; *EFEL*, p. 7. Cf. above, p. 24.

[62] *BC*, p. 163; cf. *EPH*, p. 347.

[63] *Ibid.*, p. 164.

[64] Cf. above, p. 172.

[65] *BC*, p. 164.

[66] Cf. above, p. 133. The Church herself is an *event*, 'taking place again and again' (*MCO*, p. 301; cf. below, p. 187). All must be present: 'The Church is a communion of ministries all of them existing simultaneously and in interdependence' (*BTD*, p. 35). This simultaneity would preclude the same person from acting in *two* capacities in the liturgy; cf. above, pp. 20-21, 22, for Peter Damian's view.

the *actual personal presence* of the members of the local church, in which *every* initiated Christian occupies a specific *ordo*.[67] This is how Zizioulas places 'the entire matter of Ordination outside the dilemma of choosing between *ontological* and *functional*',[68] that is, how he understands the 'functional' as having 'ontological' weight.[69]

Though there is debate among exegetes about the precise meaning of 'corporate personality',[70] we have seen that Zizioulas' own understanding of the term is clear: the one and the many are *mutually constitutive*.[71] In order to be clear about the 'one' and the 'many' in this configuration, we must look to the Trinity. Zizioulas considers that the Cappadocians were the first to consider the question of God's being '*in itself*', rather than 'in relation to the world, as was the case even still with St Athanasius'.

> 'What is it that causes divine being to *be* and to be particular beings? The analogy of Adam ... and not the οὐσία (ὑπερκειμένη or ὑποκειμένη) was applied ... to this question. ... God's being, the Holy Trinity, is not caused by divine substance but by *the Father*, i.e. a particular being. The one God is the Father.'[72]

The 'one' in God is the Father, thus the 'one' in corporate personality is not the total, overall unity, but the specific person at the heart of the 'many'. Moreover, the 'many' include the 'one'; the 'one' is one of the 'many' and does not stand outside them. Thus, the 'many' in the Trinity are *three*

---

[67] *OAS*, p. 36: 'It is a mistake to call the lay members of the Church "non-ordained". Baptism and especially confirmation (chrismation) ... *inevitably and immediately* leads the baptised person to the eucharistic community in order to assume his particular "*ordo*" there. The laity ... exist *together with* the other orders.' Cf. the next note.

[68] *BC*, p. 164. Cf. *BC*, p. 227, n. 47, and *EQA*, p. 48, n. 37, also *OAC*, p. 189: 'We must be brave enough to put aside these dilemmas and seek our understanding of ordination along different lines, namely those suggested by the notion of communion.' Cf. below, pp. 275-276.

[69] Cf. above, p. 172.

[70] Cf. above, p. 171, n. 31.

[71] For Christ, cf. above, pp. 166-168; for the Trinity, cf. above, p. 145.

[72] *OBP*, pp. 39-40. Cf. *PRCE*, pp. 41-42.

(not *two*), just as, in ecclesiology, Christ is *one of the Church.*[73]
With regard to ecclesiology, Zizioulas recently said the following.

> 'We need to find the golden rule, the right balance between the
> "one" and the "many", and this I am afraid cannot be done
> without deepening our insights into Trinitarian theology. The
> God in whom we believe is "one" by being "many (three)", and
> is "many (three)" by being "one".'[74]

Corporate Personality in the New Testament Eucharist

Zizioulas notes the switching between the singular and the
plural in the following passage from John's Gospel.

> 'Truly, truly, I say to you, *we* speak of what *we* know, and bear
> witness to what *we* have seen; but you do not receive *our*
> testimony. If *I* have told you earthly things and you do not
> believe, how can you believe if *I* tell you heavenly things? No one
> has ascended into heaven but he who descended from heaven,
> *the Son of Man.*'[75]

He comments as follows. 'It is clear that this anomaly of syntax
cannot be explained except by ecclesiology.'[76]

The key to an explanation lies in recognising that here, as
very frequently elsewhere, Jesus speaks as the *Son of Man,* a title
which gives 'perhaps the most authentic reflection of Jesus'
self-conscious'.[77] As we have seen, the Son of Man is the
eschatological gathering of the Saints with Christ, appearing in

---

[73]Cf. above, p. 140.

[74]*NUS,* p. 345. Though Zizioulas on one occasion implies that the 'many'
in the Trinity are only the Son and the Spirit (*BTD,* p. 34), this unequivocal
statement of 'the golden rule' expresses his view in its full rigour: the 'one'
must be included in the 'many'.

[75]Jn. 3: 11-13, quoted with the emphases given in *EQA,* pp. 34-35 and *BC,*
p. 147; cf. *PRCE,* p. 37.

[76]*EQA,* p. 35; cf. *BC,* p. 147.

[77]*PRCE,* p. 38. Cf. O. Cullmann, *The Christology of the New Testament*
(hereafter, *Christology*), pp. 65, 160. Zizioulas makes a reference to this book
of Cullmann in his description of the link between corporate personality and
the Eucharist in the Gospels (*BC,* p. 230, n. 64). We shall indicate points of
convergence between their respective accounts.

order to judge the world.[78] Zizioulas bids us recognise the scriptural evidence for the Eucharist being the occasion of such appearances.

'If the sixth chapter of this Gospel [John's] refers to the Eucharist, as the mainstream of tradition and exegesis seems to accept, it is significant that the dominant figure there is that of the "Son of Man".'[79]

Most characteristic of the Son of Man is that 'it is he who has descended from heaven (Jn. 3:13)'.[80]

'That is why the fourth Gospel describes the Eucharist as the eating not simply of the flesh of Christ, but of the flesh of the *Son of Man*: "unless you eat the flesh of the Son of Man and drink his blood, you have no life in you".'[81]

Because the Church exists definitively in and derivately from the Eucharist, Zizioulas sees simply 'another way of saying' what Jesus teaches here in the axiom, 'No salvation outside the Church', which Cyprian stated 'and which seems to be presupposed throughout the early church'.[82]

The Son of Man 'takes into himself everyone who eats this bread, thus fulfilling his role as the corporate Son of Man'.[83] Abiding in him, which he enjoins in Jn. 13-17, depends upon eucharistic participation, as is conveyed not only by the Last

---

[78]Cf. above, p. 168; also *EQA*, p. 33. With slight qualification, Cullmann endorses Manson's exegesis of the Son of Man (*Christology*, p. 154, n. 3; cf. p. 158, n. 3).

[79]*EQA*, p. 33; cf. *BC*, p. 146.

[80]Zizioulas' emphatically corporate understanding of this passage may be contrasted with de Lubac's interpretation of Eph. 4: 9-10 as indicating the descent of the *individual* Christ. Cf. above, pp. 43, 57, 64-65.

[81]*EAQ*, p. 33, with reference to Jn. 6: 53; cf. *BC*, pp. 146-147. We may contrast de Lubac's clarification of Augustine, that Christians are not the eucharistic body of Christ (*Splendour*, p. 112; cf. above, p.78).

[82]*ECC*, pp. 34, 32. We have seen that, although de Lubac does not give the axiom a specifically eucharistic interpretation, nevertheless like Zizioulas he does apply it to something concrete, namely the visible, earthly Church, and not simply to the heavenly Church; cf. above, p. 17, n. 76.

[83]*BC*, p. 147, with reference to Jn. 6: 56. The likeness to Augustine's (eucharistic) dictum in this passage must be qualified by the comment above, in n. 81.

Supper context of these chapters, but also in Jn. 6.[84] The climax of Jn. 13-17, in the prayer that 'they all may be one', looks towards the 'eschatological unity of all in Christ', of the 'many' in the 'one', but it is a prayer fulfilled in each Eucharist.[85] We recall that this fulfilment occurs in a transient *event*, when, as it were, the eschatological Son of Man *touches* earthly, historical reality. The Eucharist is 'the *moment* in the Church's life when, through the Holy Spirit, the "eschaton" enters history'.[86]

As well as the Son of Man, the other key corporate personality apparently invoked by Jesus to explain himself, and similarly presented in the scriptures as *eucharistically* accessible, is the Servant of God. The 'principal characteristic' of the Servant of God is as follows:

> 'he it is who takes upon himself the sins of the "many" (Is 40-55) in such a way that he is fully identified with the "many" to the extent that several exegetes have even seen in this figure the "corporate personality" of the People of God'.[87]

That this corporate personality is actualised in the Eucharist emerges from the striking fact that all of the accounts of the Last Supper use Servant terminology.

> '[W]hen he explains the meaning of the meal, our Lord does not simply identify the bread and the wine with his body and his blood, but he links this identification to another notion: it is "for" or "in the place of" the "many" or "you" that he offers himself (Mt. 26: 28; Mk. 14: 24; Lk. 22:20; 1 Cor. 11:25).'[88]

Zizoulas points out that 'primitive liturgical canticles' and 'the most ancient eucharistic prayers which we possess' show that the linking of the Eucharist with the 'tradition of the Servant

---

[84]*EQA*, p. 34, with reference to Jn. 6: 56.

[85]Cf. *BC*, p. 147.

[86]*EQA*, p. 31 (my italics). Cf. above, pp.168-169.

[87]*Ibid.*, p. 32. Zizioulas does not cite any specific exegetes, but Cullmann would be one; cf. *Christology*, p. 54.

[88]*Ibid.*, p. 31; *BC*, p. 146. Cf. Cullmann, *Christology*, p. 64.

of God' quickly became established in the liturgy of the early Church.[89]

We may note finally the testimony which he presents from Paul[90] to the *realism* of the Christian's identification with Christ, an identification explicable by a rigorous understanding of the corporate personality, Christ, who fulfils both the tradition of the Son of Man and that of the Servant of God. First, though it was *Christians* whom Paul persecuted, Christ himself said to him: 'why do you persecute *me*?'[91] In so saying, Christ echoed his teaching about the coming of glory of the *Son of Man*: 'as you did it to one of the least of these my brethren, you did it to *me*'[92] Secondly, it is Christ who is the suffering Servant, yet Paul sees his own sufferings as completing 'what is lacking in Christ's afflictions',[93] indeed as a *share* in Christ's sufferings,[94] co-suffering with him in order to be co-glorified.[95] Zizioulas would equally say of the scripture passages cited regarding this second point what he characteristically says of those cited with respect to the first, namely that sermons normally take their message to be 'moral' or 'mystical', when in fact it is *'ontological'*.[96]

Corporate Personality for a Scriptural Synthesis

Zizioulas distinguishes two ways in which the New Testament speaks of the relationship between Christ and the Holy Spirit.[97] From them flow two different understandings, both of the Church and of apostolicity, as *dispersion* or *convocation*.[98]

---

[89]*Ibid.*, p. 32, where Zizioulas cites first Phil. 2: 6-11, and then *1 Clement* 59: 2-4 and the *Didache* 9: 2; 10: 2, as examples of the two respective categories of sources. It is presumably the occurrence of παῖς, that is, child or *servant*, which Zizioulas is noting in the latter two works (cf. Bihlmeyer, pp. 6 and 66-67).

[90]I draw the content of this paragraph from *PRCE*, p. 38.

[91]Acts 9: 4. Cf. above, p. 95.

[92]Mt. 25: 40; cf. *IED*, p. 144. Zizioulas again refers to Manson's exegesis.

[93]Col. 1: 24.

[94]Phil. 3: 10.

[95]Rom. 8: 17.

[96]*PRCE*, p. 38. Cf. above, pp.137, 156.

[97]E.g. *BC*, pp. 127-128; *IED*, pp. 141-145; *PRCE*, pp. 22-23.

[98]E.g. *BC*, pp. 172-175, 179-180; *IED*, *passim*.

According to the first, Christ gives or sends the Spirit and according to the second, Christ himself as the work of the Spirit, that is, the Spirit gives us Christ.

The first way is found particularly in the Gospel of John, where it is said that '*there was no Spirit yet*, for Christ had not yet been glorified'.[99] The coming of the Spirit is presented as identical with Christ giving the Spirit to his disciples.[100] Christ himself invites the thirsty to drink the 'living water' of the Spirit from his breast,[101] an invitation which has been linked to the water flowing from Christ's side on the Cross.[102] Christ is 'the Truth'[103] and the Spirit is 'the Spirit of Truth',[104] so again Christ appears as the source of the Spirit.

The second way is found in the Synoptic Gospels, where the Spirit is related to Christ as 'the one who *constitutes his very identity as Christ*, either at his baptism (Mark) or at his very biological conception (Matthew and Luke)'.[105] It is said that 'the heavenly Father will give the Holy Spirit to those who ask him', as if it is not Jesus Christ but the Father who gives the Spirit directly.[106] Likewise Paul teaches that the Father raised Jesus from the dead by the Holy Spirit.[107]

Can it be said both that Christ gives the Spirit and that the Spirit gives Christ? Zizioulas says that the answer must be Yes, because both approaches appear in the New Testament and indeed even in the same books.[108] The New Testament itself is their synthesis. But *how* may such a synthesis be conceived? Zizioulas indicates that the synthesis requires there to be a

---

[99]Jn. 7: 39; cf. *BC*, p. 127.

[100]Jn. 20: 22; cf. *PRCE*, p. 22.

[101]Jn. 7: 37-38; cf. *PRCE*, p. 22.

[102]Jn. 19: 34; cf. *PRCE*, p. 23, where Zizioulas also refers to Jn. 3: 34, in which Christ is called the one who 'gives the Spirit'.

[103]Jn. 14: 6; cf. *PRCE*, p. 23.

[104]Jn. 14: 17; 15: 26; 16: 13; cf. *PRCE*, p. 23.

[105]*BC*, pp. 127-128.

[106]Lk. 11: 13; Mt. 7: 15; cf. *PRCE*, p. 23.

[107]Rom. 8: 11; cf. *PRCE*, p. 23.

[108]Cf. *BC*, p. 128: 'Both of these views could co-exist happily in one and the same Biblical writing, as is evident from a study of Luke (Gospel and Acts), John's Gospel, etc.'

'dimension of communion' in Christology. It involves the '"corporate personality" of Christ', that is, the fact that 'Christ is not just an individual, not "one" but "many"'.[109] However, he does not explain precisely *how* corporate personality fits both of the models of activity we have described and thereby integrates them. Let us now see how.

It can easily seem that, having spoken of the need for a synthesis between the two models, Zizioulas in fact works only with the second, for he presents the Holy Spirit always as the one acting upon history; the Spirit formed Christ and the Church ever lives epicletically. However, this view excludes the view that Christ himself gives the Spirit only as long as we persist in thinking of Christ and the Church separately and not as one, as the corporate personality Christ. Zizioulas would wish us to recast the statement just made as follows: the Spirit, acting *on* history, formed and *ever forms* the *corporate personality* Christ *in* history.[110] This eschatological corporate personality becomes an earthly, historical reality only epicletically. Not for a moment is Christ to be separated from the Church, that is from the eschatological company of the Saints.

Now, corporate personality has a structure. As we have seen, its archetype is the Trinity, in which the Father is the *cause*.[111] Correspondingly, in the Church, Christ is the *cause*. The Spirit gives us Christ, that is, the Spirit forms the corporate personality Christ. The one and the many are *all* the work of the Spirit. The fact that the many exist by the Spirit and yet are causally dependent upon Christ is aptly expressed by saying that Christ, the 'one', *gives* the Spirit to the 'many'. Thus a corporate understanding of Christ enables and requires *both* of the following to be said: the Spirit forms Christ and Christ gives the Spirit. In other words, corporate personality can indeed offer

[109] *BC*, pp. 130-131.

[110] Cf. *ibid.*, p. 130: 'The economy . . . in so far as it assumed history and has a history, is *only one* and that is the *Christ event*. . . . The Spirit is the *beyond* history.' This is Zizioulas' understanding of the 'indivisible but *not undifferentiated*' activity of the Triune God *ad extra* (*BC*, p. 129, n. 13; *TSE*, p. 39, n. 30).

[111] Cf. above, pp. 159-165

a synthesis of the two ways in which the Scriptures speak of the relationship between Christ and the Spirit.

In the third corresponding reality which Zizioulas aligns with the Trinity and the eschatological Church, namely the local church,[112] even though the Spirit breaks upon the whole community, including the bishop, alike in the Eucharist, Zizioulas nevertheless speaks of the bishop, as 'giving it the Holy Spirit, the charismata'.[113] He thereby confirms the explanation we have just given of the scriptural synthesis which corporate personality offers, especially since he comments that 'the paradox in the office of bishop . . . is the very paradox of Christ's position in the Eucharist'.[114] We must now see how an ecclesiological synthesis can follow, on the same basis of the one and the many.

---

[112]Cf. above, p. 135.

[113]*EPH*, p. 345, Equivalently, Zizioulas adds, with regard to the bishop: 'none else can give the Spirit to the community, none else can ordain'.

[114]*Ibid.*, p. 345.

Chapter 9

The Eucharist, The Church

'She [the Church] is what she is by becoming again and again what she will be.'[1]

There could be no clearer statement by Zizioulas of his view that the Church's centre of gravity lies in the future, not in the past. Her roots and her continuity lie *ahead*. By the bluntness of his following statement about the occasion of the Church's *becoming*, namely the Eucharist, Zizioulas intends to emphasise this complete reversal of the everyday notion of historical causality.

'[T]he Eucharist is not a sacrament but the manifestation of the eschatological community in its totality.'[2]

The interpretation we have just made of this passage is confirmed by Zizioulas' similar statement about Ordination.

'The "grace" of sacramentalism is a "possessed" and "transmitted" object. In this sense Ordination is not a sacrament.'[3]

Like the Eucharist, Ordination receives its meaning and content from the future, not from the past. We have seen that Zizioulas interprets the Ignatian *hosper* to mean that the

---

[1]*MCO*, p. 301; cf. below, n. 14. Zizioulas' *future* orientation marks a significant correction of J. Romanides, who says that in the Eucharist the Church 'is continuously becoming what she *is*' ('The Ecclesiology of St Ignatius of Antioch', pp. 64-65, my italics).

[2]*ECC*, p. 34.

[3]*OAS*, p. 39.

historical gathering of the local church around its bishop is *exactly the same as* the future gathering of the whole ('catholic') Church around Christ for eternity.[4] Because the historical eucharistic gatherings are the places where the eschatological gathering really exists until it is lastingly established, to be assigned a place in the local church's Eucharist, which is the meaning of Ordination,[5] is, indeed, to assume an identity in that eternal gathering. The *hosper* significantly reappears when Zizioulas describes the effect of Ordination.

> 'The ordained person is distinguished from the rest in that he is "like" (*hosper*) or "in the place of" (*eis topon*) a particular person in the very kingdom of God.'[6]

We shall see which particular persons in the future Kingdom each eucharistic *ordo* manifests when we examine the structure of the local church. For the present, let us recall that Zizioulas locates the Kingdom in the *future* in order to stress that it gathers into itself and consummates the *whole* of God's historical purpose. He considers that the Book of Revelation, 'more than any other writing of the New Testament, offers an idea of the eucharistic celebration in the early Church'[7] and points out that, in 'the icon of the kingdom' which it paints, 'the lamb on the table is slain'.

> 'The eucharistic vision of the kingdom does not leave history behind it, it involves it. It is not a Platonic vision that the icon brings.'[8]

This happens because the Holy Spirit, who makes present the Kingdom, is not only the one who announces the things to come, but also the one who recalls for the Church 'all that Christ said and did'.[9] Equally, this twofold work of the Spirit

---

[4] Cf. above, p. 169.
[5] Cf. above, pp. 178-179, and below, pp. 275-276.
[6] *OAS*, p. 38.
[7] *EQA*, p. 40.
[8] *EAH*1, p. 34.
[9] *EQA*, p. 24, with reference to Jn. 16: 13 and 14: 26, respectively. Zizioulas notes the *eucharistic* context of these teachings of Jesus in the farewell discourse of John's Gospel.

makes it clear that, as we have seen, what is recalled in the Eucharist is not just Christ's work of the past, but that work brought to its completion in the things to come.[10] Thus, in the power of the Spirit:

'the Church's *anamnesis* acquires the eucharistic paradox which no historical consciousness can ever comprehend, i.e. the *memory of the future*'.[11]

'Remembering the second coming is very important existentially',[12] says Zizioulas, in what we may certainly take to be a reference to *freedom*. Significantly, he warns that if the Church is understood as 'a historically given reality — an institution', then it is 'a provocation to freedom'.[13] Whatever I encounter coming down to me from the historical past is necessarily something that, at least at first, excludes me and stands outside me as a *given object*. Zizioulas insists that someone's becoming a Christian in a local church is not their assimilation into such an already constituted object, rather it is their becoming part of its eschatological *re*constitution in the Eucharist, when they and the other members encounter and affirm themselves from within the all-embracing Christ-event made present there.[14]

---

[10] Cf. above, pp. 135-136. Criticising H. Lietzmann's view (in *Messe und Herrenmahl*, 1926) that the early Church had two types of Eucharist, one (Pauline) imbued with the sadness of Calvary from the Last Supper and one in the joy of Christ's fellowship and post-Resurrection meals, Zizioulas says: 'the persistent vision of "the lamb who has been sacrified" does not suppress the light, the colour and the songs which surround the eucharistic experience in the Apocalypse' (*EQA*, pp. 28-29). Cf. the similar criticism of Lietzmann by Y. de Montcheuil, 'Signification eschatologique du repas eucharistique', particularly pp. 24-26, 33-36.

[11] *BC*, p. 180, with reference to the Orthodox liturgical prayer: 'Remembering the cross, the resurrection, the ascension *and the second coming*. Thine own of Thine own we offer Thee' (Zizioulas' italics). Cf. reference to this prayer also in *BC*, p. 169; *VEM*, p. 87; *EQA*, p. 31. Meyendorff praises the 'brilliant clarity' of this expression by Zizioulas of 'the essential meaning of the eucharistic celebration' (*Catholicity and the Church*, p. 27).

[12] *FTCR*, p. 11.

[13] *DGT*, p. 28.

[14] Cf. *BC*, p. 217, n. 21: 'the Church's historical existence' is 'her constant charismatic reconstitution'.

Christ is a 'corporate personality', says Zizioulas, immediately adding in explanation that he is 'the all-inclusive being'.[15] If he is to include me now and present history, then he must be a *future* and not a *past* reality.

Original sin has fragmented creation into objects. Zizioulas considers that Christ cannot save creation from this predicament if he himself comes as another individual object.[16] Christianity is all about the overcoming of this object-ification in the communion-event of Christ. A common feature of the many '-ism's which Zizioulas criticises[17] is a concession to the terminology of *objects* in describing the workings of Christianity. We have seen him reject 'sacramentalism' as a view which makes 'grace' an 'object'.[18] Likewise, 'ontologism' is the approach which would try to explain the Church as an object in herself[19] and Ordination in terms of its effect upon the ordained individual in himself, as an isolated object.[20] 'Collectivistic universalism' is an understanding of local churches in the worldwide Church as objective *parts* which are to be added together, rather than as coincident circles.[21]

Zizioulas' attention to *time* as God's creation is of particular interest to us here. Time itself is now fragmented by sin into objective parts and stands in need of redemption. Zizioulas fears that the common appreciation of '*Heilsgeschichte*', since Cullman, fails to heed the means by which time is redeemed. This appreciation is 'linear', he says, considering 'Creation, Old Testament interventions, the Incarnation, . . . the Ministry and the Cross of Christ, . . . the Resurrection, . . . the Church, . . . the second coming' all as successive 'stages'. This conception 'fits in very well with . . . the unredeemed concept of

---

[15] *MCO*, p. 300.

[16] Cf. *BC*, p. 182: '*Christ without his body is not Christ but an individual of the worst type.*'

[17] Cf. above, pp. 70-71, for the '-ism's of de Lubac.

[18] Cf. above, p. 187.

[19] *BC*, p. 217, n. 21: 'ecclesiological ontologism' considers 'the Church's being' as 'the intrinsic source of her actions'.

[20] *Ibid.*, pp. 233, 235. Cf. below, p. 276.

[21] *PDC*, p. 149; cf. *BC*, p. 158, n. 66. Also, above, p. 170.

time'.[22] However, the Church's ministry ought not to be envisaged as occupying an 'interim' period, while the accomplishment of God's work is awaited. On the contrary, 'it exists as an expression of the *totality* of the Economy'.[23] Indeed, this totality is what becomes present in advance, in the period of the Church, in order to heal broken time by, as it were, filling its gaps.[24] The Church shows forth in her life 'a time which does not move from the earlier to the later, from the old to the new, through the intermediary of *nothing, but through that of the future kingdom*'.[25]

Historicism is the general name given by Zizioulas to the many instances which he sees of the failure to appreciate that only the future Kingdom gives continuity to time, and that nothing of Christ can be possessed and transmitted from fragment to fragment through time, but only received and re-received. One of its forms is the 'institutionalism'[26] which we described above and which envisages the Church propagating in history, instead of being constantly reconstituted. 'Linear historicism' is that approach to Apostolic Succession which forgets that 'every episcopal Ordination is a fresh Pentecostal event, taking place . . . always within the eucharistic community'.[27] With its view of the Church progressively advancing towards the Kingdom, 'historical determinism' equally neglects the fact that, in the Eucharist, 'the Kingdom *in its fulness* enters into history'.[28]

---

[22]*FTCR*, p. 4. Cf. above, p. 57, for de Lubac on Cullmann.

[23]*BC*, p. 211.

[24]In *ESLT*, p. 6, Zizioulas recalls Aristotle's statement: ἅπαν ἐν κρόνω κινεῖται, ἐν δὲ τῷ νῦν μηθέν (*Physics*, Z 10, 241a 15). He says that Aristotle regards the 'in between' the earlier and the later as 'crucial for the concept of time' and that he refers to it here 'with two words which seem to be contradictory, the word νῦν (now) and the word μηθέν (nothing)'. Zizioulas clearly regards νῦν and μηθέν as being in apposition in Aristotle's statement, so as to mean that the now is nothing, contrary to the statement's apparent meaning, namely that everything moves in time, but nothing (moves) in the now, which J. Barnes more freely renders as follows: 'motion is always in time and never in a now' (*The Complete Works of Aristotle*, vol. 1, p. 406).

[25]*ESLT*, p. 20.

[26]*GIE*, p. 266. Cf. above, p. 189.

[27]*PDC*, p. 149. Cf. below, pp. 262-263.

[28]*EQA*, p. 68, n. 52.

Man is powerless to bring in the Kingdom.[29] Therefore, if the inbreaking Kingdom is the very bond of continuity in the Church's historical life, she must acknowledge her powerlessness to guarantee her own life. Zizioulas says that his approach abolishes 'historical causality' and recognises 'divine activity' as 'the sole cause of the Church's existence in history'.[30] The Apostles received the Spirit from Christ and yet they had to invoke the Spirit afresh upon the seven,[31] as the Church has to invoke the Spirit afresh in each Eucharist. God alone provides the continuity between these events and His absolute *freedom* must be respected.

> 'In an epiclectical context, history ceases to be in itself a guarantee for security. The *epiclesis* means ecclesiologically that the Church *asks to receive from God what she has already received historically in Christ as if she had not received it at all*, i.e. as if history did not count in itself.'[32]

In short, nothing of Christ is carried into the present from the past, it is only received again in the present from the future. Zizioulas considers that 'notions of historical causality' particularly characterised 'scholastic medieval theology'.[33] The following comment reveals his belief that such notions are tainted with *monism* which, with its view of God-and-the-world as the primary given object, we may regard as the essential '-ism' that Zizioulas opposes.

> 'The Incarnation does not bind God to history. Pneumatology and eschatology, by conditioning Christology and history liberate God from history. The future decides about history and the future is kept in God's freedom.'[34]

We may well doubt that anyone has ever actually subscribed to all the '-ism's which Zizioulas condemns, but they serve to

[29] Cf. *DPE*, pp. 96-97.
[30] *PDC*, p. 147.
[31] *BC*, p. 185, cf. *Acts* 6: 1-6.
[32] *Ibid.*, p. 185. Cf. de Lubac: 'in the spiritual order it is an illusion to think that anything can be absolutely acquired, once for all' (*Sources*, p. 65).
[33] Cf. *EAH*1, p. 39.
[34] *Ibid.*, p. 37.

indicate his own theological stance clearly and precisely. As we have seen, de Lubac rejects monism just as clearly as Zizioulas.[35] However, he lacks the unqualified orientation to the *future* which Zizioulas considers necessary for Christianity's defence against monism.[36] De Lubac's own need for such an orientation emerges specifically in his eucharistic theology.[37]

Zizioulas would express the delicate interplay of freedoms, which he substitutes for notions of historical causality, as follows. He would refer to the scene of Pentecost and say that what happens in the Eucharist is that the bishop and people freely express, by their coming together *epi to auto*, their desire to be Christ, and God freely endorses this desire by the inbreaking of the Spirit to form the corporate Christ.[38] God's free will in creation, across space and time, *is* the corporate Christ, and man finds his freedom by affirming himself and all things in this gift of God.[39]

We may emphasise again the *threefold* correspondence which Zizioulas envisages,[40] by noting his statement that it is 'the proper and specific function of the Spirit' to render '*the life of God* a reality here and now' in 'an event of communion'.[41] It is in the strict sense of this triple correspondence of the Trinity, Christ and the Eucharist, which are all *communion-events,* that Zizioulas says, of the eternal life nourished in the earthly, local gathering around the bishop, that it is 'the life of God in Christ'.[42]

---

[35]Cf. above, Chapter Two.

[36] Zizioulas considers that the monistic view of the Greeks both made creation unthinkable and looked to the past for an explanation of historical events in terms of an unfolding causality, '*for the very same reason*' (*HCH*, p. 418, n. 1).

[37]Cf. his inability to *integrate* memorial and anticipation (above, p. 89).

[38]In personal discussions, Zizioulas has confirmed this elaboration of the following unpublished statement. '*C'est seulement dans le rassemblement du peuple dispersé que l'Esprit est donné (voir Actes 2: 17).*' (*EFEL*, p. 6; cf. p. 1 for the phrase *epi to auto*. This phrase, which reinforces the sense of 'together', originates in 1 Cor. 11:20 and recurs throughout Zizioulas' writings; e.g. *BC*, p. 148.)

[39]Cf. above, pp. 148-149; below, p. 243.

[40]Cf. above, pp. 135, 185-186; below, p. 252.

[41]*PDC*, p. 148 (my italics).

[42]*EQA*, p. 57. Cf. above, p. 160, n. 79; pp. 177-178.

'In the Eucharist the Church becomes a reflection of the eschatological community of Christ, the Messiah, an image of the Trinitarian life of God.'[43]

Accordingly, for Zizioulas, far from its being determined merely pragmatically: 'the basic structure of the Church herself is organically connected with her essence'.[44] It is a structure imparted by the Eucharist of the local church.[45]

The Local Church

'The Church was always understood as the great mystery of the plan of God for the final destiny of the world, a mystery which was celebrated in the Eucharist and of which one became partaker as a member of a concrete local community.[46]

This summary by Zizioulas of the belief of 'the ancient Church' makes it clear that what becomes present in the Eucharist is the world as it will be. He speaks elsewhere of 'the eternal design of the Holy Trinity to draw man and creation to participation in God's very life'.[47] This inclusion of 'creation' is highly significant, because it excludes the notion that God's interest in the world is restricted to man. Rather, God intended man to be creation's *priest*.[48] It is this role, which will be his when God's design is accomplished in eternity, that he already exercises in the Church when he is part of her 'eucharistic movement':

'which relates the world to God by "referring" it to God as *anaphora* and by bringing to it the blessings of God's life and the taste of the Kingdom to come'.[49]

Zizioulas says that, in the Holy Spirit, Christ 'can now minister to this pre-eternal plan of God for creation *in* or

---

[43]*BC*, p. 254; cf. *ibid.*, p. 220 and *DGT*, pp. 28-29.
[44]*MOC*, p. 193. Cf. above, p. 98, for de Lubac's view.
[45]Cf. *ORT*, pp. 8, 11.
[46]*EDO*, pp. 35-36.
[47]*BC*, p. 211.
[48]Cf. above, pp. 30, 132; below, Conclusion.
[49]*BC*, p. 221.

rather *as* the Church'.[50] We may, therefore, appreciate the wider context of the corporate personality Christ. The local community around the bishop is identified in the Eucharist with Christ surrounded by the eschatological Church, *corporately offering creation to God.* Though Zizioulas' concern to show the realisation of corporate personality in the Eucharist means that he does not always mention creation, it is always in the context of ministry to the latter that the former is envisaged.

There are four orders which, he says, 'have survived in history as constitutive for the Eucharist': the bishop, the presbyters, the deacons and the laymen.[51] In short, we shall see that these four orders have their roles to play in the differentiated manifestation of what we may call life as God intends it, in the eschatological Kingdom. But it is essential to remember that the Eucharist is the dialectical encounter of this reality with life as it actually is: 'the dialectic between history and eschatology . . . is so central . . . to the Eucharist'.[52] The presbyters emerge as having, additionally, a vital *judgmental* role, which witnesses to this dialectical encounter.

> 'As far as we can reconstruct this structure [of the early eucharistic community] from the pieces of evidence that we possess, we can see that in the centre of the *synaxis* of the "whole Church" and behind the "one altar" there was the throne of the "one bishop" seated "in the place of God" or understood as the living "image of Christ". Around his throne were seated the presbyters, while by him stood the deacons helping him in the celebration, and in front of him the "people of God".'[53]

Zizioulas' footnote references from this summary are mainly Ignatian. As we shall see, he regards Ignatius as most representative of the first three centuries. Zizioulas indicates Ignatius' use of two distinct typologies with regard to the earthly bishop; in one he represents God (the Father) and in the other he

[50] *Ibid.*, p. 211.
[51] *EPH*, pp. 343-344, with reference to Ignatius of Antioch, *Smyr.*, 8 and *Magn.*, 6 (Bihlmeyer, pp. 90, 108). Cf. also, *BC*, pp. 152-153, 221-223; *EQA*, pp. 41-43; *GIE*, pp. 255-257; *EOT*, pp. 46-50.
[52] *BC*, p. 258.
[53] *Ibid.*, pp. 152-153.

represents Christ. Both of these typologies find expression in the threefold correspondence which we have noted in Zizioulas' account of the Eucharist.[54] However, they do so with an important qualification. It is only *via* his identification with Christ that the bishop is identified with the Father. In the context of this latter identification, another ministry might represent Christ, indeed Ignatius suggested the deacon,[55] but he never assigned the representation of the Holy Spirit to any ministry. Perhaps because of such attendant complications, the typology of the bishop as the Father was not pursued, as Zizioulas notes.[56] He considers that it is better to leave it as the background and focus on the Christocentric typology which is the immediate referent of the liturgy.[57]

With regard to the achievement of corporate personality, of the one and the many, in the Eucharist, Zizioulas dwells upon the bishop and the laity, whose *Amen* 'always formed an integral and indispensable part of the Eucharist'.[58] Its occurrence in the New Testament itself shows, he maintains, that from the first the gathered Christian community was marked by a fundamental structural distinction 'between those who lead the eucharistic community by offering the Eucharist and those who confirm or seal this action with their "Amen"'.[59] The freedom of personhood is experienced in this response to Christ.

> 'The people of God gathered together in the Eucharist realise their freedom under the form of affirmation alone: it is not the "yes" and the "no" together which God offers in Christ, but only the "yes", which equates with the eucharistic "Amen" (2 Cor. 1: 19-20).'[60]

[54] Cf. above, n. 40, also pp. 193-194.

[55] Williams says that 'Zizioulas omits to mention that Ignatius speaks of the *deacon* as imaging Christ' ('Review', p. 104). Ignatius does so in the context of identifying the bishop with the Father, in *Magn.* 6: 1, a text which Zizioulas does cite (*BC*, p. 152, n. 48; p. 177, n. 21), though not for its reference to deacons.

[56] Cf. *EPH*, p. 345, n. 31a: 'the Christological image prevailed (cfr. Hippolytus and ancient Liturgies).'

[57] For these comments, I draw on personal discussions with Zizioulas.

[58] *TPR*, p. 192. No other order can say the 'Amen' (*BTD*, p. 34).

[59] *ECC*, p. 30; cf. 1 Cor. 14: 16.

[60] *BC*, p. 121; cf. above, pp. 149-150.

In the eschatological, one-many relationship between Christ and the Saints, which is realised in history in the eucharistic assembly, the eucharistic gifts are '*agia*' (holy things) for the '*agoi*' (holy people).[61]

> 'Eucharistic communion is . . . at the same time *communio in sacris* and *communio sanctorum.*'[62]

In an eschatological context where *all* is holy, there is, we may say, a parity between holy gifts and holy people, not a causality.[63] The encounter which takes place in the Eucharist is not that of the risen Christ with his historical people, but that of the eschatological corporate personality of Christ–and–the–Saints with historical reality.[64] It would seem that, for Zizioulas, the holy gifts are, as it were, one half of the eschatological commerce between Christ and the Saints; the gifts are the outgoing of Christ to the Saints, their corresponding outgoing to Christ being their 'Amen'.

The eucharistic gifts, given by the bishop to his community, are *spiritual* gifts, 'a *spiritual food* and a *spiritual drink* (1 Cor. 10: 3)'. By its insistence, the sixth chapter of John's Gospel leaves no doubt that the bread and wine really and truly become the body and blood of Christ, but it also makes clear that this 'change (*metabole*)' is the work of the Holy Spirit.[65] As the work of the Spirit, this change cannot be something which relates just to an object, outside a specifically communitarian context. All 'objectification' of the Eucharist, seeing in it for instance 'a miracle which manifests the

---

[61] *EQA*, pp. 58-59. Zizioulas says that Christ gave his disciples a 'diagram' of the Kingdom, of the one and the many, when he gathered them for the Last Supper (*BC*, p. 206).

[62] *EQA*, p. 76. In contrast, de Lubac sets up a *causal sequence* here. He considers that it is *communio in sacris* which brings about the *communio sanctorum* (*CMys*, p. 31); cf. *TOcc*, p. 16. Cf. above, p. 79.

[63] Cf. above, p. 72. De Lubac says that eucharistic realism and ecclesial realism 'depend on each other', but as adequated 'cause' and 'effect', respectively (*CMys*, p. 283).

[64] Cf. below, pp. 267-268, 277.

[65] *EQA*, pp. 56-57, with particular reference to Jn. 6: 63: 'It is the *Spirit* that gives life, the flesh is of no avail' (Zizioulas' italics). Cf. above, pp. 131, 153.

power of God', is 'impossible'.[66] Thus, the *eucharistic elements*
are not the primary presence of Christ around whom the many
gather; the *bishop* is, and the holy gifts are the appropriate gifts
which he gives to the holy people.

It is when the perspective is widened to take in the rest of
creation, as we noted above is necessary, that Zizioulas introduces the deacons. In the liturgy the people offer not just their
Amen to Christ, 'each one of them brings with him the elements
of his own life or the gifts of creation that have been entrusted
to him'.[67] Zizioulas presents the deacons as those whose ministry points to the existence of this wider context; they 'reveal
the relation of the mystery of the Church to creation as a
whole'.[68] The deacon does this by acting in 'a double movement' between the bishop and the people: 'on one hand, he
offers the gifts of the world to the bishop so that they may
become Eucharist and, on the other hand, he offers the
Eucharist to the world as communion in the life of God'.[69]

As the laity represent the multitude of the Saints around the
throne in the Kingdom, so we may see the presbyters representing the elders who lead the heavenly praise.[70] However, it is as
we move now to consider the eucharistic *dialectic* between this
eschatological reality and present historical reality that the
ministry of the presbyters particularly emerges.

With regard to ecumenical strategy, Zizioulas recently said
the following.

> 'We have to ask ourselves constantly whether what unites or
> divides us matters eschatologically, whether it affects the des-
> tiny of God's world as He has prepared it in Christ.'[71]

He considers that the early Church provides us with a ready
test: the Eucharist. As the interface between the eschaton and

---

[66] *Ibid.*, pp. 56-57; cf. *BC*, p. 160, n. 70. We have seen de Lubac's complaint
that the scholastics changed the Eucharist from a mystery into a miracle
(above, p. 79).

[67] *GIE*, p. 259.

[68] *Ibid.*, p. 257.

[69] *EQA*, p. 42; cf. *BC*, p. 222; *EGA*, p. 72.

[70] Cf. Zizioulas' reference to Rev. 4: 4 in *BC*, p. 153, n. 50.

[71] *NUS*, p. 348.

history, the Eucharist is, as it were, a *filter* through which only what matters eschatologically can pass. It tests whether something bears the stamp of this fallen world or that of the world to come, in which we shall share the life of God.[72] For instance, 'all credal and conciliar formulations' cannot be said to have been received *ecclesially* unless and until 'they become integral parts of the eucharistic community'.[73] Further, Zizioulas believes that 'all other forms of the life of the Church can take place in partial groups, but not the Eucharist',[74] because division into partial groups is incompatible with the universal gathering of the last days which the Eucharist must manifest; 'natural divisions' cannot be given 'an eschatological affirmation' by being allowed to enter the Eucharist.[75]

All in all, the world really passes into *judgment* in the Eucharist.[76] It is not that the Church condemns the world, but rather that the world, which is brought as a whole into the Eucharist by the laity to be offered to God, inevitably there encounters the filter we have mentioned: 'it is by being *assumed* that the world is judged'.[77] This judgement and that of the Church's own members are the tasks which Zizioulas would restore to the presbyters, whom he presents as:

> 'the *synedrion* of the community portraying in liturgical as well as in actual terms the important and lost dimension of judgement which relates both *ad intra* and with the world'.[78]

---

[72]Cf. *BC*, p. 21, also p. 61 and n. 61.

[73]*TPR*, p. 191; cf. *BC*, p. 191.

[74]*EFEL*, p. 8: '*Toutes les autres formes de vie de l'Eglise peuvent être réalisées pour des groupes partiels, mais non pas l'Eucharistie.*'

[75]*ECC*, p. 34; cf. *BC*, pp. 151-152; *EQA*, pp. 39-40. Of a eucharistic gathering deliberately manifesting such divisions, Zizioulas comments: 'I would even say that it ceases to be [the] Eucharist, but I know that that would provoke many objections' (*GIE*, p. 268). The Eucharist must be '*a catholic act of a catholic Church*' (*BC*, p. 145).

[76]*EQA*, pp. 58-59.

[77]*BC*, p. 224.

[78]*Ibid.*, pp. 222-223.

He highlights the scriptural evidence for the community's responsibility to judge its members[79] and then looks to the Fathers.

> '[W]e may infer from Ignatius, the Syriac *Didascalia Apostolorum*, Tertullian and other sources, [that] the entire eucharistic assembly would be transformed into a court and the bishop surrounded by the council of presbyters (the Ignatian *synedrion episcopou*) would pass the final judgement so that the matters dividing the faithful would be settled in view of the eschatological act of communion in the life of the Kingdom through the Eucharist.'[80]

Zizioulas considers that 'the phenomenon of early councils' of bishops can only be understood on the basis of this 'primitive conciliarity' exercised within individual local churches.[81]

There is an exemplary period to which Zizioulas would direct our gaze. Its upper bound is the fourth century and it begins with the dawn of the post-apostolic age.[82] He maintains that fundamental principles unite this period in a coherent ecclesiological witness, as follows. All the sources of this period, starting with the *Didache*, *1 Clement* and Ignatius, regarded *episkope*, singly or collectively exercised stably and locally, as 'the focal ministry with the help of which the churches realised and expressed their communion with the Apostolic Church'.[83] What distinguished this period from that which followed was its association of *episkope* with celebration of the Eucharist[84] and what distinguished it from the preceding period was its option 'for the ultimate authority of the local church'.[85]

Let us consider the latter distinction first.

> 'A curious but crucial and decisive fact of the Church's history is that the transition from the apostolic to the post-apostolic

---

[79] In *EQA*, p. 59, Zizioulas refers to 1 Cor. 5, Mt. 5: 23, Mt. 18. In *DCS*, pp. 34-36, he sets 1 Cor. 5 in the eucharistic context of the whole letter.

[80] *CECB*, p. 3.

[81] *BC*, p. 156, with reference to *DCS*.

[82] Cf. above, p. 125.

[83] *EEE*, p. 36; cf. pp. 31-32.

[84] *Ibid.*, pp. 38-39.

[85] *Ibid.*, p. 41.

Church [took] place not through a series of missionary del-
egates, but via the local communities. It was by making each
local church a full and catholic church, capable of judging any
"universal" minister, that the Christians of that time moved to
a state of existence in which the apostles were no longer
present.'[86]

Zizioulas considers that 'an identification of the whole Christ
and the whole Church with the local episcopal community' is
'a key idea' in Ignatius' thought.[87] He implies that a scriptural
indication of the transition to this situation is provided by
Diotrephes' putting himself first and refusing to acknowledge
the authority of John. Here is a local church coming of age,
'judging' John and rejecting an itinerant, 'universal' minister
as its link with the apostolic Church, in favour of a stable, local
ministry.[88]

Both the disappearance of the apostolic generation and the
fall of Jerusalem prompted the change from a unitary Church
which looked up to the historical Jerusalem to a Church for
which, in each place, 'Jerusalem is the Eucharist'.[89] Zizioulas
thinks that 'the post-apostolic generation opted in a way that
led naturally to the Ignatian notion of episcopacy' since, if the
local church can give a final judgement on matters and if the
Eucharist is the context for such judgements,[90] then it is a
'natural consequence' to see the eucharistic community as
'portraying the Kingdom of God on earth' and therefore to

[86] *Ibid.*, p. 32.
[87] *BC*, p. 144, n. 3.
[88] *EEE*, p. 32; cf. 3 Jn.
[89] *PRCE*, p. 26. Zizioulas thinks that a significant scriptural indication of this
transition taking place is the terminological progression from 'the apostles
and presbyters' in Jerusalem (Acts 15: 6) to 'James and the presbyters' (Acts
21: 18) in Jerusalem. The Ignatian scheme of 'the bishop and the presbyters'
in each locality then marks the next step, (*BC*, p. 195, n. 87; cf. p. 175, n. 16
and *DCS*, pp. 36-38). Williams finds his argument 'very thin' ('Review', p.
104). However, in context, Zizioulas intends only to suggest that the standard
missionary approach to apostolic succession needs a convocational *corrective*
(cf. *BC*, p. 195, n. 87). Cf. below, Conclusion.
[90] *EEE*, p. 41; cf. *DCS*, pp. 34-36.

cast into particular relief 'one of the presbyters or *episkopoi* to become *ho episkopos*',[91] 'the image of God or Christ'.[92]

In the West, Hippolytus clearly distinguished the bishop from the surrounding presbyters and saw him *both* as '*alter Christus*', 'giving the Spirit, feeding the people, by presiding over the Eucharist, etc.', and also as '*alter apostolus*', in terms similar to those used in *1 Clement*. Zizioulas sees here 'the first synthesis' in the office of bishop between the Christological (cf. Ignatius) and apostolic (cf. *1 Clement*) elements of *episkope*.[93]

Cyprian decisively altered this Ignatian-Hippolytan imagery:

> 'the eschatological image of the apostolic college surrounding Christ . . . is changed to become an image of the apostolic college surrounding its head, *St Peter*'.

The episcopal throne is no longer the throne of God or Christ, but the *cathedra Petri*.[94] However, although Cyprian thereby crucially impairs the ecclesial image of the Kingdom and 'leads to the search for a "vicarius Christi" outside or above the apostolic — and the episcopal — college',[95] his concept retains the vital eschatological element of convocation, 'each episcopal church' is the image of 'the apostolic college *in its entirety*'.[96] Moreover, he recognises the fulness of each local church; each is the 'catholic Church', each bishop is 'the successor of Peter'[97] and 'directly responsible to God for his community'.[98] As it were, Peter and the apostles preside in each local church.

Regarding now the transition into the fourth century, we may note a link between two major points of decline which Zizioulas indicates. In the first three centuries, when the Church 'had no identity recognised by the State', it was obvious

---

[91] *Ibid.*, p. 33.

[92] *Ibid.*, p. 35.

[93] *Ibid.*, pp. 34-35; cf. *BC*, p. 195.

[94] *BC*, pp. 168, 200; reference to Cyprian, *Ep.* 40 (43), 5 (PL 4, 336); *De unit.* 4 (PL 4, 500).

[95] *Ibid.*, p. 203, n. 114.

[96] *Ibid.*, p. 201 (my italics).

[97] *EEE*, p. 35.

[98] *BC*, pp. 200-201, n. 106; pp. 155-156, n. 59; reference to Cyprian, *Ep.* 52 (55), 21 (PL 3, 787A).

to her members that the source of her identity lay with God in Heaven. It went without saying that she was 'an *eschatological community*'. Christians lived in eucharistic expectation of the Kingdom, which would come purely as God's gift. Zizioulas suggests that official recognition by the State produced a dangerous impression that human effort could bring in the Kingdom.[99] In other words, official recognition blurred the essential *dialectic* between this age and the age to come and so lessened the judgmental aspect of the Eucharist. Since a judgmental role had traditionally been exercised by the presbyteral college, such a development would fit well with another aspect of the Constantinian era which he highlights, namely the fact that, by establishing parishes and individual presbyters as eucharistic presidents, 'the Church turned him [the presbyter] into a bishop, and thus lost the presbyter'.[100]

> 'The parish as it finally prevailed in history made redundant both the deacon and the bishop. (Later, with the private mass, it made redundant event he laity.)'[101]

Already in his doctoral thesis, Zizioulas quoted A. Schmemann's description of the rise of the parish as 'one of the most radical changes that ever took place in the Church', a change which, strangely, has remained 'virtually unnoticed'.[102]

Apostolic Succession, Councils and Primacy

In 1974, Zizioulas drew the following analogy.

> '[J]ust as on the anthropological level the Spirit does not create individuals but persons in communion, in the same way ecclesiologically no individualistic isolation of the local community is conceivable in the Spirit. This is shown in the structure of the Church in two ways: (a) by a communion in time through Apostolic Succession, and (b) by a communion in space through conciliarity.'[103]

---

[99]*DPE*, pp. 97-98.
[100]*EEE*, p. 39.
[101]*BC*, p. 250.
[102]*UC*, p. 25, n. 70; cf. A. Schmemann, 'Towards a Theology of Councils', p. 177.
[103]*PDC*, p. 149.

Focusing on communion in space,[104] we may note that there is a tension in this analogy because, whereas Zizioulas recognises the unity of persons in the local church as the many forming a differentiated unity-of-complementarity around the one in their midst who holds them apart in unity,[105] he describes the unity of local churches as a coincident, or overlapping, unity-of-identity.[106] This latter description dates from 1969.[107] We shall see that Zizioulas has gradually moved towards resolving this tension in the direction of recognising a need for the local churches throughout the world to be configured as a one-many unity around a genuinely primatial local church. How this move qualifies *conciliarity* will become apparent.

Let us follow Zizioulas' movement. In 1969, he said that episcopal collegiality 'does not represent a *collective* unity, but a *unity in identity*'[109] and he made the following reference to the confirmatory practice of the early Church.

> 'The fact that in each episcopal ordination at least two or three bishops from the neighbouring churches ought to take part tied the episcopal office and with it the local eucharistic community in which the ordination to it took place with the rest of the eucharistic communities in the world in a fundamental way.'[109]

He added that this fact 'must have been . . . one of the basic factors in the appearance of episcopal conciliarity',[110] that is, in the coming together of bishops in councils.

---

[104]For Zizioulas on Apostolic Succession, cf. above, p. 191, and below, pp. 262-263; also, P. McPartlan, 'Eucharist and Church: the Contribution of Henri de Lubac', pp. 856-858.

[105]Cf. above, pp. 23-24, 140-143.

[106]Cf. above, p. 170.

[107]For date, see Zizioulas' Full Bibliography of Published Writings, n.8.

[108]*BC*, p. 168.

[109]*Ibid.*, p. 155 (cf. p. 202); reference to Hippolytus, *Apost. Trad.* 2; Council of Arles, c. 20; 1 Nicaea, c. 4 and 6, etc. Zizioulas comments: 'This is a fundamental point which N. Afanasiev has failed in his eucharistic ecclesiology to see and appreciate'; cf. below, p. 227.

[110]*BC*, p. 155.

'[C]onciliarity is born out of the Church's belief that eucharistic communion in a certain community is a matter that concerns all communities in the world.'[111]

Conciliarity, then, expresses a relationship between communities which is reminiscent of that within a corporate personality, where all are implicated in what happens to any particular member. Are we dealing here with a corporate personality? We have seen that true corporate personality demands that there be a specific and stable 'one' at the heart of the configuration, constituted by the many and yet also giving identity to the many.[112] We have also seen that this 'one' must be present *in the same manner* as the many, such that, for instance, the central presence of Christ, the 'one', in the eucharistic gathering is not the eucharistic elements, but the bishop, who stands as a human being among human beings.[113] If Zizioulas were to think that the 'oneness' binding communities/bishops was conciliarity, that is the practice of holding councils, then we could not be dealing with a corporate personality, for 'oneness' in this context must itself be a community/bishop. The following statement shows clearly that he does *not* think that Orthodoxy has replaced oneness in the Pope with oneness in conciliarity.

'The council is not present in Orthodox theology as a substitute for the Roman Catholic Pope, and this for the simple reason that the council cannot play the role of the Pope or replace his ministry.'[114]

A comparison suggests itself: as the gifts are the *currency* for the relationship between Christ-the-one (the bishop) and Christ-the-many (the people) in the Eucharist, so councils are the *currency* for the relationship between the one community/bishop of Rome and the many communities/bishops around the world.

---

[111] *Ibid.*, p. 156, n. 62.
[112] Cf., e.g., above, pp. 177-178.
[113] Cf. above, pp. 197-198.
[114] *BC*, p. 133.

But for this comparison we need *positive* evidence that Zizioulas considers the one primatial community/bishop and the many communities/bishops to be *mutually constitutive*, as the concept of corporate personality demands. Zizioulas has, in fact, provided such evidence with increasing clarity. In 1981, he used canon 34 of the *Apostolic Canons* to derive 'two fundamental principles' opposing a conciliarist understanding of Orthodoxy.

> 'The first principle is that in every province there must be *one* head — an institution of unity. . . . The local bishops/churches can do nothing without the presence of the "one". On the other hand . . . the "one" cannot do anything without the "many".'[115]

With regard to the first principle, he added that there is need for 'the ministry of the πρωτος (the first one)' to express 'the *oneness* of the Church' amidst 'the "many" (the heads of the local churches)'. These comments are rather general. The vital topic of whether the relations between the one and the many are *constitutive* is broached in comment upon the second principle. After the pattern of a 'pneumatologically conditioned Christology', Zizioulas said, we must recognise every 'one' as 'many': 'the multiplicity is not to be subjected to the oneness; it is constitutive of the oneness'.[116]

In 1984, Zizioulas drew attention to the 'mutual interdependence' which canon 34 teaches and he alluded to the question of the one *complementarily* constituting the many by speaking of the 'indispensability' of primacy. The communion of local churches 'does not exclude but necessitates primacy', a primacy which is 'not simply a primacy of honour'.

> 'Nor is the Primus simply *primus inter pares*; there is content in his function . . . you cannot do without him.'[117]

It was in 1988 that Zizioulas most directly asserted the complementary dependence of the many upon the one. Summarising the 'most fundamental principles' of Tradition, he said that

---

[115] *Ibid.*, p. 135. For date, see Zizioulas' Full Bibliography, n. 33.
[116] *Ibid.*, p. 136.
[117] *EOT*, p. 52.

there is 'a ministry of primacy inherent in all forms of conciliarity'.

> 'An ecclesiology of communion, an ecclesiology which gives to the many the right to be themselves, risks being pneumatomonistic if it is not *conditioned* by the ministry of the "one".

> 'The "many" always *need* the "one" in order to express themselves.'[118]

Then, taking the example of 'a patriarch in relation to a synod in the Orthodox Church', he said: 'the many without the one are inconceivable'. 'The *primus* . . . gives its theological status to the synod.'[119]

We may conclude that Zizioulas does consider that local bishops/churches properly align in a one-many configuration. That his thought reaches to a single *worldwide* one and not just to a one in each province is clear from his statements about the need for a *universal* one.

> 'Ecclesial identity must involve . . . (a) a ministry of unity on the local level; (b) a ministry of unity on the universal level.'[120]

This point is also made in the following statement, which is a more recent formulation of the analogy with which we started this section.[121] Since it dates from 1982, amid the clarifications which we have been detailing, the 'just as' and 'in the same way' may be taken to justify the interpolation which I have given in square brackets.

> 'Just as the many individual members of a local church must be united in and through the ministry of the One (the bishop, representing Christ) in the same way the many local churches must be united into one [i.e. in and through one local church] for their Eucharist to be proper ecclesiologically. Ecclesial unity on a universal level is essential for the Eucharist.'[122]

---

[118]*NUS*, p. 344 (my italics).
[119]*IEC*, p. 380; i.e. the *primus* gives to the synod its theological status.
[120]*CIEI*, p. 14; cf. *IEC*, p. 381.
[121]Cf. above, p. 203.
[122]*EPH*, p. 347.

The conclusion from our interpolation would be that the universal ministry exists in order to serve *each local Eucharist*. This conclusion finds confirmation as follows. Zizioulas considers that councils are concerned with the 're-reception' of truth for their own times.[123] As we have seen, the reception and re-reception of conciliar formulation ultimately takes place in the local Eucharist.[124] Zizioulas significantly refers to the need for a 'ministry of universal reception' which will underpin conciliar activity, serving the process of reception and, we may add, thereby serving the local Eucharist. The 'classical model of reception', which he adds is 'not at all out of date', is as follows:

> 'each local church receives the gospel and re-receives it con-stantly through the ministry of the *episkope* acting in commun-ion with the faithful and with the other local churches in conciliar decisions *through a universal ministry*'.[125]

Our suggested comparison between the eucharistic gifts and councils seems justified. As the bishop is the stable centre of the local church, which is regularly active in the giving and receiving of gifts, so the primate is the stable centre of the communion of bishops, which is periodically active in councils.

Zizioulas comments that 'one should not hesitate to seek such a ministry in the Bishop of Rome'.[126] However, we must be clear about the sense in which such a ministry would be 'Petrine'. We have seen Zizioulas approvingly interpreting Cyprian as teaching that Peter and the apostles constitute *one* leadership which presides in each of the *many* local churches.[127] Thus the pope would stand among the bishops not as Peter among the apostles, but as a definitive Peter in his own local

---

[123]Cf. *CWU*, p. 23. Zizioulas uses the example of the Council of Alexandria (362) to maintain that conciliarity is not about the submission of one party to the others but about the re-reception of the truth by all.

[124]Cf. above, p. 199.

[125]*TPR*, pp. 193, 192 (my italics).

[126]*Ibid.*, p. 192.

[127]Cf. above, p. 202.

church, constituting and enabling their manifold presence as Peter in their own local churches, with each local presbyterium representing the apostolic college.[128] Let us recall the characteristic of the one-many configuration which we noted above, namely that, after the pattern of Christ, the bishop may be said to *give* the Spirit to his community, even though he himself receives the Spirit *with* them, because they depend existentially upon him.[129] By now applying this same characteristic to the one-many configuration of local churches worldwide, we see a way of saying, as de Lubac wishes to say, both that jurisdiction is part of the episcopal Ordination which the pope receives like the other bishops, and also that they receive their jurisdiction *from him.*[130]

However, the transition from corporate personality within each local church to corporate personality among the worldwide local churches must be made with caution. Though, as we have seen, Zizioulas certainly appears to favour the transition, he has not clearly indicated *how* it may be made. We stand here on the frontier of his thought, which we shall investigate further in the next chapter. As the prerogative of the 'one' among the 'many', primacy must belong to a bishop among bishops (or, equivalently, to a local church among local churches) and it must also observe all the *reciprocity* of dependence which the essential constitutive mutuality of one-many entails. While we must say that, *within* the local church, the 'many' simply do not exist without 'one' (as there is no Christian without Christ), it does not seem that we can say the same *among* the local churches, for each of them has a certain fulness as the icon of the Kingdom, even though it can never be this in deliberate isolation.[131]

---

[128]Cf. *IEC,* p. 379. Zizioulas comments that these two views are 'entirely different', the first being characteristic of 'a universalist ecclesiology'. Given that Vatican II espoused this picture (e.g. *Lumen Gentium,* n. 22), yet also recognised 'the fulness and catholicity of the local diocese' (e.g. *Lumen Gentium,* n. 26), Zizioulas wonders whether 'the council operated with two ecclesiologies at the same time, one universalist and the other local'.

[129]Cf. above, p. 186.

[130]Cf. above, p. 117.

[131]Cf. *BC,* pp. 156-157, 257.

All the local churches in the worldwide configuration are *identical* as icons of the Kingdom, whereas Christian persons within the local church are utterly differentiated by their charisms. The full number of members of a local church, in all the orders, ought to be present for the Eucharist,[132] but Zizioulas criticises the tendency, in Cyprian's time, to attach importance to the 'great number' of bishops attending councils: 'care for the number [of bishops] . . . represents a clear tendency towards a universal ecclesiology'.[133] While believing that separation from the communion of the local church is precisely the action from which each Christian is discouraged by the principle of 'No salvation outside the Church',[134] with regard to the schismatic separation of local churches themselves from the worldwide communion, Zizioulas admits that it is something 'which, to my knowledge, ecclesiology has not yet explained at all'.[135]

Nevertheless, we have seen that, particularly in recent years, Zizioulas has been increasingly explicit about the necessity of primacy. It is always *rooted*: 'it should be exercised by the head of a local church'. 'This would assure that universal catholicity does not bypass or contradict the catholicity of the local church.'[136] In fact, primacy *underpins* the catholicity of the local church by underpinning its Eucharist. What Zizioulas has written on primacy may be seen as developing the insight of J. J. von Allmen to which he favourably referred in 1974, three years after de Lubac had done likewise, as we have seen.

> '[T]he words of Christ to Peter concerning his particular task in the Church are situated in Luke — and perhaps in the rest of the Gospels — in the context of the Last Supper.'[137]

[132]Cf. above, p. 178, 195.

[133]*DCS*, p. 43. Cf. not *all* other bishops, but only two or three, are required for an episcopal Ordination (above, p. 204).

[134]Cf. above, p. 181.

[135]*GIE*, p. 269.

[136]*TPR*, p. 192.

[137]*BC*, p. 203, n. 115; reference to J. J. von Allmen, 'L'Eglise locale parmi les autres Eglises locales', particularly p. 529f. Cf. above, pp. 114-115, for de Lubac's reference to this insight.

He commented that this point had 'many important implications', perhaps making the Petrine task 'ultimately acceptable to those who hold a eucharistic as well as a historical approach to the continuity of the Church'. At that time, however, his thoughts were still at an early stage, as he acknowledged: 'this requires further elaboration'.[138]

[138]*Ibid.*, p. 203, n. 115.

Chapter 10

Russian Theology

There are three modern theologians with whom Zizioulas engages at some length. All are Russian Orthodox and, being part of the Dispersion, all taught for lengthy periods in Paris.[1] They are Georges Florovsky (1893-1979), Vladimir Lossky (1903-1958) and Nicolas Afanassieff (1893-1966). We shall examine these encounters, and the issues involved in them, in turn. A number of these issues are of prime importance for our overall comparison between Zizioulas and de Lubac, with whom he has not explicitly engaged at length.

Georges Florovsky

'One can evolve the whole body of Orthodox belief out of the Dogma of Chalcedon.'[2]

This statement by Florovsky foreshadows Zizioulas' own focus on the centrality of the Chalcedonian formula[3] and indicates another area of influence upon his student in addition to those we have already noted.[4] One consequence of this statement is the need to associate *ecclesiology* with the Christological kernel of belief. A principle of Florovsky, which

---

[1]Florovsky taught at the Orthodox Institut S. Serge (1925-1948), Lossky at the Ecole des Hautes-Etudes of the Sorbonne (1945-1958) and Afanassieff at S. Serge (1930-1966).
[2]Florovsky, 'Patristic Theology and the Ethos of the Orthodox Church', p. 24.
[3]Cf. above, pp. 150-153.
[4]Cf. above, pp. 126-127, 129-130.

Zizioulas first stated in his doctoral thesis of 1965, is as follows.

'The theology of the Church is but a chapter and a vital [*capital*] chapter of Christology. Without this chapter, Christology itself would be incomplete.'[5]

The second sentence here foreshadows Zizioulas' emphatic assertion in 1974: '*Christ without His body is not Christ but an individual of the worst type*'.[6] However, Zizioulas is clearly saying something much stronger than Florovsky, relating not merely to the incompleteness of Christ-*ology* if we neglect consideration of the fruition of Christ's work in and through the Church, but to the incompleteness of *Christ himself* if the Church is not included as part of his very definition. Zizioulas makes such statements on the two-fold basis of the scriptural constitution of Christ by the Spirit and the scriptural characteristics of the Spirit's work.[7] It is from his understanding of the relationship between Christ and the Spirit that the difference between his ecclesiology and that of Florovsky arises, as he clearly indicates.

'Florovsky indirectly raised the problem of the synthesis between Christology and Pneumatology, without however offering any solution to it. In fact there are reasons to believe that far from suggesting a synthesis, he leaned towards a Christological approach in his ecclesiology.'[8]

Zizioulas' embryonic synthesis of Christology and Pneumatology may be found in his programmatic address of 1966, even though he mentions the Spirit there only once.

'The fundamental character of the Eucharist consists in the fact that it is a gathering [*rassemblement*] and an act and that the *total mystery of Christ*, the whole Christ [*le Christ total*] and the salvation of the world is revealed, lived and concentrated in it.'[9]

In these words, Zizioulas expressed that the whole mystery of God's activity in history bears the name *Christ*. But he did not

[5] *UC*, p. 14, n. 38; quotation from Florovsky, 'Le corps du Christ vivant', p. 12. Cf. *BC*, p. 124; also above, p.xviii.
[6] *BC*, p. 182.
[7] Cf. above, p. 167.
[8] *BC*, p. 124.
[9] *VEM*, p. 85.

thereby exclude the Spirit, for it is the Spirit who empowers *all* of this activity, never from within history but always cutting across history afresh, *penetrating* it with the eschatological mystery of the 'new creation' in Christ, that is with the *totus Christus.*

> 'The eschatological penetration is not a historical development which can be understood logically and by experience; it is a *vertical descent* of the Holy Spirit, by the *epiclesis* — that epiclesis which is so fundamental and so characteristic in the Orthodox liturgy — which transfigures the "present age" and transforms it in Christ into the "new creation".'[10]

Hence, Christians (and indeed the whole new creation) are nothing other than *Christ*, whose differentiated manifestation *is* the Eucharist.[11]

In marked contrast with Zizioulas' assertion of the ever repeated inbreaking of the Holy Spirit, who never enters the channels of history, is the following statement by Florovsky.

> 'The Holy Ghost does not descend upon earth again and again, but abides in the "visible" and historical Church.'[12]

Florovsky often speaks of the Spirit *abiding.*[13] To Zizioulas, such a statement is an unacceptable *historicisation* of the Spirit. Zizioulas affirms that 'every ordination . . . requires the Pentecostal event as its context'.[14] He thereby understands a *new* Pentecostal inbreaking. When Florovsky says that 'the sacramental life of the Church is the continuation of Pentecost', his meaning is quite otherwise. He envisages an historical perpetuation of the *one* Pentecost.

> 'The descent of the Spirit was a supreme revelation. Once and for ever, in the "dreadful and inscrutable mystery" of Pentecost, the Spirit-Comforter enters the world in which he was not yet present in such a manner as now He begins to dwell and abide.

---

[10]*Ibid.*, p. 91.
[11]Cf. *EPH*, p. 335; also above, pp.142-143.
[12]Florovsky, 'The Catholicity of the Church', p. 45.
[13]E.g. *ibid.*, pp. 37, 47. Cf. below, p. 220.
[14]*BC*, p. 185, n. 45. Cf. *EQA*, p. 23, for Pentecost and the Eucharist.

An abundant spring of living water is disclosed on that day, here on earth, in the world which had been already redeemed and reconciled with God by the Crucified and Risen Lord.'[15]

In these sentences, the redemption and reconciliation of the world with God are presented purely as the work of Christ. Florovsky asserts that the 'starting point' for ecclesiology is 'Christ, the God incarnate'. We must take into account 'the total dogma of the Incarnation', that is to say, 'including the glory of the Risen and Ascended Lord, who sitteth on the right hand of the Father'.[16] All of this is thus treated by him as the concern and achievement of Christ himself, which is *then* opened up to others by the Holy Spirit, who comes into history to bridge the gap between believers and Christ. Florovsky admitted the ecclesiological difficulty of integrating the two approaches to the Church which would speak of her as being '*in Christ*' and '*in the Spirit*', respectively. He said: 'one does not see yet quite clearly, how this could and should be done.'[17] However, we may say that an understanding of Christ and the Spirit as being *both* active *in* history only contributes to the difficulty, for it dictates what actually prevents a full integration between the formulae 'in Christ' and 'in the Spirit', namely, the giving of 'precedence, or preference' to one or the other.[18] Florovsky thinks that precedence must be given to the ascended Christ. The Church is his 'continuous presence . . . in the world'.

'The crucial and ultimate problem of Ecclesiology is precisely to describe and explain the mode and character of this "Presence".'[19]

Zizioulas has responded to this challenge with a synthesis which excludes any notion of demarcation between Christ and the Spirit *in* history. The Holy Spirit acts *upon* history, not *in* history, in order to bring to bear upon history its own fulfil-

[15]Florovsky, 'The Church: Her Nature and Task', p. 62.
[16]Florovsky, 'Christ and His Church', p. 165.
[17]*Ibid.*, pp. 163-165.
[18]Cf. *ibid.*, p. 165.
[19]*Ibid.*, p. 168.

ment, that is the *totus Christus,* Christ's historical work brought to its eschatological fulness: '[the Holy Spirit] is the person of the Trinity who actually realises in history that which we call Christ'.[20]

It is significant that, while praising the Christological emphasis in the West of Augustine, whose *totus Christus, caput et corpus* (the whole Christ, head and body) he regarded as a 'glorious phrase',[21] Florovsky focused upon Nicholas Cabasilas as a great exponent of 'the Christological approach or attitude' in the East.[22] Geoffrey Wainwright notes that Cabasilas 'finds no place for the second advent among the mighty acts of Christ which he sees represented by the various ceremonies in the course of the liturgy'. What Cabasilas understands as 'shown forth by the liturgical action' is rather 'the most significant events between the Lord's incarnation and Pentecost'.[23]

Wainwright explicitly contrasts the understanding of Maximus the Confessor, who saw the 'descent of the priest from the sacerdotal throne' after the Gospel as 'the image ($\epsilon i \kappa \omega \nu$) and type ($\tau \upsilon \pi o \varsigma$)' of the End when 'Christ will descend with his angels'. Then, 'with the great entrance of the holy mysteries heaven is entered'.[24] We have seen how indebted to Maximus is Zizioulas in seeing the eucharistic *anamnesis* as the *memory of the future,* such that the whole of God's historical purpose, up to its consummation in the Second Coming, is made present in the Eucharist.[25]

In contrast, Florovsky clearly understands the liturgical *anamnesis* to embrace only the past. In the following quotation, he hails the *anamnesis* for making present and permanently efficacious the salvific acts of Christ in the past, by which he fulfilled the promise of the Old Testament.

[20] *BC,* pp. 110-111.
[21] 'Christ and His Church', p. 163; cf. B. Bobrinskoy, 'Présence réelle et communion eucharistique', p. 413 and n. 44. Florovsky said: 'St Augustine is a Father of the Church universal and we must take his witness in account' ('The Doctrine of the Church and the Ecumenical Problem', p. 156).
[22] *Ibid.,* p. 163: Cabasilas' treatise on the *Life of Christ* is 'admirable'.
[23] G. Wainwright, *Eucharist and Eschatology,* p. 90; reference to Cabasilas, *Liturgiae expositio* (PG 150, 368-492).
[24] *Ibid.,* p. 73.
[25] Cf. above, pp. 149, 189.

'Christians are bound to look back to the mighty events which are the foundation of their faith and hope: Incarnation, Cross and Resurrection, Pentecost. But these individual elements of the past are, at the same time, paradoxically present in the Church here and now. The Incarnation of the Word is at once an historical event of the past which can and should be "remembered" in the ordinary way, and also *an abiding presence* of the Lord which can be directly perceived and recognised at all times and at any particular time by the eye of faith in the Church. This changes radically the meaning and character of *anamnesis* in Christian worship. . . . The accomplishment of the Promise was not just an extra event in the homogeneous sequence of happenings. It was an "event" indeed, but it was an event *which never passes.* . . . The acknowledgement of the Presence is inseparably coupled with the memory of the Past. This paradoxical coincidence of Past and Present constitutes the distinctive and unique characteristic of the Christian "memory", which reaches its culmination in the Eucharistic *anamnesis* or "commemoration". . . . Worshippers are, as it were, *taken back* to the Upper Room and made participants of the same sacred supper.'[26]

Here there is no mention of the future. Florovsky's exclusive emphasis on the presence of the *past* rather than that of the *future* indicates that he sees a sharp distinction between what the past and the future hold. For Florovsky, the *totus Christus* lies *ahead* as the full application of the achievement of the individual Christ, this individual achievement being what stands, ever-effectively, in our past. For Zizioulas, who sees Christ as essentially corporate because of his constitution by the Spirit, the *totus Christus* exists in principle from Christ's very conception, even though its full realisation awaits the last day. Florovsky says of Christ, evidently perceived as an individual (that is, apart from the Church),[27] that the Church is 'the purpose and goal of His "coming down", for us men and for our salvation'.[28]

[26]Florovsky, 'The Worshipping Church', quotation on pp. 28-29 (*Florovsky's* italics).

[27]Cf. above, p. 17, n. 73.

[28]'Christ and His Church', p. 167.

For Zizioulas, the *totus Christus* is what comes down. We have seen the great emphasis which he gives to Christ's teaching in John's gospel that the one who has descended from heaven is the *Son of Man*, that is the *corporate* Christ.[29] Moreover, in every Eucharist it is the same *corporate* Christ who is present, for us to communicate in him. For Florovsky, on the contrary, the Eucharist and indeed all the sacraments are the means by which Christians participate in the past achievement of Christ; all of them 'imply an intimate participation in Christ's death and resurrection and a personal "communion" with him'.[30]

If Christ is always considered to be present from the future, when he will be manifestly corporate, then there is a possibility that it may be perceived that he is *intrinsically* corporate. However, if he is considered to be present *from the past*, as he is so resolutely by Florovsky and de Lubac, then he will be perceived only individually, and the Church will be seen, in a second phase, as 'the extension and the "fulness" of the Holy Incarnation'.[31] Lelouvier likens Florovsky's view to 'the happy formula of Bossuet: "the Church is *Jesus Christ spread abroad and communicated,* . . . Jesus Christ in his fulness"'.[32] We have seen that Bossuet's formula is one of the expressions for the Church most quoted by de Lubac, from his earliest writings.[33]

---

[29]Cf. above, p. 181.

[30]'Christ and His Church', p. 167. In 1923, the Roman Catholic theologian, Maurice de la Taille published in Paris a monumental tome in which he explained the ultimate meaning (*res tantum*) of all the sacraments as union with Christ in his Passion (*Mysterium Fidei de Augustissimo Corporis et Sanguinis Christi Sacrificio atque Sacramento*, p. 581, n. 1). Therefore, all the other sacraments are 'either a preparation for the Eucharist, or a safeguard of the eucharistic life in us' (De la Taille, *The Mystery of Faith and Human Opinion Contrasted and Defined*, p. 30).

[31]'The Church: Her Nature and Task', p. 64.

[32]Y. N. Lelouvier, *Perspectives russes sur l'Eglise. Un théologien contemporain: Georges Florovsky*, p. 64. Lelouvier gives the quotation as from Bossuet, *Lettre à une demoiselle de Metz* (Ed.Lachat, vol. 27), p. 310.

[33]Cf. above, p. 60. It is notable that Florovsky and de Lubac wrote on the *catholicity* of the Church at around the same time. Florovsky's paper, 'The Catholicity of the Church', first appeared in 1934; de Lubac's book, *Catholicism*, was first published in 1938, but was based on talks given from 1932 onwards.

The fact that Zizioulas never actually uses the Latin phrase, *totus Christus*, so favoured by Florovsky and de Lubac, is perhaps explained by the fact that both of these latter theologians apply the Augustinian term to an understanding of Christ's *own* saving work as the Mystery in which human beings *then* participate as his Body. De Lubac refers to the *totus Christus* as 'the end . . . of the mystery',[34] whereas Zizioulas insists on a *simultaneity* of the Head and the Body:

> 'the mystery of the Church is essentially none other than that of the "One" who is simultaneously "many" — not "One" who exists first of all as "One" and *then* as "many", but "One" and "many" at the same time'.[35]

De Lubac's understanding that the Christ-event rises from its achievement in history in order to overarch the whole of history, ever-effectively,[36] corresponds closely with Florovsky's teaching that the 'sacramental *anamnesis*' means that 'each Eucharistic celebration is actually *the Last Supper* itself'.[37] There is no duplication or repetition involved, but rather a continuous access to one historical saving mystery of perennial relevance. By means of the sacramental *anamnesis*, 'worshippers' have 'an actual and immediate encounter . . . with the ever abiding Lord'. Thereby disclosed is the 'ultimate mystery of Christian existence', which Florovsky immediately specifies by saying: 'The Body is never separated from the Head.'[38] Zizioulas is concerned to emphasise that neither is the Head ever separated from the Body and to show that this *mutual* dependence is the ultimate mystery which the Eucharist discloses.

Like de Lubac, Florovsky expresses the one-way dependence of Christians on Christ in terms of Christ *indwelling* each member of his Body,[39] and it is presumably Christ's coming

---

[34] *CMys*, p. 34.
[35] *BC*, p. 112.
[36] Cf. above, p. 63.
[37] Cf. above, p. 217.
[38] 'The Worshipping Church', pp. 29-30.
[39] Cf. *ibid.*, p. 30: the Body of Christ is 'a corporation of them who dwell in him and in whom Christ himself is dwelling and abiding'. For de Lubac, cf. above, pp. 19, 52-53, 60-61.

progressively to indwell his members that Florovsky is envisaging when he says that 'the ultimate is being realised within the stress of historical happenings and events'.[40] The 'ultimate' here is the Church '*in statu patríae*',[41] that is, the 'Bride'[42] who is 'still *in statu viae*'.[43] She is the '*eschatological*' reality of which Florovsky says the following.

> 'What is "not of this world" is here "in this world", not abolishing this world, but giving it a new meaning and a new value, "transvaluating" the world, as it were.'[44]

Underpinning this vision of Florovsky is his conviction that 'the Spirit abides in the Church'.[45] Zizioulas' view is quite different. The Spirit does not abide in the Church from the past, but rather breaks upon her historical life from the future. Accordingly, eschatological reality does not drive history continually from within, but rather draws it from without in dialectical encounters:

> 'it confronts history already now with a *presence from beyond history* . . . [the] *presence* of the Kingdom here and now.'[46]

For Zizioulas, as we have seen, this confrontation occurs in the eucharistic event and makes of each Eucharist Jerusalem in its entirety.[47] With his historicisation of the Spirit, on the contrary, Florovsky seems to understand the Church as the extension of the one historical Jerusalem, such that any particular church can only be a *part* of the great gathering. He says that, having descended at Pentecost, the Spirit then abides in the Church.[48] Through the bishops, Pentecost is extended to

---

[40]'The Church: Her Nature and Task', p. 68.

[41]*Ibid.*, p. 68; reference to Augustine, *In Joann.* 124, 5 (PL 35, 1974; corrected reference). The terminology actually used by Augustine in this passage is as follows. '*Duas itaque vitas . . . novit Ecclesia . . . una in via, altera in patria. . . .*'

[42]Cf. *ibid.*, footnote 19 (p. 123) to p. 67.

[43]Cf. above, n. 41.

[44]'The Church: Her Nature and Task', p. 68.

[45]*Ibid.*, p. 68.

[46]*BC*, p. 174, n. 11.

[47]Cf. above, p. 201.

[48]Cf. above, p. 214.

gather the whole Church into a unity of 'incorporation' into 'the *Apostolic* community'.[49]

> 'In the episcopacy Pentecost becomes universal and continuous. . . . The Apostolic Succession is not so much the canonical as the mystical foundation of Church unity.[50]

In this remarkable last sentence, Apostolic Succession occupies the role which both de Lubac and Zizioulas would certainly attribute to the Eucharist. Florovsky would effectively be making the same point if he then stipulated that the bishops are the primary eucharistic celebrants, but this he emphatically does not; for him, the Eucharist is not the bishop's direct concern. Florovsky distinguishes the priest's office from the 'higher' office of the bishop, which in itself secures 'the universal and catholic unity of the whole Church in space and time'. The priest celebrates the Eucharist: 'it is as the celebrant of the Eucharist that the priest is the minister and builder of Church unity'. But the bishop has 'a power of sacramental action beyond that possessed by the priest', for he can *ordain* the priests who then celebrate the Eucharist; thus, 'the bishop as "ordainer" is the builder of Church unity on a wider scale'. The priest's concern is with the sacrament of the Last Supper, the bishop's is with the sacrament of Pentecost and these two sacraments 'cannot be merged into one another'.[51]

De Lubac's early assertion that '[o]ur churches are the "upper room" where not only is the Last Supper renewed but Pentecost also'[52] stands as a firm rejection of any such attempt to envisage the bishop as someone *above* the Eucharist, uniting the Church in a way *independent* of the Eucharist. However, in that he still looks *backwards* in the Eucharist, the Christ who is present there is still understood *as an individual.*

---

[49]'The Church: Her Nature and Task', p. 59.
[50]*Ibid.*, p. 66.
[51]*Ibid.*, p. 66.
[52]*Catholicism*, p. 48. Cf. also above, pp. 101-102.

Vladimir Lossky

Lossky was the first to respond to Florovsky's call in 1936 'to restore in ourselves *the patristic spirit*'.[53] With reference to Lossky's *Essai sur la Théologie Mystique de l'Eglise d'Orient*, which appeared in 1944, Lelouvier says: 'Florovsky could only congratulate Lossky . . . for having attempted in the West the first Eastern theological synthesis entirely drawn from Byzantine tradition and free from Latin influences'.[54] Rowan Williams notes Lossky's debt to Florovsky,[55] but also his distinctiveness.

> 'Generally, Florovsky is far closer than Lossky to the *ipsissima verba patrum*, less willing to revise or extend patristic concepts: Lossky appears as the more original mind of the two.'[56]

There is one topic in particular which manifests Lossky's originality. With regard to the problem 'indirectly raised' by Florovsky, namely that of a synthesis between Christology and Pneumatology, Zizioulas says that Lossky was 'the Orthodox theologian who was destined to exercise the greatest influence on this subject in our time'.[57] Lossky tackled this problem by means of the distinction, so characteristic of his theology, between nature and person. He said:

> 'The work of Christ concerns human nature which He recapitulates in His hypostasis. The work of the Holy Spirit, on the other hand, concerns persons, being applied to each one singly. . . . The one [Christ] lends His hypostasis to the nature, the other gives His divinity to the persons.'[58]

By comparing Lossky's next statement with one by Zizioulas we can begin to perceive the difference between them. Lossky adds:

---

[53]Cf. above, p. 130.

[54]Lelouvier, *Perspectives russes sur l'Eglise*, p. 35.

[55]R. Williams, *The Theology of Vladimir Nikolaievich Lossky: An Exposition and Critique*, p. 281.

[56]*Ibid.*, p. viii.

[57]*BC*, p. 124.

[58]Lossky, *The Mystical Theology of the Eastern Church* (hereafter, *Mystical Theology*), pp. 166-167.

'Thus, the work of Christ unifies; the work of the Holy Spirit diversifies.'[59]

Zizioulas' understanding *seems* to be the same, when he says that the Eucharist has a '*Christological* aspect', in that it '*unifies*' the Church 'by uniting all the ministries "in common"', and also a '*Pneumatological* aspect', in that it '*diversifies*' the Church 'by creating orders and ministries which cannot substitute one for another'.[60] However, the fact that Zizioulas speaks of *aspects*, as of two sides of the same coin, marks a difference, for here the Christological and the Pneumatological exactly *coincide*, though in a differentiated manner: the Holy Spirit forms and Christ is what is formed. Hence he can say, not just with Lossky that Christ unites and the Holy Spirit diversifies or divides, but that the Holy Spirit *both* unites and divides.

'the Holy Spirit is not only a power which unites, but also a power which "divides".... The Holy Spirit unites precisely when He divides.'[61]

The explanation is that the Holy Spirit always forms Christ, and Christ is a differentiated being, a corporate personality, divided in unity and united in division.[62] Whenever the Holy Spirit breaks in the effect is always the same.

Lossky does not share this view of the Spirit's activity, nor of the corporate character of Christ. He considers that there are two *different* comings of the Spirit:

'one was effected by the breath of Christ when He appeared to His apostles on the evening of the day of His resurrection (Jn. 20: 19-23); the other by the personal coming of the Holy Spirit on the day of Pentecost (Acts 2: 1-5).'[63]

---

[59] *Ibid.*, p. 167.

[60] *EFEL*, p. 10: '*D'une part, elle [l'Eucharistie] unifie en réunissant tous les ministères "en commun". D'autre part, elle diversifie, en créant des ordres et des ministères dont aucun ne peut remplacer un autre. Dans le premier cas, nous pouvons parler d'un aspect christologique de l'Eucharistie, dans le second d'un aspect pneumatologique ou charismatique.*'

[61] *GIE*, p. 259.

[62] Cf. *OAS*, p. 35: 'the Church through ordination is "united in division" — *sundiairoumene*: St Maximus the Confessor'. Also, *BC*, p. 220.

[63] *Mystical Theology*, p. 167.

In this statement, Lossky is doubly distancing himself from the West. First, he says that there would be no distinction between these two comings 'did not the Eastern Church acknowledge the independence (as to His eternal origin) of the hypostasis of the Holy Spirit in relation to the Son',[64] so he is implicitly rejecting the Western *Filioque*. Then, secondly, whereas de Lubac would consider that Pentecost brings the *incarnate Christ* personally to birth in Christians, in whom he then abides, this being his justification for considering the Church as the Incarnation continued,[65] Lossky states that Pentecost brings the *Holy Spirit* (and hence the Trinity) personally to dwell within Christians and that statements linking the Church to the Incarnation will have to be changed accordingly.

> 'Pentecost is not a "continuation" of the Incarnation. It is its sequel, its result. The creature has become fit to receive the Holy Spirit and He descends into the world and fills with His presence the Church which has been redeemed, washed and purified by the blood of Christ.'[66]

Christ having done *his* work on the stage of history, the Holy Spirit enters upon the same stage. Indeed Lossky refers to 'The Economy of the Son' and 'The Economy of the Spirit'.[67]

His objection to the view which de Lubac has of the Church is something that Lossky made quite explicit.

> '[T]o see in the Church solely "an extension of the Incarnation", a continuation of the work of Christ, as is so often stated, is to forget Pentecost and to reduce the work of the Holy Spirit to a subordinate role, that of an emissary of Christ, a liaison between the Head and the members of the Body.'[68]

He explained the dangers he saw in such a role for the Holy Spirit in a highly significant form. If the Spirit is just the bond of union between Christ and human persons, then 'either they

---

[64] *Ibid.*, p. 169.
[65] Cf. above, pp. 60-61.
[66] *Mystical Theology*, p. 159; cf. pp. 168-171.
[67] These are the titles of the seventh and eighth chapters, respectively, of *Mystical Theology*. See p. 155 for the transition between the two.
[68] Lossky, *In the Image and Likeness of God*, p. 177.

would be annihilated in being united to the Person of Christ, or else the Person of Christ would be imposed upon them from without', thereby compromising the 'freedom' with which Christians in fact acknowledge him.[69] The former danger possibly threatens de Lubac;[70] the latter danger is a vivid anticipation of the concern of Zizioulas for *freedom*.[71]

Zizioulas thinks that the Person of Christ is an objective provocation to freedom unless Christ is recognised as being *corporate*, such that he is acknowledged *from within*.[72] However, Lossky maintains that our freedom is preserved by means of the indwelling Spirit manifesting to us 'the Deity of the Son' which we can then freely acknowledge.[73] In that Christ still remains a distinct, objective reality here, Zizioulas would not accept that freedom is preserved in Lossky's scheme. Indeed, while praising Lossky for making 'contemporary theology more conscious of the importance of Pneumatology', Zizioulas criticises his stress on the *Filioque* as '*the* crucial problem between the East and the West',[74] and generally thinks that Lossky's approach renders the synthesis of Christology and Pneumatology 'so difficult that it must be abandoned'.[75] Zizioulas implies that the idea of an 'economy of the Spirit' is an overreaction to the view of the Spirit as just a 'satellite' of the 'self-defined' Christ-event and he adds that it makes it hard to

---

[69] *Mystical Theology*, pp. 169-170.

[70] Cf. D. Brown, *Continental Philosophy and Modern Theology*, p. 188. Brown recalls the belief of Teilhard de Chardin that we must be transformed into Christ, because 'in a real sense, only one man will be saved: Christ, the head and living summary of humanity' (*Le milieu divin*, p. 136), and he comments of Teilhard: 'one laments his failure to pursue further his own claim that personal identity can be preserved in such a union'. We may compare de Lubac's repeated quotation from Augustine, *In ps.* 26, 2, 23 (PL 36, 211): '*Erit unus Christus, amans seipsum*' (*Catholicism*, pp. 53, 177; cf. *RTeil*, p. 159).

[71] Cf. e.g. above, pp. 146-150. Zizioulas presents the first step (cf. the first leavening) towards preserving God's freedom as that of distinguished the uncreated God from His creation. Lossky also emphasises this primordial distinction (*Mystical Theology*, p. 88).

[72] Cf. above, p. 189; below, pp. 242-243.

[73] *Mystical Theology*, p. 170.

[74] *DGT*, p. 20. Cf. above, pp. 125-126, 157-158, 164.

[75] *BC*, p. 125.

understand 'the biblical assertion that the Church is the Body of Christ, and not of the Spirit'.[76]

The economy, says Zizioulas, 'in so far as it assumed history and has a history, is *only one* and that is the *Christ event*'.[77] However, the Christ-event here is emphatically not 'self-defined' by Christ himself. On the contrary, in the Spirit, the Church is part of his definition.[78] The Spirit's one unchanging activity has been, we may say, first, to make Christ the Church and now to make the Church Christ. In Lossky's vision, the two phases of salvation are marked by a different presence of the Spirit, 'functional' and 'personal', respectively,[79] such that it can be said of the Spirit that, in the Kingdom, 'the multitude of the saints will be His image'.[80] In Zizioulas' distinctive synthesis, the multitude of the saints is simply *the corporate Christ*.[81]

Nicolas Afanassieff

Afanassieff coined the term 'eucharistic ecclesiology'[82] for the understanding of the Church which flows from his basic principle: 'where there is a eucharistic assembly, there Christ abides, and there is the Church of God in Christ'.[83] Zizioulas

[76] *PDC*, p. 144; cf. *ORT*, p. 8.

[77] *BC*, p. 130.

[78] Cf. above, pp. 166-167.

[79] Cf. *Mystical Theology*, p. 167. O. Clément notes Lossky's eventual preference (in lectures of 1956) for 'one Logo-Pneumatic economy', instead of two economies (*Orient-Occident. Deux passeurs: Vladimir Lossky et Paul Evdokimov*, pp. 48, 63).

[80] *Ibid.*, p. 173.

[81] Cf. above, p. 167. Likewise, whereas Lossky rejects Congar's assertion that 'the catholicity of her head is the principle of the catholicity of the Church', so as to maintain the distinct role of the coming of the Holy Spirit at Pentecost (*In the Image and Likeness of God*, pp. 176-177), Zizioulas firmly states that 'it is *Christ's* unity and it is *his* catholicity that the Church reveals in her being catholic' (*BC*, p. 159).

[82] Cf. Afanassieff, 'Réflexions d'un orthodoxe sur la collégialité des évêques', p. 15.

[83] Afanassieff, 'Una Sancta', p. 459. Zizioulas refers to this article in *UC*, pp. 17, 197; *BC*, p. 155; *EPH*, p. 339.

quotes this principle in an abbreviated form, 'wherever the Eucharist is celebrated there is the Church',[84] and comments that, in itself, it is 'an authentically Orthodox theological principle'.[85] However, he considers that Afanassieff's ecclesiology tends towards the narrow view that 'it is sufficient to "celebrate" the Eucharist for there to be the Church', a view which simply reverses the unilateralism of the scholastics and risks finding no place for such traditional elements of the Church as the profession of true faith and repentance for sins.[86]

Since Zizioulas associates the safeguarding of these latter two elements with local churches' mutual relations in councils[87] and with the ministry of presbyters,[88] respectively, we may anticipate two of his specific criticisms of Afanassieff's eucharistic ecclesiology. First, he says that it 'would lead to the conclusion that each local church celebrating the Eucharist is a full church regardless of its unity with the other churches'.[89] We recall that, as an icon of the Kingdom, the local church *coincides* with other local churches across time and space.[90] Its identity as an icon of the Kingdom depends not only upon its internal composition but also upon its manifestation of this *coincidence* by apostolic succession and conciliarity.[91] Zizioulas is particularly critical of Afanassieff's failure to heed the manifestation of this fact in the canonical manner of episcopal Ordination, by two or three neighbouring bishops.[92] Secondly, Zizioulas complains that Afanassieff's principle envisages 'the

---

[84]*EOT*, p. 44; cf. *BC*, p. 24; *EPH*, p. 339; *ORT*, pp. 2, 8.

[85]*ORT*, p. 2. For a detailed study of Afanassieff's theology and its context, cf. Aidan Nichols, *Theology in the Russian Diaspora: Church, Fathers, Eucharist in Nikolai Afanas'ev, 1893-1966*.

[86]*Ibid.*, p. 8; cf. above, p. xvii. In *UC*, p. 198, Zizioulas says that 'the extreme elevation' of Afanassieff's principle leads to the antithesis which Rudolph Sohm introduced between religion ($\theta\rho\eta\sigma\kappa\epsilon\dot{\iota}\alpha$) and law ($\delta\dot{\iota}\kappa\alpha\iota o\nu$).

[87]Cf. above, p. 208.

[88]Cf. above, pp. 199-200.

[89]*EOT*, pp. 50-51; *BC*, pp. 24-25. Cf. above, pp. 203, 209.

[90]Cf. above, p. 170.

[91]Cf. above, p. 203.

[92]Cf. above, p. 204, n. 109.

parish where the Eucharist takes place as a complete and "catholic" Church' even though it structurally lacks some of the ministries required for 'catholicity'.[93]

Thus, Zizioulas alleges that Afanassieff's principle leads to a neglect of structures both between and within local churches. Zizioulas himself does not investigate a possible link between these two dangers; however, following our study of Florovsky and Lossky, which indicated that both of them consider Christ *as an individual,* we may perceive one. Since it is a link which focuses on the very section of Afanassieff's principle that Zizioulas habitually omits when he presents it,[94] it is perhaps a link that Zizioulas himself has not fully appreciated. Afanassieff progresses from the Eucharist to the Church via an intermediate, bridging term: where there is a eucharistic assembly, *there Christ abides,* and there is the Church of God in Christ and, moreover, it is 'in the eucharistic gifts' that Christ abides.[95] Zizioulas himself would feel unable to distinguish such a middle term, he would say: wherever there is a eucharistic assembly, there abides Christ surrounded by the Saints, that is Christ and the Church, the corporate Christ. He would not envisage any *progression* from Christ himself to the corporate Christ, as occurs in the full principle of Afanassieff, because for Zizioulas Christ is corporate from the outset.

Since, as Zizioulas does note, a concentration on what happens objectively to the eucharistic elements is characteristic of scholasticism,[96] we may now say that such a focus characterises *both* of the unilateralisms which he rejects. Moreover, it is also characteristic of de Lubac, who attempts to overcome both unilateralisms *sequentially,* by saying that the Church makes the Eucharist which *in its turn* makes the Church,[97] because for him, as we have seen, the sequence passes through the eucharistic elements.[98] It is because he regards the Eucha-

---

[93] *BC,* p. 24. Cf. above, p. 203; also, pp. 104-105.

[94] Cf. above, pp. 226-227.

[95] Afanassieff, 'L'Eucharistie, principal lien entre les Catholiques et les Orthodoxes', p. 338.

[96] Cf. *ENO,* pp. 166-169.

[97] Cf. above, pp. xv, xvi-xvii.

[98] Cf. above, pp. 79-80, 103-104.

rist not primarily as the elements but as the gathered local church[99] that Zizioulas is able decisively to overcome the unilateralisms by *integrating* the two halves of de Lubac's double principle.[100]

Thus, it would seem that Afanassieff, too, is operating with an understanding of Christ as an individual who *then* becomes corporate. We have seen in our study of de Lubac's similar understanding[101] that an individual Christ who then becomes corporate does so in an *atomistic* way, that is by entering identically into each of his faithful and assimilating them individually to himself; they are *identically* Christ rather than *differentiatedly* Christ. The latter is Zizioulas' vision of the local church,[102] but we may now go on to see that the former is that of Afanassieff. We shall then turn to relations *between* local churches.

With regard to the early centuries, Afanassieff says: 'no church could live without its *proestos*'.[103] O. Rousseau notes that Afanassieff 'retains untranslated certain terms such as *proestos, proïstamenos* to signify the president of the assembly without wishing to determine them particularly'.[104] Afanassieff says that the following is the 'chief postulate' of eucharistic ecclesiology: 'there can be no local church without the ministry of the *proestos*'.[105] However, Afanassieff asserts that the *proestos* was no more specifically *priestly* than each and every one of the community: 'all were priests there and there were no priests who were such by a special title'. '[W]hat differentiated them [the *proestotes*] was not the sacerdotal charism, granted by God to each member of the Church, but that of *proestos*.'[106] The prime characteristic of Christians is that, while there are other specific gifts given to some, *all* are priests. Moreover, since it is 'as [a] priest' that each serves 'God, his Father',[107] we may say

---

[99]Cf. above, pp. 72, 133, 197-198.
[100]Cf. above, pp. xvi-xvii.
[101]Cf. e.g., above, pp. 60-66.
[102]Cf. above, pp. 140, 142, 223.
[103]Afanassieff, *L'Egise du Saint-Esprit* (hereafter, *L'Eglise*), p. 192.
[104]O. Rousseau in the preface to *L'Eglise*, p. 11.
[105]*L'Eglise*, p. 196.
[106]*Ibid.*, p. 197.
[107]*Ibid.*, p. 197.

that it is as a *priest* that each is most configured to Christ. It is, then, most significant to note that, for Afanassieff, all are priests *equally, undifferentiatedly.* At the level of this most intimate relationship with Christ, Afanassieff denies that there was any articulation of the local church into one and many, that is, into ministerial priesthood and common priesthood.

Paul omits ministerial priesthood from his lists of specific ministries, because, says Afanassieff, it is 'the common ministry of the People of God'. It 'culminates in Christ' who is the one and only 'High Priest'; no earthly minister is accorded the title High Priest in 'apostolic times'. In his own concrete community, the *proestos* is truly their *pastor,* but not their High Priest, because in their eucharistic assembly 'the fulness of the Church is manifested . . . and the whole Church officiates through the intermediary of the High Priest who is Christ'.[108] Afanassieff thus has no notion of a mystical identification between the concrete community around the bishop and the whole Church around Christ. Originally, precisely *as proestos,* the *proestos* had the sacerdotal task of merely *manifesting* 'the sacerdotal ministry of the people in the course of the eucharistic assembly'.[109] As it were, he emerged from the people so as to stand 'before God at the head of the people',[110] absolutely like them in that prime gauge of Christ-likeness, namely priesthood. To borrow a term from the parallel which Afanassieff sets up and to which we shall shortly turn, in terms of priesthood, the *proestos* has simply a *priority* in the midst of the community, all of whom equally are priests.

Afanassieff considers that Ignatius of Antioch was the first to attribute the dignity of High Priesthood to the *proestos,* that is to the bishop. He has a priestly ministry not shared with others but proper to himself. In contrast with the priestly aspect of the New Testament *proestos,* the ministry of the Ignatian bishop 'was proper to him, it had ceased to be a function of the ministry of the presbyters and of that of the people'.[111]

[108] *Ibid.,* pp. 304-306.
[109] *Ibid.,* p. 324; cf. p. 300.
[110] *Ibid.,* p. 196.
[111] *Ibid.,* p. 308.

Afanassieff criticises the 'doctrine of consecration', which scholastic theology pressed further and which regarded the bishop, presbyter and deacon as having not just 'higher degrees' of the common priesthood of the people but a distinct consecration. This doctrine, he says, isolated these higher orders and obscured the idea of a common priesthood 'which was already weakened by the formation of higher degrees of the priesthood'.[112] Apparent in these comments is Afanassieff's conviction that the *unity* of the people depends on the *sameness* of their priesthood. This is an *atomistic* unity; all are one because all are the same. Differentiation isolates and divides.

Quite other is Zizioulas' view of the community as 'united in division' through ordination,[113] that is, as a necessarily differentiated manifestation of Christ. He complains that, 'in spite of his eucharistic ecclesiology', Afanassieff 'has not managed to escape from the dilemma between "ontological" and "functional"' understandings of ministry in the Church.[114] We have seen Zizioulas' view that only an ontology in which being is communion rises above this dilemma; we experience such an ontology in the eucharistic community.[115] In the article which Zizioulas is here criticising, Afanassieff describes a *twofold* work of the Spirit: 'we enter into the Church by the Spirit and we are her members of the Spirit'. The Spirit imparts a unity and a diversity. But, crucially, it is not a unity-in-diversity but a primary unity *underlying* a secondary diversity.

> 'Neither the diversity of gifts, nor the diversity of ministries destroys the ontological unity, because the diversity within the Body is not of an ontological nature but of a functional nature.'[116]

Unity within the local church comes from the ontological priesthood that all have identically in common. Only at the secondary, functional level is there complementarity.

---

[112] *Ibid.*, pp. 300-301.

[113] Cf. above, p. 223.

[114] *EQA*, p. 48, n. 37, with reference to Afanassieff, 'L'Eglise de Dieu dans le Christ', p. 19. Cf. *BC*, p. 226.

[115] Cf. above, pp. 178-179; below, pp. 275-276.

[116] Afanassieff, 'L'Eglise de Dieu dans le Christ', p. 19.

The parallel to which we referred above, is that which Afanassieff sets up by likening the regrettable emergence of the bishop as something *different* (not identically a priest with the others) within the communion of the local church to the emergence of the metropolitans and ultimately of the patriarchs as something different (not identically bishops with the others) in the communion of churches.[117] As before *within,* so here *between* the local churches, his implication is that differentiation harms unity whereas sameness secures it.

Afanassieff stresses the fulness of the local church, in contrast with 'universal ecclesiology', which, he says, sees the local churches as *parts* of the Church.

> 'The Eucharist is where Christ dwells in the fulness of His Body: the Eucharist could never have been offered in a local church if it had been no more than one part of the Church of God. Where the Eucharist is, there is the fulness of the Church.'[118]

Since all the churches are 'indwelt by the Church of God', their unity is something 'absolutely *sui generis*'.

> '[T]he unity was not the result of separate parts reuniting, but it was the unity of one and the same Church. Each local church united in itself all the local churches because it possessed all the fulness of the Church of God, and all the local churches together were united, because they were always this same Church of God.'[119]

There is a profound sameness of local churches conveyed by these words of Afanassieff. Nevertheless, he does think that within this communion of like churches, there was and must be a church which takes *priority* in witness to the Church and to the churches. Its witness 'has a sovereign value'; 'this church holds a two-fold priority, of authority and love, which means it makes a sacrificial gift of itself to the others'.[120] Afanassieff is careful to distinguish *priority,* which claims no power over other churches, from *primacy.* As we saw earlier, he maintains that

---

[117] *L'Eglise*, pp. 301-302; cf. above, p.230.
[118] Afanassieff, 'The Church which presides in love', p. 76.
[119] *Ibid.*, p. 78.
[120] *Ibid.*, p. 79.

'either concept almost excludes the other',[121] and finds a prime example of the exercise of such a *priority* in the letter of Clement of Rome, in which the church of Rome was not 'laying down the law' but bearing witness to the unacceptability of the actions of the church of Corinth in the Church of God.[122]

Afanassieff states that 'the foundations of universal ecclesiology were formulated for the first time by Cyprian of Carthage'. Such an ecclesiology attributes the 'fulness of ecclesial *esse*' no longer to the local churches, one of which has a priority, but to the universal (i.e. worldwide) Church, one of whose bishops necessarily exercises primacy, that is 'a unique, personal power founded on rights'.[123] Zizioulas repeatedly refutes this allegation of Afanassieff against Cyprian, on the grounds that Cyprian maintained that each bishop was directly responsible to God for his own community.[124]

However, Zizioulas does not bring fully to light the real issue, which is that of whether being equally answerable vertically to God for their own churches precludes the bishops from having in their midst one whose horizontal role is truly unique and personal. It would seem that Afanassieff cannot conceive of a way in which these two realities might be compatible; for him there can be no primacy with a unique and personal role within a communion of full local churches, there can only be a priority. The compatibility of these two realities is an extremely important insight of Zizioulas, who, as we saw in the last chapter, considers that the one-many configuration applies not only *within* but also *among* local churches in the world.[125] Each church is equally full in itself but they all depend upon this configuration in order to be fully themselves. Their unity derives not from their sameness but from their existence in this differentiated configuration.

---

[121]*Ibid.*, p. 81; cf. above, p. 119.

[122]*Ibid.*., p. 92.

[123]*Ibid.*, pp. 107-109.

[124]*BC*, pp. 155-156; 200-201; cf. above, p. 202. We have already seen de Lubac's objection to Afanassieff's interpretation of Cyprian; above, pp. 106-107.

[125]Cf. above, pp. 204-211.

It was clear that this insight is one which Zizioulas is still striving to articulate adequately. This perhaps explains why the content of Zizioulas' responses to Afanassieff sometimes fails to bear out the evident conviction with which the responses are made. This insight is the key to distinguishing the ecclesiology of Zizioulas from that of Afanassieff. It rests upon the notion of corporate personality, which Zizioulas regards as a motif running through the whole of Christianity, from its heart which is the *corporate* Christ. No one more than Afanassieff serves to highlight the practical implications of this motif in the ecclesiology which Zizioulas has elaborated.

We may end by explicitly applying this Zizioulan insight to some otherwise puzzling points of encounter between himself and Afanassieff. Zizioulas suggests that Afanassieff's view of the fulness of the local church does not heed the necessary unity between the churches, but implies rather their independence.[126] In fact Afanassieff approvingly describes the situation in the early Church as one in which the local church 'could not live apart from the other churches' and 'could not shut itself in or refuse to be acquainted with happenings in other churches'.[127] Zizioulas' real objection is, perhaps, that the necessary unity between the churches is a *differentiated* one and not just one of utter sameness in which all indwell each.

Similarly, Afanassieff's assertion that, in ecclesiology, 'one plus one is still *one*',[128] which seems to be just an alternative to Zizioulas' description of local churches as '*full circles* which cannot be added to one another but *coincide* with one another',[129] is in fact an assertion of an undifferentiated oneness which we have seen Zizioulas does not accept. Zizioulas' differentiated oneness distinguishes local churches as a one-many worldwide configuration, which *is* the *universal* Church. The necessity of each local church being in this configuration in order to be itself is, perhaps, what Zizioulas is fundamentally

---

[126]Cf. above, p. 227.
[127]'The Church which presides in love', p. 78.
[128]*Ibid.*, p. 75.
[129]*BC*, p. 158, n. 66. Cf. above, p. 170.

expressing when he complains that Afanassieff only deepens the division between the local church and the universal Church, when 'eucharistic ecclesiology must be able to overcome this division'.[130]

---

[130]*ORT*, pp. 8-9. Zizioulas regards 'local versus universal' as a 'false dilemma' which other Orthodox theologians, such as Meyendorff, also 'perpetuate' (*BC*, p. 202, n. 112).

Part Three

Dialogue

Chapter 11

Beginning and End

'I did not ask to be born.'[1]

'[W]ho consulted me when I was brought into the world?'[2]

In these strikingly similar ways, de Lubac and Zizioulas, respectively, express the rebellion in man which they, with their marked existential emphasis, are concerned to address as theologians. For Zizioulas, it is a rebellion against the givenness of one's own existence, that is, against 'the ontological necessity which exists in the biological hypostasis'.[3] *Freedom* is what man seeks, but 'how can a man be considered absolutely free when he cannot do other than accept his existence?'[4] For de Lubac, the rebellion is more specifically against the givenness of a moral code inscribed in man's conscience and the givenness of God on whom man's creaturely existence depends.

For both de Lubac and Zizioulas, this objective givenness is something to be overcome, and it is Christ who enables the overcoming. Zizoulas sets Christ in this role when, with admitted *bluntness*, he says that, for a Christian, 'God in himself has no authority'. 'It is *only in Christ* that He becomes authoritative.'[5] Equally bluntly, de Lubac says that if God were to remain

---

[1]De Lubac, *MédPVM*, p. 266, cf. p. 260. Blondel introduced *L'action (1893)* similarly (p. vii).

[2]Zizioulas, *BC*, p. 51, n. 45.

[3]*Ibid.* p. 51, n. 45.

[4]*Ibid.*, p. 42.

[5]*OCA*, p. 163.

only an external, legislating power, 'we would have the right to revolt':

> 'moreover, if I may venture the apparent blasphemy which is directed only at an idol, we ought to curse God'.[6]

In fact, he goes on, we have no right to revolt, because the creaturely dependence in which moral obligation is rooted is actually God's invitation to the freedom of intimacy. With Augustinian allusions, he explains that revolt against God is ultimately 'a revolt against myself', condemning myself to 'something worse than death'.

> 'How can I reject God without, so to speak, emptying me of myself? *Deus interior intimo meo.* "Emancipation" would be the opposite of liberation, because service is the opposite of slavery. *Servire Deo, regnare.*'[7]

Thus, regarding the statements of rebellion with which we started, while for Zizioulas they are simply honest recognitions of the condition in which we are born, that is into the world which Original Sin has collapsed into objects, for de Lubac they indicate a personally sinful *collaboration* with Original Sin. De Lubac maintains that, if we enter into ourselves, we find there 'a certain disorder'.

> 'Deep within us, there is a disharmony which prevents us from feeling in tune with the exigencies of having-to-exist.'[8]

We have the choice, either of rebelling against our existence and so perpetuating the disharmony, or of rejecting the disorder by assenting to our existence. If we do the latter, we begin 'to reestablish harmony in ourselves' and 'only then will we have the right to demand light'. We do, indeed, thereby set out upon a long road, 'but ... perhaps we shall see the dawn already breaking and there will be given to us the presentiment of the state of perfect freedom'.[9] The way to 'freedom properly so

---

[6] *MédPVM*, p. 260.
[7] *Ibid.*, p. 262; cf. above, p. 41.
[8] *Ibid.*, p. 263.
[9] *Ibid.*, pp. 263-264.

called' is by using my free will to ratify, 'at whatever price', the 'natural consent' which I discover in myself 'under the appearance of slavery',[10] but which is really the 'sacred *nisus*' or '*élan*' constituting humanity made in the image of God and inviting each of us to be *like* Him.[11]

Mere obedience to God is not enough, says de Lubac. It keeps me 'under the yoke' and is unworthy 'of Him and of me'.[12] Quoting Gabriel Marcel, de Lubac later said that 'each one of us is in a position to recognise that his own essence is a *gift*, that it is not a *datum*'.[13] Accordingly, the assent we give to our existence must be 'a gift, the gift of oneself', 'a return of love'.

> '[T]he more total it is, the more it exalts the personal life of the one who gives himself, divinising and eternalising him.'[14]

In terminology identical to de Lubac's, his friend, de Montcheuil, said that the Christian God is primarily *moral*, calling us to a relationship. Even someone who claimed to accept everything that the Church teaches about God 'would really be an atheist' if God was considered just as One infinitely powerful from whom an egoistical happiness could be obtained by various actions, and not as the 'moral ideal'.[15]

> 'God is not a being who is posited as a fact ... only *then* to discuss His attitude with regard to us.'[16]

The Christian God is only known properly as the giver of the invitation which constitutes our being. Our being does not *precede* this relationship. However, as we have just seen, it is our

[10] *Ibid.*, p. 261.

[11] *Ibid.*, pp. 258-259 and n. 2.

[12] Cf. *ibid.*, p. 261.

[13] *MSup*, p. 100; quotation from G. Marcel, *The Mystery of Being*, vol. 2, 'Faith and Reality' (hereafter, *Mystery*), p. 173. Cf. above, p. 145.

[14] *MédPVM*, p. 259.

[15] De Montcheuil, 'Dieu premièrement moral', p. 44. This text, which dates from the 1920s, remained unpublished until recently.

[16] *Ibid.*, p. 44 (my italics). Lack of a felt moral imperative (cf. *ibid.*, p. 42) is presumably what makes the proofs of God's existence often ultimately ineffective (cf. de Lubac, *Athéisme*, p. 109, and Marcel, *Mystery*, p. 176).

response which determines whether this relationship confers eternal life.

Zizioulas' and de Lubac's different attitudes to the statements of rebellion with which we started this chapter, as honest and sinful, respectively, amount to the same endorsement of an *élan* in man, a drive to freedom in a truly personal existence. For Zizioulas, the statement is a sign of this *élan* at work, whereas for de Lubac it is a sign of the *élan* being renounced. Like de Lubac, Zizioulas thinks that, given the *élan*, rejection of God involves rejection of myself. 'Personhood . . leads to God — or to non-existence.'[17] As we have seen, freedom presents man with two options, 'either to annihilate the "given" or to accept it as *idion thelema*'. However, since creation is God's *thelema* and not man's, man can perform this acceptance 'only by *identifying his own will with that of God*'.[18] De Lubac also stresses that 'everything is explained on the basis of [the] divine Will'[19] and we have seen him assert that mere *obedience* to this will is not adequate. Zizioulas explains his view in remarkably similar terms, with, like de Montcheuil, a keen awareness of the proximity of atheism.

> 'Christianity throughout the centuries has tried to conceive this [identification of wills] in terms of *obedience* of man to God. It has failed because it has been unable to maintain freedom in and through this obedience. Man has felt like a slave and rejected the yoke of God. Atheism sprang out of the very heart of the Church.'[20]

Like de Lubac, Zizioulas recognises that the state of true freedom which we seek can only be attained by a *second gift*: '[it] can only be realised from outside human existence'.[21] He echoes one of the most frequent refrains in de Lubac's writings when he immediately adds: 'the mystery of man reveals itself fully only in the light of Christ'.[22] The second gift is Christ.

---

[17] *HCH*, p. 432.
[18] *Ibid.*, p. 433; cf. above, p. 147.
[19] *MédPVM*, p. 259.
[20] *HCH*, p. 433.
[21] *Ibid.*, p. 433. Cf. above, p.40, n. 83.
[22] *Ibid.*, p. 433; cf. above, p. 12.

However, the different attitudes which Zizioulas and de Lubac have to our opening expressions of rebellion indicate an important difference in their understandings of Christ. It seems that de Lubac rejects the rebellion because the question in which Zizioulas expresses it cannot be answered, at least not directly. I must *first* accept my existence as a *gift*, thereby conforming my will to that of God in creating me.[23] Then my subsequent striving may be blessed with the second gift of being caught up into the sonship of Christ. Zizioulas accepts the question because it *can* be answered. When Christ appears, so do I beside him,[24] to find him is to find myself simultaneously, to embrace him is to embrace myself also, for Christ is *corporate.*

In that de Lubac can only urge us to accept our given existence as a *gift*, we must say that it still remains a *given*. Only a corporate understanding of Christ, such as that of Zizioulas, gives the possibility of truly overcoming our givenness by actually entering into God's *giving* of our existence, for that giving is an intrinsic part of His giving of *Christ*, whom we are free to accept or not.[25] Whereas de Lubac considers that, having first accepted our existence, we may then attain freedom by accepting and begetting the individual Christ, that is, the Son enfleshed,[26] true freedom for Zizioulas must involve our begetting ourselves, as it were, *and this we can do* in begetting Christ, for Christ is *corporate.* Moreover, this is what we do do in the Eucharist, foretasting there the heavenly identity which God has intended for us from all eternity in Christ. Zizioulas would respond, it seems, to the opening rebellious question by saying that, in each Eucharist, *God* consults us about our existence, by offering it to us afresh, for our affirmation, in Christ.

Zizioulas' stance depends explicitly upon a particular view

[23]That this first action on our part is itself effected by God's grace is implicit when de Lubac emphasises that he himelf ought not to be interpreted in a semi-Pelagian fashion (*MédPVM*, p. 264, n. 11).

[24]Cf. Zizioulas' important acceptance of Manson's exegesis of the appearance of the Son of Man to judge, in Matthew's gospel (above, p. 168).

[25]Cf. above, pp. 148-150, with particular reference to n. 23.

[26]Cf. above, p. 53.

of the relationship between history and eschatology and, implicitly, upon a particular understanding of the relationship between Christ and the Spirit. Let us now compare him with de Lubac on these two issues, the latter first.

Christ and the Spirit

In the early article which we have been studying, de Lubac says that the *élan* which constitutes humanity 'drives the whole of creation to reenter for ever . . . into the bosom of the Eternal Trinity'.[27] The only indication he gives of his meaning is his double quotation of the statement that 'God is love',[28] with the affirmation that this explains our destiny.[29] It means that God is 'pure generosity' and therefore that 'we truly discover Him, as the God of our soul, only along a path at least begun [*ébauché*] in generosity'.[30] In other words, if we make the outgoing option of generosity, we shall not find Him wanting.

De Lubac's exposition of the Trinitarian structure of the Apostles' Creed clarifies his understanding of the principle that God is love, and enables us to see, so to speak, the *shape* or *pattern* of this love and generosity into which we are invited. Echoing his earlier work, he says of the 'extrinsicist doctrines' which support 'a faith of pure obedience' that 'they stifle Christian liberty' and are 'an intolerable yoke'.[31] He recalls Augustine's distinction: true Christian faith is not simply '*credere Deum* ("to believe God [exists]")', nor '*credere Deo* ("to believe God")', but rather '*credere in Deum* ("to believe in God")'.[32] To say 'I believe *in* God' means 'I hand myself over to him completely' in a personal commitment.[33] It expresses a 'drive

[27] *MédPVM*, p. 259. Here as elsewhere, de Lubac does not develop the cosmic dimensions of his statement (cf above, p. 30). It is the reentry of *humanity* into the Trinity that he will examine.

[28] *Ibid.*, pp. 259, 265.

[29] *Ibid.*, p. 259.

[30] *Ibid.*, p. 265.

[31] Cf. *Faith*, p. 102.

[32] *Ibid.*, p. 67 (the bracketed clarifications are not contained in the French original). De Lubac refers, for example, to Augustine, *In Joann.* 29, 6 (PL 35, 1631); *In ps.* 77, 8 (PL 36, 988-989).

[33] *Ibid.*, p. 70; cf. pp. 68, 155.

[*élan*] *in Deum*'.[34] Moreover, this act is 'our *reply* to His summons',[35] 'in a word, it is Amen to God',[36] and in particular to his 'salvific act'.[37] Christian faith is 'the reply given by man to God who has come to him in Christ'.[38]

This later account opens with de Lubac's assertion that 'the mystery of the Trinity' has revealed to us 'a completely new perspective: the basis of being is communion'.[39] He appears to be in profound agreement with Zizioulas, whose major publication bears the title, *Being as Communion*. However, the degree of agreement can be assessed only when the *pattern* of the communion which de Lubac envisages is known. We have seen that the pattern of communion, or *koinonia,* as Zizioulas understands it, is *one-many*; in the Trinity, the one is the Father and the many are (the Father and) the Son and the Spirit.[40] In Zizioulas' explanation of the statement that 'God is love', there is a balance or symmetry between the Son and the Spirit.

> 'When we say that "God is love", we refer to the Father, that is, to that person which "hypostasises" God, which makes God to be three persons.'[41]

He dramatically conveys the balance or symmetry between the Son and the Spirit when, distinguishing again the Father, he says that *both* of them, the Son and the Spirit, 'call Him "Father"'.[42]

The balance and symmetry of this view instantly contrast with de Lubac's explanation of the words of St John that 'God is love'. They refer, he implies, to the *Spirit* and not, as Zizioulas has just said, to the *Father*.

---

[34] *Ibid.*, p. 189.
[35] *Ibid.*, pp. 70, 189 (my italics).
[36] *Ibid.*, p. 71.
[37] *Ibid.*, p. 82.
[38] *Ibid.*, p. 150; quotation from R. Guardini, *The Life of Faith*, p. 24.
[39] *Ibid.*, p. x.
[40] Cf. above, pp. 179-180.
[41] *BC*, p. 46, n. 41.
[42] *Ibid.*, p. 48.

'At the heart of being, there is ecstasy, a going-out from self. This is "in the unity of the Holy Spirit", the perfect circumincession of Love.'[43]

By singling out the Holy Spirit in this way, as the *unity* in the Trinity, de Lubac conveys that the ecstatic going-out from self pertains primarily to the Father and, in response, to the Son. We may compare Gréa's view that it is the 'circumincession', not of Father, Son and Spirit, but of the Father and the Son, which is the pattern for the Church's life.[44] The Trinity, adds de Lubac, reveals that 'the plenitude of personal existence coincides with the plenitude of giving' and, manifesting his conviction that the 'Trinity in itself' is the 'Trinity for us', de Lubac immediately passes to our situation and again singles out the Holy Spirit, as the one who will expand our natural desire 'into the hope of loving even as God Himself loves'.[45] Overall, we may say that de Lubac is using a *one-to-one* pattern of Trinitarian communion, focusing on the personhood of the Father and the Son in the unity of the Holy Spirit, such that our destiny becomes that of entering, by the action of the Holy Spirit, into the total self-giving which binds the Father and the Son in love.

This pattern is confirmed when de Lubac repeats St John's '*Deus caritas*' to summarise a passage in which von Balthasar says that the constitution of Being is manifested in the Incarnation. It is shown to be an unceasingly-giving Love ('*die weiter-schenkende Liebe*'). God's sign of Himself in Christ culminates, in death and 'Godforsakenness' ('*Gottleere*'), that is, on the *Cross*.[46]

De Lubac's endorsement of von Balthasar's focus upon the revelatory climax of the Cross is of the utmost significance. Zizioulas would agree with de Lubac in the following basic statement of theological principle.

---

[43]*Faith*, p. ix.

[44]Cf. above, p. 112. Gréa indicates that there is 'circumincession' in the hierarchies in *L'Eglise*, p. 135. He does say that the 'society of the Father and the Son', which is the pattern for the other two hierarchies (pp. 130, 133), is a society 'in the Holy Spirit' (p. 130), but this is still not to see the Holy Spirit precisely as one of the society of Trinitarian persons.

[45]*Faith*, p.x. De Lubac here aligns with Rahner's 'vice-versa'; cf. above, p. 157.

[46]*Ibid.*, p. 53; reference to von Balthasar, *Glaubhaft ist nur Liebe*, pp. 95-96.

'The mystery of the Trinity, which illumines the mystery of human existence, is wholly contained in the mystery of Christ.'[47]

But we have seen that, for Zizioulas, this means that the *one-many* Christ reveals the *one-many* Trinity.[48] For Zizioulas, the Cross is *not* a manifestation, so to speak, of the corporate Christ, and therefore *not* a manifestation of God's inner being. We are here at the nub of the distinction between Zizioulas and de Lubac. For de Lubac, the Resurrection so endorses the witness and achievement of the Cross[49] that it serves to throw the *latter* into higher relief as the culmination of Christ's revelation. In this sense, the Cross is an end, the place from which 'we are brought to the Father' in the union imparted there with our fellow believers.

'The apostolic group can be explained only through the attraction coming from the Cross and the movement of believers going to Jesus to become "his own". All who climb to Calvary meet there; Christ gives us to one another; he is the bond between us'.[50]

The unity we have there at the Cross is the unity of the Trinity. De Lubac praises the 'admirable sign, which splendidly combines the faith's Christological and redemptive expression and its Trinitarian one', namely the sign of the *Cross.*[51]

In sharp contrast, Calvary is rather the backdrop to the Resurrection for Zizioulas. In itself it is a *failure*. If it were the end, then, rather than bringing salvation, Christ too would finally fail to escape 'the tragic aspect of the human person'.[52] Moreover, it is impossible to build a bridge between de Lubac's focus on the Cross and Zizioulas' conception of the corporate Christ, so as to say, for instance, that we all died with Christ on the Cross and thereby passed to a salvation which we now simply *realise* in our historical lives, because, as we have seen,[53]

---

[47] *Ibid.*, p. xi.

[48] Cf. above, pp.185-186, 193-194, 195-196.

[49] Cf. above, p. 63.

[50] *Faith*, p. 189; quotation from A. Manaranche, *Prêtres à la manière des apôtres*, pp. 95-96.

[51] *Ibid.*, p. 34.

[52] *BC*, pp. 54-55 and n. 49.

[53] Cf. above, pp. 174-177.

death *invalidates* corporate personality. Only in his Resurrection *life* is Christ a corporate personality, our 'first-born brother'.[54] Since the New Testament 'was written by those who had accepted Jesus' Resurrection as a historical fact', it presents him already beforehand as a corporate personality (for example at the Last Supper[55]), but it does so *retrospectively*, from the standpoint of the Resurrection and ultimately from the standpoint of the *eschata*.[56]

Zizioulas regards Christ's death as the necessary historical prelude or preparation for his Resurrection, which itself is what opens up hope for the future, where Christians' centre of gravity lies. The Eucharist is 'the perpetuation of the post-Resurrection meals' which Christ had with his disciples.

> 'During the Resurrection appearances and in the form of meals shared with Christ, the disciples experienced a sense of time which was bound to affect the entire existence of the early Church. . . . The time of the Church is the time of the *free* realisation of the eschaton.'[57]

In the historical Economy, God has worked to establish moments or events, which themselves occur in history, but in which God is revealed in a way in which He is not at other times. It was 'from the realm of worship and not from historical revelation' that St Basil took his doxology, praising 'the Father with the Son and with the Spirit'.[58] Contrasting '*Theologia*' and '*Oikonomia*', Zizioulas says the following.

> 'The safest theology [i.e. *Theology*] is that which draws not only from the Economy, but also, and perhaps mainly, from the vision of God as He appears in worship.'[59]

---

[54] *BC*, p. 182; cf. p. 108.

[55] *Ibid.*, pp. 145-148, 230; cf. p. 174, n. 13 and p. 206. Cf. above, pp. 180-183.

[56] *Ibid.*, pp. 113-114 and n. 116.

[57] *ESLT*, pp. 13-14. Cf. *EQA*, pp. 29-31; also, above, p. 189, n. 10. Regarding freedom, cf. above, p. 192.

[58] *BC*, p. 179, n. 30. Cf. above, pp. 158-159, 177-178.

[59] *TSE*, pp. 38-40. We make the bracketed insertion on the assumption that the safest theology is that which is nearest to true knowledge of God in Himself, i.e. to Theology.

De Lubac likewise locates in the fourth century the first use of 'the two contrasted but combined expressions, "economy" and "theology",' for the divisions of 'sacred science'.[60] In the following statement, he seems to accord fully with Zizioulas:

> 'if the economy has really opened to us the way which leads to theology; the latter always keeps, in the last analysis, . . . the finest meaning that it has in Christian language: worship and silent adoration in thankful acknowledgement of the unfathomable Mystery'.[61]

However, unlike Zizioulas, de Lubac is not here envisaging, as it were, a *rhythm* in the flow of history itself, whereby the historical economy, unfolding from the past, opens up into historical events of worship, which have a quite distinct capacity to reveal the immanent Trinity, from our destiny in the future. Rather, there is, in his view, one continuous historical flow of the economic activity of Father, Son and Spirit, which itself accords with and so reveals their immanent relations, so that the immanent Trinity is found by retracing that historical flow back to its fountainhead, which we have seen to be the Cross. Worship, specifically in the Eucharist, centres *there*, as, in the power of the Spirit, we enter into Christ's Sacrifice and so come to the Father.

Zizioulas' view is dramatically *different.* It appears that, for him, the Cross is an event in the preparatory Economy which tells us *nothing* about Theology. As he vigorously explains, the Son becomes an historical being, with a beginning and subject to death, utterly unlike his situation in the immanent Trinity, and the Spirit raises the incarnate Son from death, rescuing him from his historical fate and performing a salvific role which it is nonsensical to attribute to the Spirit in the immanent Trinity.[62] From death, which is the downfall of corporate personality, the Spirit raises Christ,[63] constituting him as a

---

[60]*Faith*, p. 41.

[61]*Ibid.*, pp. 52-53 (corrected translation).

[62]Cf. *PRCE*, pp. 29-33, 43, 45-47.

[63]Zizioulas stresses that this is the teaching of Scripture, Rom. 8: 11; e.g. *PRCE*, pp. 23, 31, 32.

corporate personality, indeed as *the* corporate personality, whose undying immanent personal identity, as Son, is 'implanted' in humanity[64] as 'the basis and "hypostasis" of the person for every man'.[65]

Zizioulas would fully agree with de Lubac's following quotation from de Montcheuil, stressing the necessity of rooting Christ's saving activity in his ontological identity.

> 'We must know who Christ is in himself if we want to understand his function.'[66]

De Lubac makes this point in order to argue that the economic activity of all three Persons of the Trinity is rooted in their immanent identity: 'the "economy" itself has meaning . . . only if there is presupposed in the background a "theology"'.[67] However, the quotation is not itself relevant to the argument, since it affirms the rooting of the Son's economic activity in his *economic* identity as Christ, God-made-man. The fact that it would be relevant if Christ's identity were simply that of the Son extended, as it were, enfleshed, into the economy leads us to conclude that the latter is de Lubac's view. It is a view which Zizioulas wishes to reject by affirming the 'freely undertaken modes of action' of the Son and the Spirit in order to execute the Father's will for the salvation of the world.[68]

Precisely within such a view does Christ's being find an explanation in terms of a *communicatio idiomatum*, which we have indeed seen de Lubac use to explain the Church.[69] Zizioulas will not accept *communicatio idiomatum* to explain Christ,[70] nor, *a fortiori* to explain the Church.[71] As Christ himself is a *new* creation, moulded by the Son and the Spirit

---

[64] *PRCE*, pp. 45, 46.

[65] *BC*, p. 54; cf. above, p. 177.

[66] *Faith*, p. 48; quotation from de Montcheuil, *Leçons sur le Christ*, p. 53. Cf. above, p. 73.

[67] *Ibid.*, p. 44.

[68] *PRCE*, p. 30; cf. above, pp. 157-158.

[69] Cf. above, p. 95.

[70] Cf. *BC*, p. 109; *MCO* p. 302.

[71] Cf. above, p. 96.

according to the will of the Father, so this new creation is *immediately* corporate. The one constituting the many would be compatible with *communicatio idiomatum.* The latter is excluded and Christ's newness underlined by Zizioulas' emphasis that the many also constitute the one: 'Christ without his body is not Christ'.[72]

For Zizioulas, in the Eucharist, the one-many life of the (immanent) Trinity is manifested and experienced in the one-many life of Christ. This summary helps us to appreciate that Zizioulas' sharp distinction between the immanent Trinity and the economic Trinity is actually made in order to forge a bond between them as intimate as that which de Lubac would require, though quite differently conceived. The summary in fact bluntly presents the distinction: in the Trinity, the *Father* is the One, whereas in the corporate personality Christ it is *Christ* who is the One. However, the (one-many) *structures* of the Trinity and of the corporate Christ are identical, and the Chalcedonian doctrine that the 'I' of Christ is the 'I' of the eternal Son means that the corporate Christ does not stand as a separate reflection of the Trinity but rather is drawn to it, such that in Christ we do indeed share the life of the Trinity.

Pictorially, we may imagine that Zizioulas breaks the extension which de Lubac makes of the immanent communional axis of the Father and the Son in the Spirit into the economy, where, again in the Spirit, Christ unites with his Bride. However, having broken this single line into two, Zizioulas then places the two sections in parallel and finds them mystically identified in the Eucharist. In order to account for Zizioulas' understanding of the Spirit's position in the immanent Trinity and for his view of Christ in the midst of the Church in the economy, it is better to envisage two *discs* in parallel and then mystically identified; that centred on the Father, who is surrounded by the Son and the Spirit, and that centred on Christ, who is surrounded by the Church.

In fact, just as de Lubac's view involves a further historical prolongation of the one axis into the mission which Christ has

[72] *BC,* p. 182; cf. above, p. 167.

'passed on' to the hierarchy,[73] its 'origin' being 'in the divine processions themselves',[74] so Zizioulas makes a further break, so as to distinguish, and then mystically identify with the other two, a *third* section, which must be rendered as a third disc, namely that centred on the bishop, who is surrounded by his church. We have seen that, for Zizioulas, the local church around the bishop in the Eucharist is *exactly the same as* the Church around Christ.[75] Appreciating now his full vision of three tiers mystically identified, to which we have already alluded,[76] we may say that our life as persons in Christ is *exactly the same as* the life of the divine Persons in the Trinity.[77] Pictorially, we may also note the contrast between Zizioulas' three horizontal discs, mystically identified, and Grea's three descending hierarchies,[78] which so readily align sequentially as three stages of the single axis which de Lubac envisages, extending from God's inner life into history.

In 'the language of scholasticism', de Lubac affirms that 'the (internal) "processions" of the Persons of the Trinity are known to us only through their (external) "missions"';[79] but Zizioulas refers to Gregory of Nazianzus in saying that, on the basis of the Theology that arises from *worship*, 'we cannot say . . . what the difference is between generation and procession'.[80] Like de Lubac, Zizioulas recognises that the Economy indicates a progression in 'God's coming to us': 'the initiative starts with the Father, passes through the Son and reaches us

---

[73] *Splendour*, pp. 101-102. Cf. above, p. 103.

[74] *Ibid.*, p. 71.

[75] For this translation of the Ignatian '*ὥσπερ*', cf. above, p. 169 (with reference to *BC*, p. 149).

[76] Cf. above, pp. 135, 185-186, 193-194, 196. The identification of the first and third discs takes place only *via* the second, as we noted in our mention of the two Ignatian typologies (above, pp. 195-196).

[77] I owe this extension of the Ignatian '*ὥσπερ*' to personal discussions with Zizioulas.

[78] Cf. above, p. 111.

[79] *Faith*, p. 41.

[80] *TSE*, p. 40. Zizioulas' reference to Gregory of Nazianzus, '*Or.* 33', does not seem relevant to this point. Perhaps, *Or.* 31, 8 (PG 36, 141B) or 32, 5 (PG 36, 180B) is intended.

in the Holy Spirit'.[81] However, whereas the undisputed fact that economically the Spirit 'is sent by Christ as Christ was sent by the Father'[82] is revelatory of God's inner being for de Lubac, it is not for Zizioulas. For Zizioulas, it reveals, rather, how God has worked to establish (essentially eucharistic) events which themselves are revelatory of His inner being. For de Lubac, the Eucharist takes us, in the Spirit, to the incarnate Son on the Cross, and thence to the Father. For Zizioulas, the Eucharist takes us to the heavenly banquet, which the corporate Christ, established by triumph *over* the Cross, celebrates.

In short, de Lubac envisages us being gathered to God back along the way in which He has come to us. However, rather like a one-way valve, which blocks an attempt to reverse the flow, is Zizioulas' view of history. How God has come to us historically is *not* the way in which we shall return. Zizioulas' reason, as we have seen, is that how God has come to us historically does not reveal God as He is, and it is God *as He is* who is our destiny. The way God has come to us is, as it were, along a single channel: from the Father, through the Son, to us in the Holy Spirit. We have seen that this *does* reflect God's inner being for de Lubac, who envisages a one-to-one model of Trinitarian communion, between the Father and the Son in the unity of the Holy Spirit. The Father-Son axis is extended into the axis of the economy; the Son becomes incarnate and the Spirit overshadows him and goes ahead of him to draw others to him in the Bride whom he seeks. Let us recall what we have said before about de Lubac's view of the unity of Christians, that, because it considers that it is the same Christ in each that makes all one, it risks effectively collapsing Christians *atomistically* into a coincident identity as Christ's Spouse.[83] We may now see that this collapse results from the gathering of all into de Lubac's single, extended axis. If I may venture another image: the collapse, in relation to Christ, is like that of all the points of an open umbrella, to the *same* position in relation to the tip, when it is folded.

[81] *Ibid.*, p. 38.
[82] *Faith*, p. 131.
[83] Cf. above, pp. 65-66, 92-93, 95-96.

The individualism which still affects de Lubac's system, in spite of his stand against it, results from this coincidence.[84] It can be overcome only if personhood is understood as conferred not only in relation to God, but also in relation to one another. We have seen that the former is de Lubac's view.[85] We may now perceive that the complementary reference to one another, sideways, as it were, cannot exist in the narrowness of the single axis. It is by breaking the axis and broadening each of its sections into the discs I have described, that Zizioulas offers a remedy to individualism. The immanent, one-to-one Trinitarian axis of the Father and the Son in the Spirit is broadened into a vision of the Father surrounded by the Son and the Spirit, which is the one-many pattern for Christ surrounded by the Church and the bishop surrounded by his church.

As long ago as 1938, de Lubac showed that he does not historicise the Holy Spirit. He foreshadowed Zizioulas' later statement that 'Pentecost is the natural atmosphere of the Eucharist'[86] when, as we have seen, he himself stressed the regular inbreaking of the Spirit afresh.

> 'Our churches are the "upper room" where not only is the Last Supper renewed but Pentecost also.'[87]

Both affirm that it is the Holy Spirit who forms Christ in the Eucharist, as it was the Spirit who formed Christ in Mary's womb.[88] However, for de Lubac, this is the individual Christ in the eucharistic elements, who is present from the past in order to be then received the same by all, according to an historically sequential understanding of how the Church making the Eucharist progresses into the Eucharist making the Church.[89]

Zizioulas' breaking of the axis entails the elimination of even this instance of historical progression. As we have seen, he

[84]Cf. above, pp. 66-67.
[85]Cf. above, pp. 19-20, 48.
[86]*EQA*, p. 23.
[87]*Catholicism*, p. 48; cf. above, p. 221.
[88]For de Lubac, cf. *Catholicism*, p. 48. *Faith*, p. 131: 'Jesus himself depends on the Spirit, in whom he exults'. For Zizioulas, cf. *BC*, p. 211.
[89]Cf. above, pp. 79-80, 103-104; below, p. 262.

considers that Christ's formation by the Spirit means that he is *immediately* corporate, constituted by the eschatological community of the Saints.[90] Accordingly, in the Eucharist, Christ is present not sequentially, in the elements through the action of the bishop and then in the people, but simultaneously in the configuration of the bishop surrounded by his church and in the spiritual gifts they share.[91]

For Zizioulas, all of history hangs upon the eschaton. That is, all of creation's meaning and history's purpose derives from God's will, which can be summarised as '*the incarnate Christ*',[92] namely Christ who 'contains by definition the eschata, our final destiny, ourselves as we shall be'.[93] The Spirit brings this unchanging will of God to bear upon history in what Zizioulas calls '*καιροί*' , which the Spirit opens up. Christ's own earthly life was full of such '*καιροί*', when, in the power of the Spirit, he freely shaped his humanity in accordance with his divine personhood and purpose. The Spirit now opens up such moments in the life of the Church, eucharistic moments of our free response to the fulness of God's will.[94] Such moments are also, indeed primarily, moments of God's sovereign freedom and hence of the delicate interplay of freedoms to which we have already referred.[95] 'God is not bound by His past', says Zizioulas, praising Irenaeus' role in the patristic development of the notion of '*καιρός*' to explain what the ancient world could not conceive, namely that an event could be 'both good and replaceable'.[96] Contrary to the Greek understanding of history's centre of gravity lying at its start[97] and significantly different from de Lubac's reading of Irenaeus, namely that history's centre of gravity is located in the Incarnation,[98]

[90]Cf. above, pp. 166-167.
[91]Cf. above, pp. 197-198.
[92]*BC*, p. 97. Cf. above, p. 149.
[93]*Ibid.*, p. 183. Cf. above, p. 168
[94]*PRCE*, pp. 46-51.
[95]Cf. above, p. 193.
[96]*ESLT*, p. 12.
[97]Cf. above, p. 193, n. 36.
[98]Cf. above, p. 56.

Zizioulas looks towards the future.

'The past is not binding precisely because there is a future event which gives the past its meaning.'[99]

Von Balthasar well illustrates the two latter, contrasting views. In accord with what we have seen to be de Lubac's understanding,[100] he himself presents the individual Christ as the 'norm' of history. It is then by the work of the Spirit that 'the individual historical existence of Christ can be so universalised as to become the immediate norm of every individual existence', a norm which is 'inward' to 'every life'.[101] From his position in the 'centre' of history, Christ reveals 'in this one particular *kairos*... the meaning of every *kairos* that can ever be'.[102] They will all, we may deduce, be actualisations of the individual Christ. However, presenting the views of Maximus, so favoured by Zizioulas, von Balthasar notes that, of the 'three great pivots of the world's history', namely Original Sin, the Incarnation and Christ's Parousia, it is the *third* which particularly occupies him.

'The general concept of Parousia remains the fundamental category in the philosophy of history of the Greek Fathers.'[103]

History and Eschatology

We have seen de Lubac's view that the Eucharist is an anticipation, '*in mysterio nostro*'.[104] In other words, it is *forward* that we must look for our unity in the heavenly Jerusalem, our Mother. However, a tension exists in de Lubac's account from the fact that he describes this heavenly Mother, '*Mater caelestis*',[105] as effective upon us, not, in fact, from the future, but from the

[99]*ESLT*, pp. 12-13.
[100]Cf. above, pp. 56-67.
[101]Von Balthasar, *A Theology of History*, pp. 79-80.
[102]*Ibid.*, p. 86.
[103]Von Balthasar, *Liturgie cosmique*, pp. 127-128.
[104]*CMys*, pp. 83-84. Cf. above, p. 75.
[105]*Splendour*, p. 54.

past, as we may see in the following way. He says that the 'fatherhood of her spiritual leaders' is the 'privileged expression' of the 'motherhood of the Church',[106] thereby aligning the latter with the Apostolic Succession of the bishops, which he presents with pronounced historical emphasis, as coming into the present from the past. The bishops are, he says, 'those whose line extends from the beginning, assuring not only the authentic transmission of a doctrine, but also the propagation of a life'.[107] The impression, here, of historical growth from the past is reinforced by de Lubac's incorporation of Louis Bouyer's description of the local churches of which the bishops have charge as having been 'propagated' from the original local church of Jerusalem 'by planting cuttings, as it were, from the main shoot'.[108]

Likewise, de Lubac speaks of the '*Ecclesia sanctorum*' as 'something essentially eschatological', but then adds that that does not mean 'merely "to come"'.[109] For an explanation of how it is already present, we may look to his following words.

'Since the fact of Christ and his resurrection, "time-after [the metachronic] is already present in the interior of time"'.[110]

Again it is a picture of the organic growth of something planted within time that he paints. Moreover, his designation of Christ's own achievement as that which has initiated this growth, combines with what we have just seen, that the effective presence of the eschatological reality is the bishops, whose mission, we recall, perpetuates that of Christ,[111] to indicate that the eschatological reality which de Lubac actually envisages as active in history is *Christ.* As we said previously, de Lubac regards the eschatological reality present in the Eucharist as

---

[106]*Motherhood*, p. 113. Cf. McPartlan, 'Eucharist and Church', pp. 855-857.

[107]*Ibid.*, p. 86.

[108] L. Bouyer, *The Church of God*, p. 279; quoted by de Lubac, *Motherhood*, p. 207.

[109]*Splendour*, p. 80.

[110]*ChPM*, p. 52; the incorporated quotation is from B. C. Butler, *The Idea of the Church*, p. 218, with reference to which the bracketed amendment is given. Cf. Florovsky's view, above, p.20.

[111]Cf. above, pp. 251-252.

the individual, risen Christ gathering his people into the Church, his Spouse, which is still a projection for the future.[112]

Whereas de Lubac presents the eschatological reality as something now *continuously* present inside time, for Zizioulas it is something present only as a regular *visitation*. Why this is so becomes apparent when, in sharp contrast with de Lubac's view of the eschaton as present *within* history, Zizioulas says that eschatology 'confronts history ... with *a presence from beyond history* . . .[the] *presence* of the Kingdom here and now'.[113] Whereas, for de Lubac, the eschatological reality is the individual Christ who, having been definitively manifested, has ascended and now comes down again in a second phase to fill al,[114] for Zizioulas it is the corporate Christ of the Kingdom, who still *awaits* his definitive manifestation, on the last day. Zizioulas repeatedly emphasises the Johannine teaching that 'the coming of the Logos is a *visitation* from above and consists in establishing God's *tabernacle* in history so that we may see the glory of God'.[115] Until the last day, this tent must be repeatedly pitched as the eschatological reality visits history 'to open it up in a communion-event'.[116]

The separability of Christ from the Church, such that he can be conceived without her, is what underlies de Lubac's two-phase account, in which Christ comes to indwell his Bride in the second phase of his work. We have noted that the Church as Bride is not an image which Zizioulas develops.[117] We may initially suggest that this is because, although the image well conveys her dependence on him, it does not adequately convey his complementary dependence on her. We have seen that de Lubac's own use of it raises problems which are resolved if we apply Zizioulas' concept of Christ and the Church as mutually constitutive,[118] each being inconceivable without the other. In

[112]Cf. above, p.113.

[113]*BC*, p. 174, n. 11. Cf. above, p.20.

[114]Cf. above, p. 57.

[115]*EAH*1, p. 34 (my italics). Cf. *BC*, p. 114 and p. 179, n. 27, both in reference to Jn. 1: 14.

[116]*BC*, p. 100.

[117]Cf. above, p. 90.

[118]Cf. above, pp. 93-97.

fact, Zizioulas' most recent account of their interdependence indicates that, more deeply, it is its implication that there may be an hypostasis of the Church herself that renders bridal imagery unacceptable to him. With admitted paradox, he explains his conviction that the Church's identity 'is Christ's own identity':

> 'there is no hypostasis of the Church. The Church has no hypostasis of its own. This makes Christ's identity dependent on the existence of the Church, which is paradoxical, for though the Church has no hypostasis of its own, it is a factor which conditions Christ's identity: the one cannot exist without the many'.[119]

As if to emphasise his point, Zizioulas here abandons all trace of the female terminology which he otherwise readily adopts for the Church on account of her *motherhood*.[120]

Importantly, we have also now seen that safeguarding the distinction between the created and the uncreated, that is between nature and the supernatural, for which de Lubac regards the bridal image as indispensable,[121] is achieved in Zizioulas' system without it.[122] Zizioulas can, as it were, safely position Christ on *our* side of this divide, in the midst of the Church, constituting her and being constituted by her, not only without any Adoptionist danger, on one hand,[123] but also,

---

[119]*MCO*, pp. 302-303.

[120]Zizioulas acknowledges that, 'in early patristic literature, the image of the Church as mother is often employed', its spirit being 'precisely that in the Church a birth is brought about; man is born as "hypostasis", as person' (*BC*, p. 56). We note immediately that he differs from de Lubac in his understanding of this image. For Zizioulas, the Church is mother because in her man is born again, into the corporate Christ. For de Lubac, as we have seen, she is mother because she brings the individual Christ to birth in man (cf. above, pp. 52-53, 66). Zizioulas has no doctrine of indwelling (cf. below, p. 279), which in fact tends to be associated also with bridal imagery (cf. above, pp. 15-19, for de Lubac, and pp. 219-220 for Florovsky) and, thereby, with a two-phase account of salvation. The doctrine of indwelling forms a bridge between the images of the Church as mother and bride, respectively.

[121]Cf. above, p. 29.

[122]Cf. above, Chapter Seven.

[123]Cf. above, p. 168.

on the other hand, without any monistic danger of the Church becoming some sort of divine emanation, necessarily created at the generation of the Son, because of his utter refusal to read back the data of the economy into the immanent Trinity.[124] Instead, what we have in the economy are, to reiterate, the 'freely undertaken modes of action' of the Son and the Spirit, in order to execute what is the Father's free will, namely the salvation of the world.[125]

The fact that de Lubac envisages Christ on God's side of the created/uncreated divide, whereas, for Zizioulas, he has crossed this divide, suggests that the encounter between these two theologians is not so much an encounter between modern Catholic and Orthodox theologies as a modern echo of that between the ancient theological schools of Alexandria and Antioch, which, as J. N. D. Kelly relates, had 'Word-flesh' and 'Word-man' Christologies, respectively.[126] We have several times noted de Lubac's affinity with a Word-flesh Christology,[127] and have had to verify that Zizioulas avoids the Adoptionism which traditionally threatens Word-man Christology. We may recall that, though de Lubac stresses the importance of history,[128] history was less respected in Alexandria than in Antioch, and that, though Zizioulas can sometimes appear to envisage an eschatological Christ who is not fully rooted in history,[129] it is the school of Antioch which 'deserves credit for bringing back the historical Jesus'.[130] In fact, we have contrasted the views that de Lubac and Zizioulas have of eternity, in which time is escaped for the former but redeemed for the latter.[131] However, with regard to the overall purpose of this book, we should note that, differences between them notwithstanding, *both*

[124]Cf. above, pp. 157-159.

[125]Cf. above, p. 250.

[126]Cf. J. N. D. Kelly, *Early Christian Doctrines*, p. 302; but cf. above, p. 125.

[127]Cf. above, p. 53; p. 59, n. 41 and p. 250; also, below, p. 292.

[128]Cf. above, pp. 3-4 and p. 76, n. 10.

[129]Cf. above, pp. 191-192, e.g. 'the Incarnation does not bind God to history'; and pp. 257-258, e.g. 'eschatology . . . confronts history . . . with *a presence from beyond history*'.

[130]Kelly, *Early Christian Doctrines*, p. 302.

[131]Cf. above, pp. 45-49.

schools contributed much to the life of the one Church of the Fathers.

Regarding Christ and the Church as inseparable, Zizioulas integrates de Lubac's two phases of salvation into *one*. He considers that already in the life of Christ, as now in the life of the Church, it was the one purpose of God, as a totality, namely *'the incarnate Christ'*,[132] which was operative, breaking upon history, from the future, in events whereby it salvifically lifted history up to itself. The following statement, which de Lubac endorses, appears to express what de Lubac envisages taking place in the second phase. 'With Jesus, eschatology has entered into history.'[133] However, Zizioulas' desire to amend the vision of an entry into history in a second phase so as to envisage, rather, the free *tabernacling* of the same eschatological reality, first in Christ's life and then in the life of the Church, is what he conveys as follows.

> 'I agree with the view that the incarnation introduces eschatology into history but this does not mean that the eschatological God has been enclosed by history. The eschaton must be allowed to reaffirm itself anew, and this is the essence of the Eucharist as I understand it. Otherwise the eschaton does not determine history but history captures the eschaton.'[134]

We shall see in the next chapter how Zizioulas' resolve to free the eschaton from history, so that it can condition history in dialectical encounters, responds to de Lubac's desire to explain the Church in dialectical terms. For de Lubac, as we have seen, Christ is free from history in the sense that he has risen to overarch history.[135] However, de Lubac describes Christ as then entering into the fabric of history again to gather the Church. Zizioulas' account of the Spirit rescuing Christ from the fate of history[136] implicitly understands Christ as *corporate*, for that is what follows from his constitution as Christ

[132]*BC*, p. 97. Cf. above, pp. 90, 149, 255.

[133]*Sources*, p. 199; quotation from P.B. (Pierre Benoit ?), review article, 'Bulletin; Nouveau Testament', p. 284. Cf. above, p. 257.

[134]*EAH*2, p. 73; cf. above, p. 192.

[135]Cf. above, pp. 57, 62-63.

[136]Cf. above, p. 249.

by the Spirit, his body being the eschatological Church.[137] Therefore, Christ is present always as from the end of history. In other words, he is definitively freed from history by being inseparable from the Church, one and many, mutually constitutive.

Two examples may serve to indicate the contrast between Zizioulas' view of the end, as really present now to the Church on earth, and de Lubac's view of the end, as still a future projection for the Church as she encounters now the real presence of Christ himself. First, whereas Zizioulas emphatically says that 'there is no room for the slightest difference between the worshipping eucharistic community on earth and the actual worship in front of God's throne',[138] it is our historical *distance* from this worship that de Lubac highlights when he says:

'[w]e are all *on our way* to the sanctuary of heaven and the liturgy of eternity'.[139]

Significantly, de Lubac says this in the context of sequentially describing the eucharistic action of the hierarchy to make the Eucharist which 'in its turn' makes the Church.[140]

Secondly, we may note that this sequence pursued to its end is what de Lubac understands by the term *teleiosis*. He says that the sacraments, and especially the Eucharist, are 'the sacred benefits by which *teleiosis* (completion, final perfection) is obtained'.[141] For Zizioulas, however, the being perfected, or brought to completion, which *teleiosis* expresses with regard to the sacraments is not a long-term goal but rather the achievement of the liturgy itself, in which the end comes to meet and mould us. With reference to '$\tau\epsilon\lambda\epsilon\iota\omega\sigma\iota\varsigma$' in 'the Greek patristic tradition', he says the following about Ordination in particular.

---

[137]Cf. above, pp. 166-167.
[138]*BC*, p. 233.
[139]*Splendour*, p. 104 (my italics).
[140]Cf. *ibid.*, pp. 104-106.
[141]*Faith*, p. 113.

'Precisely because of the identification of the eucharistic community, into which one is ordained, with the worshipping community before the throne of God, ordination is not something of a *temporal* nature, but of *eschatological decisiveness.*'[142]

At the centre of the eschatological Church worshipping before God's throne stands Christ, for the bishop, who is ordained into the central position in the eucharistic community which is identified with the worshipping community is identified with Christ. It is indeed through this eucharistic identification that he becomes a successor of the apostles.

'The bishop becomes *alter apostolus* (through the imposition of hands of already ordained bishops) by becoming at the same time *alter Christus* (through the occupation of his eucharistic throne).'[143]

By asserting that 'apostolic succession goes through the concrete episcopal community',[144] Zizioulas breaks any historical transmission of apostolicity and roots in *eschatology* the role which historical succession plays in the Church; he roots Christ in the Church and the bishop in his church.

In this chapter, we have seen de Lubac's emphatically *retrospective* view of Apostolic Succession: the bishops propagate life in their continuation of the mission which Christ received from the Father.[145] In this light, it would appear to be the individual bishops whom de Lubac has in mind when he refers to the sacramentality of the Church.

'If Christ is the sacrament of God, the Church is for us the sacrament of Christ; she represents him in the full and ancient meaning of the term, she really makes him present.'[146]

We noted in Chapter One that de Lubac's precise meaning is not clear, for there are two possible interpretations of this

---

[142]*BC*, p. 234.
[143]*BTD*, pp. 31-32.
[144]*BC*, p. 166. Zizioulas notes the naming of the new bishop's local church in his very Prayer of Consecration; e.g. *BC*, p. 166 and p. 239, n. 92.
[145]Cf. above, pp. 251-252, 256-258.
[146]*Catholicism*, p. 28.

passage: one taking the Church's priests to be those intended by 'the Church' and the other regarding the whole people, including the priests, as those intended.[147] Both interpretations flow, *in their distinction*, from understanding Christ as an individual.

With his *corporate* understanding of Christ, Zizioulas clarifies the ambiguity by offering a synthesis of these views. The bishop surrounded by the people is the sacrament of Christ surrounded by the eschatological Church. In Zizioulas' emphatically *prospective* view, '[i]t is the *eschatological* Christ that the bishop is an εἰκών of',[148] 'the manifestation of the arrival of Christ on earth',[149] surrounded by his own as the corporate Son of Man.[150] The intrinsically differentiated local church, centred on the bishop, is the sacrament of the intrinsically differentiated 'catholic' Church, centred upon Christ; in it 'the "catholic" Church is fully present and real'.[151]

Zizioulas' corporate understanding of Christ, which offers this resolution of the Church's sacramentality to de Lubac, rests, as we have seen, on a powerful and precise Pneumatology, according to which the Holy Spirit does not flow out of the historical Christ in order to gather us back to him in unity, but rather breaks upon us as it broke upon him, too, in order to fulfil God's will by actually forming that which *is* God's will and one historical purpose, namely the corporate Christ of the last day.

---

[147]Cf. above, pp. 22-23
[148]*BTD*, p. 30.
[149]*Ibid.*, p. 35.
[150]Cf. above, p. 168.
[151]*BC*, p. 233, n. 71.

Chapter 12

The Beating *Heart of the Church*

De Lubac and Zizioulas both criticise Cullmann, as we have seen, for presenting *Heilsgeschichte* simply as an ongoing flow,[1] not recognising that there is a reality *overarching* history and conditioning it by descending to it. For de Lubac, this reality is Christ himself in his Calvary sacrifice, whereas, for Zizioulas, it is the corporate Christ of the Parousia.[2] Both understand the conditioning to occur in a Chalcedonian fashion, according to what we have called the *Chalcedonian shift*. For de Lubac, it occurs by Christ himself encountering individual Christians and *indwelling*,[3] whereas, for Zizioulas, it occurs by the corporate Christ encountering local eucharistic assemblies and only *tabernacling*.[4] We must now clarify what kind of conditioning is envisaged in the latter case and what advantages it offers over the former.

Baptism, Penance and the Eucharist

Gaëtan Baillargeon seriously criticises Zizioulas as follows.

'Our Western sensibility hesitates in the face of the almost absolute identity between Christ and the Church which John Zizioulas proposes; for him there is no distance between Christ and the Church. The historical reality of the Church *in via* finds hardly any place; the view of a Church which gathers a sinful

[1]Cf. above, pp. 57, 190.
[2]Cf. above, p. 89.
[3]Cf. above, pp.51-56, 257-259.
[4]Cf. above, pp. 150-153, 169-170, 257-259.

people, a Church called to conversion, is almost absent or dimmed [*occulté*] by a strong eschatological emphasis.'[5]

This criticism is mistaken.[6] Zizioulas' careful account, far from setting up an 'almost absolute identity' already between Christ and the pilgrim Church of sinners, actually respects Baillargeon's concerns. He does indeed say that 'the Church is part of the definition of Christ' and that 'you cannot have the body of the individual Christ (the One) without having simultaneously the community of the Church (the Many)', but the Church of which he is speaking is not the Church *on earth*, but rather 'the eschatological company of the "Saints"'. The Church on earth is not yet this company, which is why Zizioulas immediately adds that the identification of the Church with Christ is something which the Church on earth, in history, can experience only *momentarily*, namely in the Eucharist.

'The Eucharist is the only occasion *in history* when these two coincide.'[7]

More recently, within a few lines Zizioulas three times referred to the Eucharist as a 'moment', when the head of the earthly community becomes 'the image of Christ' and the members are '*hagioi*'.[8]

The thrust of Zizioulas' 'strong eschatological emphasis' is not to make an abiding identification between the pilgrim Church of sinners and the Church of heaven, but rather to make the *momentary* identification of the earthly community around the bishop with the heavenly Church around Christ. It is precisely this regularly experienced identification which repeatedly prompts the Church *in via* to conversion. By being already regularly cast, as we may say, in the role of the heavenly

---

[5]G. Baillargeon, 'Jean Zizioulas, porte-parole de l'Orthodoxie contemporaine' (hereafter, 'Porte-parole'), p. 192. Cf. Baillargeon's thesis, *Perspectives orthodoxes*, pp. 255-256.

[6]It has recently been disputed by Constantin Agoras also, in his own wide-ranging critique of Baillargeon's appraisal of Zizioulas ('Vision ecclésiale et ecclésiologie', p. 111).

[7]*EPH*, p. 342 (my italics).

[8]Cf. *MCO*, p. 298.

Church around the glorified Christ who yet bears the marks of having been slain,[9] the members of the earthly community are called to repent for what still makes them unfit for that place, namely their own lack of acceptance of 'the very scandal of the crucified Son of Man'.[10]

The eucharistic foretaste of the return of the Son of Man cannot fail to be an occasion of judgment. Far from dispensing with the need for reconciliation, as Baillargeon suggests, Zizioulas explicitly locates it in the Eucharist.[11] There it finds its 'context' and 'purpose'.[12]

> 'How can we understand the place of the sacrament of reconciliation in the life of the Church and that of sinners . . . if this identity between Christ and the Church is absolutely maintained?'[13]

To this question by Baillargeon, we may reply that the lack of distance between Christ and the (eschatological) Church is exactly what prompts the members of the earthly community to a repenting awareness, in the Eucharist, of the contrast between themselves as they are and themselves as God wills them to be.

In short, Baillargeon implies that for Zizioulas the heavenly Church is already present and realised in an abiding way in the earthly Church. He asks: 'although the Holy Spirit introduces the *eschaton* into history, is there not a difference between eschatology and history?'[14] Our last chapter amply shows that Zizioulas himself regards this difference as fundamental. Baillargeon suggests that Zizioulas might adopt a Chalcedonian solution to the problem of the relationship between the historical and the eschatological Church. He recalls the Chalcedonian formulation and then says:

[9]*EAH*1, p. 34. Cf. above, p. 188.

[10]Cf. *ECC*, p. 24.

[11]Cf. above, pp. 195, 198-200. Thus, P. Vallin's criticisms that Zizioulas neglects the *judgmental* aspect of Christ's return and the *critical* dimension of every epiclesis cannot be accepted (review of *EE*, p. 386).

[12]*CECB*, p. 3.

[13]*Perspectives orthodoxes*, p. 256.

[14]*Ibid.*, p. 257.

'If this same model of union was transposed to the Church in its being and its life, could it not be said that in the Eucharist, by the Holy Spirit, the Church *in via* and the eschatological Church are united "without separation" (which is already strongly developed in John Zizioulas) but also "without confusion", that is to say without the Church *in via* losing its historical, incomplete and imperfect character?'[15]

We have seen that Zizioulas *does* adopt a Chalcedonian solution to this problem. However, importantly, the Chalcedonian shift which he envisages does not bring into union the two realities which Baillargeon suggests, namely the Church *in via* and the eschatological Church, with Christ standing distinct from both, but rather the local church *around the bishop* and the eschatological Church *around Christ*. Baillargeon seems not to heed adequately the intrinsic inseparability of Christ and the Church, one and many, whose bond is mirrored in that of the bishop and his church in the Eucharist.[16]

Baillargeon is also unhappy with Zizioulas' view of Baptism.

'[I]s there not, with John Zizioulas, an overvaluing of the Eucharist to the detriment of Baptism?'[17]

The following statement makes clear the decisive nature of Baptism for Zizioulas.

'As death and resurrection in Christ, Baptism signifies the decisive passing of our existence from the "truth" of individualised being into the truth of personal being. The resurrectional aspect of Baptism is therefore nothing other than *incorporation into the community*.'[18]

Baillargeon himself quotes this statement, but comments that it is an indication of Zizioulas' strong identification between the Church and Christ,[19] which we have seen him criticise. In the following statement, we may see, therefore, Baillargeon's ecumenically prompted desire[20] not only to give Baptism

---

[15] *Ibid.*, p. 257.
[16] Cf. above, p. xxi.
[17] 'Porte-parole', pp. 191-192; cf. *Perspectives orthodoxes*, p. 254.
[18] *BC*, p. 113.
[19] *Perspectives orthodoxes*, pp. 193-194.
[20] Cf. *ibid.*, p. 254.

priority over the Eucharist in defining Christianity, but also to loosen the bond between personhood and the concrete community. He says that he favours 'a Christian anthropology in which Baptism would contribute to Christian identity' and suggests that there are the beginnings of such an approach in the following comment by Zizioulas.

> 'This adoption of man by God, the identification of his hypostasis with the hypostasis of the Son of God, is the essence of Baptism.'[21]

However, in fact, there are no beginnings to be sought here for the satisfaction of Baillargeon's desire, because Zizioulas *immediately* explains that the place where this new hypostasis is 'realised in history' is 'in the Church',[22] and that means *in a concrete community*, for the following reasons. First, Zizioulas clarifies that this new hypostasis is 'a historical *experience*, even though it is not permanent'[23]; secondly, the experience he intends is the *Eucharist*, which, as we have just seen, is the only occasion in history when the identification in Christ of the Church with the Son's hypostasis is a reality; thirdly, the Eucharist is 'understood properly as a community'.[24]

Zizioulas gives no support for finding a meaning in Baptism other than in the eucharistic practice to which, by definition, it and Chrismation '*inevitably and immediately*' lead.[25] Baillargeon appears to be seeking recognition of the *abiding status* which Baptism gives to the individual Christian, a status which enables his eucharistic participation, but which itself must be *primary*, since the Eucharist is only a transient celebration in which the Christian may or may not take part. The Eucharist, he seems to say, is just an *event* whereas Baptism confers membership of the *institution* which celebrates this event. Bluntly, for Zizioulas, the Christian has *no* abiding status in this world. The place where he stands is the future and that status

---

[21] *Ibid.*, p. 255; the quotation is found in *BC*, p. 56.
[22] *BC*, p. 56.
[23] *Ibid.*, p. 58, n. 53.
[24] *Ibid.*, p. 213. Cf. above, p. 73.
[25] *OAS*, p. 36; cf. *BCE*, p. 651. Also, above, p.179, n. 67.

is an historical reality only in the Eucharist. Having claimed his true, future identity when Baptism and Confirmation (or Chrismation) first introduced him to the Eucharist,[26] the Christian then clings to that identity by living from Eucharist to Eucharist. For Zizioulas, the Eucharist is nothing less than '*the reality which makes it possible for us to exist at all*'.[27]

In this world, the Christian never grasps that identity so as to *keep* it. Already in his programmatic address, Zizioulas referred to the 'ontological grace' of the Eucharist as something 'acquired *only to be lost again* until the last day when it will be acquired definitively'.[28] Nevertheless, it is precisely this relationship with the eschaton, characterised by the rhythmic acquiring and losing of his eschatological identity, which *defines* the Christian in history. He is not more stably defined by other criteria, such as Baptism. The Christian has what we may call, paradoxically, a *rhythmic stability*. For Zizioulas, it is by the rhythmic acquiring and losing of our eschatological identity in the Eucharist that the stability expressible as 'our deification in space and time'[29] is imparted.

Nearly twenty years later, Zizioulas admitted the paradox as follows.

> 'I can say that for the Orthodox the Church is not an institution but an event — which sounds Protestant to Roman Catholic ears. Or I can say the opposite, namely that the Church is an institution and not an event — which would cause total confusion to the ecumenical listener. Indeed, such terms as "event" or "institution" or even "Church" can mean totally different things, depending on the theological presuppositions that lie behind them.'[30]

To one who thinks that stability means an abiding identity, Zizioulas says that the Church is not an institution but an event.

---

[26]Cf. also *TLU*, pp. 164-165: 'one of the faithful who has received Baptism but not Confirmation is not yet a "layman", he does not yet occupy the *ordo* which falls to him [*qui lui revient*] in the community'.

[27]*EPL*, p. 193.

[28]*VEM*, p. 91 (my italics).

[29]*Ibid.*, p. 91.

[30]*MCO*, p. 294.

To another who thinks that events are transient glimpses of what saves but does not change us, he says that the Church is an institution and not an event.

In summary, Zizioulas says of the Church: 'everything is permanent and non-permanent'.[31] A comparison with de Lubac and Barth highlights the distinctiveness of his view. Like de Lubac, Zizioulas is committed to man's divinisation, and, like Barth, he is committed to Christ's coming into history only in events; yet these two tenets are mutually exclusive for the two Western theologians. De Lubac says that we are divinised by 'the active presence in us of the Spirit'.[32] We have seen that the Spirit works to form Christ[33] and therefore we note the equivalence of de Lubac's belief that Christ was born of Mary so as to be born in Christians:[34] we are divinised by the indwelling of Christ. We may now link Barth's firm rejection of the notion of divinisation[35] with his denial of 'the Saviour's birth in our soul', for which de Lubac criticises him, as we have seen.[36] In contrast with de Lubac's view of Christ *abiding* and transforming, Barth envisages *events* in which Christ preaches to the Church. Such proclamation, by the coming together of God's Word and human utterance, requires for its explanation 'the Christological doctrine of the two natures',[37] but is *transient*, as Barth memorably conveys in a quotation from Luther.

> '[The] preaching of the Gospel is not an eternal, lasting, static doctrine, but like a moving shower of rain which strikes what it strikes and misses what it misses. Nor does it return or halt, but is followed by the sunshine and warmth which lick it up.'[38]

Zizioulas states that, because of the Fall, 'the world ultimately consists of a fragmented existence in which beings are

[31] *PRCE*, p. 28.
[32] *BCat*, p. 42 (cf. p. 41); quotation from Bouyer, *Le Père invisible*, p. 288.
[33] Cf. above, p. 254.
[34] *MMys*, p. 71. Cf. above, pp. 52-53.
[35] Cf. Barth, *Church Dogmatics* IV/2, pp. 77-83.
[36] *MMys*, p. 55. Cf. above, pp. 53-54.
[37] Barth, *Church Dogmatics*, I/1, p. 52.
[38] *Ibid.*, p. 49; quotation from Luther, *Fastenpostille* 1525, W.A., 17[II], p. 178, 1.28.

particular *before* they can relate to each other: you first *are* and then relate'.[39] Sin has made the world fall apart into individual objects,[40] which then may or may not enter into relation, just as, we may imagine, one may or may not link separate blocks of wood with strings. It is notable that this picture of the effect of sin can be used as a basis for *both* de Lubac's and Barth's accounts of the salvific effect of Christ. For de Lubac, the individual Christ saves by coming to indwell those who will accept him, by being born in the blocks, as it were. For Barth, the individual Christ comes to shower the blocks with the assurance of salvation. For both, the blocks persist, and in them occur the processes of increasing internalisation of the mystery of Christ for the former and ever greater thanksgiving and obedience for the latter.

De Lubac's Christ abides and transforms. Barth's Christ visits and does not transform. Both of these views have their respective coherence on the basis of our model of the blocks. Zizioulas' distinctiveness is rooted in his rejection of the blocks. His Christ is corporate, with an existence for which an alternative model is required, as we shall see below; one involving a 'fundamentally different . . . *way of relating*'.[41] This Christ visits, with, at his side, us as we shall be,[42] in dialectical (eucharistic) encounters with the realm of the blocks. Accordingly, there are *two* steps to be taken from the shared ontology of de Lubac and Barth to that of Zizioulas. Our fallen existence as blocks is what Zizioulas calls the *biological* hypostasis. In Baptism man is born into the one-many *ecclesial* hypostasis. However, the fact that this identity is not abidingly assumed and that, for instance, man continues 'to be born and to die in accordance with his biological hypostasis', means that 'another ontological category' is needed to express what we have called the *rhythmic* Christian existence, from foretaste to foretaste of the ecclesial hypostasis. This further category is what Zizioulas calls the *sacramental* or *eucharistic hypostasis*.[43]

[39] *BC*, p. 103.
[40] Cf. *HCH*, p. 425.
[41] *CECB*, p. 4.
[42] Cf. above, pp. 168, 243.
[43] Cf. *BC*, pp. 53-59, for the three hypostases named in this paragraph.

We have seen Zizioulas' eucharistic theology criticised for its lack of attention to Baptism.[44] De Lubac's eucharistic theology is similarly criticised.[45] However, the low profile of Baptism in his writings has a different cause, namely that he envisages the possible conferral of the second gift outside the visible Church, that is, without Baptism.[46] The cause in Zizioulas' writings is that he passes swiftly *through* Baptism, as it were, to what Baptism serves to inaugurate, namely eucharistic foretastes of the second gift.

> 'The new life that is born out of Baptism is made manifest only in the Eucharist.... It is not until the baptised is made a member of the eucharistic community that he or she acquires and realises the new life.'[47]

For Zizioulas, what we are as Christians is what we are, strictly speaking, only in momentary, eucharistic events in this world; but these events are *ontologically definitive*. The Christian lives in them and out of them.[48] Whereas it is an *abiding* identity that de Lubac attributes to the Christian in referring to him as a '*vir ecclesiasticus*',[49] it is a *rhythmic* identity that Zizioulas conveys by his description of the '*homo eucharisticus*'.[50] Correspondingly, we may say that Zizioulas would refine de Lubac's description of the Eucharist as the heart of the Church[51] and present it as

---

[44]Cf. above, p. 268.

[45]Cf. S. Wood, *The Church as the Social Embodiment of Grace in the Ecclesiology of Henri de Lubac*, p. 300: 'De Lubac has not attempted a systematic theology. Were he to do so, however, there are a couple of points that have not yet received an adequate accounting within a eucharistic theology. The first is an adequate theology of Baptism.'

[46]Cf. above, p. 41; also accounts such as that given by de Lubac in *DGod*, pp. 109-110, where, without mention of Baptism, he dramatically describes the outcome of man's fidelity, even amid perplexity, to the *élan* of his being. 'Then, to our astonishment, the Gift of God intervenes. It is the second gift.'

[47]*EPL*, p. 192.

[48]The local eucharistic community, that is, strictly, the local community, in the eucharistic event, is 'his existential milieu here and now' (*BC*, p. 237).

[49]Cf. above, pp. 12, 21.

[50]*EPL*, p. 203.

[51]Cf. above, p. xvi.

her *beating* heart, the ecclesial life it sustains being one marked by gathering and dispersal, week by week, in each place.

Blocks and Strings and Spiders' Webs

Let us now improve the model we used in the last chapter for the one-many structure of communion and then examine, in the next section, the consequence of the fact that this structure only pertains properly to the Eucharist and therefore rhythmically to the Church on earth.

Refining the model of a disc,[52] we may consider a spider's web (most helpfully envisaged in a horizontal plane), in which the web of relations links the beings represented by its junctions or points. A marked advantage of this model is that *link* is readily seen to be too *weak* a term, for a point in a network of lines is *defined* by the lines which meet there, joining it to other points. Here the relational web *constitutes* the points, *as junctions;* no point *exists* until there are such relational lines. Relationship or communion is ontologically decisive: the difference between being and not being. We have a model which faithfully shuns that which Zizioulas wishes to shun, namely the view that 'you first *are* and then relate'.[53]

Moreover, the model has a definite *structure.* If Zizioulas simply said that being result from communion, then a simple lattice would serve as a model. Although Zizioulas esteems the insights of Martin Buber, particularly in distinguishing individuality from personhood,[54] ultimately he parts company from the latter on the grounds that 'communion is not a relationship understood for its own sake'. Zizioulas will not reject a system in which *substance* is primary only to embrace one in which *communion* is, for both deny the priority of the particular, the primacy of the *person.*

---

[52]Cf. above, 251-252.
[53]*BC*, p. 103. Cf. above, p. 272.
[54]*Ibid.*, p. 226, cf. pp. 164-165, with reference to Buber, *I and Thou*, p. 62.

'Just like "substance", "communion" does not exist by itself: it is the *Father* who is the "cause" of it.'[55]

To say that 'God is love' is to say not that the nature of God is love and therefore that God is a communion of persons, but rather that the *Father* is love,[56] who 'out of love freely begets the Son and brings forth the Spirit'.[57] Accordingly, our model must have a source and focus, as in a spider's web. Every point there is radially connected to the centre as well as being laterally connected to other points. If the central point is removed the whole structure disintegrates. But likewise, the centre, as a *point*, exists only in relation to the points around it, to which it gives being. It and they are mutually constitutive.

Applying the model of the web to the local church, we may appreciate that Ordination either introduces someone into the web, into the *ordo* of layperson by Baptism and Confirmation, or alters their position in the web. For example, Ordination as a bishop would move a Christian ordinarily from a presbyteral point to the focal episcopal point. Such moves are clearly *transfers* and not *additions* of anything, in line with Zizioulas' opinion that it is 'very questionable' to say that the bishop 'somehow possesses the "fulness of priesthood"'.[58] All that the points have in common is membership of the net, which each has only in the specificity of its own position, in line with Zizioulas' rejection of the 'priesthood of all believers' if this means something that everyone shares in the community *prior* to the differentiation brought about by 'particular charismata (= ordinations)',[59] and especially if it is taken to designate an underlying identity as *laity* which all have in the

---

[55] *Ibid.*, pp. 17-18. In what may be seen as a defence of Buber against this criticism by Zizioulas, von Balthasar comments about the 'I-Thou' relationship that Buber does not erect it 'into a general univocal principle'; 'it is . . . a principle which Buber regards as decisively indicative of the relationship of the creature to God' (*Martin Buber and Christianity*, p. 113).

[56] Cf. above, p. 245.

[57] *BC*, p. 41.

[58] *BTD*, p. 25. According to the view here questioned, the bishop can, in consequence, 'perform every sacramental function in the Church'.

[59] *OAS*, p. 36.

community, instead of the laity being recognised as a specific *ordo* alongside the other specific *ordines*.[60] Each Christian is priestly exactly 'according to the charisma given to him'.[61] Points are distinguished not by gradation but, as in the Trinity, purely by '*specificity of relationship*'[62] and the realisation that *relationship*, which we have already seen to be ontologically decisive, here actually indicates ministerial *function* enables us to perceive what Zizioulas means when he speaks of no longer having to choose *between* 'ontological' and 'functional' understandings of ministry, as a *dilemma*.[63]

The ontology which Zizioulas is explicitly opposing is that according to which Ordination confers a charism subsequently *possessed* by the individual concerned,[64] such that he can be 'understood in himself'.[65] We have seen that de Lubac would never say that the Christian can *possess* grace and then be understood in himself. Grace cannot be 'separated from its Source' as something 'which man would appropriate to himself.'[66] However, this very quotation may serve to focus Zizioulas' objection, for the direction in which de Lubac would direct us to seek understanding of each Christian is clearly *vertical*, in relation to the divine Source, whereas it is primarily *horizontal* for Zizioulas, in relation to his fellow Christians. 'The way to God has to pass *through* the relationship with the neighbour.'[67] The Christian comes to God by the mystical identification of the horizontal tier of his primary ecclesial relations with the other two tiers which we saw above.[68] The Eucharist is not 'the vertical relation of each with God', but rather 'the communal, catholic expression of the total Church'.[69] Zizioulas' applica-

---

[60]Cf. *MOC*, p. 191.

[61]*OAC*, p. 192. Cf. *GIE*, p. 259: 'The multiplicity of people and the multiplicity of ministries are correlative.'

[62]*PDC*, p. 151; cf. *OAS*, p. 37.

[63]E.g. *BC*, p. 164. Cf. above, p. 179.

[64]Such ontology is what Zizioulas calls 'ontologism' (*BC*, pp. 233-234; *OAS*, p. 37). Cf. above, p. 190.

[65]*OAC*, p. 189.

[66]*BCat*, p. 42. Cf. above, p. 44.

[67]*ECC*, p. 37.

[68]Cf. above, p. 252.

[69]*VEM*, p. 84.

tion of this scheme to monasticism sharply contrasts with de Lubac's account of the horizontal relations between monks *via* their individual relationships with God.[70]

'The monk had to find γέρων, a spiritual father, to whom he would offer his full obedience. It is interesting to note that all this involved a *horizontal* relationship and not an individual relationship with God. The event of communion that character-ises all charismatic life lies at the heart of asceticism.'[71]

Saward adopts the vertical approach of de Lubac when he says, in criticism of Zizioulas, that the primary effect of Ordina-tion is that 'it places the minister in a permanent relation to the person of the Word made flesh'.

'Zizioulas is right to stress the minister's relation to the Body, but he neglects somewhat his relation to its Head, for it is the latter relation that is the foundation of the former.'[72]

In fact, Zizioulas does not relate the minister to 'the Body' in the sense intended by Saward. Recalling the tiers, we must say, with regard to the bishop, that Zizioulas relates him to the *local church*, which in its Eucharist is mystically identified with the Body as the bishop is there identified with Christ the Head. Saward's criticism is based on the view that if priesthood is not exclusively derived from Christ then it must be exclusively derived from the Christian community, and that the latter is not acceptable.[73] However, this dichotomy arises out of the separation of Christ from the Church which is precisely what Zizioulas most fundamentally opposes.

It is with regard to the *horizontal* dimension that we may say that de Lubac aligns with the view that Zizioulas criticises: 'you first *are* and then relate'.[74] We may model this view precisely with the blocks mentioned earlier, where the secondary, hori-zontal relations are represented by strings which *link* the

---

[70]Cf. above, p. 20.
[71]*CMBC*, p. 20.
[72]J. Saward, review of *BC*, p. 47.
[73]Cf. *ibid.*, p. 47.
[74]*BC*, p. 103. Cf. above, pp. 272, 274.

blocks, but manifestly do not determine the *existence* of the blocks themselves.

Zizioulas considers that the horizontal relations between Christians *are* determinative and exist in the web of the eucharistic event. It is at these moments that Christians, in communities, strictly *are* the Body of Christ. From the close reading which Zizioulas often recommends of chapters 10-14 of the First Letter to the Corinthians, he deduces that 'for St Paul the Body of Christ is literally composed of the charismata of the Spirit (charisma = membership of the Body)'.[75] Moreover, since these chapters 'in one way or another treat directly of the Eucharist',[76] he concludes that the charisms 'only find their proper place in this Pentecostal gathering'.[77] It is *from the Eucharist* that Christians 'return into the world rejoicing and full of charisms',[78] which they will exercise there *by extension*.[79] St Paul's emphasis on *love* in chapter 13 of this letter ought to be recognised as pointing to the charisms' place *ontologically* in the Body of Christ and therefore *historically* in the Eucharist.[80]

The charismata are '*absolutely relational notions*',[81] that is, they pertain to each Christian specifically as a member of the local church. Since each charism is a gift of the Spirit, Zizioulas equivalently says that no Christian 'can possess the Spirit as an individual, but only as a member of the community'.[82] As the local community in the Eucharist is the Body of Christ, so also it, strictly, is the Temple of the Spirit. As Zizioulas interprets such texts as Paul's statement that the mystery is 'Christ in you' to mean 'you' not as many individuals but as a single corporate unit, such that the mystery is Christ *as a community*,[83] so also he maintains that, although it is commonly assumed to do so, the New Testament never refers to Christians as temples of the

---

[75] *BC*, p. 111. Cf. *OAC*, p. 189; *PDC*, p. 150.
[76] *EQA*, p. 45. Cf. above, p. 133, n. 54.
[77] *BCE*, p. 651. Cf. *BC*, p. 188, n. 58; *EQA*, pp. 45-46, 69.
[78] *VEM*, p. 91.
[79] *EQA*, p. 46.
[80] Cf. *OAC*, p. 189; *BC*, p. 227, n. 48.
[81] *Ibid.*, p. 189.
[82] *ECC*, p. 27.
[83] Cf. above, p. 143.

Spirit, in the plural. Rather, it is local communities which the epistles address and acknowledge, each as a Temple of the Spirit.[84]

We may contrast de Lubac's view that Christ is born in Christians through the active presence of the Spirit in them, which understands the Spirit to be present in *each* Christian since Christ is born in each,[85] with the view of Zizioulas, for whom Christ is present as the local eucharistic community by the inbreaking of the Spirit upon the assembly. Whereas de Lubac considers that, in the Spirit, Christ comes to save the fallen human blocks by being born into each, Zizioulas envisages salvation by the blocks' regular experience, in the Spirit, of a quite different life as points in the web of Christ. Unlike blocks, points offer no volume in which to dwell; Zizioulas never speaks of Christ indwelling each Christian.[86]

There are two limitations of de Lubac's view. First, it indicates no essential unit in which Church members live, no definitive existential milieu, no structural articulation of the Church, other than that which serves to initiate and strengthen the life of the indwelling Christ in her members and then to reflect the communality of the life engendered. The model of unity which it uses is a coincident unity-of-identity, where all are one because of the same Christ in each.[87] We have suggested that this model pays little attention to the horizontal component of the personhood of Christians, namely their relations with one another, and that respecting this component requires a model in which they would be held apart in a differentiated unity-of-complementarity by Christ in their midst, as one of the many.[88]

---

[84]I am indebted for this point to personal discussions with Zizioulas. The singular form ('temple', 'building', . . .) is indeed notable in 1 Cor. 3: 16-17; 1 Cor. 3: 9; 2 Cor. 6: 16; Eph. 2: 21-22. However, 1 Cor. 6: 19 ('your body is a temple of the Holy Spirit within you') does seem in context to be a teaching directed to *individual* Christians, to whom Paul has just said: 'Do you not know that your bodies are members of Christ?' (v. 15)

[85]Cf. above, p. 271.

[86]Cf. above, p. 259, n. 120, and below, pp. 283-285.

[87]Cf. above, pp. 15-19.

[88]Cf. above, pp. 66-67, 96, 254.

The latter is the model of unity which Zizioulas applies to the local church. Though he then speaks of these local churches themselves being in a coincident unity-of-identity, we have seen that his criticisms of Afanassieff manifest an emerging conviction that there is a differentiated oneness, not only *within* each local church, but also, in a certain way, *among* local churches.[89] Accordingly, he has been moving towards understanding the worldwide configuration of local churches as *one-many*.[90] In this configuration, local churches are held apart in unity, such that each can fulfil its task, which is to engage all the particularities of a given geographical locality, in order to *transcend* them, 'by bringing all these natural and cultural particularities up to God in the unity of the one Body of His Son'.[91] A 'eucharistic approach to life' means 'accepting and sanctifying the material world and not undermining its importance in any way'.[92] We may note that these comments serve to refute Baillargeon's criticism that Zizioulas gives 'little space' to 'relations with cultures and with the world'.[93]

The second problem with de Lubac's view of Christ lastingly indwelling the members of the Church is that it is difficult then to distance him adequately from their sins. Intolerably, he can seem implicated, as he can also in any errors of the hierarchy if they are deemed to propagate Christ's life and teaching in the emphatically historical way which de Lubac describes.[94] Contrary to the view that Christians bear Christ within them and that Christian ministers additionally bear Christ through history, in blocks upon blocks, as it were, Zizioulas proposes the view that bishop and people *are* Christ, in their respective orders, in the web of the Eucharist *and only then*. All the Church's members, life, words and action must be tested there.[95]

---

[89]Cf. above, pp. 233-235.
[90]Cf. above, pp. 204-211.
[91]*EII*, p. 149. Cf. *BC*, pp. 253-259; *OAC*, p. 192.
[92]*ECC*, p. 35.
[93]Baillargeon, 'Porte-parole', p. 192.
[94]Cf. above, pp. 256-257.
[95]Cf. above, pp. 198-200, 265-268.

People of God and Body of Christ

Both de Lubac and Zizioulas explicitly recognise the danger of 'ecclesiological monophysitism', but their understandings of this danger are diametrically opposite. For de Lubac, it is 'an exaggerated assimilation of the Church with Christ',[96] whereas Zizioulas says that 'we risk becoming monophysite in ecclesiology' if we *separate* the Church from Christ, in the (mistaken) belief that 'Christ does not draw his identity from his relation with the Church'.[97] At the start of this chapter, we saw how Zizioulas manages both to identify the Church with Christ and also to give full place to the need for the Church on earth to repent. We may now see how this view offers an original contribution to the long-running debate about the relative merits of the terms 'Body of Christ' and 'People of God' for the New Testament Church.[98]

De Lubac urges us to recognise that the Church is 'made up of men'.

> 'She is (or ought to be) wholly subject to Christ; she is a people, often unfaithful and unsubmissive. In her members she is a sinner.'[99]

His reference to the Church as 'a people' in this context might lead us to expect that he would favour the description of the pilgrim Church on earth as the People of God. However, he does not. He considers that the second chapter of *Lumen Gentium*, which gives the Church this name, does not fully heed 'the traditional dialectic between the two Testaments'. It gives, he says, the impression of 'continuity rather than transforma-

---

[96] *ChPM*, p. 24, n. 35.

[97] *MCO*, p. 299; cf. above, pp. 258-259. Ecclesiological monophysitism here means seeing the Church as purely *human*. I draw on personal discussions with Zizioulas for confirmation of this interpretation, which differs from the normal meaning which 'monophysite' has in theology, namely 'of a purely *divine* nature'.

[98] For the debate in Roman Catholic theology, cf. Ratzinger, *Das neue Volk Gottes*, pp. 75-104; Congar, *Le concile de Vatican II*, pp. 109-161; McNamara, *The Church*, pp. 9-35.

[99] *ChPM*, p. 24.

tion'.[100] He is concerned to avoid what he calls 'the mistake made by certain Protestant ecclesiologies', which fail 'to take account of and draw the consequences of the Christian novelty'.[101]

De Lubac's view is that this newness or 'novelty' makes the Church the Body of Christ and that this single image serves to convey *both* the identification with and the distinction from Christ which a balanced ecclesiology needs.

> 'The image of the Church as a body is ambivalent [*ambivalente*], making, as it does, a single organism of Jesus Christ and his Church but signifying at the same time the subjection of the members to the head.'[102]

However, *ambivalence* is a weaker term than *paradox,* and de Lubac is committed to there being genuine and manifold *paradox* inherent in the mystery of the Church. He says that there are three paradoxes or antitheses, which are actually all 'facets of the same basic paradox':

> 'the Church is of God (*de Trinitate*) and she is of men (*ex hominibus*); she is visible and invisible; she is of this earth and this time and she is eschatological and eternal'.[103]

But the image which de Lubac suggests to express the basic paradox, that of the body, involves no paradox of two apparently contradictory features, but simply the ambivalence of a single organism in which the members are subjected to the Head. Thus, there appears to be a tension between the paradox he desires and the image he describes.

By reducing the paradox to a mere ambivalence, de Lubac suggests that its poles are not fully distinct, as would be

---

[100]*Ibid.*, pp. 42, 43. De Lubac thinks that 'a just equilibrium' was established in the final text of *Lumen Gentium* by the fact that this second chapter follows an initial chapter on 'the mystery of the Church' (*ibid.*, pp. 44-45). He himself remarkably foreshadowed this opening of *Lumen Gentium* in his *Méditation sur l'Eglise,* in 1953, the opening chapter of which was entitled 'L'Eglise est un mystère'.

[101]*Ibid.*, p. 25. Cf. above, p. 56.

[102]*Ibid.*, p. 24.

[103]*Ibid.*, p. 23; cf. *Catholicism,* p. 27 (quoted above, p. 91).

required for a genuine dialectic. We have just seen de Lubac warn that emphasis on continuity between the Old and the New Testaments can mar their proper dialectic. Recalling now his own statement that there is 'an underlying continuity' between the Church's temporal and eternal reality[104] and noting that continuity is strongly conveyed by the element of *indwelling* in the following account, we may suspect this indwelling of being what compromises the ecclesiological dialectic.

> 'In one way, for the people of God envisaged as still on pilgrimage through the obscurity of this world, it is altogether a matter of the "not-yet". But in another way — one that cannot be disassociated from the first — for the Church considered as a gift from above and the habitation of Christ and his Spirit [*habitée par le Christ et son Esprit*], we are faced with the "already-present".'[105]

De Lubac's doctrine of indwelling derives from his view that Christ is not dependent upon the Church, that he stands distinct from her and comes, in a second phase, to indwell her members. De Lubac speaks firmly of 'the distance [*distance*] to be kept between the head of the body and the other members'.[106] The Church then has a 'borrowed splendour' from her head, which on earth she sometimes 'disguises . . . in a shabby garment'.[107] This metaphor eloquently conveys the distance between Christ and the Church, the glow she acquires from his indwelling and the effect of sin, which is to cloud that glow, such that only a 'penetrating regard' discloses 'the beauty of her face'.[108] What will happen on the last day, we conclude, is that all disguises will be removed so that her beauty shines unclouded, though still as a reflection of Christ who

---

[104] *Splendour*, p. 52.

[105] *ChPM*, p. 52.

[106] *Ibid.*, p. 41. De Lubac adds that the distance is well conveyed by reference to the Church as the People of God, but he insists, nevertheless, that it is 'an essential characteristic of the idea of the Body of Christ'.

[107] *Ibid.*, p. 25.

[108] *Ibid.*, p. 25.

remains at a certain distance from her. What she will be then is what she now already is internally, waiting for the day of its full maturation and manifestation.

The interaction between what the Church already is and what she will be, between the *Ecclesia ex hominibus* and the *Ecclesia de Trinitate*, is overshadowed in de Lubac's approach by the distance which remains between her and Christ in *both* of her states. Zizioulas' distinctive approach to this interaction derives from his recognition of Christ's dependence upon the Church, that is, upon the *Ecclesia de Trintate*. Indeed, as we have seen, he presents Christ as one of the Church, the *Ecclesia sanctorum*.[109] By so doing, he invests the ecclesiological interaction with the distance which de Lubac defends, now seen as a distance not between Christ and the Church in both of her states, but rather between the *corporate* Christ and the Church *on earth*. Moreover, by centring the Church on earth on the *bishop* in each locality (and not on Christ, as such), he *completely* distinguishes the interacting poles, such that they can be in a genuinely dialectical relationship.

De Lubac seeks an ecclesiological dialectic but the continuing distance between Christ and the Church is what dominates in his account. With his corporate understanding of Christ, Zizioulas transforms this distance into the service of the dialectic itself, such that the local church around the bishop is really distinct from the heavenly Church around Christ and mystically identified with the latter only in the Eucharist. Christ is distanced from the earthly sins and errors of Christians and their bishops, but not from the Church.

For de Lubac, the Church on earth is already inwardly the Body of Christ and the dialectic works itself out in her historical growth. Taking into account the preparation for this process in the Old Testament, he speaks overall of the need to distinguish 'three main epochs and three successive conditions of the Church'.[110] On this theme, he refers in this context to Methodius

---

[109]Cf. above, pp.140, 180.
[110]*Splendour*, p. 41.

of Olympus[111] and, elsewhere, to Ambrose[112] and Maximus.[113] The latter reference is of particular interest to us because it is to a text which Zizioulas frequently quotes, as in the following passage.

'The things of the Old Testament are shadow (σκιά); those of the New Testament are image (εἰκών); and those of the future state are truth (ἀλήθεια).'[114]

Zizioulas' freeing of the eschaton from history, by means of his corporate understanding of Christ,[115] enables genuinely dialectical encounters between them which correspond to Maximus' view of the future truth and its present *eikon* with a rigour which de Lubac's organic view, based on the individual and then indwelling Christ, is unable to achieve.

Yves Congar and Joseph Ratzinger both give more recognition to the title *People of God* for the Church than de Lubac does. However, like him, they consider the Church to be essentially the Body of Christ and they give organic accounts of this identity historically developing.

Congar says that Protestant thought does not properly recognise the dialectic which characterises the pilgrim Church: 'the *not yet* diminishes or overshadows the truth of the *is now*'.[116] Since the Incarnation, Easter and Pentecost, the People of God has become the Body of Christ.[117] He particularly associates

---

[111]*Ibid.*, p. 41, n. 2; reference to Methodius, *Convivium decem virginum*, 5, 7 (PG 18, 109C), on the actual Church between the 'shadows' of the Law and the 'truths' of the future. Methodius uses the same triad of σκιά, εἰκών and ἀλήθεια as Maximus (see below, n. 113).

[112]*PSpir*1, p. 33; reference (without specific citations) to Ambrose on 'the progression *umbra* (Old Testament) — *imago* (New Testament) — *veritas* (in patria)'. *CMys*, p. 219, n. 55, specifies Ambrose, *In ps. 38*, 25 (PL 14, 1051-1052) and *De excessu fratris sui Satyri*, 2 (= *De fide resurrectionis*), n. 109 (PL 16, 1347).

[113]*CMys*, p. 219, n. 55; reference to Maximus, *Sch. in Eccl. Hier.*, 3, 3, 2 (PG 4, 137D); cf. *ibid.*, p. 213, n. 22.

[114]*BC*, p. 99; quotation from Maximus as in previous note. Also, *ESLT*, pp. 15-17; *CMBC*, p. 18. Cf. McPartlan, 'Eucharist and Church', pp. 856-857.

[115]Cf. above, pp. 261-262.

[116]Congar, 'The Church: The People of God', p. 14.

[117]Cf. *ibid.*, p. 16.

this new identity with the indwelling of the Spirit, in the Church herself and in each Christian.[119] Nevertheless, on her historical journey, her members are 'sinful and weak'[119] and it is the Eucharist which strengthens their new identity.

> 'The People of God says: *congregatio fidelium*, assembly of believers. This assembly brings about the Eucharist. . . . And then the Eucharist makes the Body of Christ; the Eucharist moulds the People of God into the Body of Christ.'[120]

Ratzinger identifies the Eucharist as that which gives the Church her new identity: 'this meal appears as the original foundation [*Quellgrund*] of a new Israel and as its lasting centre'.[121] Christians are 'the new People of God'; *new*, in that they are God's people *as the Body of Christ*.[122] The latter is an inner, growing identity, as Ratzinger makes clear by saying that, in the Eucharist, the Church 'confirms and fulfils her invisible identity [*Wesen*] as the Body of Christ'.[123] Until she reaches her goal, she 'continually needs purification and renewal', which is a fact conveyed by the concept of the People of God. Without this corrective, as in the Roman Catholic ecclesiology of the Body of Christ several decades ago, 'a definitive quality was ascribed to all the Church's official statements and actions so that any criticism could appear as an attack on Christ himself'.

> 'The Christological difference, it was said, must once again clearly be brought out: the Church is not identical with Christ but stands over against him.'[124]

However, if this is said of the Church in this world, where she is already, though invisibly, the Body of Christ, it appears that Ratzinger acknowledges that, even in eternity, when this iden-

---

[118]Cf. *ibid.*, p. 15.

[119]*Ibid.*, p. 15.

[120]Congar in a discussion recorded in John H. Miller (ed.), *Vatican II: An Interfaith Appraisal*, pp. 231-232.

[121]Ratzinger, *Das neue Volk Gottes*, p. 79.

[122]*Ibid.*, p. 82; cf. p. 85.

[123]*Ibid.*, p. 85.

[124]Ratzinger, *Church, Ecumenism and Politics*, p. 16.

tity alone will apply, there will *still* be a distance between Christ and the Church; she will still stand over against him. In other words, the sin of the pilgrim people does not *cause* the distance, but only compounds it. Thus, with Ratzinger, as with de Lubac (and Congar), we do not find the two concepts of the Body of Christ and the People of God *fully distinguished*, so as to enable a genuine dialectic between them, the reason being that all three consider there to be a permanent distance between the Church and Christ, who does not depend on her as she depends on him.

Zizioulas' distinctive approach to the relationship between these concepts has already been indicated: there is identification between Christ and the eschatological Church and distance between that corporate entity and each local church around its bishop in this world. The Eucharist gathers the latter and makes it into the former. It 'gathers in one place "together" the scattered People of God' and 'this People "gathered together" and celebrating the Eucharist becomes "the Church of God",'[125] which is synonymous with the Body of Christ for Zizioulas.[126] 'The eucharistic community is the Body of Christ *par excellence*,'[127] says Zizioulas, by which he understands a *rhythmic* attainment, for, as we have seen, the identity experienced in the Eucharist is immediately lost again, to be abidingly acquired only on the last day.[128] While still being 'the People of God journeying in history', in the Eucharist, where she 'lives the presence of Christ', the Church 'becomes what she is delayed in being [*ce qu'il lui tarde d'être*]'.[129] In short, the People of God is *rhythmically* the Body of Christ.

---

[125] *EFEL*, pp. 5, 4, respectively: '*L'eucharistie rassemble le peuple de Dieu dispersé en un lieu "en commun"*'; '*ce peuple "réuni en commun" et célébrant l'eucharistie devient "l'Eglise de Dieu"*'.

[126] 'Church of God' means 'an image or sign of the Trinity' (*DGT*, p. 29), which we are as the Body of Christ in the Eucharist (cf. above, pp. 193-194; also, n. 127 below).

[127] *BC*, p. 114. Zizioulas continues, '. . . simply because it incarnates and realises our communion within the very life and communion of the Trinity'.

[128] *VEM*, p. 91. Cf. above, p. 270.

[129] *EQA*, p. 31.

Equivalently, for Zizioulas, the Church on earth is rhythmically the Kingdom of God. The fact that this identification is *rhythmic* removes the 'fears' which Zizioulas regards as 'to some extent behind the reaction of the Reformation against the medieval Church'. These fears result when the identification is thought to *abide* in history,[130] such that *all* of the Church's historical statements and actions assume the definitive character of the Kingdom.[131] 'By being the *eikon* of the Kingdom the Church is at the same time maximalised and minimalised.' She is maximalised by her identification with Christ and the Kingdom, but minimalised in that she does not *possess* this identity, but only rhythmically experiences it *from the future*: 'she has no *hypostasis* of her own but draws her identity from Christ and the Kingdom to come'.[132]

Christ and the Kingdom to come are not *two* realities in this latter quotation, but *one*. Ultimately this is the key to Zizioulas' position and to the way in which he avoids the problems which we have noted with regard to the Body of Christ being an abiding reality in this world.[133] If Christ is an individual, whose historical achievement is past, then he can come to abide in creatures, taking them as his Body and leading them to their destiny. However, the Body of Christ does not yet exist and so cannot abide in history if their destiny is his achievement, which it is if Christ is intrinsically *corporate*.

---

[130]Cf. *BC*, p. 185.
[131]Cf. Ratzinger's comments quoted above, p. 286.
[132]*MCO*, p. 300.
[133]Cf. particularly, above, p. 280.

Conclusion

The existential emphasis of both of the theologians we have considered[1] makes it appropriate to conclude by comparing their views of the relationship between the Church and the world.

The Church and the World

'The Church is essentially missionary because what we call her *missions* are nothing other than the first means by which she fulfils her *mission*.'[2]

'Through Ordination the Church becomes the community which *relates the world to God*—and this is essentially what mission should mean. Mission is not a method ... but an *attribute* related to the nature of the Church.'[3]

Both de Lubac and Zizioulas, respectively, here express their conviction that mission is essentially bound up with the nature of the Church. However, there is a significant divergence of meaning between them. For de Lubac, the Church's mission is to the world of humanity, bringing Christ to men, whereas for Zizioulas her mission is to the world of creation, acting as *Christ* and lifting it to God.[4] This contrast underlies the striking difference between de Lubac's view that each Christian must preach the Gospel, giving this gift to others so as 'to participate in the divine Life, which is Gift',[5] and Zizioulas' opinion that 'the celebration of the sacraments, especially the

---

[1]Cf. above, pp. 10-13, 130-138, respectively.
[2]De Lubac, *FTMiss*, p. 17; cf. above, p. 98.
[3]Zizioulas, *OAC*, p. 190; cf. *BC*, pp. 224-225.
[4]Cf. *BC*, p. 211.
[5]*FTMiss*, p. 41. Cf. P. McPartlan, 'Henri de Lubac – Evangeliser', p. 345.

Eucharist' is, for the Church, 'perhaps more crucial than the preaching of the Word'.

> 'For the sacraments involve *all* creation in the being of the Church — not only humans — and the Church becomes in this way the very core and nucleus of the destiny of the world.'[6]

De Lubac likewise says that 'in her very visibility the Church is the vital nucleus around which gather from age to age, and in ways often hidden from us, *all* those who are to be saved', but his vision is of the Church's position among *humanity*, as 'the soul of this great *human* body',[7] rather than the Church at the interface between God and *all* of His creation, with her members acting 'as priest of creation, because of and in the name of the priesthood of Christ, the High Priest *par excellence*'.[8] Though de Lubac recalls St Paul's doctrine that God's purpose is 'to reunite [ἀνακεφαλαιώσασθαι] all things in Christ',[9] thereby forming the Body of Christ, he immediately omits all creation beneath man in saying of Christ that he is the one in whom 'man and God, man and man, are in communion and achieve union'.[10] Zizioulas, on the other hand, with emphasis, omits *nothing* from the union of the Body of Christ, effected in the Eucharist.

> 'The Eucharist accepts and sanctifies *all* of creation "recapitulated" in the one Body [*dans le corps unique*] of the "first-born of creation".'[11]

It is because Zizioulas places relations between human beings within the fuller context of the relationship between God and creation through humanity, that verbal proclamation of the Gospel, which of its nature impinges only on human beings, is placed by him firmly within the context of the Eucharist which reaches to embrace all creation.

[6] *MCO*, p. 296.
[7] *Splendour*, p. 177 (my italics). Here, as elsewhere (e.g. *Faith*, p. ix), de Lubac recalls the teaching of the *Epistle to Diognetus*, 6 (Bihlmeyer, pp. 144-145).
[8] *EQA*, p. 71.
[9] *Catholicism*, p. 10 (amended translation), with reference to Eph 1: 9-10.
[10] *Ibid.*, p. 11.
[11] *EQA*, p. 70.

'The Eucharist calls man to bring [*rapporter*] the whole world back to God; it *is* itself this offering to God, an *anaphora*. It follows that the Eucharist is inseparably linked to proclamation of the *Word of God* which calls man, and through him all creation, to come back [*faire retour*] to God (*metanoia*).'[12]

As we saw earlier, de Lubac's emphasis on the practical centrality of the Eucharist in the Church, whereby he affirms that 'Christ *in his Eucharist* is truly the heart of the Church',[13] appears to be compromised by a parallel emphasis on the Scriptures.[14] We may now say that if the salvific emphasis is purely on man then this duality threatens. By placing man in his unique position with regard to the whole of creation, Zizioulas offers a way of esteeming the Scriptures firmly *within* a eucharistic focus, a way moreover which should commend itself to de Lubac in that it also responds to what he has acknowledged as gaps in his vision, namely his lack of an adequate integration of man into the universe and of the universe into the Kingdom, gaps which are clearly related.[15]

We may further suggest that the historical weakness of the Orthodox mission to *people*, which Zizioulas admits,[16] is the result of an improper minimising of *this* mission within a proper mission to creation. That Zizioulas himself is emphasising his overall context and not just neglecting the ministry of the word must not be forgotten by those, such as Congar, who legitimately criticise the low profile which the latter has in his writings: '[i]t is true that the Word was made flesh, but it also spoke!'[17] A fair summary would be that, in his vigorous reaction against the Church's presence in the world becoming just 'an ambo without a sanctuary',[18] Zizioulas himself has not sufficiently rehabilitated the ambo within the sanctuary.

---

[12]*Ibid.*, p. 70.

[13]*Splendour*, p. 113 (my italics). Cf. above, pp. 13, 70.

[14]Cf. above, pp. 72-73.

[15]Cf. above, pp. 30, 48-49.

[16]*BC*, p. 182 and n. 36.

[17]Congar, 'Bulletin d'ecclésiologie', p. 89. Cf. Baillargeon, 'Porte-parole', p. 192.

[18]*VEM*, p. 90. Cf. above, pp. 133, 138.

De Lubac follows Augustine in teaching that the Eucharist gathers and constitutes the Church.[19] The remarkable absence from Augustine's major writings of the verse about recapitulation in Paul's Letter to the Ephesians[20] justifies us in attributing de Lubac's difficulty in integrating all of creation into the Kingdom at least partly to the influence of Augustine. For Augustine, 'Christ as man' is the *way* by which men come to 'Christ as God', that is not to Christ in his glorified humanity but 'to the Word who was in the beginning God with God'.[21] The Word is 'the wholly spiritual food of the angels' which man desires and which the Incarnation has made accessible to him.[22] Augustine's accent is on man's *release* from materiality, rather than on the Incarnation as the means whereby embodied man might be enduringly established in the enfleshed Christ at the interface between the spiritual and material creation, as priest of the latter.

Zizioulas stresses that the Eucharist constitutes the 'catholic Church': 'in a way which involves the whole creation in it, and not just human beings or angelic powers'.[23] He considers that, particularly by his understanding of time, Augustine cuts man off from the material creation.

'Under the influence of modern existentialist philosophies which in this respect go back to St Augustine, the concept of time has been associated mainly with what man experiences psychologically as time. Augustine seems to have been the first one to deduce time from the self-interpretation of presence, as a study of Book XI, chapters 13-29 of his *Confessions* shows. . . . This understanding of time, valid as it may be to some extent, introduces a dichotomy between man and nature. . . . [W]e

[19] *Splendour*, p. 106. Cf. above, p. 105.

[20] Augustine makes no reference to Eph. 1:10 in his *Confessions, Tractates on John, City of God, De Trinitate* and *Enarrationes in Psalmos*. In contrast, Irenaeus quotes or alludes to this verse five times: *Adv. Haer.* 1, 3, 3 (PG 7, 473A); 1, 10, 1 (549B); 3, 16, 6 (925 C, D); 3, 21, 9 (954C); 5, 20, 2 (1178B).

[21] Augustine, *In Joann.* 13, 4 (PL 35, 1494). Cf. above, p. 59.

[22] Camelot, 'Réalisme et symbolisme dans la doctrine eucharistique de s.Augustin', p. 401, with reference to Augustine, *Enarr. in Psalm 134*, 5: 'In order that man might eat the bread of angels, the Creator of the angels made himself man' (PL 37, 1742). Cf. below, n. 30.

[23] *MCO*, p. 302; cf. *CECB*, p. 5.

must try to work out an approach which would make room for creation as a whole and not only for man's experience of time, as if only man existed in the world or as if time would not have really existed if there was no man to experience it.'[24]

We have seen that Zizioulas considers that man's communion with God in Christ occurs when he goes out of himself to offer creation to God through the hands of the bishop in the Eucharist.[25] Diametrically opposed is Augustine's understanding that each encounters God by entering into himself. Jean Guitton refers to the two occasions which Augustine describes in his *Confessions* 'when, so to speak, he had touched eternity'.[26] In Augustine's account of the second occasion, there is concentrated 'his whole conception of the relationship between eternity and time'.[27] The eternity fleetingly experienced by him and Monica was not God's eternity but 'their eternity in God',[28] the *aevum*. Taking the earlier, similar occasion when Augustine returned into himself to be that when he heard the words, '*non me in te mutabis sicut cibum carnis tuae, sed tu mutaberis in me*',[29] we may confirm that de Lubac's application of them to the public encounter with the incarnate Christ in the Eucharist is a multiple alteration of their original context.[30]

By linking experience of the *aevum* with the Eucharist in this way, de Lubac moves towards reflecting the bond between the *aeon* and the Eucharist in the writings of Basil, which Zizioulas

---

[24]*ESLT*, pp. 2-3; but cf. also, above, p.47.

[25]Cf. above, p. 198.

[26]J. Guitton, *Le Temps et l'Eternité chez Plotin et Saint Augustin*, p. 194, with reference to Augustine, *Confessions*, 7, 17, 23 (PL 32, 744-745); 9, 10, 24 (PL 32, 774).

[27]*Ibid.*, p. 197.

[28]*Ibid.*, p. 198.

[29]That is, taking the occasions described in *Confessions* , 7, 17, 23 (PL 32, 744-745) and 7, 10, 16 (PL 32, 742), to be the same.

[30]Cf. above, p. 68. Camelot considers that even texts in which Augustine speaks of eating the bread of angels, such as that mentioned above in n. 22, do not refer directly to eucharistic eating: 'it is much less a question here of eucharistic bread than of the Incarnation and of the spiritual contacts of faith and love which it permits with the Word' ('Réalisme et symbolisme dans la doctrine eucharistique de s. Augustin', p. 401).

notes,[31] as did Daniélou.[32] However, whereas Zizioulas immediately defines 'the new *aeon*' as 'the new earth and the new
heaven',[33] de Lubac's admitted inability to integrate 'this
terrestrial world into the eternal Kingdom'[34] shows that, for
him, rather than bringing the material creation into the *aevum*,
the link serves to make of the Eucharist an experience of
Augustinian *abstraction* from material creation.

Congar indicates the dangers of such an abstraction. He
considers that recent centuries lost 'the realisation that Christianity presents a *hope*, a total hope, even for the material
world'. This separated Christianity provoked a reaction.

> 'Confronted by religion without a world, men formulated the
> idea of a world without religion.'[35]

These comments convey humanity's natural solidarity, not
only internally but also with the material world, and its instinctive rejection of the notion that anyone or even anything is
dispensable. They imply that de Lubac's overriding conviction
that God calls *all* human beings to the same supernatural
destiny and does not just select some for a higher beatitude
than that intended for the rest,[36] is better secured if that one
destiny itself is not seen as different from the fate of the
material world as a whole.[37] It is easier to acknowledge that all
are called to the same beatitude if that beatitude is envisaged
as the fulfilling of man's role on this created earth where the
call is experienced than as extraction from it.

Thus we see that by his contribution to a topic on which, as
we have recalled, de Lubac has admitted his own limitations
(namely, both the integration of man into the universe and

---

[31]*ESLT*, p. 17. Cf., without reference to Basil, *DPE*, p. 98; *CMBC*, p. 13.

[32]J. Daniélou, *The Bible and the Liturgy*, pp. 262-266, with reference to Basil,
De Spiritu sancto, 27, 66 (PG 32, 192 A-B) and *Ho. Hex.*, 2, 8 (PG 29, 49D-52B).
Daniélou says that, in Basil's theology of Sunday, 'the Church's day of the
eucharistic celebration' is 'the eschatological day of the age to come' (p. 266).

[33]*CMBC*, p. 13.

[34]*Athéisme*, p. 149. Cf. above, p. 49.

[35]'The Church: The People of God', p. 10.

[36]Cf. above, Chapter Two.

[37]Cf. above, pp. 130-132.

that of the universe into the Kingdom), Zizioulas is able to consolidate one of de Lubac's basic principles (namely, that all receive the same call to supernatural beatitude). We shall note other such instances below, in the final section.

Let us note now the role which Zizioulas' corporate understanding of Christ plays in this contribution. De Lubac's conviction that God calls *all* human beings to the same supernatural destiny is founded on the unity of mankind. If there is salvation for anyone, there must be salvation for Adam, 'who is in us all', and hence salvation for all, in principle, at least.

> 'If several of them [the Fathers] held so strongly . . . that Adam was saved, one of the reasons for it was undoubtedly that they saw the salvation of its head as the necessary condition of the salvation of the human race.'[38]

In his wider perspective, Zizioulas considers not that the salvation of some requires that of all, but that the salvation of man requires that of creation as a whole.

> 'The salvation of man and the transformation of nature and of creation are one, since in the thought of the Greek Fathers man is a "microcosm", whose destiny is inseparably connected with that of creation.'[39]

Zizioulas' wider perspective regards man as situated at 'the focal point of unity between God and creation in Christ'.[40] Man does not primarily stand over against Christ,[41] but rather, in Christ, he stands over against God and creation. The above mention of *Adam's* headship by de Lubac manifests his different view. He refers to the human race 'as a single being' *distinct* from Christ.

> 'With the first sin it was this being, whole and entire, which fell away, which was driven out of Paradise and sentenced to a bitter exile until the time of its redemption. And when Christ at last appeared, coming as the "one bridegroom", his bride, once again, was the "whole human race".'[42]

[38] *Catholicism*, p. 2.
[39] *ORT*, p. 17.
[40] *MCO*, p. 302.
[41] Cf. Ratzinger's comment about the Church, quoted above, p. 286.
[42] *Catholicism*, pp. 1-2; cf. above, p.15.

Though de Lubac does not use the expression, we may say that Adam is here being treated as the corporate personality of humanity: when Christ descends salvifically into Hell, 'the first man alone is mentioned'.[43] Zizioulas would agree that the human race is a single human being, but he would stipulate that that man is *Christ.* The human race holds together not in Adam, from the past, but in Christ, from the future. Adam himself becomes a corporate personality only in Christ.[44] Humanity does not stand as corporate personality to meet Christ and neither does the Church.[45] The Christian is a microcosm, not of that which encounters Christ, but of *Christ.*[46] Outside of Christ, humanity and the Church are scattered individuals.

It is *as Christ* that humanity, in the form of the Church or rather churches, assumes its proper role *vis-a-vis* both God and creation. This is the role which Zizioulas sees humanity exercising in the Liturgy, which is an encounter with Christ only within the wider context of participating in Christ's ministry to God's creation. He considers that the latter point is attested by the fact that 'all ancient eucharistic liturgies began their eucharistic prayer or canon with thanksgiving for *creation* in the first place, and only afterwards for redemption through Christ.'[47]

For Zizioulas, *all* Christians, in their respective orders in the Eucharist, exercise the priesthood of Christ; *complementarily* they *are* Christ the Priest,[48] situated between God and His creation. There Christ stands not outside them but in their midst, constituting them and being constituted by them. There,

---

[43] *Ibid.*, p. 2.

[44] Cf. above, p. 171; p. 174, n. 41.

[45] Cf. above, p. 94.

[46] Cf. above, pp. 90, 95, 142-143.

[47] *PGC*1, p. 4. Zizioulas continues: 'In certain cases, like that of the eucharistic liturgy commented upon by St Cyril of Jerusalem in his *Mystagogical Catecheses*, the thanksgiving for creation seems to be the only point of the eucharistic canon, with no mention at all of the sacrifice of Christ.' Cf. *CEE*1, p. 162. Yarnold notes that there is sacrificial terminology and reference to 'offering the slain Christ' in the *Mystagogical Catecheses* (*The Awe-Inspiring Rites of Initiation*, p. 91, n. 16). However, Zizioulas' point is simply to illustrate 'how central the reference to creation was in the ancient liturgies' (*PGC*1, p. 5).

[48] Cf. above, pp. 275-276.

between God and His creation, stands the corporate Christ, utterly differentiated in unity.

Of course, Zizioulas would not deny that there is growth in the Christian life, but he gives little attention to it, apparently because he considers that, *theologically*, it is of secondary importance, even a distraction. We may appreciate his view as follows. If Christ is understood as an *individual* whom each Christian identically interiorises, then Christians are distinguished primarily by the extent to which this growth is completed in each. If Christ is understood as *corporate* then Christians are distinguished primarily by the ways in which they are Christ, in their respective orders, and only secondarily by the extent to which they have each grown into these charismatic identities.

Complementary Critique

In his concern to emphasise that Christ is intrinsically corporate and that salvation is not the same undifferentiated gift to each but rather a differentiated gift to all, in the form of local communities, Zizioulas has undoubtedly neglected to treat certain questions which a rounded theological presentation would require, such as how human beings grow not only *in* faith, as Christians, but *to* faith. Both of these are questions which, of their nature, must involve some consideration of human beings over against Christ. De Lubac has given considerable attention to both of these matters,[49] but Zizioulas has yet to indicate how they may be treated within his system.

As we noted earlier, de Lubac dwells on the *moral* as well as the *ontological* barriers to the salvific achievement of personhood.[50] However, Zizioulas focuses only upon the latter barriers.[51] Consideration also of the *former* is particularly necessary in a theological approach as existential as that of Zizioulas.

---

[49] E.g. in *MMys* (cf. above, pp. 53-54) and *DGod* (cf. above, p. 273, n. 46), respectively. On both points, see also *MédPVM* (cf. above, Chapter Eleven).

[50] Cf. above, p. 17.

[51] Cf above, pp. 127-128, 137-138, 156, 183, 278. Zizioulas refers to morality only in the context of those who are already Christians. For them, moral conduct is 'a prolongation of liturgical experience' (*VEM*, p. 89).

He believes that a 'preoccupation' which has 'never abandoned Western Christianity' is that expressed in the question
on which the Pelagian controversy centred: 'how much do we
contribute to our salvation — something or nothing?' While
Zizioulas evidently considers such a question, which 'never
arose in the Greek Fathers',[52] to be a distraction, to dismiss it
altogether would be to remove what can be, in fact, a pointer
to the value of his own vision. De Lubac's view of salvation
being imparted by the indwelling of Christ in his people is
obviously a secure defence against Pelagianism. Zizioulas offers a view in which Pelagianism is rejected by an equally firm
stress that salvation is found only in strict dependence upon
Christ,[53] but without the need for a doctrine of indwelling
which we have maintained itself causes difficulties both in
defending the ecclesiological dialectics and in stipulating
more than a minimal structure for the celebration of the
Eucharist.[54]

Zizioulas' approach may be characterised as one which
seeks to reset the bones of theology. Much flesh needs to be put
upon these reset bones. For instance, having reset the Eucharist at the centre of the Christian life and the other sacraments
within it, Zizioulas must show not only how to rehabilitate the
ministry of the Word and the Church's mission to humanity,[55]
but also how to elaborate what he admits that the Eastern
tradition can seem to ignore, namely 'the *ethical* implications
of the Eucharist in particular and sacramental life in general'.[56]
His preoccupation with stressing that ethics are not the bones
of Christianity has so far prevented him from providing even
ethical flesh for the sacramental bones. Having stated that 'an
entire sociological theory and practice can be developed out of
the Eucharist',[57] it is particularly important that he, as an

---

[52]*EAH*1, p. 32. Rejecting theological anachronisms as they impinge upon
the East as well as the West, de Lubac says that 'St Thomas was no more an early
Baianist than the Greek Fathers were Pelagians' (*MSup*, p. 35).

[53]Cf. above, pp. 242-243.

[54]Cf. above, pp. 22, 97, 113-114, 279-280, 283.

[55]Cf. above, pp. 289-291.

[56]*EAH*1, p. 37 (my italics).

[57]*Ibid.*, p. 36. Cf. above, n. 51.

Eastern theologian, shows *how*, because, as he himself says, the risk which traditionally faces the East is that of 'undermining mission and involvement in history and being satisfied with a beautiful liturgy without bothering to draw its social and ethical implications'.[58]

The latter statement is an admission that the historical evidence for the possibility of maintaining a vigorous mission to humanity when the eschaton captures history, as Zizioulas insists it must,[59] is slight. The evidence suggests, paradoxically, that when history brought to its completion is so resolutely seen as the reality dominating history, something essential to the very drive of history towards its completion is lost. He must, therefore, explain in more detail than he has so far that this is not necessarily so and that, far from rendering history redundant, the eucharistic inbreaking of the eschaton provides the vital means whereby, as the flow of history continues, Christians can discern what is truly of God and build upon it.[60]

Respect of the flow of history is what finds expression in de Lubac's emphasis on the Church's mission to humanity in the power of the Spirit. In his extensive study of Pneumatology, Yves Congar likewise attributes the Church's historical spreading to the gift of the Spirit, 'whose coming was the beginning of the apostolic mission and testimony'.[61] In an appendix to the following chapter, he gives a summary of Zizioulas' view of apostolicity and declares himself to be 'fundamentally in agreement with it'. In the Eucharist what is actualised is the 'consummation' of the mystery of Christ. Congar expresses that it is the consummation of the historical economy by his statement that '[t]he Omega truly comes from the Alpha'. He adds that he would 'stress this more than Zizioulas does',[62] but

---

[58]*Ibid.*, p. 39; cf. above, p. 291.

[59]Cf. above, p. 261.

[60]Cf. above, pp. 198-200, 284. As I have already suggested, Zizioulas is in a strong position to defend his attention to history (cf. above, p. 260).

[61]Congar, *I Believe in the Holy Spirit*, vol. 2, p. 24.

[62]*Ibid.*, p. 51, with reference to Zizioulas, 'La continuité avec les origines apostoliques dans la conscience théologique des Eglises orthodoxes'; cf. Zizioulas' Full Bibliography, n. 18.

the implication that he is only modifying the balance of Zizioulas' account is contradicted by Zizioulas' subsequent assertion that Congar's statement actually reverses his meaning.[63] Zizioulas therefore maintains nothing less than that the Alpha comes from the Omega. It is within the boldness of this view that he must clarify that history still has the space, as it were, really to *happen*.

Zizioulas' need to correct so radically this interpretation of his eschatology by a Western theologian as appreciative of him as Congar shows how thoroughly foreign his theological approach is to the Western mind. Indeed, because of the strict unity of eschatology and Christology in his theology, it is legitimate to apply to his view of eschatology the description which he himself gave to the notion by which Christ is to be understood, namely that of corporate personality: it is 'a scandal to our Western minds'.[64] Zizioulas' use of 'our' here indicates, significantly, that he wishes to be counted among those who are scandalised. Criticism of his use of the notion of corporate personality must not forget that he presents it simply as one which the Bible seems to enjoin,[65] whatever may be its difficulties. The ongoing exegetical debate about whether the Bible does actually enjoin this concept[66] clearly has considerable relevance for Zizioulas and his theology.

That Christ, the one, should be immediately and inherently corporate, that is, many, such that he and the Church can be said to be *mutually* constitutive, certainly runs counter to the understanding which comes more readily to the Western mind, namely that Christ is one who, in due course, becomes many. We have attributed such an understanding to de Lubac.[67] It may now be seen as another example of his respect for the flow of history, for in history Christ does indeed come to be known progressively by, and realised progressively in, the multitude of humanity. To the ready translation of this un-

---

[63]I draw on personal discussions with Zizioulas for this point.
[64]*MCO*, p. 299. Cf. above, p. 166.
[65]Cf. *ibid.*, p. 299.
[66]Cf. *above*, p. 171, n. 31.
[67]Cf. above, pp. 60-62.

doubted fact into a view of Christ as an individual who progressively becomes corporate as he takes new *individuals* to himself, Zizioulas offers an alternative translation: Christ is corporate from the outset and is progressively realised in new *communities*. However, for Zizioulas fully to counter the former, instinctive, translation, he must show that his view can fully account for the historical missionaries who originally set out to gather those communities.

One person whose absence from Zizioulas' writings is strongly apparent in comparison with de Lubac is Mary. For an Orthodox theologian to be almost silent on the Mother of God is surprising. Zizioulas makes the excuse that the historical period which he regards, ecclesiologically, as exemplary, namely from the post-apostolic age to the fourth century,[68] is one which just predates the flourishing of Marian doctrine and devotion.[69] Much impetus for the latter came from the Council of Ephesus, in 431, which formally endorsed the title '*Theotokos*' for Mary.[70] Undoubtedly, also, Zizioulas has theological objections to the position which Mary often occupies in (Western) ecclesiology. For many reasons, as we have seen, whereas both de Lubac and Teilhard de Chardin tend to locate Mary at the centre of a Church which is viewed in distinction from Christ,[71] not only as his bride but also as his mother,[72] with Mary as the archetype for his indwelling in all,[73] Zizioulas firmly locates Christ himself at the centre of the Church and dispenses with the notion of indwelling.[74]

Nevertheless, one early Father who did give prominence to Mary, as the new Eve, is Irenaeus, and Zizioulas does, on one occasion, state that ecclesiology can begin from this very point.[75] Since Irenaeus envisages an historical progression in which Mary reverses Eve's disobedience and brings about

---

[68]Cf. above, p. 200.
[69]I draw on personal discussions with Zizioulas for this point.
[70]Cf. DS 251, 252.
[71]Cf. above, p. 64, n. 75; p. 67, n. 90; p. 96.
[72]Cf. above, p. 259, n. 120.
[73]Cf. above, p. 53.
[74]Cf. above, p. 279.
[75]*PRCE*, p. 46.

salvation for all, instead of death,[76] if Zizioulas were to incorporate Mary into his ecclesiology in this way, he would be better equipped to refute those who allege that he himself neglects history.

Catholicity

If Zizioulas' reaction against definitions of Christianity in terms of ethics and preaching the Word has, in the sense we have described above,[77] been an overreaction, we may also say that de Lubac's reaction against anthropocentrism, by applying in all spheres the corrective implicit in the Augustinian dictum on which we have focused,[78] has been an overreaction, in the sense that he considers that personhood is conferred upon human beings only in relation to God through Christ who stands above them. We have seen that this overreaction causes tensions in de Lubac's system by having seen that many tensions are resolved if Zizioulas' concept of the corporate Christ is adopted, such that human beings are persons in relation to one another in the Church around Christ in their midst and *thereby* in relation to God, this eschatological personhood being tasted in the eucharistic gathering of the local church around the bishop.

As we saw in Chapter Eleven, Zizioulas' three-tier scheme is no less theocentric than de Lubac's view of the single axis, in which each Christian relates to the Father through the individual Christ, but it maintains that each person has vertical relations with the tiers above him only in the differentiated context of his horizontal relations with the persons of his own tier, which is identified with the higher tiers in the Eucharist. We suggested there[79] that this scheme eradicates the individualism of 'the detestable "I"'[80] from human relationships with God, as de Lubac himself strove to do, but without full success.

---

[76]Cf. Kelly, *Early Christian Doctrines*, p. 494.

[77]Cf. above, pp. 291, 298-299.

[78]Cf. particularly pp. 67-73; also pp. 29-30 and 41, for the change from anthropocentrism to theocentrism.

[79]Cf. above, pp. 253-254.

[80]Cf. above, p.14.

We have seen that corporate personality is the key to Zizioulas' system. It is greatly to be hoped that he will devote a major study to this theme, explicitly gathering around their strictly theological source the many aspects of corporate personality, scriptural, patristic, philosophical, ethical and sociological, which either have found expression already in his occasional writings or still await development. Zizioulas' corporate understanding of Christ must clearly be set at the heart of an exposition of his thought, as I have sought to do in this study, for, as we have seen, it is the kernel of the resolution which, as we may now briefly recall,[81] he offers to a remarkable number of the lingering tensions in the pioneering theological achievement of de Lubac, one of the leading Western theologians of this century.

'What a complexity of dialectics!' exclaims Zizioulas, as he describes the simultaneous identification and yet distance between the bishop surrounded by his people and Christ surrounded by the Church before the Father in the Trinity.[82] We have seen in Chapter Twelve that, with his intrinsically corporate understanding of Christ, Zizioulas can strengthen the dialectics with which de Lubac, the champion of paradox in theology, expresses the mystery of the Church. This he does by making Christ inseparable from the future Church, that is, by making Christ–and–the–Church the inseparable future reality which, as God's will, is what encounters and moulds history throughout its course. Though de Lubac has always distinguished the uncreated God from the created world as firmly as Zizioulas does,[83] he then considers that God encounters the world in the *individual* Christ, present in his *past* victory, in order to draw human beings into the future Church, his Bride. We saw in Chapter Four that, with a *corporate* concept of Christ, Zizioulas renders inseparable the memorial and anticipatory aspects of the Eucharist which, having separated Christ from the Church in this way, de Lubac cannot fully integrate as he desires.

---

[81] Cf. also, above, pp. 291, 292-295.
[82] *MCO*, p. 298.
[83] Cf. above, Chapters Two and Seven, respectively.

The fact that de Lubac has acknowledged, either personally or by association with the general trend of Western theology, respectively, his limitations in the two areas of eschatology[84] and Pneumatology,[85] within which Zizioulas' concept of the corporate Christ is located,[86] indicates, at least in principle, his openness to this concept. This book is structured not simply to show a progress from de Lubac to Zizioulas, but rather to highlight the contribution which Zizioulas can make, from a fuller development of areas of de Lubac's acknowledged limitations, via the corporate Christ, to a fuller realisation of de Lubac's own aims. The contribution is strongly evident when, by way of the corporate Christ, Zizioulas identifies the Eucharist and the Church, such that not only are the two halves of de Lubac's ecclesiological principle that the Church makes the Eucharist and the Eucharist makes the Church aligned and integrated,[87] but also apparent barriers to his mystical synthesis are removed.[88]

We have seen that Zizioulas' contribution to de Lubac is still developing in the particularly practical area of a *eucharistic* justification for a genuine primacy among the bishops, in accordance with the scriptural insight of von Allmen,[89] such that, though all receive their jurisdiction from God at their episcopal Ordination, it can be said that they do so in dependence upon one in their midst.[90]

The dialogue initiated between de Lubac and Zizioulas in this book is, indeed, capable of much development. The path established here between them needs consolidating, not least by further investigation of the differences between de Lubac's coincident unity-of-identity and Zizioulas' differentiated unity-of-complementarity, for the benefit of all who share the existential concern of both theologians.

---

[84]Cf. above, pp. 48-49.
[85]Cf. above, p. 74.
[86]Cf. above, pp. 166-167.
[87]Cf. above, pp. xv-xvii, 254-255.
[88]Cf. above, pp. 72-74.
[89]Cf. above, pp. 114-115, 210.
[90]Cf. above, pp. 208-209.

When it is recalled that the initial contribution was from de Lubac to Zizioulas, in the form of much of the latter's initial patristic and eucharistic inspiration,[91] then the context of this study is complete. Aware of their *mutual* contributions, my aim has been to highlight what de Lubac would fully have agreed with Zizioulas in saying:

'the authentic catholicity of the Church must include both the West and the East'.[92]

---

[91]Cf. above, pp. xiii-xvii.
[92]*BC*, p. 26; cf. above, p. 6.

De Lubac Bibliography

For a complete bibliography up to 1974, cf. Karl H. NEUFELD and Michel SALES, *Bibliographie Henri de Lubac S.J.* (Johannes Verlag, Einsiedeln, 1974²). Neufeld and Sales have corrected and updated this bibliography to 1989 in an appendix to Henri de Lubac, *Théologie dans l'histoire*. Vol. II, *Questions disputées et résistance au nazisme* (Desclée de Brouwer, Paris, 1990), pp. 408-416.

WORKS CITED IN THE TEXT
(The abbreviations used in the text are indicated)

Note: For ready distinction from Zizioulas' bibliography, I give no abbreviations of de Lubac's works purely as capital initials. For instance: *BC* is a Zizioulas reference, but *BCat* is a de Lubac reference.

Amida = *Amida* (Seuil, Paris, 1955).
AMTh = *Augustinianism and Modern Theology* (Geoffrey Chapman, London, 1969); translation of *Augustinisme et théologie moderne* (Aubier, Paris, 1965).
AMys = *Affrontements Mystiques* (Témoignage Chrétien, Paris, 1950).
Aspects = *Aspects of Buddhism* (Sheed and Ward, London, 1953); translation of *Aspects du bouddhisme I* (Seuil, Paris, 1951).
Athéisme = *Athéisme et sens de l'homme* (Cerf, Paris, 1968).
BCat = *A Brief Catechesis on Nature and Grace* (Ignatius, San Francisco, 1984); translation of *Petite catéchèse sur nature et grâce* (Communio-Fayard, Paris, 1980).
BTCorr = *Pierre Teilhard de Chardin-Maurice Blondel: Correspondence* (Herder and Herder, New York, 1967); translation of *Blondel et Teilhard de Chardin: Correspondence commenté* (Beauchesne, Paris, 1965).
BWCorr = *M. Blondel-J. Wehrlé: Correspondence* (Aubier, Paris, 1969), 2 vols.
Catholicism = *Catholicism* (Universe Books edition; Burns & Oates, London, 1962); translation of *Catholicisme* (Cerf, Paris, 1947⁴). Latest edition of the original: *Catholicisme* (Traditions chrétiennes 13; Cerf, Paris, 1983⁷).

ChPM = *The Church: Paradox and Mystery* (Alba House, New York, 1969); translation of *Paradoxe et mystère de l'Eglise* (Aubier, Paris, 1967).

CMys = *Corpus Mysticum* (Aubier, Paris, 1949²).

CPég = *Claudel et Péguy* (written by de Lubac and Jean Bastaire) (Aubier, Paris, 1974).

DCDieu = *De la connaissance de Dieu* (Témoignage Chrétien, Paris, 1945¹; 1948²).

DGod = *The Discovery of God* (Darton, Longman & Todd, London, 1960); translation of *Sur les chemins de Dieu* (Aubier, Paris, 1956).

DHAth = *Le drame de l'humanisme athée* (Cerf, Paris, 1983⁷).

DHBeat = 'Duplex hominis beatitudo (Saint Thomas, I, II, q. 62, a. 1)', *Recherches de science religieuse* 35 (1948), pp. 290-299.

EFem = *The Eternal Feminine* (Collins, London, 1971); translation of *L'Eternel Féminin* (Aubier, Paris, 1968).

ExMéd *I/1, I/2, II/1, II/2* = *Exégèse Médiévale* (Aubier, Paris): Part I, vols. 1, 2 (1959); Part II, vol. 1 (1961), vol. 2 (1964).

ESPaul = 'L'Eglise dans saint Paul', *La Vie Spirituelle* 68 (1943), pp. 470-483.

EVat = *Entretien autour de Vatican II* (France Catholique-Cerf, Paris, 1985).

Faith = *Christian Faith* (Geoffrey Chapman, London, 1986); translation of *La Foi chrétienne* (Aubier, Paris, 1970²).

FTeil = *The Faith of Teilhard de Chardin* (Burns & Oates, London, 1965); translation of *La prière du Père Teilhard de Chardin* (Librairie Arthème Fayard, Paris, 1964).

FTMiss = *Le fondement théologique des missions* (Seuil, Paris, 1946). Reprinted in *Théologie dans l'histoire*, II, pp. 159-219.

HEsp = *Histoire et esprit* (Aubier, Paris, 1950).

Images = *Images de l'Abbé Monchanin* (Aubier, Paris, 1967).

Lettres = *Lettres de monsieur Etienne Gilson au Père de Lubac* (Cerf, Paris, 1986).

MédPVM = 'Méditation sur le principe de la vie morale', *Revue apologétique* 65 (1937), pp. 257-266.

Mémoire = *Mémoire sur l'occasion de mes écrits* (Culture et vérité, Namur, 1989).

Mistica = *Mistica e mistero cristiano* (Opera omnia, vol. 6; Jaca Book, Milano, 1979).

MMys = 'Mystique et mystère', in the collection *Théologies d'occasion* (Desclée de Brouwer, Paris, 1984), pp. 37-76.

Moehler = 'Moehler et sa doctrine sur l'Eglise', *L'Union Apostolique* 77 (1939), pp. 372-377.

Motherhood = *The Motherhood of the Church* (Ignatius, San Francisco, 1982); translation of *Les églises particulières dans l'Eglise universelle* (Aubier, Paris, 1971).

Motif = 'Le motif de la création dans «l'Etre et les êtres»', in *TOcc*, pp. 425-432; an article first published in the *Nouvelle revue théologique* 65 (1938), pp. 220-225.

MSup = *The Mystery of the Supernatural* (Geoffrey Chapman, London, 1967); translation of *Le mystère du surnaturel* (Aubier, Paris, 1965).

MSur = 'Le mystère du surnaturel', *Recherches de science religieuse* 36 (1949), pp. 80-121. Reprinted in *Théologie dans l'histoire*, II, pp. 71-107.

NFRel = 'Un nouveau «front» religieux', in H. de Lubac, J. Chaine, L. Richard, J. Bonsirven, *Israel et la foi chrétienne* (Librairie de l'université, Fribourg, 1942), pp. 9-39. Reprinted in *Théologie dans l'histoire*, II, pp. 250-281.

NMan = 'The New Man: The Marxist and the Christian View', *The Dublin Review* 442 (1948), pp. 5-35; translation of 'L'idée chrétienne de l'homme et la recherche d'un homme nouveau', *Etudes* 255 (1947), pp. 3-25, 145-169, which appeared most recently in *Le drame de l'humanisme athée* (Cerf, Paris, 1983[7]).

Paradoxes = *Paradoxes of Faith* (Ignatius, San Françisco, 1987); combined translation of *Paradoxes* (Livre français, Paris, 1946) and *Nouveaux paradoxes* (Seuil, Paris, 1955), which are now published together as *Paradoxes suivi de Nouveaux paradoxes* (Seuil, Paris, 1983).

PDDog = 'Le problème du développement du dogme', *Recherches de science religieuse* 35 (1948), pp. 130-160. Reprinted in *Théologie dans l'histoire*, II, pp. 38-70.

PSpir 1 & 2 = *La postérité spirituelle de Joachim de Flore* (Lethielleux, Paris): tome 1, de Joachim à Schelling (1979); tome 2, de Saint-Simon à nos jours (1981).

QMys = Review of *Qu'est-ce que la mystique?* (Cahiers de la nouvelle journée 3; Paris, 1925), in *Livres et Revues* 17 (1925), pp. 405-406.

RCAnt = *Résistance chrétienne à l'antisémitisme* (Fayard, 1988).

RDiv = *La révélation divine* (Cerf, Paris, 1983[3]).

RTeil = *The Religion of Teilhard de Chardin* (Collins, London, 1967); translation of *La pensée religieuse du Père Teilhard de Chardin* (Aubier, Paris, 1962).

SComm = 'Sanctorum Communio', *Théologies d'occasion* (q.v.), pp. 11-35.

Sources = *The Sources of Revelation* (Herder and Herder, New York, 1968); translation of *L'Ecriture dans la Tradition* (Aubier, Paris, 1967).

Souvenirs = 'Souvenirs (1940-1945)', in Αλεξανδρινα, Mélanges offerts à Claude Mondésert (Cerf, Paris, 1987), pp. 9-13.

SPChr = 'Sur la philosophie chrétienne', *Nouvelle revue théologique* 63 (1936), pp. 225-253; quoted here from its revised republication in de Lubac, *Recherches dans la foi* (Beauchesne, Paris, 1979), pp. 125-152.

Spirito = *Spirito e libertà* (Opera omnia, vol. 13; Jaca Book, Milano, 1981).

Splendour = *The Splendour of the Church* (Sheed and Ward, London, 1956); translation of *Méditation sur l'Eglise* (Aubier, Paris, 1953^2). Latest edition of the original: *Méditation sur l'Eglise* (Théologie 27; Desclée de Brouwer, Paris, 1985).

STPDieu = Review of Daniélou, *Le Signe du Temple ou de la Présence de Dieu*, in *Cité Nouvelle* (1942), vol. 2, p. 715.

Surnaturel = *Surnaturel* (Aubier, Paris, 1946). New edition, with Preface by Michel Sales and translation of all Latin and Greek quotations: *Surnaturel* (Desclée de Brouwer, Paris, 1991).

SVDis = 'Sur un vieux distique', in *Théologies d'occasion* (q.v.), pp. 117-136.

ThDH1 = *Théologie dans l'histoire*. Vol. I, *La lumière du Christ* (Desclée de Brouwer, Paris, 1990).

ThDH2 = *Théologie dans l'histoire*. Vol. II, *Questions disputées et résistance au nazisme* (Desclée de Brouwer, Paris, 1990).

TMAp = *Teilhard, missionnaire et apologiste* (Prière et Vie, Toulouse, 1966).

TOcc = Théologies d'occasion (Desclée de Brouwer, Paris, 1984).

Trois = Trois jésuites nous parlent (Lethielleux, Paris, 1980).

Zizioulas Bibliography

In Zizioulas' FULL BIBLIOGRAPHY OF PUBLISHED WRIT-INGS which follows after this listing, all of his published articles in their various translations are shown, as far as possible. In the present listing, which indicates how his published and unpublished writings are identified by abbreviations in the text, the articles which appear in the collection, *Being as Communion*, are not identified separately. A selection of reviews of Zizioulas' books is appended.

WORKS CITED IN THE TEXT
(Two capital initials are used for books, three for published articles and four for unpublished material.)

BOOKS

BC = *Being as Communion. Studies in Personhood and the Church* (Darton, Longman and Todd, London, 1985).

EE = *L'être ecclésial* (Labor et Fides, Genève, 1981).

UC = Ἡ Ἑνότης τῆς Ἐκκλησίας ἐν τῇ θεία Εὐχαριστία καί τῷ Ἐπισκόπῳ κατά τούς τρεῖς πρώτους αἰῶνας (The Unity of the Church in the Holy Eucharist and in the Bishop in the First Three Centuries) (Athens, 1965).

PUBLISHED ARTICLES

BCE = 'Some Reflections on Baptism, Confirmation and Eucharist', *Sobornost*, series 5, number 9 (1969), pp. 644-652.

BTD = 'The Bishop in the Theological Doctrine of the Orthodox Church', in Richard Potz (ed.), *Kanon* VII: *Der Bischof und seine Eparchie*, Jahrbuch der Gesellschaft für das Recht der Ostkirchen (Verlag des Verbandes der wissenschaftlichen Gesellschaften Osterreichs, Wien, 1985), pp. 23-35.

CCC = 'The Contribution of Cappadocia to Christian Thought', in Frosso Pimenides, Stelios Roïdes (eds.), *Sinasos in Cappadocia* (National Trust for Greece: Agra Publications, 1986), pp. 23-37.

CEE1 = 'Christologie et existence: la dialectique crée-incrée et le dogme de Chalcédoine', *Contacts* 36 (1984), pp. 154-172.

CEE2 = 'La réponse de Jean Zizioulas' (to reactions to the above article), *Contacts* 37 (1985), pp. 60-72.

CSC = '(Communal Spirit and Conciliarity:) A Comment', in S. C. Agourides (ed.), *Procès-Verbaux du Deuxième Congrès de Théologie Orthodoxe* (Athènes, 1978), pp. 140-146; reply to N. A. Zabolotsky, 'Esprit Communautaire et Conciliarité (Sobornost)', *ibid.*, pp. 129-140.

CWU = 'Conciliarity and the Way to Unity — An Orthodox Point of View', in *Churches in Conciliar Fellowship* (Conference of European Churches, Geneva, 1978), pp. 20-31.

DCS = 'The Development of Conciliar Structures to the Time of the First Ecumenical Council', in *Councils and the Ecumenical Movement* (World Council of Churches Studies 5; World Council of Churches, Geneva, 1968), pp. 34-51.

DGT = 'The Doctrine of God the Trinity Today: Suggestions for an Ecumenical Study', in Alasdair I. C. Heron (ed.), *The Forgotten Trinity. 3 A Selection of Papers Presented to the BCC Study Commission on Trinitarian Doctrine Today* (BCC/CCBI, London, 1991), pp. 19-32.

DMJ = 'Discours du métropolite Jean de Pergame', La célébration du millénaire du «baptême» de la Russie au siège du Patriarcat oecuménique, *Istina* 33 (1988), pp. 197-203.

DPE = 'Déplacement de la perspective eschatologique', in G. Alberigo, *et al.*, *La chrétienté en débat* (Cerf, Paris, 1984), pp. 89-100.

EAH 1 = 'Eschatology and History', in T. Wieser (ed.), *Cultures in Dialogue*, Documents from a symposium in honour of Philip A. Potter (Geneva, 1985), pp. 30-39.

EAH 2 = 'Eschatology and History', extracts from the above paper and comments by Zizioulas in the discussion which followed ('one of the most animated exchanges during the symposium'), in T. Wieser (ed.), *Whither Ecumenism?* (World Council of Churches, Geneva, 1986), pp. 62-71, 72-73.

ECC = 'The Early Christian Community', in Bernard McGinn, John Meyendorff, Jean Leclerq (eds.), *Christian Spirituality: Origins to the Twelfth Century* (Routledge and Kegan Paul, London, 1986), pp. 23-43.

EDO = 'The Ecumenical Dimensions of Orthodox Theological Education', in *Orthodox Theological Education for the Life and Witness of the Church* (World

Council of Churches, Geneva, 1978), pp. 3-40.

EEE = 'Episkopé and Episkopos in the Early Church: A Brief Survey of the Evidence', in *Episkopé and episcopate in ecumenical perspective* (Faith and Order Paper 102; World Council of Churches, Geneva, 1980), pp. 30-42.

EGA = 'Die eucharistische Grundlage des Amtes, in Reinhard Thöle, Ilse Friedeberg (eds.), *Philoxenia*, Band II (Flacius-Verlag, Fürth, 1986).

EII = 'Ecclesiological Issues Inherent in the Relations between Eastern Chalcedonian and Oriental non-Chalcedonian Churches', in Paulos Gregorios, William H. Lazareth (eds.), *Does Chalcedon Divide or Unite? Convergence in Orthodox Christology* (World Council of Churches, Geneva, 1981), pp. 138-156.

ENO = 'Die Eucharistie in der neuzeitlichen orthodoxen Theologie', in *Die Anrufung des Heiligen Geistes im Abendmahl* (Otto Lembeck Verlag, Frankfurt am Main, 1977), pp. 163-179.

EOT = 'The Ecclesiology of the Orthodox Tradition', *Search*, vol. 7, part 2 (Winter, 1984), pp. 42-53.

EPH = 'The ecclesiological presuppositions of the holy Eucharist', *Nicolaus* 10 (1982), pp. 333-349.

EPL = 'Eucharistic Prayer and Life', *Emmanuel* 85 (1979), pp. 181-196, 201-203.

EQA = L'euchariste: quelques aspects bibliques', in J. Zizioulas, J. M. R. Tillard, J. J. von Allmen, *L'eucharistie* (églises en dialogue 12; Mame, 1970), pp. 11-74.

GIE = 'Les groupes informels dans l'Eglise', in Y. Congar *et al.*, *Les groupes informels dans l'Eglise* (University of Strasbourg, Cerdic Publications, Strasbourg, 1971).

GRM = 'God Reconciles and Makes Free — An Orthodox Comment', *Bulletin* (of the Department of Theology of the World Alliance of Reformed Churches and the World Presbyterian Alliance), vol. 10, number 2 (1970), pp. 7-8.

HCH = 'Human Capacity and Human Incapacity', *Scottish Journal of Theology* 28 (1975), pp. 401-448.

IEC = 'The Institution of Episcopal Conferences: An Orthodox Reflection', *The Jurist* 48 (1988), pp. 376-383.

IED = 'Implications ecclésiologiques de deux types de pneumatologie', in *Communio Sanctorum*, Mélanges J. J. von Allmen (Labor et Fides, Genève, 1981), pp. 141-154.

MCO = 'The Mystery of the Church in Orthodox Tradition', *One in Christ* 24 (1988), pp. 294-303.

MOC = 'The Meaning of Ordination: A Comment', *Study Encounter* 4 (1968), pp. 191-193.

NUS = 'The Nature of the Unity We Seek — The Response of the Orthodox Observer' (reply to the keynote address of the Archbishop of Canterbury to the 1988 Lambeth Conference), *One in Christ* 24 (1988), pp. 342-348.

OAC = 'Ordination and Communion', *Study Encounter* 6 (1970), pp. 187-192.

OAS = 'Ordination — A Sacrament? An Orthodox Reply', *Concilium* (English Edition), vol. 4 (Ecumenism), 1972, pp. 33-39.

OBP = 'On Being a Person. Towards an Ontology of Personhood', in Christoph Schwöbel and Colin E. Gunton (eds.), *Persons, Divine and Human* (T. & T. Clark, Edinburgh, 1991), pp. 33-46. This paper was first read to the fourth meeting of the BCC/DEA Study Commission (see below, under *CMOR*), in March, 1985.

OCA = 'On the Concept of Authority', *The Ecumenical Review* 21 (1969), pp. 160-166.

OEE = 'Orthodox Ecclesiology and the Ecumenical Movement', *Sourozh*, number 21 (August, 1985), pp. 16-27.

OPB = 'Orthodox-Protestant Bilateral Conversations: Some Comments', *The Orthodox Church and the Churches of the Reformation* (Faith and Order Paper 76; World Council of Churches, Geneva, 1975), pp. 55-60.

ORT = 'Ortodossia', in *Enciclopedia del Novecento*, vol. 5 (Istituto della Enciclopedia Italiana, Roma, 1980), pp. 1-18.

PDC = 'The Pneumatological Dimension of the Church', *International Catholic Review-Communio* 1 (1974), pp. 142-158.

PGC1 = 'Preserving God's Creation. Three Lectures on Theology and Ecology, I', *King's Theological Review* 12 (1989), pp. 1-5.

PGC2 = 'Preserving God's Creation, II', *King's Theological Review* 12 (1989), pp. 41-45.

PGC3 = 'Preserving God's Creation, III', *King's Theological Review* 13 (1990), pp. 1-5.

ROA = 'Reflections of an Orthodox (on common witness and proselytism), *The Ecumenical Review* 23 (1971), pp. 30-34.

TLU = 'Tradition liturgique et unité chrétienne', *Revue de l'Institut Catholique de Paris*, No. 36 (Octobre-Décembre, 1990), Tirage special: *Centenaire de la Faculté de Théologie*, pp. 157-170.

TPR = 'The Theological Problem of "Reception"', *One in Christ* 21 (1985), pp. 187-193.

TSE = 'The Teaching of the 2nd Ecumenical Council on the Holy Spirit in Historical and Ecumenical Perspective', in J. S. Martins (ed.), *Credo in Spiritum Sanctum* (Libreria Editrice Vaticana, Roma, 1983), vol. 1, pp. 29-

54.
VEM = 'La vision eucharistique du monde et l'homme contemporain', *Contacts* 19 (1967), pp. 83-92.

UNPUBLISHED MATERIAL

(Page references in the text are to manuscripts in the present author's possession.)

CECB = 'The Church as Eucharistic Community and the Basis of Law'; Paper prepared for the Faith and Order Commission of the World Council of Churches, March, 1974.

CIEI = 'Confessional Identity and Ecclesial Identity: the nature of the unity we seek'; Paper read to the Colloque at the Monastère de Chevetogne on the theme «Identité confessionnelle et traditions ecclésiales», 22-26 August 1983.

CMBC= 'The Church as the "Mystical" Body of Christ'; Paper presented to the annual meeting of the Académie Internationale des Sciences Religieuses, Crete, 1985.

CMOR = 'Christian Monotheism and Other Religions'; Paper presented to the fifth meeting of the British Council of Churches/Division of Ecumenical Affairs Study Commission on Trinitarian Doctrine Today, November 1985 (including notes of the discussion which followed).

EFEL= 'L'eucharistie, foyer de l'église locale'; Lecture to the Conference on 'Les paroisses dans l'Eglise d'aujourd'hui', Louvain-la-Neuve, 14-16 September 1981.

ESLT = 'The Existential Significance of Liturgical Time'; Paper presented to the students and Faculty of Theology, Durham University, 1982.

FCTR = 'From the Cross to the Resurrection'; Lecture to the Seminar on Orthodox Theology and Worship, Bossey, 1980.

FRIT= 'The Filioque in Relation to the Immanent Trinity'; Paper read to the International Commission for Anglican-Orthodox Theological Dialogue, 1990.

PRCE = 'Pneumatology in Relation to Christology and Ecclesiology'; The present author's notes from this course of lectures by Zizioulas at the Pontifical Gregorian University, Rome, March-April, 1984.

REVIEWS OF ZIZIOULAS' BOOKS (Selection)

UC: BORI, Pier Cesare, 'L'unité de l'Eglise durant les trois premiers siècles', *Revue d'histoire ecclésiastique* 65 (1970), pp. 56-68.

PARSONS, Stephen, review in *Sobornost* 8 (1972), pp. 270-279.

EE: BOBRINSKOY, Boris, 'Jean Zizioulas, théologien de l'Eglise', *SOP* (Service orthodoxe de presse) n. 112 (Novembre 1986), pp. 11-13.

CONGAR, Yves, review in 'Bulletin d'ecclésiologie', *Revue des sciences philosophiques et théologiques* 66 (1982), pp. 88-89.

VALLIN, P., review in 'Bulletin d'histoire de l'Eglise et d'ecclésiologie', *Recherches de science religieuse* 71 (1983), pp. 385-386.

BC: McPARTLAN, Paul, review in *Sobornost* 9: 1 (1987), pp. 78-81.

SAWARD, John, review in *New Blackfriars* 67 (1986), pp. 45-48.

WILLIAMS, Rowan, review in *Scottish Journal of Theology* 42 (1989), pp. 101-105.

John D. Zizioulas
Full Bibliography of Published Writings

BOOKS

(1) 'Η'Ενότης τῆς 'Εκκλησίας ἐν τῇ Θεία Εὐχαριστία καί τῷ 'Επισκόπῳ κατὰ τοὺς τρεῖς πρώτους αἰῶνας (The Unity of the Church in the Holy Eucharist and in the Bishop in the First Three Centuries) (Athens, 1965).

(2) L'être ecclésial (Labor et Fides, Genève, 1981); hereafter referred to as *EE*.

(3) *Being as Communion* (Darton, Longman and Todd, London, 1985); hereafter referred to as *BC*.

ARTICLES
(Translations are indicated only where precise details can be given.)

(1) 'Jerusalem', in *Encyclopedia of Religion and Ethics*, vol. 6 (Athens, 1964) (in Greek).

(2) 'Ignatius I (Saint) Patriarch of Constantinople (846-858, 867-877 A.D.)' and 'Thyateira — Church of', in *Encyclopedia of Religion and Ethics*, vol. 6 (Athens, 1964) (in Greek).

(3) 'La vision eucharistique du monde et l'homme contemporain', *Contacts* 19 (1967), pp. 83-92.

In German, 'Die Welt im eucharistischer Schau und der Mensch von Heute', *Una Sancta* 4 (1970), pp. 342-349. Reprinted in *Philoxenia*, hrsg. 1, (Friedeberg, Marburg/Lahn, 1973), pp. 24-34.

In Italian, *Simposio Cristiano* (Milano, 1975), pp. 301-310.

In Serbian, *Teoloski Pogleti* 6 (1973), pp. 37-45.

(4) 'The Meaning of Ordination: A Comment', *Study Encounter* 4 (1968), pp. 191-193.

(5) 'The Development of Conciliar Structures to the Time of the First Ecumenical Council', in *Councils and the Ecumenical Movement* (World Council of Churches Studies 5; World Council of Churches, Geneva, 1968), pp. 34-51.

In German, 'Die Entwicklung konziliarer Strukturen bis zur Zeit des estern ökumenischen Konzils', *Konzile und die ökumenische Bewegung* (Studien des ökumenischen Rates, Nr. 5, Genf., 1968).

(6) 'On the Concept of Authority', *The Ecumenical Review* 21 (1969), pp. 160-166.

In Czech, *Krestanska revue* 41 (1974), pp. 6-13.

(7) 'Some Reflections on Baptism, Confirmation and Eucharist', *Sobornost*, series 5, number 9 (1969), pp. 644-652.

(8) 'La communauté eucharistique et la catholicité de l'Eglise', *Istina* 14 (1969), pp. 67-88. Reprinted as Chapter Three of *EE*.

In English, 'The Eucharistic Community and the Catholicity of the Church', *One in Christ* 6 (1970), pp. 314-337. Reprinted as Chapter Four of *BC* and in J. Meyendorff and J. McLelland (eds.), *The New Man* (Agora Books, New Brunswick, New Jersey, 1973), pp. 107-131.

In German, 'Abendmahlsgemeinschaft und Katholizität der Kirche', in W. Pannenberg *et al.*, *Katholizität und Apostolizität*, Beiheft zu *Kerygma und Dogma* 2 (1971), pp. 31-50.

In Serbian, *Glasnik* 52 (1971), pp. 110-121.

(9) 'God Reconciles and Makes Free — An Orthodox Comment', *Bulletin* (of the Department of Theology of the World Alliance of Reformed Churches and the World Presbyterian Alliance), vol. 10, number 2 (1970), pp. 7-8.

(10) 'Ordination and Communion', *Study Encounter* 6 (1970), pp. 187-192.

In French, 'Ordination et communion', *Istina* 16 (1971), pp. 5-12. Reprinted as Chapter Five of *EE*.

(11) 'L'eucharistie: quelques aspects bibliques', in J. Zizoulas, J. M. R. Tillard, J. J. von Allmen, *L'eucharistie* (églises en dialogue 12: Mame 1970), pp. 11-74.

(12) 'Ecclesiological Issues Inherent in the Relations between Eastern Chalcedonian and Oriental non-Chalcedonian Churches', *The Greek Orthodox Theological Review* 16 (1971), pp. 144-162. Reprinted in Paulos Gregorios, William H. Lazareth (eds.), *Does Chalcedon Divide or Unite? Towards Convergence in Orthodox Christology* (World Council of Churches, Geneva, 1981), pp. 138-156.

(13) 'Les groupes informels dans l'Eglise', in Y. Congar *et al.*, *Les groupes informels dans l'Eglise* (University of Strasbourg, Cerdic Publications, Strasbourg, 1971).

In German, *Die Spontanengruppen in der Kirche* (Paul Pattloch Verlag, Aschatteburg, 1971), pp. 171-190.

In English, R. Metz (ed.), *Informal Groups in the Church*, Papers of the Second CERDIC Conference, University of Strasbourg, 1971 (Pittsburgh Theological Monographs Series, 7; Pittsburgh, 1975).

(14) 'Reflections of an Orthodox (on common witness and proselytism), *The Ecumenical Review* 23 (1971), pp. 30-34.

(15) 'Ordination — A Sacrament? An Orthodox Reply', *Concilium* (English edition), vol. 4 (Ecumenism), 1972, pp. 33-39.

In French, 'L'ordination est-elle un sacrement? Réponse d'un orthodoxe', *Concilium* (French edition) 4 (1972), pp. 41-47.

Also in other language editions of *Concilium*.

(16) 'Priesteramt und Priesterweihe im Licht der östlich-orthodoxen Theologie', in Karl Rahner and H. Schlier (eds.), *Questiones Disputatae* 50, *Der priesterliche Dienst — V.Amt und Ordination in ökumenischer Sicht* (Herder, Freiburg-Basel-Wien, 1973), pp. 72-113.

In English, Chapter Six of *BC*.

(17) 'Die pneumatologische Dimension der Kirche', *Internationale Katholische Zeitschrift* 2 (1973), pp. 133-147.

In English, 'The Pneumatological Dimension of the Church', *International Catholic Review* 2 (1973), pp. 82-90 and again in *International Catholic Review-Communio* 1 (1974), pp. 142-158.

(18) 'La continuité avec les origines apostoliques dans la conscience théologique des églises orthodoxes', *Istina* 19 (1974), pp. 65-94. Reprinted in the Proceedings of the *Académie internationale des sciences religieuses* for 1974 and as Chapter Four of *EE*.

In English, *St Vladimir's Theological Seminary Quarterly* 19 (1975), pp. 75-108 and as Chapter Five of *BC*.

(19) 'Human Capacity and Human Incapacity', *Scottish Journal of Theology* 28 (1975), pp. 401-448.

(20) 'Orthodox-Protestant Bilateral Conversations: Some Comments', in *The Orthodox Church and the Churches of the Reformation* (Faith and Order Paper 76; World Council of Churches, Geneva, 1975), pp. 55-60.

(21) 'Eucharistic Prayer and Life', *Emmanuel* 81 (1975), pp. 462-470. Again in *Emmanuel* 85 (1979), pp. 191-196, 201-203.

In Dutch, 'Eucharistisch Gebed en leven', *Rond de Tafel* 31 (1976), pp. 54-66.

(22) 'Hellenism and Christianity: The Encounter of Two Worlds', in *The History of the Hellenic Nation*, vol. 6 (Athens, 1976), pp. 519-559 (in Greek).

(23) 'Die Eucharistie in der neuzeitlichen orthodoxen Theologie', in *Die Anrufung des Heiligen Geistes im Abendmahl* (Otto Lembeck Verlag, Frankfurt am Main, 1977), pp. 163-179.

(24) 'The Local Church in a Eucharistic Perspective'. *In Each Place, Towards a Fellowship of Local Churches truly united* (World Council of Churches, Geneva, 1977), pp. 50-61. Reprinted as Chapter Seven of *BC*.

In French, Chapter Six of *EE*.

(25) 'From *Prospeion to Prosopon:* The Contribution of Patristic Theology to

the Concept of the Person', *Charisteria. Studies in Honour of Metropolitan Meliton of Chalcedon* (Institute of Patristic Studies, Thessaloniki, 1977), pp. 287-323 (in Greek).

In French, Chapter One of *EE*.

In English, Chapter One of *BC*.

(26) 'Verité et communion dans la perspective de la pensée patristique grecque', *Irenikon* 50 (1977), pp. 451-510. Reprinted as Chapter Two of *EE*.

In German, 'Wahrheit und Gemeinschaft in der Sicht der griechischen Kirchenväter', *Kerygma und Dogma* 26 (1980), pp. 2-49.

In English, Chapter Two of *BC*.

In Spanish, *Selecciones de Teologia* 71 (1979), pp. 251-271.

(27) '(Communal Spirit and Conciliarity:) A Comment', in S. C. Agourides (ed.), *Procès-Verbaux du Deuxième Congrès de Théologie Orthodoxe* (Athènes, 1978), pp. 140-146; reply to N. A. Zabolotsky, 'Esprit Communautaire et Conciliarité (Sobornost)', *ibid.*, pp. 129-140.

(28) 'Conciliarity and the Way to Unity — An Orthodox Point of View', in *Churches in Conciliar Fellowship* (Conference of European Churches, Geneva, 1978), pp. 20-31.

Also in the French and German editions of the same.

Again in German, *Die Zeichen der Zeit* 1/2 (1979), pp. 30-39.

(29) 'The Ecumenical Dimensions of Orthodox Theological Education', in *Orthodox Theological Education for the Life and Witness of the Church* (World Council of Churches, Geneva, 1978), pp. 3-40.

(30) 'Ortodossia', in *Enciclopedia del Novecento*, vol. 5 (Istituto della Enciclopedia Italiana, Roma, 1980), pp. 1-18.

(31) 'The Synodal Institution: Historical, Ecclesiological and Canonical Problems', in *Studies in Honour of Metropolitan Barnabas of Kitros* (Athens, 1980), pp. 1-30 (in Greek).

(32) 'Episkopé and Episkopos in the Early Church: A Brief Survey of the Evidence', in *Episkopé and episcopate in ecumenical perspective* (Faith and Order Paper 102; World Council of Churches, Geneva, 1980), pp. 30-42.

In French, 'Episkopé et Episkopos dans l'Eglise primitive' *Irenikon* 56 (1983), pp. 484-502.

In Spanish, 'Episkopé y episkopos en la Iglesia primitiva', *Selecciones de teologia* 24 (1985), pp. 54-62.

(33) 'Cristologia, pneumatologia e istituzioni ecclesiastiche: un punto di vista ortodosso', *Cristianesimo nella storia* 2 (1981), pp. 111-127.

In English, Chapter Three of *BC*.

In French, in G. Alberigo (ed.), *Les Eglises après Vatican II* (Beauchesne, Paris, 1981), pp. 131-148.

(34) 'Two Ancient Traditions Concerning Apostolic Succession and their

Theological Significance', in *Studies in Honour of Prof. G. Konidaris* (Athens, 1981), pp. 683-712.

(35) 'God and the World: The Problem of Transcendence in Greek Philosophy and Patristic Thought', in *Epopteia*, Studies in Memory of Prof. N. Karmiris (Athens, 1981).

(36) 'Implications ecclésiologiques de deux types de pneumatologie', in *Communio Sanctorum*, Mélanges J. J. von Allmen (Labor et Fides, Genève, 1981), pp. 141-154.

(37) '"Created" and "Uncreated": The Philosophical and Theological Background of the Doctrine of Chalcedon', *Synaxis* (1981).

In French, 'Christologie et existence: la dialectique crée-incrée et le dogme de Chalcédoine', *Contacts* 36 (1984), pp. 154-172.

(38) 'Response of John Zizioulas' (to reactions to the above article), *Synaxis* (1982).

In French, 'La réponse de Jean Zizioulas', *Contacts* 37 (1985), pp. 60-72.

(39) 'The ecclesiological presuppositions of the holy Eucharist', *Nicolaus* 10 (1982), pp. 333-349.

(40) 'The Teaching of the 2nd Ecumenical Council on the Holy Spirit in Historical and Ecumenical Perspective', in J. S. Martins (ed.), *Credo in Spiritum Sanctum* (Libreria Editrice Vaticana, Roma, 1983), vol. 1, pp. 29-54.

(41) 'Déplacement de la perspective eschatologique', in G. Alberigo, *et al.*, *La chrétienté en débat* (Cerf, Paris, 1984), pp. 89-100.

In Italian, 'Il mutamento di collocazione della prospettiva escatologica', *Cristianesimo nella Storia* 5 (1984), pp. 119-130.

In Spanish, 'El desplazamento de la perspective escatologica', *Selecciones de teologia* 24 (1985), pp. 184-186.

(42) 'The Ecclesiology of the Orthodox Tradition', *Search*, vol. 7, part 2 (Winter, 1984), pp. 42-53.

(43) 'The Bishop in the Theological Doctrine of the Orthodox Church', in Richard Potz (ed.), *Kanon* VII: *Der Bischof und seine Eparchie*, Jahrbuch der Gesellschaft für das Recht der Ostkirchen (Verlag des Verbandes der wissenschaftlichen Gesellschaften Osterreichs, Wien, 1985), pp. 23-35.

(44) 'Orthodox Ecclesiology and the Ecumenical Movement', *Sourozh*, number 21 (August, 1985), pp. 16-27.

(45) 'The Theological Problem of "Reception"', *Bulletin—Centro pro Unione* 26 (1984), pp. 3-6.

Again in *One in Christ* 21 (1985), pp. 187-193.

In Italian, 'Il problema teologico della "Recezione"', *Studi Ecumenici* 3 (1985), pp. 197-208.

(46) 'Eschatology and History', in T. Wieser (ed.), *Cultures in Dialogue*, Documents from a symposium in honour of Philip A. Potter (Geneva, 1985), pp. 30-39.

(47) 'Eschatology and History', extracts from the above paper and comments by Zizioulas in the discussion which followed, in T. Wieser (ed.), *Whither Ecumenism?* (World Council of Churches, Geneva, 1986), pp. 62-71, 72-73.

(48) 'Die eucharistische Grundlage des Amtes, in Reinhard Thöle, Ilse Friedeberg (eds.), *Philoxenia*, Band II (Flacius-Verlag, Fürth, 1986).

(49) 'The Early Christian Community', in Bernard McGinn, John Meyendorff, Jean Leclerq (eds.), *Christian Spirituality: Origins to the Twelfth Century* (Routledge and Kegan Paul, London, 1986), pp. 23-43.

(50) 'The Contribution of Cappadocia to Christian Thought', in Frosso Pimenides, Stelios Roïdes (eds.), *Sinasos in Cappadocia* (National Trust for Greece: Agra Publications, 1986), pp. 23-37.

(51) 'Le mystère de l'Eglise dans la tradition orthodoxe', *Irénikon* 60 (1987), pp. 323-335.
The English original text, with additional final paragraphs on 'the cosmic dimension of the Church', 'The Mystery of the Church in Orthodox Tradition', *One in Christ* 24 (1988), pp. 294-303.

(52) 'Discours du métropolite Jean de Pergame', La célébration du millénaire du «baptême» de la Russie au siège du Patriarcat oecuménique, *Istina* 33 (1988), pp. 197-203.

(53) 'The Nature of the Unity We Seek — The Response of the Orthodox Observer' (reply to the keynote address of the Archbishop of Canterbury to the 1988 Lambeth Conference), *One in Christ* 24 (1988), pp. 342-348.

(54) 'Las conferencias episcopales — reacciones ecumenicas. Causa nostra agitur? Punto de vista ecumenico', in *Naturaleza Y futuro de las Conferencias episcopales*, Actas del Coloquio internacional de Salamanca (Salamanca, 1988).
In English, 'The Institution of Episcopal Conferences: An Orthodox Reflection', *The Jurist* 48 (1988), pp. 376-383.

(55) 'Preserving God's Creation. Three Lectures on Theology and Ecology', *King's Theological Review* 12 (1989), pp. 1-5, 41-45; 13 (1990), pp. 1-5.

(56) 'Tradition liturgique et unité chrétienne', *Revue de l'Institut Catholique de Paris*, No. 36 (Octobre-Décembre, 1990), Tirage spécial: *Centenaire de la Faculté de Théologie*, pp. 157-170.

(57) 'The Doctrine of God the Trinity Today: Suggestions for an Ecumenical Study', in Alasdair I. C. Heron (ed.), *The Forgotten Trinity. 3 A Selection of Papers Presented to the BCC Study Commission on Trinitarian Doctrine Today* (BCC/CCBI, London, 1991), pp. 19-32.

(58) 'On Being a Person. Towards an Ontology of Personhood', in Christoph Schwöbel and Colin E. Gunton (eds.), *Persons, Divine and Human* (T. & T. Clark, Edinburgh, 1991), pp. 33-46.

General Bibliography

Anonymous, 'L'évêque d'après les prières d'ordination', in Y. Congar and B. Dupuy (eds.), *L'Episcopat et l'Eglise universelle* (q.v.), pp. 739-780.

AA.VV., *La sainte Eglise universelle. Confrontation oecuménique* (1948).

—*Mystery and Mysticism* (Blackfriars, London, 1956).

—*Etudes sur le sacrement de l'ordre* (Cerf, Paris, 1957).

—*Le concile et les conciles* (Chevetogne/Cerf, 1960).

—*L'Infallibilité de l'Eglise* (Chevetogne, 1962).

—*L'homme devant Dieu, Mélanges offerts au père Henri de Lubac* (Théologie 56, 57, 58; Aubier, Paris, 1963), 3 vols.

ACERBI, Antonio, *Due ecclesiologie: ecclesiologia giuridica ed ecclesiologia di comunione nella 'Lumen gentium'* (Dehoniane, Bologna, 1975).

ADAM, Karl, *Das Wesen des Katholizismus* (Schwann, Düsseldorf, 1936).

AFANASSIEFF, Nicolas, 'La doctrine de la primauté à la lumière de l'ecclésiologie', *Istina* 2 (1957), pp. 401-420.

—'Le concile dans la théologie orthodoxe russe', *Irenikon* 35 (1962), pp. 316-339.

—'L'Infallibilité de l'Eglise du point de vue d'un théologien orthodoxe', in AA.VV., *L'Infallibilité de l'Eglise* (q.v.), pp. 183-201.

—'Una Sancta', *Irenikon* 36 (1963), pp. 436-475.

—'L'Eucharistie, principal line entre les Catholiques et les Orthodoxes', *Irenikon* 38 (1965), pp. 337-339.

—'Réflexions d'un orthodoxe sur la collégialité des évêques', *Le Messager Orthodoxe* 29-30, I-II (1965), pp. 7-15.

—'L'Eglise de Dieu dans le Christ', *La Pensée Orthodoxe* 13 (1968), pp. 1-38.

—'The Church which presides in love', in J. Meyendorff, N. Afanassieff, R. P. A. Schmemann, N. Koulomzine, *The Primacy of Peter* (Faith, Leighton Buzzard, 1973[2]), pp. 57-110.

—*L'Eglise du Saint-Esprit* (Cerf, Paris, 1975).

AGORAS, Constantin, 'Vision ecclésiale et ecclésiologie', *Contacts* 43 (1991), No. 154, pp. 106-123.

ALLCHIN, A. M., 'Foreword' to Lars THUNBERG, *Man and the Cosmos* (q.v.), pp. 7-9.

von ALLMEN, Jean Jacques, 'L'Esprit de vérité vous conduira dans toute la vérité', in AA.VV., *L'Infallibilité de l'Eglise* (q.v.), pp. 13-26.

—'L'Eglise locale parmi les autres églises locales', *Irenikon* 43 (1970), pp. 512-537.

St Thomas AQUINAS, *Opera omnia* (ed. S. Fretté; Paris, 1871-1879), 32 vols. *Summa theologiae*, with commentary by CAJETAN [Thomas de Vio], vols. 4-12 of the *Opera omnia* (Rome, 1882-1971), 48 vols.

ARISTOTLE, *De caelo* (Clarendon, Oxford, 1922).

—*Physica* (Clarendon, Oxford, 1973).

—*The Complete Works of Aristotle* (trans. J. Barnes; Princeton University Press, 1985), 2 vols.

ARNOU, R., 'Unité numérique et unité de nature chez les Pères, après le Concile de Nicée', *Gregorianum* 15 (1934), pp. 242-254.

AUDET, J. P., 'Review' [of J. de Fraine, *Adam et son lignage: Etudes sur la "personnalité corporative" dans la Bible (Desclée de Brouwer*, Bruges, 1959)], *Revue biblique* 67 (1960), pp. 297-298.

de BACIOCCHI, J., *L'Eucharistie* (Desclée, Tournai, 1964).

BACON, Gratien, 'La pensée de Bossuet sur l'eucharistie, mystère d'unité, *Revue des sciences religieuses* 45 (1971), pp. 209-239.

BAILLARGEON, Gaëtan, *Perspectives orthodoxes sur l'Église-Communion, L'oeuvre de Jean Zizioulas* (Éditions Paulines, Montréal and Médiaspaul, Paris, 1989).

—'Jean Zizioulas, porte-parole de l'Orthodoxie contemporaine', *Nouvelle Revue Théologique* 111 (1989), pp. 176-193.

von BALTHASAR, Hans Urs, *Liturgie cosmique* (Théologie 11; Aubier, Paris, 1947).

—*Martin Buber and Christianity* (Harvill, London, 1961).

—*Glaubhaft ist nur Liebe* (Johannes Verlag, Einsiedeln, 1963).

—*A Theology of History* (Sheed and Ward, London, 1963).

—*The Theology of Karl Barth* (Anchor, New York, 1972).

—'The Achievement of Hneri de Lubac', *Thought* 51 (1976), pp. 7-49.

—'Cento domande a von Balthasar', interview in the Italian magazine, *30 Giorni*, 6 June 1984, pp. 8-18, 75-78.

von BALTHASAR, H. U., and CHANTRAINE, G., *Le cardinal Henri de Lubac: l'homme et son oeuvre* (Lethielleux, Paris, 1983).

BARAÚNA, G., (ed.), *L'Eglise de Vatican II* (Unam Sanctam 51 a, b, c; Cerf, Paris, 1966), 3 vols.

BARTH, Karl, *Dogmatics in Outline* (SCM, London, 1949).

—*Christmas* (Oliver and Boyd, Edinburgh and London, 1959).

—'The Church', in CALLAGHAN, Daniel J., OBERMANN, Heiko A., O'HANLON, Daniel J., (eds.), *Christianity Divided* (Sheed and Ward, London, 1962).

—*Church Dogmatics*, I/1 (T. & T. Clark, Edinburgh, 1975); I/2 (1956); IV/ 2 (1958).

BENEDETTI, G., 'L'antropologia teologica nella riflessione teologica di H. de Lubac', in MARRANZINI, A., (ed.), *Dimensione antropologica della teologia* (Ancora, Milano, 1971), pp. 439-457.

BENKO, Stephen, *The Meaning of Sanctorum Communio* (SCM, London, 1964).

BENOIT, Pierre, (?; article signed 'P.B.'), 'Bulletin: Nouveau Testament', *Revue biblique* 49 (1940), pp. 273-290.

BERTHOLD, George Charles, Translation and Notes for MAXIMUS CONFESSOR, *Selected Writings* (q.v.).

de BÉRULLE, Pierre, *Oeuvres complètes du Cardinal de Bérulle* (Maison d'institution de l'Oratoire, Montsoult, 1960), 2 vols.

BIHLMEYER, Karl, *Die apostolischen Vater* (Mohr, Tübingen, 1956).

BLANCHARD, J. P., *Méthode et principes du père Teilhard de Chardin* (Vieux Colombier, Paris, 1961).

BLONDEL, Maurice, *L'action (1893)* (Presses universitaires de France, Paris, 1950).

L'action (Librairie Felix Alcan, Paris, 1936, 1937), 2 vols.

Exigences philosophiques du christianisme (Presses universitaires de France, Paris, 1950).

BLOOMFIELD, M. W., 'Joachim of Flora', *Traditio* 13 (1957), pp. 249-311.

BOBRINSKOY, Boris, 'Présence réelle et communion eucharistique', *Revue des sciences philosophiques et théologiques* 53 (1969), pp. 402-420.

—*Le Mystère de la Trinité, Cours de théologie orthodoxe* (Cerf, Paris, 1986).

BOSSUET, Jacques Bénigne, *Oeuvres oratoires* (ed. J. Lebarq; Lille and Paris, 1890-1921), 7 vols.

BOTTE, Bernard, 'L'Ordre d'après les prières d'Ordination', in AA.VV., *Etudes sur le sacrement de l'ordre* (q.v.), pp. 13-35.

—'La Collégialite dans le Nouveau Testament et chez les Pères apostoliques', in AA.VV., *Le concile et les conciles* (q.v.), pp. 1-18.

—'Caractère collégial du presbytérat et de l'épiscopat', *ibid.*, pp. 97-124.

—'The Collegial Character of the Priesthood and the Episcopate', *Concilium*, vol. 4 (Ecumenism), number 1 (1965), pp. 88-90.

BOTTE, Bernard (ed.), *La Tradition Apostolique* (Sources Chrétiennes 11; Cerf, Paris, 1946).

BOULARAND, E., 'La consécration épiscopale est-elle sacramentelle?', *Bulletin de littérature ecclésiastique* 54 (1953), pp. 3-36.

BOUYER, Louis, 'Mysterion', in AA.VV., *Mystery and Mysticism* (q.v.), pp. 18-32.

—'Mysticism. An essay on the history of a word', *ibid.*, pp. 119-137.

—*The Paschal Mystery* (George Allen & Unwin, London, 1951).

—*The Spirituality of the New Testament and of the Fathers* (Burns & Oates, London, 1963).

—'Préface' to A. GRÉA, *L'Eglise et sa divine constitution* (q.v.), pp. 7-10.

—*Le Père invisible* (Cerf, Paris, 1976).

—*The Church of God* (Franciscan Herald, Chicago, 1982).

—*Mysterion. Du mystère à la mystique* (O.E.I.L., Paris, 1986).

BRITISH COUNCIL OF CHURCHES/DIVISION OF ECUMENICAL AFFAIRS STUDY COMMISSION ON TRINTARIAN DOCTRINE TODAY (hereafter, BCC/DEA Study Commission), Minutes of meetings (unpublished); 11-12 November 1983; 8-9 June and 16-17 November 1984; 8-9 March, and 15-16 November 1985; 20-21 June and 21-22 November, 1986; 14-16 June 1987.

BRITISH COUNCIL OF CHURCHES, *The Forgotten Trinity. 1. The Report of the BCC Study Commission on Trinitarian Doctrine Today* (British Council of Churches, London, 1989).

BROWN, David, *Continental Philosophy and Modern Theology* (Blackwell, Oxford, 1987).

BROWN, Raymond E., 'The Pater Noster as an Eschatological Prayer', *Theological Studies* 22 (1961), pp. 175-208.

BROWN, Raymond E., and MEIER, John P., *Antioch and Rome* (Geoffrey Chapman, London, 1983).

BUBER, Martin, *I and Thou* (T. & T. Clark, Edinburgh, 1958).

BURKE, T. Patrick, (ed.), *The Word in History* (Collins, London, 1968).

BUTLER, Basil Christopher, *The Idea of the Church* (Darton, Longman & Todd, London 1962).

—*The Theology of Vatican II* (Darton, Longman & Todd, London, 1981²).

CAJETAN, see under St Thomas AQUINAS.

CAMELOT, P. Th., 'Réalisme et symbolisme dans la doctrine eucharistique de s.Augustin', *Revue des sciences philosophiques et théologiques* 31 (1947), pp. 394-410.

—'A l'éternel par le temporel (*De Trinitate*, IV, xviii, 24)', *Revue des études augustiniennes* 2 (1956), pp. 163-172.

—«Sacramentum» Notes de théologie sacramentaire augustinienne', *Revue Thomiste* 57 (1957), pp. 429-449.

—See also under Ignatius of Antioch.

CERFAUX, L., 'Review' of A. Lieske, *Die Theologie der Logosmystik bei Origenes* (1938), in *Ephemerides Theologicae Lovaniensis* 16 (1939), pp. 148-149.

—*La théologie de l'Eglise suivant saint Paul* (Unam Sanctam 10; Cerf, Paris, 1942, 1948²).

CHAILLET, Pierre, *et al., L'Eglise est une; hommage à Moehler* (Bloud & Gay, 1939).

CIOLA, Nicola, *Paradosso e mistero in Henri de Lubac* (Pontificia Università Lateranense, Rome, 1980).

—'Il recente pensiero di H. de Lubac', *Rassegna di teologia* 23 (1982), pp. 277-293.

CLEMENT, Olivier, *L'Eglise orthodoxe* (1965).

—'Le dimanche et le Jour éternel', *Verbum Caro* vol. 20, n. 79 (1966), pp. 99-124.

—'Liminaire', *Contacts* 19 (1967), pp. 1-3 (author identified as 'O.C.').

—*Orient-occident, Deux passeurs: Vladimir Lossky et Paul Evdokimov* (Labor et Fides, Genève, 1985).

COLSON, Jean, *L'épiscopat catholique. Collégialité et primauté dans les trois premiers siècles de l'Eglise* (Unam Sanctam 43; Cerf, Paris, 1963).

CONGAR, Yves M.-J., *Chrétiens désunis* (Unam Sanctam 1: Cerf, Paris, 1937).

—*Esquisses du mystère d l'Eglise* (Unam Sanctam 8; Cerf, Paris, 1941).

—'Bulletin d'ecclésiologie 1939-1946', *Revue des sciences philosophiques et théologiques* 31 (1947), pp. 77-96.

—'Structure du sacerdoce chrétien', *La Maison Dieu* 27 (1951), pp. 51-85.

—'Ecclesia ab Abel', in *Abhandlungen über Theologie und Kirche, Festschrift für Karl Adam* (Patmos, Dusseldorf, 1952), pp. 79-108.

—'The Church: the People of God', *Concilium*, vol. 1, number 1 (1965), pp. 7-19.

—*L'ecclésiologie du haut Moyen-Age* (Cerf, Paris, 1968).

—*L'Eglise de saint Augustin à l'époque moderne* (Cerf, Paris, 1970).

—'La personne «Eglise»', *Revue Thomiste* 71 (1971), pp. 613-640.

—*Ministères et communion ecclésiale* (Cerf, Paris, 1971).

—'Rudolf Sohm nous interroge encore', *Revue des sciences philosophiques et théologiques* 57 (1973), pp. 263-294.

—Bulletin d'ecclésiologie' *Revue des sciences philosophiques et théologiques* 66 (1982), pp. 87-119.

—*I Believe in the Holy Spirit*, 3 vols. (Geoffrey Chapman, London, 1983).

—*Essais oecuméniques* (Centurion, Paris, 1984).

—*Le concile de Vatican II* (Beauchesne, Paris, 1984).

—*Diversity and Communion* (SCM, London, 1984).

—*Fifty Years of Catholic Theology, Conversations with Yves Congar* (SCM, London, 1988).

CONGAR, Yves M.-J., (ed.), *La collégialité épiscopale* (Unam Sanctam 52; Cerf, Paris, 1965).

CONGAR, Y., and DUPUY, B., (eds.), *L'épiscopat et l'Eglise universelle* (Unam Sanctam 39; Cerf, Paris, 1964).

COPPENS, J., 'Review' [of J. de Fraine, *Adam et son lignage* (see under J. P. Audet)], *Ephemerides Theologicae Lovaniensis* 36 (1960), pp. 488-490.

CRISTIANI, Marta, 'La controversia eucaristica nella cultura del secolo IX', *Studi Medievali* 9 (1968), pp. 167-233.

CULLMANN, Oscar, *Christ and Time* (SCM, London, 1962³).

—*Peter: Disciple, Apostle, Martyr* (SCM, London, 1962²).

—*The Christology of the New Testament* (SCM, London, 1963²).

D., 'Ein Weg zur Bestimmung des Verhältnisses von Natur und Gnade', *Orientierung* 14 (1950), pp. 138-141.

D.T.S., 'Chronique religieuse', *Irenikon* 23 (1950), pp. 407-447.

DALMAIS, Irénée-Henri, 'La théorie des «logoi» des créatures chez s.Maxime le confesseur', *Revue des sciences philosophiques et théologiques* 36 (1952), pp. 244-249.

—'Preface', to MAXIMUS CONFESSOR, *Selected Writings* (q.v.), pp. xi-xiv.

DANIÉLOU, Jean, 'Christianisme et histoire', *Etudes* 254 (September, 1947), pp. 166-184.

—*The Bible and the Liturgy* (Darton, Longman & Todd, London, 1956).

—*The Lord of History* (Longman's, Green and Co., London 1958).

DENZINGER, H., and SCHÖNMETZER, A., *Enchiridion Symbolorum Definitionum et Declarationum de Rebus Fidei et Morum* (Herder, 1976³⁶).

DIX, Gregory, *The Shape of Liturgy* (Dacre, Westminster, 1945²).

DUCHESNE, L., *Christian Worship; its origin and evolution* (SPCK, London, 1927⁵).

DULLES, Avery, *The Catholicity of the Church* (Clarendon, Oxford, 1987).

ETEROVIĆ, Nikola, *Christianesimo e religioni secondo H. de Lubac* (Città Nuova, Roma, 1981).

FESSARD, Gaston, 'Théologie et histoire', *Dieu vivant* 8 (1947), pp. 39-65.

FIDDES, Paul, 'The Atonement and the Trinity', unpublished paper presented to the BCC/DEA Study Commission (q.v.).

FIGURA, Michael, *Der Anruf der Gnade. Über die Beziehung des Menschen zu Gott nach Henri de Lubac* (Johannes Verlag, Einsiedeln, 1979).

—'Henri de Lubac: teologia della pienezza della fede', *Communio* (Italian edition) no. 58 (1981), pp. 73-84.

FLANNERY, Austin (ed.), *Vatican Council II. The Conciliar and Post Conciliar Documents* (Dominican Publications, Dublin, 1980).

FLOROVSKY, Georges, 'The Catholicity of the Church', in *Bible, Church, Tradition: An Eastern Orthodox View*, Collected Works, vol. 1 (Nordland, Belmont, 1972), pp. 37-55.

—'The Church: Her Nature and Task', *ibid.*, pp. 57-72.

'[Origen, Eusebius and] The Iconoclastic Controversy', in *Christianity and Culture*, Collected Works, vol. 2 (Nordland, Belmont, 1974), pp. 101-119.

—'*Cur Deus Homo*? The Motive of the Incarnation', in *Creation and Redemption*, Collected Works, vol. 3 (Nordland, Belmont, 1976), pp. 163-170.

—'Patristic Theology and the Ethos of the Orthodox Church', in *Aspects of Church History*, Collected Works, vol. 4 (Nordland, Belmont, 1975), pp. 11-30.

—'The Fathers of the Church and the Old Testament', *ibid.*, pp. 31-38.

—'St Athanasius' Concept of Creation', *ibid.*, pp. 39-62.

—'The Patristic Age and Eschatology: An Introduction', *ibid.*, pp. 63-78.

—'Western Influences in Russian Theology', *ibid.*, pp. 157-182.

—'The Ways of the Russian Theology', *ibid.*, pp. 183-209.

—'Patristics and Modern Theology', in H. Alivisatos (ed.). *Procès-Verbaux du Premier Congrès de Théologie Orthodoxe* (Athens, 1939).

—'Le corps du Christ vivant', in AA.VV., *La sainte Eglise universelle. Confrontation oecuménique* (q.v.).

—'The Doctrine of the Church and the Ecumenical Problem', *The Ecumenical Review* 2 (1950), pp. 152-161.

—'Orthodox', in Pehr Edwall, Eric Hayman, William D. Maxwell (eds.), *The Ways of Worship* (SCM, London, 1951), pp. 53-65.

—'La Bible et l'Eglise', *Dieu Vivant* 21 (1952), pp. 97-105.

—'Christ and His Church. Suggestions and Comments', in *1054-1954. L'Eglise et les Eglises.* Etudes offerts à Lambert Beauduin, vol. 2 (Chevetogne, 1955), pp. 159-170.

—'Le future concile de l'Eglise Romaine', *Le Messager Orthodoxe* 6, II (1959), pp. 3-8.

—'The Worshipping Church', Introduction to Mother Mary and Kallistos Ware (trans.), *The Festal Menaion* (Faber, London, 1969), pp. 21-37.

FORTE, Bruno, *La chiesa nell'eucaristia* (M. D'Auria, Napoli, 1975).

FORTINO, E., 'Pan-Orthodox decision on the Catholic-Orthodox dialogue — Towards the next meeting of the joint commission', *Osservatore Romano* (English edition), 16 February 1987, p. 8.

de FRAINE, J., *Adam and the Family of Man* (Alba, New York, 1965).

FREY, C., *Mysterium der Kirche, Öffnung sur Welt* (Göttingen, 1969).

FUCHS, Josef, 'Origines d'une trilogie ecclésiologique à l'époque rationaliste de la théologie', *Revue des sciences philosophiques et théologiques* 53 (1969), pp. 185-211.

GARRIGOU-LAGRANGE, R., 'La nouvelle théologie où va-t-elle?', *Angelicum* 23 (1946), pp. 126-145.

GARRIGUES, J. M., le GUILLOU, M. J., RIOU, A., 'Le caractère sacerdotal dans la tradition des Pères grecs', *Nouvelle revue théologique* 93 (1971), pp. 801-820.

GILSON, Etienne, *L'Esprit de la philosophie médiévale* (Vrin, Paris, 1932).
—*The Christian Philosophy of Saint Augustine* (Victor Gollancz, London, 1961).

GRACIAS, A., *The spiritual sense of Scripture according to Henri de Lubac* (Pontificia Universitas Gregoriana, Rome, 1975).

GRAHAM, Aelred, 'St Augustine's Doctrine of Grace', *The Eastern Churches Quarterly* 6 (1945-1946), pp. 228-247.

GRÉA, Adrien, *L'Eglise et sa divine constitution* (Casterman, Paris, 1965).

GRELOT, P., *Sens chrétien de l'Ancien Testament* (Desclée, Tournai, 1962).

GROOTAERS, J. (ed.), *Primauté et collegialité. Le dossier de Gérard Philips sur la Nota Explicativa Praevia (Lumen Gentium, Chap. III)* (University Press, Leuven, 1986).

GUARDINI, Romano, *The Life of Faith* (Catholic Book Club, London, 1961).

le GUILLOU, M. J., *Christ and Church. A Theology of the Mystery* (Desclée, New York, 1966).

GUITTON, Jean, *Le Temps et l'Eternité chez Plotin et Saint Augustin* (Boivin, Paris, 1933).

GUNTON, Colin, 'The Person and the Individual in Western Philosophy: Some Exploratory Comments', unpublished paper presented to the BCC/DEA Study Commission (q.v.)

—'The Spirit in the Trinity: in Quest of the Unfindable', unpublished paper presented to the BCC/DEA Study Commission (q.v.).

GUNTON, Colin E. & HARDY, Daniel W. (eds.), *On Being the Church: Essays on the Christian Community* (T. & T. Clark, Edinburgh, 1989).

GUNTON, Colin E., & SCHWÖBEL, Christoph (eds.), *Persons, Human and Divine* (see under SCHWÖBEL).

de HALLEUX, A., '"L'église catholique" dans la lettre ignatienne aux Smyrnotes', *Ephemerides Theologicae Lovaniensis* 58 (1982), pp. 5-24.

—'Le IIe concile oecuménique. Une évaluation dogmatique et ecclésiologique', *Christianesimo nella storia* 3 (1982), pp. 297-327.

—'«Hypostase» et «personne» dans la formation du dogme trinitaire (ca. 375-381)', *Revue d'histoire ecclésiastique* 79 (1984), pp. 313-369, 625-670.

—'Personnalisme ou essentialisme trinitaire chez les Pères cappadociens? Une mauvaise controverse' *Revue théologique de Louvain* 17 (1986), pp. 129-155, 265-292.

HANSON, R. P. C., *Allegory and Event* (SCM, London, 1959).

HASTINGS, Adrian, (ed.), *Modern Catholicism, Vatican II and after* (SPCK, London, 1991).

HENRICI, Peter, 'Blondel and Loisy in the Modernist Crisis', *Communio* (English edition) 14 (1987), pp. 351-372.

HENRY, Paul, 'On Some Implications of the "Ex Patre Filioque Tanquam Ab Uno Principio"', *The Eastern Churches Quarterly* 7 (1948), Supplementary Issue: 'Concerning the Holy Spirit', pp. 16-31.

HERON, Alasdair, '"Person" as a Trinitarian Technical Term and the Problems of its Application to the Holy Spirit', unpublished paper presented to the BCC/DEA Study Commission (q.v.).

HERTLING, Ludwig, *Communio. Church and Papacy in Early Christianity* (Loyola University, Chicago, 1972).

HOFFMAN-AXTHELM, D., *Anschauung und Begriff. Zur historischen Einordnung von 'Nouvelle Théologie' und 'Existentialer Theologie'* (Munich, 1973).

HOLLAND, David Larrimore, 'History, Theology and the Kingdom of God: A Contribution of Johannes Weiss to 20th Century Theology', *Biblical Research* 13 (1968), pp. 54-66.

HOLSTEIN, H., *Hiérarchie et peuple de Dieu* (Beauchesne, Paris, 1970).

Saint IGNATIUS OF ANTIOCH, *Ignace d'Antioche, Lettres* (ed. P. Th. Camelot; Sources Chrétiennes 10; Cerf, Paris, 1951²).

JEREMIAS, Joachim, *The Eucharistic Words of Jesus* (SCM, London, 1966).

Pope JOHN-PAUL II, Address to the Roman Curia in the presence of a delegation from the Ecumenical Patriarchate, 28 June 1985, *Osservatore Romano* (English edition), 15 July 1985, pp. 3-5.

JOHNSON, Aubrey R., *The One and the Many in the Israelite Conception of God* (University of Wales, Cardiff, 1942).

JONES, Cheslyn, WAINWRIGHT, Geoffrey, YARNOLD, Edward, BRADSHAW, Paul, (eds.), *The Study of Liturgy* (revised edition; SPCK, London, 1992).

JUNGMANN, Josef A., *The Early Liturgy* (Darton, Longman & Todd, London, 1960).

KASPER, Walter, 'Esprit, Christ, Eglise', *L'expérience de l'Esprit: Mélanges E. Schillebeeckx* (Le Point Theologique 18; Beauchesne, Paris, 1976).

—*The God of Jesus Christ* (SCM, London, 1984).

—*Theology and Church* (SCM, London, 1989).

KELLY, J. N. D., *Early Christian Doctrines* (Adam & Charles Black, London, 1977⁵).

—'"Catholic" and "Apostolic" in the Early Centuries', *One in Christ*, 6 (1970), pp. 274-287.

KÜNG, Hans, *The Church* (Search, London, 1968).

LABOURDETTE, M., NICOLAS, M. J. and BRUCKBERGER, R. L., dominicains, *Dialogue théologique. Pièces du débat entre «La Revue Thomiste» d'une part et les RR. PP. de Lubac, Daniélou, Bouillard, Fessard, von Balthasar, S.J., d'autre part* (Les Arcades, Saint-Maximin, 1947).

LAMPERT, E., 'The Orthodox Church's Teaching of Grace', *The Eastern Churches Quarterly* 6 (1945-1946), pp. 248-258.

LANNE, Emmanuel, 'Le mystère de l'Eglise dans la perspective de la théologie Orthodoxe', *Irenikon* 35 (1962), pp. 171-212.

LASH, Symeon, 'The Trinity in present-day Eucharistic Liturgy', unpublished paper presented to the BCC/DEA Study Commission (q.v.).

LAURET, Bernard, & REFOULÉ, François, (eds.), *Initiation à la pratique de la théologie* (Cerf, Paris, 1982-1983), 5 vols.

LECUYER, J., 'Episcopat et Presbytérat dans les écrits d'Hippolyte de Rome', *Recherches de science réligieuse* 40 (1953), pp. 30-50.

LEEMING, Bernard, *Principles of Sacramental Theology* (Longman's, Green and Co., London, 1957).

LEGRAND, Hervé, 'La présidence de l'eucharistie selon la tradition ancienne', *Spiritus* 18 (1977), pp. 409-431.

—'La réalisation de l'Eglise en un lieu', in LAURET, Bernard, & REFOULÉ, François, (eds.), *Initiation à la pratique de la théologie* (q.v.), vol. 3, pp. 143-345.

LELOUVIER, Yves Noël, *Perspectives russes sur l'Eglise, Un théologien contemporain: Georges Florovsky* (Centurion, Paris, 1968).

LENGSFELD, Peter, *Adam et le Christ* (Aubier, Paris, 1970).

LIALINE, Clement, 'The Holy Ghost and the Mystical Body of Christ', *The Eastern Churches Quarterly* 7 (1948), Supplementary Issue: 'Concerning the Holy Spirit', pp. 69-94.

LIETZMANN, H., *Mass and Lord's Supper*, with an Introduction and Further Enquiry by Robert Douglas Richardson (11 fascicles; E. J. Brill, Leiden, 1953-1979).

LINDSAY, Austin J., *De Lubac's Images of the Church: A Study of Christianity in Dialogue* (Catholic University of America, 1974).

LOSSKY, Vladimir, 'The Procession of the Holy Spirit in the Orthodox Triadology', *The Eastern Churches Quarterly* 7 (1948), Supplementary Issue: 'Concerning the Holy Spirit', pp. 31-53.

—*The Mystical Theology of the Eastern Church* (James Clarke, Cambridge & London, 1957).

—*In the Image and Likeness of God* (St Vladimir's Seminary, 1974).

—*Orthodox Theology: An Introduction* (St Vladimir's Seminary, Crestwood, 1978).

—*The Vision of God* (St Vladimir's Seminary, Crestwood, 1983).

LOUTH, Andrew, *Denys the Areopagite* (Geoffrey Chapman, London, 1989).

McINTYRE, John, 'The Holy Spirit in Greek Patristic Thought', *Scottish Journal of Theology* 7 (1954), pp. 353-375.

—*The Christian Doctrine of History*, (Oliver and Boyd, Edinburgh and London, 1957).

McNAMARA, Kevin, (ed.), *The Church* (Veritas, Dublin, 1983).

McNULTY, P. *St. Peter Damian. Selected Writings on the Spiritual Life* (Faber and Faber, London, 1959).

McPARTLAN, Paul, 'Eucharistic Ecclesiology', *One in Christ* 22 (1986), pp. 314-331.

—Review of Zizioulas, *Being as Communion*, in Sobornost 9: 1 (1987), pp. 78-81.

—'Eucharist and Church: the Contribution of Henri de Lubac', *The Month* 21 (1988), pp. 847-859.

—'Mary for de Lubac and Teilhard' (Pamphlet; Ecumenical Society of the Blessed Virgin Mary, 1989).

—'The Eucharist: past event, present reality, future hope', *The New Theologian* (published by The Christian Theology Trust) 2 (1991), pp. 11-14.

—'In my end is my beginning', review of A. HASTINGS, *Modern Catholicism (q.v.)*, *The Month* 24 (1991), pp. 339-340.

—'Henri de Lubac – Evangeliser', *Priests and People* 6 (1992), pp. 343-346.

—'Tu seras transformé en moi', *Communio* (French edition) 17 (1992), no. 103, pp. 38-52.

—'Towards Catholic–Orthodox unity', *Communio* (English edition) 19 (1992), pp. 305-320.

MACY, Gary, *The Theologies of the Eucharist in the Early Scholastic Period* (Clarendon, Oxford, 1984).

MAIER, Eugen, *Einigung der Welt in Gott* (Johannes Verlag, Einsiedeln, 1983).

MANARANCHE, A., *Prêtres à la manière des apôtres* (Centurion, Paris, 1967).

MANSON, T. W., 'Entry into Membership of the Early Church', *Journal of Theological Studies* 48 (1947), pp. 25-33.

—*The Teaching of Jesus* (Cambridge University Press, 1959²).

MARCEL, Gabriel, *The Mystery of Being*, vol. 1, 'Reflection and Mystery' (Harvill, London, 1950); vol. 2, 'Faith and Reality' (1951).

MARITAIN, Jacques, *Humanisme intégrale* (Fernand Aubier, Paris, 1936).

MARTELET, Gustave, *The Risen Christ and the Eucharistic World* (Seabury, New York, 1976).

—*Les idées maîtresses de Vatican II* (Cerf, Paris, 1985²).

MASCALL, E. L., *Corpus Christi* (Longman's, London, 1953).

—*Nature and Supernature* (Darton, Longman & Todd, London, 1976).

—*Theology and the Gospel of Christ* (SPCK, London, 1977).

MASCALL, E. L. (ed.), *The Church of God* (SPCK, London, 1934).

MASURE, Eugene, *The Christian Sacrifice* (Burns Oates & Washbourne, London, 1944).

—*The Sacrifice of the Mystical Body* (Burns & Oates, London, 1954).

MAXIMUS CONFESSOR, *Selected Writings* (SPCK, London, 1985).

van der MEER, F., 'Sacramentum chez saint Augustin', *La Maison Dieu* 13 (1948), pp. 50-64.

MEREDITH, Anthony, 'The Trinity and Anthropology', unpublished paper presented to the BCC/DEA Study Commission (q.v.).

MERSCH, Emile, *Le Corps Mystique du Christ* (Museum Lessianum, Louvain, 1933), 2 vols.

—*La théologie du corps mystique* (ed. J. Levie; Louvain, 1946).

MEYENDORFF, John, *Orthodoxy and Catholicity* (Sheed & Ward, New York, 1966).

—*Christ in Eastern Christian Thought* (St Valdimir's Seminary, 1975).

—*The Orthodox Church* (St Vladimir's Seminary, Crestwood, 1981).

—*Catholicity and the Church* (St Vladimir's Seminary, Crestwood, 1983).

—'Foreword' to John Zizioulas, *Being as Communion* (q.v.), pp. 11-12.

MILLER, John, H., *Vatican II: An Interfaith Appraisal* (University of Notre Dame, 1966).

MOELLER, C., and PHILIPS, G., *The Theology of Grace and the Oecumenical Movement* (A. R. Mowbray, London, 1961).

MÖHLER, Johann Adam, *Symbolism* (Gibbings, London, 1906).

—*L'unite dans l'Eglise* (Unam Sanctam 2; Cerf, Paris, 1938).

MONCHANIN, Jules, 'L'amitié et l'amour: de la solitude à Dieu', in AA.VV., *Médicine et Adolescence* (Lavandier, Lyon, 1936).

—'L'Inde et la contemplation', *Dieu vivant* 3 (1945), pp. 15-48.

—'Théologie et mystique du Saint-Esprit', *Dieu vivant* 23 (1953), pp. 69-76.

—*Ecrits spirituels* (Centurion, Paris, 1965).

MONDIN, Battista, *I grandi teologi del secolo ventesimo:* vol. 1, 'I teologi cattolici' (Borla, Torino, 1969); vol. 2, 'I teologi protestanti e ortodossi' (Borla, Torino, 1969).

-*Le nuove ecclesiologie* (Paoline, Roma, 1980).

de MONTCHEUIL, Yves, *Problèmes de vie spirituelle* (J.E.C.F.[C. et S.], Paris, 1945).

—*L'Eglise et le monde actuel* (Témoignage Chrétien, Paris, 1945).

'Signification eschatologique du repas eucharistique', *Recherches de science religieuse* 33 (1946), pp. 10-43.

—*Aspects de l'Eglise* (Unam Sanctam 18; Cerf, Paris, 1949).

—*Leçons sur le Christ* (Epi, Paris, 1949).

—*Mélanges théologiques* (Aubier, Paris, 1951²).

—'Dieu premièrement moral', *Communio* (French edition) 13 (1988), pp. 36-45.

NEGRI, Giuseppe M., *P. Henri de Lubac. Una teologia spirituale* (Pontificia Università Urbaniana, Rome, 1982).

NICHOLS, Aidan, *Yves Congar* (Geoffrey Chapman, London, 1989).

—*Theology in the Rusian Diaspora: Church, Fathers, Eucharist in Nikolai Afanas'ev, 1893-1966* (Cambridge University Press, 1990).

NICOLAS, Marie-Joseph, 'Théologie de l'Eglise, Etude critique', *Revue thomiste* 46 (1946), pp. 372-398.

O.C.: see under Olivier CLEMENT.

O.R.: see under Oliver ROUSSEAU.

The ORTHODOX LITURGY, being the Diving Liturgy of St John Chrysostom and S. Basil the Great (SPCK, London, 1982).

PAMBRUN, James R., *The Presence of God: A Study into the Apologetic of Henri de Lubac* (University of St Michael's College, Toronto, 1978).

—'The Presence of God: A Note on the Apologetics of Henri de Lubac and Teilhard de Chardin', *Eglise et théologie* 10 (1979), pp. 343-368.

PEDERSEN, S., *Israel: Its Life and Culture* (1926).

PELCHAT, Marc, *L'ecclésiologie dans l'oeuvre de Henri de Lubac* (Pontificia Universitas Gregoriana, Rome, 1986).

'*L'Eglise Mystère de communion. L'ecclésiologie dans l'oeuvre de Henri de Lubac* (Éditions Paulines, Montréal and Médiaspaul, Paris, 1990). This is the full version of the thesis partly published in the above entry.

PELIKAN, Jaroslav, 'Introduction', to MAXIMUS CONFESSOR, *Selected Writings* (q.v.), pp. 1-13.

PHILIPS, Gérard, *L'Eglise et son mystère au IIe concile du Vatican. Histoire, texte et commentaire de la Constitution* Lumen Gentium (Desclée, Paris, 1967, 1968), 2 vols.

Pope PIUS XII, *Humani Generis*. Cf. DS 3875-3899; also *Nouvelle revue théologique* 72 (1950), pp. 840-861.

PLATO, *Republic*, with translation by Paul Shorey (William Heinemann, London, and Harvard University Press, Cambridge, Mass., 1946), 2 vols.

PRESTIGE, G. L., *God in Patristic Thought* (SPCK, London, 1964).

RAHNER, Karl, 'Concerning the Relationship between Nature and Grace', *Theological Investigations*, vol. 1 (Darton, Longman & Todd, London, 1961), pp. 297-317.

—'Remarks on the Dogmatic Treatise "*De Trinitate*"', *Theological Investigations*, vol. 4 (Darton, Longman & Todd, London, 1966), pp. 77-102.

—*The Church and the Sacraments* (Burns & Oates, London, 1963).

—*The Trinity* (Burns & Oates, London, 1970).

RATZINGER, Joseph, 'The Pastoral Implications of Episcopal Collegiality', *Concilium*, vol. 1 (Dogma), number 1 (1965), pp. 20-34.

—'La collégialité épiscopale: développement théologique', in G. BARAÚNA (ed.), *L'Eglise de Vatican II* (q.v.), vol. 3, pp. 763-790.

—*Introduction to Christianity* (Burns & Oates, London, 1969).

—*Das neue Volk Gottes* (Patmos-Verlag, Düsseldorf, 1970²).

—*Les principes de la théologie catholique* (Tequi, Paris, 1985).

—*Church, Ecumenism and Politics* (St Paul, Slough, 1988).

RAVIER, André (ed.), *La Mystique et les mystiques* (Desclée de Brouwer, Paris, 1965).

REEVES, Marjorie, *Joachim of Fiore and the Prophetic Future* (SPCK, London, 1976).

REEVES, Marjorie and GOULD, Warwick, *Joachim of Fiore and the Myth of the Eternal Evangel in the Nineteenth Century* (Clarendon, Oxford, 1987).

ROBINSON, H. Wheeler, 'The Hebrew Conception of Corporate Personality', *Zeitschrift fur die alttestamentliche Wissenschaft* Beihefte 66 (1936), pp. 49-62.

—*Redemption and Revelation* (Nisbet, London, 1942).

ROGERSON, J. W., 'The Hebrew Conception of Corporate Personality: A Re-Examination', *Journal of Theological Studies* 21 (1970), pp. 1-16.

—*Anthropology and the Old Testament* (Blackwell, Oxford, 1978).

ROMANIDES, J. S., 'Orthodox ecclesiology according to Alexis Khomiakov (1804-1860)', *The Greek Orthodox Theological Review* 2 (1956-1957), pp. 57-73.

—'The ecclesiology of St Ignatius of Antioch', *The Greek Orthodox Theological Review* 7 (1961-1962), pp. 53-77.

RONDET, Henri, *The Grace of Christ* (Newman, Westminster, 1967).

ROSATO, Philip J., 'Spirit Christology: Ambiguity and Promise', *Theological Studies* 38 (1977), pp. 423-449.

ROUSSEAU, Olivier, 'La Jérusalem céleste', *La vie spirituelle*, number 372 (April 1952), pp. 378-388.

—'Introduction', to AA.VV., *L'Infallibilité de l'Eglise* (q.v.), pp. 7-12.

—'In Memoriam: le R. P. Nicolas Afanassieff', *Irenikon* 40 (1967), pp. 291-297 (author identified as 'O.R.').

—'Préface', to Nicolas Afanassieff, *L'Eglise du Saint-Esprit* (q.v.), pp. 7-12.

RUSSO, Antonio, *Henri de Lubac: Teologia e dogma nella storia. L'influsso di Blondel* (La cultura 40; Studium, Roma, 1990).

SAGE, A., 'L'Eucharistie dans la pensée de saint Augustin', *Revue des études augustiniennes* 15 (1969), pp. 209-240.

SAWARD, John, 'Bérulle and the "French School"', in C. JONES, G. WAINWRIGHT, E. YARNOLD, *The Study of Spirituality* (q.v.), pp. 386-396.

—Review of Zizioulas, *Being as Communion*, in *New Blackfriars* 67 (1986), pp. 45-48.

SCHILLEBEECKX, Edward, 'L'instinct de la foi selon s. Thomas d'Aquin', *Revue des sciences philosophiques et théologiques* 48 (1964), pp. 377-408.

—*Christ the Sacrament of the Encounter with God* (Sheed and Ward, London, 1963).

SCHMAUS, Michael, *Dogma*, vol. 4, *The Church, its Origin and Structure* (Sheed and Ward, London, 1972); vol. 5, *The Church as Sacrament* (1975).

SCHMEMANN, Alexander, 'Towards a Theology of Councils', *St Vladimir's Seminary Quarterly* 6 (1962), pp. 170-184.

—*The Eucharist* (St Vladimir's Seminary, Crestwood, 1988).

SCHNACKERS, Hubert, *Kirche als Sakrament und Mutter. Zur Ekklesiologie von Henri de Lubac* (Peter Lang, Frankfurt am Main, 1979).

SCHULTZE, Bernhard, 'Eucharistie und Kirche in der Russischen Theologie der Gegenwart', *Zeitschrift fur Katholische Theologie* 77 (1955), pp. 257-300.

SCHWÖBEL, Christoph, & GUNTON, Colin E. (eds.), *Persons, Divine and Human* (T&T Clark, Edinburgh, 1991).

SECOND VATICAN COUNCIL *(SACROSANCTUM OECUMENICUM CONCILIUM VATICANUM II)*, *Constitutiones, decreta, declarationes* (Typis Polyglottis Vaticanis, 1974).

—see also under A. FLANNERY.

SESBOÜÉ, B., 'Eucharistie: deux générations de travaux', *Etudes* 355 (1981), pp. 99-115.

SHERWOOD, Polycarp, 'Introduction', to St Maximus the Confessor, *The Ascetic Centuries— The Four Centuries on Charity* (Ancient Christian Writers 21; Longman's, Green and Co., London, 1955), pp. 3-102.

—*The Earlier Ambigua of St Maximus the Confessor* (Herder, Rome, 1955).

SMAIL, T. A., 'The *Filioque* in Recent Theological Discussion', unpublished paper presented to the BCC/DEA Study Commission (q.v.)

SMULDERS, Peter, 'L'Eglise, sacrement du salut', in G. BARAÚNA (ed.), *L'Eglise de Vatican II* (q.v.), vol. 2, pp. 313-338.

STORMON, E. J. (ed. and trans.), *Towards the Healing of Schism. The Sees of Rome and Constantinople. Public statements and correspondence between the Holy See and the Ecumenical Patriarchate 1958-1974* (Paulist, Mahwah, 1987).

SUAREZ, Francisco de, *Tractatus de gratia Dei*, vols. 7-10 in the *Opera omnia* (ed. D. M. André; Paris, 1856-1878), 28 vols.

SWEENEY, G., 'The Primacy: The Small Print of Vatican I', *Clergy Review* 59 (1974), pp. 96-121.

de la TAILLE, Maurice, *Mysterium Fidei de Augustissimo Corporis et Sanguinis Christi Sacrificio et Sacramento* (Beauchesne, Paris, 1921).

—*The Mystery of Faith and Human Opinion Contrasted and Defined* (Sheed & Ward, London, 1934).

TARTAGLIA, Philip, 'Reflections on Trinity and Church in a Roman Catholic Context', unpublished paper presented to the BCC/DEA Study Commission (q.v.).

TEILHARD de CHARDIN, Pierre, 'La crise présente', *Etudes* 233 (1937), pp. 145-165.

—*Le milieu divin* (Collins, London, 1960).

—*Hymn of the Universe* (Collins, London, 1965).

—*Writings in Time of War* (Collins, London, 1968).

—*The Phenomenon of Man* (Collins/Fontana, London, 1970).

THUNBERG, Lars, *Microcosm and Mediator. The Theological Anthropology of Maximus the Confessor* (C. W. K. Gleerup, Lund, 1965).

—*Man and the Cosmos. The Vision of St Maximus the Confessor* (St Vladimir's Seminary, Crestwood, 1985).

TILLARD, J. M. R., 'Les sacrements de l'Eglise', in LAURET, Bernard, & REFOULÉ, François, (eds.), *Initiation à la pratique de la théologie*, vol. 3, pp. 385-466.

—*The Bishop of Rome* (SPCK, London, 1983).

—*Eglise d'églises* (Cerf, Paris, 1987).

TREMBELAS, Panagiotis N., *Dogmatique de l'Eglise Orthodoxe Catholique* (Chevetogne/Desclée de Brouwer, 1966, 1967, 1968), 3 vols.

TRETHOWAN, I., 'The Supernatural End: P. de Lubac's new volumes', *The Downside Review* 84 (1966), pp. 397-407.

VALLIN, P., review of Zizioulas, *L'être ecclesial*, in 'Bulletin d'histoire de l'Eglise et d'ecclésiologie', *Recherches de science religieuse* 71 (1983), pp. 385-386.

VANDER GUCHT, R., VORGRIMLER, H. (eds.), *Bilan de la théologie du XX siècle*, 2 vols. (Casterman, Paris-Tournai, 1970 & 1971).

VANZAN, Piersandro, SCHULTZ, Hans Jürgen (eds.), *Lessico dei teologi del secolo XX* (Mysterium Salutis Supplemento 12; Queriniana, Brescia, 1978).

VASS, G., *The Mystery of Man and the Foundations of a Theological System* (Sheed & Ward, London, 1985).

VILLAIN, Maurice, 'Un grand livre oecuménique: *Catholicisme*', in AA.VV., *L'homme devant Dieu* (q.v.), vol. 3, pp. 319-329.

VORGRIMLER, H., 'Henri de Lubac', in P. Vanzan, H. Schultz (eds.), *Lessico dei teologi del secolo XX* (q.v.), pp. 421-428. References are indicated in the text by 'Henri de Lubac (L)'.

—'Henri de Lubac', in R. Vander Gucht, H. Vorgrimler (eds.), *Bilan de la theologie del XX siècle* (q.v.), vol. 2, pp. 806-820. Reference are indicated in the text by 'Henri de Lubac (B).

WAINWRIGHT, Geoffrey, *Eucharist and Eschatology* (Epworth, London, 1971).

WALKER, Andrew, 'Fatherhood, Monarchia and Koinonia', unpublished paper presented to the BCC/DEA Study Commission (q.v.).

WARE, Timothy (Kallistos), *The Orthodox Church* (Penguin, Harmondsworth, 1980).

WEBER, J. G. (ed. and trans.), *In Quest of the Absolute: The Life and Work of Jules Monchanin* (Cistercian Studies 51; Cistercian Publications, Kalamazoo and A. R. Mowbray, London, 1977).

WEGER, Karl Heinz, *Karl Rahner. An Introduction to his Theology* (Burns & Oates, London, 1980).

WEISS, Johannes, *Jesus' Proclamation of the Kingdom of God* (SCM, London, 1971).

WILLIAMS, Jane, 'The Fatherhood of God', unpublished paper presented to the BCC/DEA Study Commission (q.v.).

WILLIAMS, Rowan, *The Theology of Vladimir Nikolaievich Lossky: An Exposition and Critique* (unpublished thesis; Oxford, 1975).

—*Eucharistic Sacrifice – The Roots of a Metaphor* (Grove Liturgical Study 31; Grove, Bramcote, 1982).

—*Authority and the Bishop in the Church*, in Mark Santer (ed.), *Their Lord and Ours* (SPCK, London, 1982), pp. 90-112.

—Review of Zizioulas, *Being as Communion*, in *Scottish Journal of Theology* 42 (1989), pp. 101-105.

WOLF, Ernst, 'Karl Barth', in Leonard REINISCH (ed.), *Theologians of our Time* (University of Notre Dame, 1964), pp. 1-16.

WOOD, Susan Karaus, *The Church as the Social Embodiment of Grace in the Ecclesiology of Henri de Lubac* (Marquette University, Milwaukee, 1986).

WORLD COUNCIL OF CHURCHES, 'The Church, the Churches and the World Council of Churches', *The Ecumenical Review* 3 (1950-1951), pp. 47-53; cf. pp. 77-78.

WYBREW, Hugh, *The Orthodox Liturgy* (SPCK, London, 1989).

YANNARAS, Christos, *The Freedom of Morality* (St Vladimir's Seminary, Crestwood, 1984).

YARNOLD, Edward, *The Awe-Inspiring Rites of Initiation* (St Paul, Slough, 1972).

—*The Second Gift. A Study of Grace* (St Paul, Slough, 1974).

Index of Names

(Bibliographies excluded. If a page number is followed by 'n.', then the reference to the person on that page occurs only in a footnote.)

Adam, K., 94, 96.

Afanassieff, N., xvii, xx, 20n., 98, 101, 105, 106-108, 113-120, 169n., 204n., 212, 226, 235, 280.

Agoras, C., 266n.

Albert the Great, St., 78n.

Alger of Liége, 82-83.

Allchin, D., 125n.

von Allmen, J. J., 113-120, 134n., 210, 304.

Ambrose, St., 83-84, 285.

Antòn, A., 9.

Aquinas, St. Thomas, 11, 30-42, 49n., 78n., 113n., 298n.

Archimedes, 51n.

Aristotle, 4, 32-34, 42, 128, 141, 144-145, 161, 191n.

Arnou, R., 20n.

Athanasius of Alexandria, St., 134, 145, 153-155, 161-163, 179.

Athenagoras, 7n.

Audet, J. P., 171n.

Augustine, St., xx, 3-5, 10, 16, 23, 30-31, 47, 49n., 52, 55, 59n., 60, 63n., 67-72, 77-78, 80-85, 86-87, 91, 94, 99, 105, 124, 131, 164n., 175, 181n., 216, 219, 220, 225n., 244n., 292-294, 302.

Baillargeon, G., xivn, xxi, 123n., 130n., 265-270, 280, 291n.

Baius, 29-30, 31, 40, 298n.

von Balthasar, H.U., 3, 5n., 9n., 12, 21n., 25n., 26n., 32n., 39, 50-51, 64, 246, 256, 275n.

Barnes, J., 191n.

Barsotti, D., 53n.

Barth, K., 53-54, 59n., 271-272.

Basil the Great, St., 20n., 124-125, 134, 141-142, 143n., 145, 155, 159, 160-165, 177-178, 179, 248, 293-294.

Bede, St., 13n.

Benoit, P., 261n.

Berengarius, 76n., 84.

Bernard, St., 20n.

Berthold, G. C., 146n.

de Bérulle, P., 54n., 60, 63-64.

Blanchard, J. P., 19n.

Blondel, M., 8-9, 12, 13, 28, 37n., 43, 44n., 52-53, 64-66, 165, 239n.

Bobrinskoy, B., 216n.

Bonaventure, St., 78n.

Bori, P. C., 123n.

Bossuet, J. B., 12n., 60n., 113n., 218.

Boularand, E., 101n.

Bouyer, L., 61, 116-117, 257, 271n.

Brown, D., 225n.